THY NATURE AND THY NAME IS LOVE

THY NATURE AND THY NAME IS LOVE

Wesleyan and Process Theologies in Dialogue

Bryan P. Stone
and
Thomas Jay Oord,
Editors

KINGSWOOD BOOKS

An Imprint of Abingdon Press
Nashville, Tennessee

THY NATURE AND THY NAME IS LOVE
WESLEYAN AND PROCESS THEOLOGIES IN DIALOGUE

Library of Congress Cataloging-in-Publication Data

Thy nature and thy name is love : Wesleyan and process theologies in dialogue / Bryan P. Stone and Thomas Jay Oord, editors.
    p. cm.
    Includes bibliographical references.
    ISBN 0-687-05220-3 (alk. paper)
    1. Methodist Church—Doctrines. 2. Process theology. I. Stone, Bryan P., 1959- II Oord, Thomas Jay.

    BX8331.3 .N38 2001
    230'.046—dc21

                                                                    2001040761

01 02 03 04 05 06 07 08 09 10—10 9 8 7 6 5 4 3 2 1

MANUFACTURED IN THE UNITED STATES OF AMERICA

In honor of

John B. Cobb Jr.

and

Schubert M. Ogden,

harbingers of this conversation

CONTENTS

INTRODUCTION

BRYAN P. STONE & THOMAS JAY OORD

John Wesley was not a process theologian. Yet for some time now a steady number of Wesleyan theologians have been drawn to the resources of process thought when inquiring into the meaning and truth of the Christian witness. This attraction is not without warrant. Both process thought and Wesleyan theology conceptualize divine sovereignty and power in such a way as to affirm human freedom and creativity. Both emphasize the priority and universality of grace, but not in such a way as to negate human responsibility. Both understand the perfecting of God's creation, in general, and human growth in grace, in particular, primarily in relational and processive terms. For both theologies, natural sensory perception is not the only, or even most important, source for human knowing. Both traditions affirm a vision of a deity whose nature and name is "love." It is not merely coincidental that many leading process thinkers over the last half-century have found themselves at home in Wesleyan religious contexts and that, at the same time, many Wesleyans have believed their fundamental theological commitments were best expressed within a process worldview.

That Wesleyans are drawn to any philosophical system might, on the face of it, seem odd, and even anathema to some. Wesley's own thought was intensely practical and rarely speculative; his concerns were shaped by the exigencies of his revival and the concrete needs of the communities he served. But Wesley also had an able, philosophical mind. His approach to thorny religious and ethical questions was deeply shaped by his own acquaintance with both classical intellectual traditions and philosophical debates of his time. If in our time, we are sometimes prone to pit theory against practice, philosophy against evangelism, or reason against faith, we will not find much help in Wesley either as an ally or as a model.

As Schubert M. Ogden argues, the Wesleyan tradition generally maintains that the "Christian witness is thoroughly reasonable." For Wesley, this implied more than a confidence in reason's usefulness for bringing coherence to theological claims and more than mere conforming of language to established patterns of logic and argumentation. However, Wesley did not advocate mere rationalism either. We find in his theology, instead, a dynamic and integral relationship between grace and knowledge. Epistemology is grounded in soteriology and thus governed by a qualified optimism about the human ability to know through reason and experience. This optimism is not a confidence in human abilities per se; it is, rather, a confidence in the power of grace to enliven our minds and quicken both our physical and spiritual senses.

The present collection of essays arises out of a conviction that there is good reason for speaking today about the distinctive contribution of Wesleyan theology to contemporary metaphysical, epistemological, and ethical debates. This contribution will undoubtedly differ from approaches generated by alternative ways of construing the God-human relationship (e.g., Reformed theology). Indeed, it is the very prevenience of grace in our world that justifies a Wesleyan confidence in experience and reason while, at the same time, pushing toward a proper humility that confesses all truth to be from God.

Wesleyans are often attracted to rigorous metaphysical inquiry without believing that this attraction is disparate with God's revelation in Christ and scripture. Consequently, many theologians in the Wesleyan tradition feel as though they need not "change hats" when engaging in philosophical inquiry. In fact, a Wesleyan doctrine of prevenient grace may even be regarded as implying a notion of "original revelation,"[1] which is the ground of all knowing and experiencing. For this reason, many Wesleyans are convinced that revelation does not stand over and against human reason and experience, and this commitment justifies a Wesleyan interest in

---

1. See Schubert M. Ogden's essay in chap. 1 and "On Revelation" in *Our Common History as Christians: Essays in Honor of Albert C. Outler*, ed. John Deschner, Leroy T. Howe, and Klaus Penzel (New York: Oxford University Press, 1975), 261–92.

what has traditionally been called "natural theology." They find no contradiction in affirming revelation and, at the same time, arguing for primary assertions in public courts of inquiry.

WESLEYANS AND PROCESS THOUGHT

Despite the fact that a number of Wesleyan theologians have been drawn to the resources of process thought, the relationship between Wesleyan theology and process thought has not been pursued in any explicit or systematic way until recently. The first published exploration of the relationship between Wesleyan theology and process thought appeared in a pair of articles in the fall 1980 edition of the *Wesleyan Theological Journal*. John Culp's essay, "A Dialog with the Process Theology of John B. Cobb Jr.," offered suggestions concerning the possible contribution that Cobb's process thought might make to Wesleyan-Holiness theology. Culp argued that Cobb's thought offers an important and helpful metaphysical basis for (1) the uniquely Wesleyan interface of grace and freedom, (2) the importance of human experience in theological reflection—without reducing experience to solipsistic subjectivism, and (3) a more constructive way of relating the crisis and progressive aspects of entire sanctification.[2] Michael L. Peterson's essay, "Orthodox Christianity, Wesleyanism, and Process Theology," which was published alongside Culp's, was more suspicious of process thought's usefulness for Wesleyan theology. Peterson came to the conclusion, with regard to the foundational doctrines of God, humanity, the kingdom of God, and Jesus Christ, that "process philosophy modifies or distorts their essential meaning to such a great extent that orthodoxy is lost."[3]

In 1983, Emory University hosted a Bicentennial Theological Consultation entitled "Wesleyan Theology and the Next Century" with the purpose of considering the relationship between Wesleyan thought and contemporary trends in theology and ethics. Of the many working groups within this consultation, one in particular

---

2. John Culp, "A Dialog with the Process Theology of John B. Cobb Jr.," *Wesleyan Theological Journal* 15.2 (1980): 33–44.

3. Michael L. Peterson, "Orthodox Christianity, Wesleyanism, and Process Theology," *Wesleyan Theological Journal* 15.2 (1980): 45–58.

explored the relationship between process thought and Wesleyan theology. Essays from this group by Schubert M. Ogden, Paul A. Mickey, Carl Bangs, Ignacio Castuera, and Sheila Greeve Davaney were included in the published collection that grew out of this consultation.[4]

Another published work focusing on the Wesleyan-process dialogue was Marjorie Hewitt Suchocki's 1987 essay, "Coming Home: Wesley, Whitehead, and Women."[5] This article explores the affinities between process thought, feminism, and Wesleyan theology, and is reprinted in the present collection to make it more accessible.

Perhaps the most important published interpretation of Wesley's theology in light of process thought to date is John B. Cobb Jr.'s book, *Grace and Responsibility: A Wesleyan Theology for Today.*[6] Although Cobb's primary purpose is to engage Wesley's eighteenth-century theology with contemporary problems and contemporary modes of thought, a process-relational vision informs his argument at several key points, such as the God-world relationship, faith, assurance, and spiritual perception.

The present volume arose from the need for further dialogue between Wesleyan theology and process theology. Although there has been a resurgence of interest in John Wesley's practical theology in recent years, there has also been a keen sense among Wesleyans that today's intellectual and social world is different from that of Wesley. Dramatic changes in the sciences, in methods of biblical interpretation, in contacts with diverse religious faiths, and in the enhancement of modern capacities to perpetrate horrendous evil, pollution, and destruction throughout the world require the task of reformulating our theology and rethinking our basic

---

4. See *Wesleyan Theology Today: A Bicentennial Theological Consultation,* ed. Theodore Runyon (Nashville: Kingswood Books, 1985). The relevant essays are Schubert M. Ogden, "Process Theology and the Wesleyan Witness," 65–75 (originally printed in *Perkins School of Theology Journal* 37.3 [Spring 1984]: 18–33); Paul A. Mickey, "Process Theology and Wesleyan Thought: An Evangelical Perspective," 76–87; Carl Bangs, "The Idea of Perfection in a Future Christian Theology," 88–94; Ignacio Castuera, "Wesley, Process and Liberation Theologies: A Test Case," 95–104; and Sheila Greeve Davaney, "Feminism, Process Thought, and the Wesleyan Tradition," 105–16. Carl Bangs's article does not really represent a dialogue between process thought and Wesleyan thought, despite its inclusion in this group of essays.
5. Marjorie Hewitt Suchocki, "Coming Home: Wesley, Whitehead, and Women," *Drew Gateway* 57.3 (1987): 31–43.
6. John B. Cobb Jr., *Grace and Responsibility: A Wesleyan Theology for Today* (Nashville: Abingdon Press, 1995).

philosophical assumptions. The present volume asks whether the resources of process thought assist Wesleyans in this task and, at the same time, whether the Wesleyan tradition offers insights from which process thinkers can benefit.

To ascertain whether Wesleyan theology and process theology can provide these resources requires the identification of sufficiently fertile points of correlation between the two traditions. Although these points of correlation often reveal important affinities, they also raise challenges and provoke conflict. All of the writers in this volume approach the subject of process thought from within the Wesleyan tradition. The volume is not, however, a mere apology for process thought by Wesleyans. Some of the essays attempt to highlight areas of tension and even incompatibility between the two traditions, while other essays are more aggressive in their attempt to move (as Cobb might say) "beyond dialogue" toward mutual transformation or creative synthesis. The essays focus on a broad range of topics, including the God-world/God-human relationship, epistemology, metaphysics, the Trinity, soteriology, consumerism, spirituality, liberation, divine and creaturely power, theodicy, aesthetics, sanctification, and feminism.

Schubert M. Ogden's contribution to the 1983 Bicentennial Theological Consultation is reprinted in chapter 1 and sets this volume's tone by tracing core commitments of both the Wesleyan witness and process theology. Ogden proposes six points of correlation from which important affinities can be traced: (1) a common commitment to defending the rational credibility of each tradition's claims, (2) reliance on a human experience that is more than a merely external sense perception, (3) a synergistic account of God and the world, and of grace and freedom, (4) an understanding of authentic existence as involving both a faithful acceptance of our acceptance by God (and, thus, a passive moment) and a loyal response to that acceptance in loving action (and, thus, an active moment), (5) a bias toward praxis, and (6) an interest in overcoming homocentrism.

As with Ogden, Marjorie Hewitt Suchocki highlights the epistemological priority that both Alfred North Whitehead and John Wesley give to the full range of human experience. Her 1987 essay reprinted in chapter 2 identifies this inclusion of experience as an important affinity between Wesleyan and process modes of thought and as an important commitment to feminism. Insofar as reason is, for Wesley, rooted in experience and thus perspectival, his thought is also open to a theological pluralism that Suchocki finds remarkably compatible with process and feminist commitments. Suchocki demonstrates the openness of the Wesleyan vision of sanctifying and perfecting love to a process-relational interpretation. A process interpretation of Christian perfection clarifies the unitive love for God and the world at the heart of Wesley's soteriology, which is likewise the ground of liberating social action.

In chapter 3, Bryan P. Stone offers a process interpretation of Wesley's understanding of sanctification by constructing a Wesleyan-process notion of the "image of God" and then clarifying the meaning of sanctification as the restoration, or perfection, of this image. For both Wesley and process thought, God is love, and our creation in God's image is centrally a creation in and for love. Christian perfection, likewise, is a perfection of love. Stone's process theology of sanctification begins with a reconstruction of Wesleyan anthropology within the distinctively process triad of community, creativity, and freedom. Insofar as we are created social, sanctification is a reorientation of our lives toward God and others in openness and inclusion. Insofar as we are created creative, sanctification is a reorientation of our lives toward the future in confidence, gratitude, and expectation. And insofar as we are created free, sanctification is a reconstitution of our lives in and for liberation.

A central point of correlation between process theology and Wesleyan theology is the relationship between God's grace and human responsibility. In chapter 4, John B. Cobb Jr. develops this correlation by noting, first, that the way the Reformers emphasized the priority of God's action relative to human freedom eroded human responsibility. Grace and freedom became a trade-off. Cobb then claims that Wesley changed the underlying assumptions of this debate by arguing that grace and freedom are not mutually incompatible. Wesley did this by offering a vision of God as internally, rather than externally, related to all humans. Grace is ever present in the human, calling forth a response and, indeed, making such a response possible, according to Cobb. Wesley's solution to

this problem interprets actual human existence as partly constituted by God's gracious activity despite the fallenness of human
nature and our own natural incapability of good action. For Cobb,
Wesley's solution is very much like that of Whitehead. For
Whitehead, the actual occasion of human experience is constituted
in part by God's immanence, and the role played by that immanence is similar to the work of grace in Wesley. We may therefore
insist with confidence on our own abilities, even as we work to better ourselves, while at the same time we live with authentic humility and recognize grace as inherent to every instance of who we are
becoming.

In chapter 5, Randy L. Maddox provides a historical overview of
how Wesley and Wesleyan thinkers who came after him construed
the nature of God given their fundamental commitment to
"responsible grace" as a model of divine/human interaction in salvation. Wesley's advocacy of a "response-able" God—a God who
both empowers human response and, at the same time, respects the
integrity of human response—compelled him to "push the edges,"
so to speak, with regard to God's temporality, foreknowledge,
omnipotence, and immutability. While subsequent British
Methodism was more conservative in reinterpreting the doctrine of
God before the courts of continental theology, American
Methodism exhibited more independence and eventually produced the kind of progressive strands in Wesleyanism that found
an openness both to personalism and, eventually, to process
thought. In the appendix to this volume, Thomas Jay Oord provides an even closer examination of the relationship between
Wesleyan theology, Boston Personalism, and process thought.

Chapters 6 and 7 contain essays that explore the importance of
trinitarian theology for Wesley, while asking about the helpfulness
of process thought in interpreting the theological significance of
the Trinity. In chapter 6, Samuel M. Powell argues that God's kind
of being is so utterly different from all other being that we know
(especially insofar as God's essence subsists in three persons) as
to render inadequate the Whiteheadian attempt to use one systematic framework and one interpretive category (the actual entity) to
describe all reality. Powell is especially suspicious of the influence
of personalism on contemporary Wesleyanism, and he argues that

it is precisely the preoccupation with God as person—a preoccupation continued in process thought—that undercuts the doctrine of God as Trinity. The emphasis upon God as person reduces the Trinity to "a puzzle about numbers: How can three be one?" Powell takes issue with the time-honored notion that the center of Wesley's theology is soteriology (understood in primarily relational and personalist terms) and suggests instead that a trinitarian ontology more adequately takes into account the plurality of reality while preserving the essential difference of God from all other beings.

Tyron L. Inbody, in contrast, maintains that it is precisely process theism's account of sociality and relatedness that allows Wesleyans to embrace the Trinity more fully and to interpret the Trinity in a way that is more consistent with Wesley's own reconceptualization of divine sovereignty in terms of justice and mercy. Inbody does not judge the Trinity to be an affirmation of the difference of God from all other beings. Rather, by appealing to Wesley's notion that human beings are "transcripts of the Trinity," Inbody argues in chapter 7 that God and humans share at least some common structure of being and that relatedness resides at the heart of that common structure. Inbody builds the case that Wesley's understanding of God's power as dynamic, relational, and persuasive helps to destabilize the classically theistic portrayal of God as static and impassible; it does this in a way that is compatible with a process-trinitarian interpretation. Rather than merely adopting the classical notion of "person" and then interpreting both God and humans accordingly, a process-trinitarian interpretation of God insists on plurality, sociality, and mutuality as fundamental to what it means to be personal. This insistence grounds contemporary concerns of equality, compassion, justice, and community in the very character of God.

One of the most notable features of process thought has been its unique approach to the problem of evil, which is understandable given its strong doctrine of creaturely freedom and reconceptualization of divine power as a persuasive lure. In chapter 8, Thomas Jay Oord draws upon the resources of process thought to develop a process Wesleyan theodicy. At the heart of this proposal is a libertarian hypothesis that Oord calls "essential free-will theism."

Along with this free-will hypothesis, Wesley's belief that God is a bodiless spirit provides the basis for claiming that God, unlike creatures possessing localized bodies, is not culpable for failing to prevent evil. God's exoneration from culpability is not, however, because of some limitation in God, or even because of divine self-limitation. God is not culpable for failing to prevent genuinely evil events, says Oord, because (1) creatures are essentially free, (2) God, as a spirit, does not possess a divine body, and (3) the essence of divinity is perfect love. The essay concludes with a doctrine of divine power that provides a basis for labeling God "almighty" without jeopardizing the proposed Wesleyan-process theodicy.

If process theism is often noted for its rejection of classical approaches to theodicy, it is also noted for its rejection of the classical doctrine of "creation out of nothing." In chapter 9, Michael E. Lodahl argues that what is at stake in the doctrine of creation out of nothing is the very heart of Christian soteriology. Insofar as process thought argues for a thoroughly social view of reality and, therefore, some degree of metaphysical necessity both to God and world, Lodahl finds here an "unacceptable dualism." Of course, most process theologians have not simply abandoned the concerns that motivated the original adoption of the doctrine of *creatio ex nihilo*; some have tried to reconstruct this doctrine in process terms. Lodahl suggests that the resources of Wesleyan theology can be especially helpful here. Wesley's reconception of God's power in terms of over-abundant, self-giving, other-receiving love leads toward a theology of *creatio ex amore* instead of *creatio ex nihilo*. If God always has a world, it is not because of some necessity imposed upon him, but because of God's own overflowing love.

In chapter 10, John Culp surveys the landscape of contemporary epistemology and asks whether a Wesleyan theology might offer a distinctive contribution. In attempting to steer a course between rationalism and fideism, Culp argues that the Wesleyan commitment to an experiential basis for knowledge, distinguished by Wesley's notion of the "spiritual sensation," is amenable to a process epistemology. Wesley's own distinctive way of thinking about God's omnipresence, power, grace, and relatedness to our lives provides an openness to natural theology while, at the same time, insisting that personal experience of God is needed for direct knowledge of God. A Wesleyan orientation toward epistemology does not claim to yield the certainty of blind belief; instead, it limits knowledge to probability because of the perspectival nature of human experience, the complexity of God and creation, and human sinfulness. The resources of process philosophy can be helpful in the development of a Wesleyan epistemology by offering an explanation of how perception includes more than sense perception and by providing an understanding of the knower and the known that defies a long-standing subject-object dualism in epistemology.

Although many Wesleyans find process thought helpful, in chapter 11, Alan G. Padgett warns against wedding any particular philosophy to Christian theology in such a way as to allow philosophy to set the terms for what counts as meaningful and true. Padgett is especially critical of any metaphysical system that presumes to explain reality within one all-encompassing system or metanarrative, which, he says, is precisely the case in Whiteheadian process metaphysics. Genuine problems arise, according to Padgett, when theology is *constrained* to a philosophical system because revelation becomes subordinated to reason; and faith is forced to justify itself in accordance with an alien rationality. For Padgett, the knowledge of God does not depend upon philosophy; Wesleyans must be cautious to give theology sufficient independence from metaphysics.

In chapter 12, Kenton M. Stiles explores the aesthetic affinities between Wesleyan and process theologies. Stiles emphasizes the notions of balance, aim, satisfaction, and wholeness in a Wesleyan doctrine of holiness, and he demonstrates how a process aesthetics can enrich that doctrine by contributing to each of these notions. A process conceptuality can help us better understand how both God and the world experience aesthetically. It can also help us better recognize "the beauty of holiness"—a beauty that is incarnate in the living form of Christ.

Of the several affinities between the Wesleyan witness and process thought suggested by Ogden in chapter 1, a "bias toward praxis" and "an interest in overcoming homocentrism" stand out in linking Wesleyan and process traditions with recent liberationist and environmental theologies. The final four chapters explore this linkage along both critical and constructive paths. In chapter 13, Theodore Walker Jr. suggests that the themes of praxis and the overcoming of homocentrism are especially challenging in offering a more "protestant" rather than ecumenical approach to the Wesleyan-process dialogue. From the standpoint of North American black theology and independent black Methodism, according to Walker, the value of process thought is to be found in its challenges to, rather than in its affinities with, mainstream white Methodism. Walker argues for the importance of a metaphysics of orthopraxis that can ground our ethical deliberations and lead us to value nonhuman creation in those deliberations.

In chapter 14, Mary Elizabeth Mullino Moore takes up the call to ground ethical deliberations in metaphysics and orthopraxis by considering, as a case study, the current deliberation of The United Methodist Church on an appropriate response to persons who are gay, lesbian, bisexual, or transgendered. In doing this, Moore undertakes a comparative analysis of the themes of compassion and hope in Wesley and Whitehead. Her analysis leads to the conclusion that all persons, regardless of their sexual orientation, should be fully accepted and included in the human community, even if Christians disagree on ethical issues of sexuality. For both Wesleyan and process-relational perspectives, argues Moore, the resolution of these problems lies less in finding agreeable mental solutions (although we should never give up hope for doing that) than in having a hopeful trust in God. That, in turn, leads us to place human well-being above particular views that we might hold. It is compassion and hope that sustain the human community through its deliberations and dilemmas.

If a Wesleyan bias toward right praxis (or, as Wesley put it, "social holiness") leads us to be concerned for the well-being of individuals above right opinions or unanimity, then process thought further challenges Wesleyans to understand the interconnectedness of reality in such a way that we become more concerned with questions of systemic and structural justice. In chapter 15, Henry James Young grounds both spirituality and social justice within a paradigm of solidarity fed by process and Wesleyan theological commitments. Young sees spirituality and social justice as "two sides of the same coin," and he argues for a more holistic conceptuality of human persons that recognizes the historical, systemic, and structural implications of who we are becoming. When interpreted within a process-relational vision, the quest for social justice drives straight to the heart of our soteriology. Christian perfection, therefore, is an integral and lifelong process that includes both personal and social transformation.

Finally, in chapter 16, Jay McDaniel and John L. Farthing explore the resources in both Wesleyan and process thought for living and thinking in postconsumerist ways. Wesley, both in his teaching and in his personal example, offers hope that life can be lived around the ideal of communal sharing. This sharing involves, on the one hand, freedom from inordinate attachments and the shackles of affluence and, on the other hand, freedom for simplicity, for the poor, and for the present. Process theology offers an understanding of God as the creative lure toward this simplicity of lifestyle. It also critiques the notions that (1) humans are skin-encapsulated egos and (2) creation is mere real estate—both of which, say McDaniel and Farthing, are foundational doctrines for the religion of consumerism. Process thought thereby lends support to Wesley's insights about the inherently social nature of our existence and further develops his incipient theology of creation.

This volume hopefully will reveal much of what process and Wesleyan theologies can learn from one another. At the center of this dialogue, however, is the passionate interest on the part of both traditions to communicate the message of God's love. Perhaps this volume may help us recognize more fully that, as Ogden has said, to speak of God's love "is not meaningful talk at all unless the structure of God in itself involves real, internal relatedness to others. This is so, at any rate, if 'love' is understood in its ordinary sense as referring, first of all, to the acceptance of others and then, secondly, to action towards others on the basis of such acceptance."[7] For both process and Wesleyan theologians, much is at stake in learning to take seriously our talk about God as love. It is out of this very vision of divine love that we are better able to give our lives, our love, our work, our play, our thoughts, and our actions—even our theology and philosophy—as acts of worship to the One whose nature and name is love.

7. See chap. 1 of the present volume.

Wrestling Jacob

(Charles Wesley)

1   Come, O thou Traveller unknown,
       Whom still I hold, but cannot see!
    My company before is gone,
       And I am left alone with thee;
    With thee all night I mean to stay,
    And wrestle till the break of day.

2   I need not tell thee who I am,
       My misery or sin declare;
    Thyself hast called me by my name,
       Look on thy hands, and read it there.
    But who, I ask thee, who art thou?
    Tell me thy name, and tell me now.

3   In vain thou strugglest to get free,
       I never will unloose my hold;
    Art thou the Man that died for me?
       The secret of thy love unfold:
    Wrestling, I will not let thee go
    Till I thy name, thy nature know.

4   Wilt thou not yet to me reveal
       Thy new, unutterable name?
    Tell me, I still beseech thee, tell;
       To know it now resolved I am:
    Wrestling, I will not let thee go
    Till I thy name, thy nature know.

5   What though my shrinking flesh complain
       And murmur to contend so long?
    I rise superior to my pain:
       When I am weak, then I am strong;
    And when my all of strength shall fail
    I shall with the God-man prevail.

6   Yield to me now—for I am weak,
       But confident in self-despair!
   Speak to my heart, in blessings speak,
       Be conquered by my instant prayer:
   Speak, or thou never hence shalt move,
   And tell me if thy name is Love.

7   'Tis Love! 'Tis Love! Thou diedst for me;
       I hear thy whisper in my heart.
   The morning breaks, the shadows flee,
       Pure Universal Love thou art:
   To me, to all, thy bowels move—
   Thy nature, and thy name, is Love.

8   My prayer hath power with God; the grace
       Unspeakable I now receive;
   Through faith I see thee face to face;
       I see thee face to face, and live!
   In vain I have not wept and strove—
   Thy nature, and thy name, is Love.

9   I know thee, Saviour, who thou art—
       Jesus, the feeble sinner's friend;
   Nor wilt thou with the night depart,
       But stay, and love me to the end:
   Thy mercies never shall remove,
   Thy nature, and thy name, is Love.

10   The Sun of Righteousness on me
       Hath rose with healing in his wings;
   Withered my nature's strength; from thee
       My soul its life and succour brings;
   My help is all laid up above:
   Thy nature, and thy name, is Love.

11   Contented now upon my thigh
       I halt, till life's short journey end;
   All helplessness, all weakness, I
       On thee alone for strength depend;
   Nor have I power from thee to move:
   Thy nature, and thy name, is Love.

12   Lame as I am, I take the prey,
        Hell, earth, and sin with ease o'ercome;
    I leap for joy, pursue my way,
        And as a bounding hart fly home,
    Through all eternity to prove,
    Thy nature, and thy name, is LOVE.[8]

CHAPTER ONE

PROCESS THEOLOGY AND THE WESLEYAN WITNESS[1]

SCHUBERT M. OGDEN

Among the stated purposes of the Bicentennial Theological Consultation is "to explore the affinities between the Methodist heritage and some of the most creative trends in contemporary theology and ethics." The assumption of this paper is that at least one of the things that could be reasonably called process theology sufficiently qualifies as just such a creative trend to justify exploring the affinities between it and the distinctively Wesleyan tradition of Christian witness.

Before we proceed with this exploration, however, it is important to be clear about some basic presuppositions. In assuming, as I do, that the process theology of which I speak is among the creative trends in contemporary theology and ethics, I naturally presuppose a certain understanding of Christian theology. According to the familiar analysis of "theology" as *logos* about *theos*, or thought and speech about God, Christian theology might be supposed to include all such thought and speech about God as is appropriate to the Christian witness of faith. But while there is certainly precedent for this very broad understanding of "Christian theology," it has long since come to be used more strictly to refer, not to all Christian thought and speech about God, but only to such as are involved in critically reflecting on Christian thinking and speaking more generally. Recognizing this, I myself use the term "Christian witness" to designate all Christian thought and speech about God (as well as the rest of Christian praxis) simply as such, thereby reserving "Christian theology" to be used in this stricter sense. Accordingly, I define the proper meaning of the second term as either the process

---

1. This essay originally appeared in *Perkins School of Theology Journal* 37 (Spring 1984): 18-33 and was later reprinted in *Wesleyan Theology Today: A Bicentennial Theological Consultation*, ed. Theodore Runyon (Nashville: Kingswood Books, 1985) and is used with permission.

or the product of critical reflection on the validity claims expressed or implied by Christian witness.

Any act of Christian witness, just like any other act of human praxis, necessarily implies, even if it may not express, certain claims to validity—for example, to the meaningfulness of what is said, to the sincerity of the speaker in saying it, to the truth of his or her assertions, or to the rightness of the norms regulative of his or her actions.[2] Moreover, every act of Christian witness expresses or implies a distinctive claim to validity—namely, the twofold claim to be at once appropriate to what is normatively Christian and credible in terms of common human experience and reason. But this claim is obviously problematic in its one aspect as well as in the other, sharp differences between Christians themselves rendering the appropriateness of their respective witnesses clearly questionable, and the even sharper differences between Christians and other interpreters of human existence serving only to cast doubt on the credibility of any of their conflicting interpretations. Thus, by its very nature, the primary level of praxis of which Christian witness is a part creates the need for the secondary level of reflection that is Christian theology. For it is only by the process of critically reflecting on witness in the way theology has the task of doing that the problematic claim to validity such witness expresses or implies can ever be confirmed.

Given this understanding of Christian theology, the assumption that process theology is one of the creative trends in contemporary theology and ethics implies at least this: Process theology is one way of critically reflecting on Christian witness so as to validate its claim to be both appropriate and credible. I stress that the only process theology I myself have ever had any interest in doing is simply a certain way of doing Christian theology in this full sense of the word. While I should not question that some so-called process theologies are quite properly taken to be only or primarily philosophical—either because they are not Christian theologies at all—being instead a new form of natural theology—or else because their main contributions are to the philosophical rather than the historical or exegetical tasks of Christian theology—still process

---

2. Jürgen Habermas, "Was heisst Universalpragmatik?" in Karl-Otto Apel, ed., *Sprachpragmatik und Philosophie* (Frankfurt: Suhrkamp Verlag, 1976), 174-79.

theology, in the only sense that I am willing to accept as proper, refers to a certain kind of Christian theology, and hence to critical reflection on the appropriateness as well as the credibility of Christian witness.

As for the other term, "the Wesleyan witness," its meaning, too, should be clearer now that some of my presuppositions have been clarified. I speak of "Wesleyan witness" instead of simply "Wesleyan thought," because I take "witness" to be appropriately the more inclusive term, covering not only speech and thought but everything else in Christian praxis. As such, it designates one important strand within the larger tradition of Christian witness that furnishes the privileged data for Christian theological reflection. Of course, there neither are nor can be any privileged data when it comes to assessing claims to credibility. By its very nature, any such claim is a universal claim, and any datum that is at all logically relevant to assessing its validity must be equally relevant with every other. But in assessing claims to appropriateness, a religious tradition is self-differentiating in assigning to some of its elements a normative authority over some or all of the others, some of the data it furnishes has a more or less privileged status in assessing any claim to be appropriate to its witness. Even so, for the Christian theologian, and hence also for the process theologian, the data furnished by any one strand of witness, such as the Wesleyan, do not and cannot have a primary normative authority. Whatever their authority for Christians who stand within this strand of tradition, they are but one of any number of such strands on whose appropriateness Christian theology has the task of critically reflecting by reference to the sole primary norm of the apostolic witness.

The other thing to note about the distinction I presuppose between witness and theology is that it is a relative, not an absolute, distinction. Just as in general the products of reflection may be integrated into contexts of praxis, thereby becoming part of the data for later reflection, so the products of theological reflection may be integrated into the contexts of Christian praxis, and thus become part of the witness on whose claim to validity subsequent theology has the task of critically reflecting.[3]

---

3. Jürgen Habermas and Niklas Luhmann, *Theorie der Gesellschaft oder Sozialtechnologie—Was leistet die Systemforschung?* (Frankfurt: Suhrkamp Verlag, 1971), 115 n. 20.

If what has been said to this point is important for understanding the argument of the paper, it is nevertheless extremely formal and at best preliminary to the exploration we have proposed to conduct. I have said that process theology is a certain kind of Christian theology, or a certain way of doing Christian theology, understood as critical reflection on the claim that is expressed or implied by Christian witness to be both appropriate and credible. But just what kind of Christian theology is process theology, and how exactly does it reflect on this distinctively Christian claim to validity? The answer to these questions may be given in two steps: first, by formally identifying process theology, and then, second, by materially describing it.

We may say formally that process theology is the kind of Christian theology that employs the insights, concepts, and methods of process philosophy and that it is in this way that it reflects on both the appropriateness and the credibility of Christian witness. By "philosophy" in general, I should explain, I mean a more or less reflective self-understanding that is comprehensive in scope and generally secular rather than specifically religious in constitution. As such, it properly includes, although it is not exhausted by, both a metaphysics and an ethics, by which I understand both a theory of ultimate reality in its structure in itself and a theory of how we ought to act and what we ought to do given the structure of ultimate reality and its meaning for us. Thus, in speaking of process philosophy, I mean just such a reflective, comprehensive, and secular understanding of existence together with the metaphysical and ethical theories that explicate its necessary implications. And in formally identifying process theology as employing the insights, concepts, and methods of process philosophy, I intend to say that it is in terms of this self-understanding and these theories that it critically reflects on the meaning and truth of Christian witness.

Yet since even this is only a formal identification of process theology, we must take the second step of materially describing it. This we may do, obviously, by means of a material description of the distinctive self-understanding of process philosophy as well as of the metaphysics and ethics that it necessarily implies. But it is equally obvious that there are certain difficulties with any such description. Aside from the fact that limitations of space increase the risk of oversimplification, what is to be rightly taken as the sources of a normative concept of process philosophy and how these sources are to be correctly interpreted are both controversial questions among those who may fairly claim the expertise prerequisite to answering them. Notwithstanding these difficulties, however, the exploration we are now conducting requires that we attempt at least a summary description of the process philosophy in whose terms the process theology expressed by this paper seeks to carry out its task as Christian theology.

For this kind of philosophy, to be a self is not merely to be continually becoming, but also to exist, in the emphatic sense in which "existence" means that one is consciously aware of one's becoming and, within the limits of one's situation, responsible for it. Thus one is aware, above all, of one's real, internal relatedness—not only to one's own ever-changing past and future, but also to a many-leveled community of others similarly caught up in time and change and, together with them, to the all-inclusive whole of reality itself. But one is also aware, relative to this same whole of reality, of one's own essential fragmentariness and of the equally essential fragmentariness of all others. With respect to both time and space, the whole alone is essentially integral and nonfragmentary, having neither beginning nor end and lacking an external environment. This is not to say, however, that the whole of reality is experienced as mere unchanging being, in every respect infinite and absolute. On the contrary, insofar as the whole is neither merely abstract nor a sheer aggregate, it must be like the self and anything else comparably concrete and singular in being an instance of becoming, or an ordered sequence of such instances, which as such is always finite in contrast to the infinite realm of possibility and relative and not absolute in its real, internal relations to others.

On the self-understanding distinctive of this philosophy, then, to be human is to live as a fragment, albeit a self-conscious and, therefore, responsible fragment, of the integral whole of reality as such. In other words, for this philosophy, the meaning of ultimate reality for us demands that we accept both our own becoming and the becomings of all others as parts of this ultimate whole and then, by serving as best we can the transient goods of all the parts, to make the greatest possible contribution to the enduring good of the whole.

As for the metaphysics that this self-understanding implies, it is in every sense antidualistic, being in one sense monistic, in another sense a qualified pluralism. It is monistic in the sense that it recognizes but one transcendental concept, or one set of such concepts, in which anything that is fully concrete and singular can and must be described. Thus for process metaphysics there are not many but only one kind of ultimate subjects of predication; and no difference between one such ultimate subject and another amounts to an absolute difference in kind, whether it be a merely finite difference between one and another part of reality or even the infinite difference between the inclusive whole of reality and any of its included parts. Even the integral whole of reality as something concrete and singular is either an instance of becoming or an individual sequence of such instances in the same sense in which this may be said of any other thing that is more than a mere abstraction or aggregate. This explains, of course, why *the* transcendental concept for such a metaphysics is precisely "process," in the sense that to be anything concretely and singularly real in the full sense of the words is to be an instance of becoming: an emergent unity of real, internal relatedness to all the things that have already become in the past, which then gives itself along with them to all the other such emergent unities that are yet to become in the future.

But if process metaphysics is in this way attributively monistic, it is nonetheless substantively pluralistic, even if in a qualified sense. This is the case insofar as it recognizes not one but many ultimate subjects of predication. Although anything fully concrete and singular is an instance of becoming of ultimately the same kind as any other, there are any number of such instances, each an emergent unity of real, internal relatedness ontologically distinct from all the others. Above all, there is the unique ontological distinction between the self and others as all mere parts of reality, on the one hand, and the one all-inclusive whole of reality, on the other. Even as each fragmentary becoming is ontologically distinct from every other, so each of them severally and all of them together are ontologically distinct from the integral becoming of the whole. And yet, as I have said, the distinction between part and whole is unique;

and this means that the pluralism of process metaphysics, real as it certainly is, is also qualified. Although "part" and "whole" are indeed correlative concepts in that each necessarily implies the other, the symmetry between their two referents presupposes an even more fundamental asymmetry between them. For while there could not be an integral becoming of the whole without the fragmentary becomings of the parts, what the whole as such necessarily implies is not *this part or that* (since all of its parts, unlike itself, are merely contingent rather than necessary), but only *some part or other*—or, if you wish to put it so, that the intensional class of parts have at least some members and thus not be a null class. On the other hand, what each and every fragmentary becoming necessarily implies is not merely *some whole or other* (since the idea of more than one whole of reality is patently incoherent), but rather the *one and only necessarily existing whole*—the one integral becoming of which all fragmentary becomings are contingent parts and but for which none of them would be so much as even possible.[4]

This brings us to the ethics of process philosophy, which, like its metaphysics, is thoroughly antidualistic. By this I mean that it recognizes at most a relative, not an absolute, difference between self-interest and interest in others and between how we are to act and what we are to do toward the others who, being consciously aware of their becomings, are insofar on the same level as ourselves, and how we are to act and what we are to do toward all those whose becomings take place at some lower, unconscious level.[5] Because even self-interest is in its way an interest in others—namely, in one's own past or future instances of becoming—and because all instances of becoming that can be affected by how we act and what we do are attributively one even if substantively many, there is only one ethical principle, or one set of such principles, governing the whole of our moral life, whether this be spoken of, as I am speaking of it here, in terms of "judgments of obligation," or, alternatively, in terms of either "judgments of virtue" or "judgments of value."[6] Of course, our moral acts themselves, if not also the modes

4. Charles Hartshorne, *A Natural Theology for Our Time* (LaSalle, Ill.: Open Court Publishing, 1967), 64-65.

5. Charles Hartshorne, *Creative Synthesis and Philosophic Method* (LaSalle, Ill.: Open Court Publishing, 1970), 198 ff.

6. Frederick S. Carney, "Theological Ethics," in Warren T. Reich, ed., *Encyclopedia of Bioethics* (New York: Macmillan, 1978) 1:429.

of our action, must be differently specified in the different situations in which we are required to act and in relation to the different others and levels of others for whom we are responsible. But for a process ethics of obligation the one thing we are obliged to do in every situation and in relation to every other is to realize as fully as we can the intrinsic good that lies in each and every instance of becoming.[7]

This means, among other things, that there is always a specifically political aspect to our moral responsibility. This is so, at any rate, if "politics" is taken in a broad sense as having to do, not only with the formation of specific structures of government and the state, but with the formation and transformation of structures of order generally. Because all becoming, and hence the realization of all intrinsic good, necessarily presupposes an order more or less permissive of emergent unities of real, internal relatedness to others, one can promote the optimal realization of intrinsic good at all levels of becoming only by forming appropriate structures of social and cultural order.[8]

So much, then, by way of a summary description of what I take to be properly meant by "process philosophy." Inadequate as it certainly is, it should be sufficient to mediate a material description of the process theology whose affinities with the Wesleyan witness we are concerned to explore. In other words, it should now be clear that such of the distinctive characteristics of process theology as warrant so speaking of it at all derive from the fact that it is in terms of the self-understanding and of the metaphysics and ethics that have just been described that it critically reflects on the meaning and the truth of Christian witness.

Proceeding with our exploration, we must now make a parallel effort to get beyond the merely preliminary clarification of the other term, "the Wesleyan witness." All that has been said so far to clarify this term is that it designates an important strand within the larger tradition of Christian witness on which any Christian theology, including process theology, has the task of critically reflecting. But, once again, we need to ask just what strand of tradition the

---

7. Charles Hartshorne, "Beyond Enlightened Self-Interest," in Harry James Cargas and Bernard Lee, eds., *Religious Experience and Process Theology: The Pastoral Implications of a Major Modern Movement* (New York: Paulist Press, 1976), 301-22.

8. Ibid., 320ff.

Wesleyan witness is and exactly how it expresses the common witness of the Christian community. And here, too, we may answer our questions in two steps: first, by identifying the Wesleyan witness formally and then, second, by essaying a material description of it.

The first step is easy enough, and we may formally identify the Wesleyan witness by saying simply that it is the testimony borne by the community of faith and witness that originates with John Wesley and that the way in which it expresses the common witness of the Christian church is in accordance with the norms that are authoritative for this particular community. But here again there are obvious difficulties in taking the second step of materially describing the Wesleyan witness. Not only do the same limits of space compel one so to simplify as to risk distortion, but there are also analogous and equally controversial questions about what is rightly understood to be normative in Wesleyan Christianity and about the correct interpretation of its norms. Moreover, whether I may fairly claim to have the expertise necessary to answer these questions is even more uncertain than in the case of the earlier questions about process philosophy. Even so, there is no way to continue our exploration without attempting a material description, however summary and inadequate, of the distinctively Wesleyan form of Christian witness.

We may begin this description by directly addressing the question of what is rightly taken to be normative for the Christian community that traces its origin to Wesley. According to Thomas Langford, who has recently discussed this question in a thoughtful way, the Methodist tradition "cannot be understood by exclusive appeal to Wesley. Although Methodism cannot be understood apart from John Wesley, it also cannot be understood except as it has moved beyond Wesley. . . . Today the Wesleyan tradition is the result of its inclusive history. . . . Beginning with Wesley, it did not stop with Wesley—this is one important mark of this tradition."[9] Having said this, however, Langford goes on to accept an analogy that C. K. Barrett cites from the work of Helmut Flender: "Just as Paul, in faithfulness, not unfaithfulness, to Jesus, had in a new

---

9. Thomas A. Langford, *Practical Divinity: Theology in the Wesleyan Tradition* (Nashville: Abingdon Press, 1983), 260f.

generation to say things that Jesus had not said, so Luke, in a third generation, had, in faithfulness to Paul, to say things Paul had not said."[10] If Langford's own statements might seem to imply that what is normative in the Wesleyan witness includes considerably more than Wesley himself, this is hardly the implication of his acceptance of Flender's analogy. On the contrary, if one applies this analogy as he presumably intends it, it is precisely faithfulness, not unfaithfulness, to Wesley that must alone finally decide whether or not any of the things that have been said by those who have followed him are normatively a part of the Wesleyan tradition.

My position is that it is just so that one ought to apply the analogy and that one rightly takes Wesley's own witness of faith to be the sole primary norm for all specifically Wesleyan witness. This is in no way to question, however, that there is indeed more to the Wesleyan tradition than simply Wesley. It lies in the very nature of a normative witness that it cannot possibly function as such except by being continually reinterpreted in each new situation. This means that there may be all sorts of things that must be said beyond anything said in the primary norm, depending on the extent of the change from the old situation to the new. Assuming, then, that there has indeed been change—in some respects, vast change—between Wesley's situation and those of his followers in the Methodist tradition, one would naturally expect that they have had to say things that he not only did not say but could not have said and that at least some of these things, also, have been and perhaps still are normative for the Wesleyan witness. To this extent, one can only agree with Langford that the Methodist tradition, even in the normative sense of the words, "cannot be understood by exclusive appeal to Wesley." This in no way alters the fact, however, that it is Wesley's witness alone that constitutes the Methodist tradition as a normative tradition and that it is always only by proving its faithfulness to this primary norm that any claim to stand in this tradition can finally be validated.

For this reason, we need only to look to Wesley's own testimony to complete a material description of the Wesleyan witness. Even then, of course, there remains the risk of oversimplification, and few points of interpretation are beyond controversy. But without

---

10. Ibid., 261.

minimizing such difficulties, I believe one may describe the Wesleyan witness sufficiently for our purposes by singling out three of the defining characteristics of Wesley's witness of faith.

First of all, his witness is characterized by a faithful restatement of catholic Christianity as recovered and reinterpreted by the Protestant Reformers. With good reason, I believe, Albert Outler has ventured to describe Wesley's distinctive doctrinal perspective as "evangelical catholicism."[11] For not only was the immediate source of his witness the tradition of Anglican divinity deriving from the English Reformation, but its "deeper wellspring," as Outler puts it, was the interpretation of the biblical witness by the Fathers of the ancient church, in whose thought and piety Wesley discovered what he came to regard as "the normative pattern of catholic Christianity."[12] At the same time, if I were to point to a single bias in many of the more recent interpretations of Wesley's witness, it would be the tendency to differentiate it far too sharply from that of the continental Reformers. Such a tendency is apparent to the point of caricature, in my opinion, in Theodore Runyon's comparison of Wesley and Luther in his introduction to *Sanctification and Liberation*.[13] But even from as generally fair and balanced an interpretation as Langford's, one would never guess that the *particula exclusiva* of the Reformers has anything like the prominence in Wesley's own formulations that it actually has.

My point, of course, is not to suggest that Wesley's witness would be even more adequately described simply as "evangelicalism." But if I have no doubt that his Christianity is substantively catholic, I am equally certain of this in the case of Luther and Calvin.[14] In him, even as in them, what is recovered and reinterpreted by the rediscovery of the gospel, and hence by *sola scriptura* and *solus Christus, sola gratia,* and *sola fide,* is the faith and witness of the early catholic church. This explains, among other things, why, like them, he everywhere assumes the authority of the Nicene

11. Outler, *John Wesley*, viii.

12. Ibid., viii, 122, 9.

13. Theodore Runyon, ed., *Sanctification and Liberation: Liberation Theologies in the Light of the Wesleyan Tradition* (Nashville: Abingdon Press, 1981), 9-48, 225-28.

14. Jaroslav Pelikan, *Obedient Rebels: Catholic Substance and Protestant Principle in Luther's Reformation* (New York: Harper & Row, 1964).

dogma of the triunity of God and the Chalcedonian dogma of the two natures of the one person Jesus Christ.

On the other hand, it is equally characteristic of Wesley's witness that these dogmas, along with other conserving articles of faith, are not so much made thematic in it as presupposed by it. Thus, while he does indeed restate classical Christology and soteriology— albeit in terms that, in important respects, are his own[15]—the center of his witness is the constituting article of salvation by grace through faith alone, which he knows Luther to have spoken of as the *articulus stantis vel cadentis ecclesiae* and the English Reformers to have called "the strong rock and foundation of the Christian religion."[16] Centering on this one theme of "salvation by faith," his preaching and teaching are typically concerned with such other evangelical themes as original sin, the use of the law, the necessity of repentance and good works, and, most distinctively of all, Christian perfection.

No doubt one reason for this "existential concentration," if I may so speak of it, is that Wesley is, above all, an evangelist whose divinity is a "practical divinity" immediately directed toward the decision of Christian faith and the formation of Christian life. But if he is therefore rightly classified as a "folk-theologian," rather than as one of "the great speculative theologians" of the front rank, one need not suppose that this is the only reason for so classifying him.[17] It is arguable, I believe, that the deeper reason for the distinctive style of his theology, very much as for that of Luther's, is his firm theoretical grasp of the existential character of Christian faith and witness, which always have to do, not with the being of God in itself, but with the meaning of God for us, and hence also with our own self-understanding and praxis. But whatever the reason for it, a second characteristic of Wesleyan witness equally defining with the first is that his evangelical restatement of catholic Christianity is ever so much more practical and existential than speculative and metaphysical.

The third characteristic defining his witness is closely related to

---

15. John Deschner, *Wesley's Christology: An Interpretation* (Dallas: Southern Methodist University Press, 1960).

16. Edward H. Sugden, ed. *Wesley's Standard Sermons,* 3rd ed. (London: Epworth Press, 1951), 1:50.

17. Outler, *John Wesley,* 119.

the second—namely, its distinctive stress within its overall existential concentration on the power of God's love in Christ to overcome the power of sin over the future as well as the guilt of sin from the past. It is just this stress, of course, that comes to expression in Christian perfection's being, as we noted, the most distinctive theme of Wesley's witness. But taking the full measure of this is not to be lightly assumed. If Langford is certainly correct that "the centering theme of Wesley's thought was grace, expressed in Jesus Christ and conveyed to individuals by the Holy Spirit," it is nevertheless important to bring out (more clearly, in my opinion, than Langford does) the distinctive nature of grace as Wesley conceives it—as always sanctifying as well as justifying, the ground of "real" as well as of "relative" change in human existence.[18] To be sure, one will not want to highlight the distinctiveness of Wesley's view by suppressing his own insistence that "faith is the condition, and the only condition, of sanctification, exactly as it is of justification" and by then contrasting it with a mere caricature of the views of the Reformer—for example, by claiming that "for Luther . . . justification provides the substructure for heaven and our relationship with God—but not for our life in this world, which is left to be dealt with on grounds other than faith."[19] But as surely as one must acknowledge that Wesley's understanding of grace and salvation is—and is intended to be—entirely in accord with the real views of the Reformers, one will as little want to miss its distinctive emphasis on the transforming effect of God's love received through faith. As Wesley consistently understands the matter, to trust in the gift of God's love, and so to accept God's prevenient acceptance of us, is always to enjoy not only freedom from the *guilt* of sin and forgiveness of the past but also—and as he insists, "at the same time . . . , yea, in that very moment"—freedom from the *power* of sin and openness for the future.[20]

These, then, are what seem to me to be the chief defining characteristics of Wesley's witness and, therefore, what may be properly taken as defining the entire tradition of witness of which his is the source. At best, of course, what emerges from such a summary

---

18. Langford, *Practical Divinity*, 260.
19. Sugden, *Wesley's Standard Sermons*, 2:453; Runyon, *Sanctification and Liberation*, 36.
20. Ibid., 2:446.

is only the primary norm of this tradition, as distinct from all the secondary attempts, more or less successful, to reinterpret this norm in succeeding situations. But if I am right that it is Wesley's witness alone that is primarily normative for this tradition, what finally measures the success of any of these attempts, alone making it part of the Wesleyan witness, is that it, too, in its own time and place restates the catholic witness to God as recovered and reinterpreted by the Reformation and, within its existential concentration on the meaning of God for us, so expresses this witness as to point, above all, to the life-transforming power of God's love.

It is time now to complete our exploration by identifying certain affinities between the Wesleyan witness thus understood and process theology as it was previously described. I shall briefly consider six such affinities, some of which are more or less clearly implied by what has been said, others of which will require us, in effect, to extend our description of one or both of our two subjects. It is well to recall at the outset some of the more formal points with which we began, so as to keep in mind throughout the discussion that, although the distinction between theology and witness is relative and not absolute, all the affinities are such as are possible between a certain kind of Christian theology and a certain strand of Christian witness, on whose meaning and truth this theology, like any other, is supposed to be the critical reflection.

1. Not the least reason for characterizing the Wesleyan witness as, in its way, "catholic" is its explicit claim for the essential reasonableness of Christianity. To be sure, Langford is entirely justified in holding that Wesley's interpreters and successors, until recently, at least, have by and large followed his lead in acknowledging Scripture as the sole primary authority for Christian witness and theology.[21] But if this acknowledgment has always sharply distinguished the Wesleyan witness from mere rationalism, it has certainly never warranted the adoption of sheer fideism. On the contrary, from Wesley on it has generally been interpreted as certainly compatible with, if not also demanding, the insistence that Christian witness is thoroughly reasonable.[22] In this, one may

---

21. Langford, *Practical Divinity*, 25f., 264f.
22. Cf. Gerald R. Cragg, ed. *The Works of John Wesley*, vol. 2: *The Appeals to Men of Reason and Religion* (Oxford: Clarendon Press, 1976), 43–90.

venture to believe, the Wesleyan tradition, like the catholic tradition more generally, rightly lays claim to the authority of Scripture. For the striking thing about Scripture is that it nowhere appeals to itself as the sufficient ground for the credibility of its claims, but points rather to God's decisive revelation and to prophetic or apostolic experience of this revelation as its explicit primal source. Further-more, it does not point even to this revelation or to such immediate experience of revelation as alone supporting the credibility of its claims, but assumes instead that its claims are credible because they represent explicitly and decisively the same existential truth that is implicitly present in all human experience and reflection.[23]

But be this as it may, insofar as the Wesleyan witness is explicit in claiming that what it says is in principle credible in rational terms, there is a close affinity between it and process theology—as well as, naturally, any other Christian theology that likewise accepts the responsibility of establishing the credibility of Christian witness in terms of common human experience and reason.

2. To say only this, however, is to assert an affinity between the Wesleyan witness and a general type of Christian theology, not process theology in particular. And there is another affinity that is very similar, in that it does indeed obtain between this witness and process theology, but hardly process theology alone. Perhaps the simplest way to formulate this affinity is to say that, while there is an important sense in which both the Wesleyan witness and process theology have their primal source in human experience, the experience in question is in both cases other and more than our external sense perception of ourselves and the world.

To put it this way, however, is not to affirm but to deny that in either case the only sense in which one can meaningfully talk about the primal source of one's witness or theology is to speak of human experience. If both cases are agreed that experience is indeed the *noetic* source of all our thought and speech about God, whether more spontaneous or more reflected, they also agree that the *ontic* source of our witness and theology is revelation: both the original revelation implied by Wesley's fundamental doctrine of "prevenient

---

23. Schubert M. Ogden, "Sources of Religious Authority in Liberal Protestantism," *Journal of the American Academy of Religion* 44.3 (1976): 413.

grace" and the decisive revelation through Jesus Christ that constitutes Christian existence.[24] In other words, process theology and the Wesleyan witness alike are objectivist not subjectivist in their understandings of experience, in that they both take it to be a primal source of our thought and speech only insofar as it is also a dependent source.

But where they are also alike is in clearly distinguishing the experience of revelation from what we ordinarily call "experience." Thus process theology contrasts the *existential* experience involved in understanding ourselves, the world, and God from the *empirical* experience involved in perceiving others and ourselves by means of our senses. Wesley, on the other hand, draws a similar contrast by way of qualifying the general empiricist dictum that "our ideas are not innate, but must all originally come from our senses." There is a difference in kind, he holds, between "external sensation" through your "natural senses," which are "altogether incapable of discerning objects of a spiritual kind," and "internal sensation" through your "spiritual senses," which are "exercised to discern spiritual good and evil." Consequently, "till you have these internal senses, till the eyes of your understanding are opened, you can have no apprehension of divine things, no idea of them at all."[25]

At this point also, then, the Wesleyan witness has a definite affinity with process theology. And yet, as I have said, process theology is hardly the only theology for which this could be claimed. A more than merely empirical understanding of experience is widely represented in recent philosophy, and a number of theologies employing the insights, concepts, and methods of different contemporary philosophies—from process philosophy and radical empiricism to existentialism and phenomenology—are all more or less similar.[26] But if process theology is not unique in its understanding of experience, the affinity between it and the Wesleyan witness still seems to be close. In fact, except for "transcendental" theologies like Karl Rahner's and Bernard Lonergan's, it may be the only contemporary

24. Schubert M. Ogden, "On Revelation," in John Deschner, Leroy T. Howe, and Klaus Penzel, eds., *Our Common History as Christians: Essays in Honor of Albert C. Outler* (New York: Oxford University Press, 1975), 261-92.

25. Cragg, *An Earnest Appeal to Men of Reason and Religion*, 56ff.

26. Schubert M. Ogden, "Present Prospects for Empirical Theology," in Bernard E. Meland, ed., *The Future of Empirical Theology* (Chicago: University of Chicago Press, 1969), 65-88.

theology in which experience at its deepest level is conceived to have the same unrestricted scope that it presumably has for Wesley.

3. There is a further point, however, where the uniqueness of process theology is generally allowed even when it is compared with such other revisionary theologies as Lonergan's and Rahner's, with which it otherwise has much in common. I refer to the understanding of God or, more exactly, of God, self, and the world that process theology has elaborated in terms of the metaphysical theory of process philosophy.

A distinctive feature of this understanding is its interpretation of "God" as properly referring to the strictly universal individual, and hence to the integral whole of reality, whose many parts are properly designated respectively as "self" and "the world." If such an interpretation is monistic enough to bear a certain resemblance to pantheism, it is nevertheless distinctively different from positions that have been traditionally so identified. By distinguishing with process philosophy between the abstract identity of the whole as the one individual sequence of integral becomings and the concrete reality of these becomings, each in itself and as an ordered sequence, process theology is able to assert the sole necessary existence of God in contrast to the radical contingency of everything else, thereby maintaining the unique ontological distinction between God, on the one hand, and self and the world, on the other. To this extent, it is undoubtedly more like traditional theism than any form of traditional pantheism, although the pluralism it asserts in thus distinguishing God from self and the world is like that of the Metaphysical theory whose terms it employs in being a qualified pluralism. God is indeed asserted to be ontologically distinct from everything else, but everything other than God, whether self or the world, is held to be absolutely dependent on God, while God is only relatively dependent on it, being dependent for neither existence nor essential identity but solely for the becoming of God's own enduring good insofar as it is internally as well as externally related to the becoming of all transient goods.

My contention is that it is just such a qualified pluralism as process theology explicitly asserts that is necessarily implied by the Wesleyan witness, and specifically by its distinctive stress on both divine and human agency. If there can be no question that this witness is in entire agreement with the Protestant Reformers in affirming that we are saved by grace alone through faith alone, it nevertheless sharply breaks with a monergistic understanding of grace according to which faith is so created in us by God's act that we are saved without any free and responsible action of our own. The question, however, is whether Wesley's clear rejection of such monergism warrants the familiar interpretations of his position as synergism.[27] My answer is that if a Wesleyan understanding of grace and freedom is properly described as "synergistic," it is so only in the sense in which process theology's understanding of God and the self may be said to be "pluralistic," which is to say, it is at most a qualified synergism that asserts a certain symmetry between grace and freedom only by presupposing an even more fundamental asymmetry between them. Thus it asserts that there is indeed a difference between God's gracious acceptance of all things and our faithful acceptance of God's acceptance, which is our own free and responsible act and not any act of God's. But it also presupposes that, whereas God would be God and would be a gracious God even if we had never existed, we could not so much as possibly exist, much less exist in faith, except for the radical prevenience of God's grace.

In sum: if the Wesleyan understanding of grace and freedom is synergistic, it nevertheless bears enough of a resemblance to monergism to imply a metaphysical understanding of God and the self that, like process theology's, is only a qualified pluralism.

4. Another feature of process theology's understanding of God, self, and the world is closely related—namely, its interpretation of the meaning of God for us as the gift and the demand of boundless love and of our authentic self-understanding, accordingly, as essentially involving an active moment of loyalty to the demand of God's love as well as a passive moment of trust in its gift. Whether talk about God's love is construed as a proper metaphysical analogy or is frankly accepted as only a symbol, it is not meaningful talk at all unless the structure of God in itself involves real, internal relatedness to others. This is so, at any rate, if "love" is understood in its ordinary sense as referring, first of all, to the acceptance of others and then, secondly, to action toward others on the basis of

---

27. E.g., Outler, *John Wesley,* 14, 16, 30, 119; Runyon, *Sanctification and Liberation,* 28.

such acceptance. Clearly, to accept others as love does is to be really, internally related to them; and not to be so related to them is not to love them at all, even in an analogical or merely symbolic sense of the word. Conversely, to conceive God, as process theology does, as the integral whole of reality that in its very structure is eminently relative as well as eminently absolute, is to do all that a theology has to do metaphysically in order to provide the basis for at least symbolic talk of God's love.

The primary meaning of such talk, however, is existential, rather than metaphysical, in that it expresses the meaning of God for us, thereby authorizing the authentic understanding of ourselves and others in relation to the whole. Thus, in speaking of the gift of God's boundless love, process theology represents the integral whole of reality as authorizing an existence in unconditional trust. Because the whole of reality is eminently absolute as well as eminently relative, it can be trusted without condition, not only to establish structures of cosmic order permissive of the optimal becoming of self and the world, but also to redeem their fragmentary becomings from the futility of sheer transience by accepting them unconditionally into its own everlasting becoming. With this in mind, process theology affirms with the Protestant Reformers that we are saved by grace alone through faith alone, in the sense that it is solely by trusting in God's love alone in all its absoluteness that we can realize our authentic existence as selves in the world.

But process theology also speaks of the demand of God's boundless love, thereby representing the same integral whole of reality as authorizing an existence in unconditional loyalty. Because the whole of reality is eminently relative as well as eminently absolute, it should be loyally served without condition, all the transient goods of self and the world being included in its own enduring good. Recognizing this, process theology also affirms—and, again, the Reformers—that the faith through which we alone are saved is an active faith that works by love, in the sense that it is only by loyally serving God's love in all its relativity that we can continue in the authentic existence that has its basis in trust.

In all of this, however, there is undoubtedly the closest affinity between process theology and the Wesleyan witness. This is clear not only from the existential concentration of this witness on the meaning of God for us, and thus on our own authentic existence, but also, and, above all, from Wesley's double insistence that faith is the only condition of justification and sanctification alike and that good works are necessary to salvation.[28] If interpreters of Wesley continue to regard this insistence as paradoxical, and, therefore, commonly tend to compose the paradox by tacitly introducing qualifications, there is not the slightest evidence, so far as I am aware, that he himself ever so regarded it. On the contrary, he constantly proceeds as though the two parts of the insistence naturally belong together, the only unnatural thing to his mind being the suppression of either of them by missing the point of the other.

The reason for this, I submit, is that Wesley is exactly like the process theologian in interpreting our authentic existence as essentially involving an active as well as a passive moment. If he himself characteristically speaks of these moments as "love" and "faith," thereby taking "faith" narrowly as referring to trust but not loyalty, he nevertheless everywhere assumes the teaching of the Edwardian Homilies that "that faith which bringeth [not forth repentance but] either evil works or no good works is not a right, pure and living faith, but a dead and devilish one, as St. Paul and St. James call it."[29] Verbal difference aside, then, the Wesleyan witness and process theology express essentially the same understanding of human authenticity: as passive acceptance of the gift of God's love as the sole ultimate ground of all reality and meaning and, on the basis of this acceptance, active obedience to the demand of God's love as the only final cause to which both self and the world exist to contribute.

5. I have appealed to Wesley's insistence that good works are necessary to salvation as confirming that he is exactly like the process theologian in understanding authentic existence to involve an active as well as a passive moment. But this is not the only thing that his insistence on the necessity of good works confirms. It also confirms the definite bias toward praxis that is one of the abiding characteristics of the Wesleyan witness.

This becomes clear as soon as one recognizes that in Wesley's view

---

28. Sugden, *Wesley's Standard Sermons*, 2:444-60.

29. *The Doctrine of Salvation, Faith, and Good Works, Extracted from the Homilies of the Church of England*, "Of the Salvation of Mankind," §13, *John Wesley*, 128.

good works properly so-called are but one of two main ways in which faith working through love comes to external expression. If they are rightly regarded as its "practical" expression, it also finds "speculative" expression in "thinking" or "opinions," which Wesley systematically distinguishes from the "walking" or "practice" proper to works. Moreover, in explaining what is and is not "a catholic spirit," he is as concerned to distinguish it from *"speculative* latitudinarianism," in the sense of "an indifference to all opinions," as to distinguish it from "any kind of *practical* latitudinarianism," such as "indifference as to public worship, or as to the outward manner of performing it."[30] In other words, for all of his insistence that a catholic spirit is an inward matter of faith and love distinct from all outward matters of either works or opinions, Wesley is as steadfastly opposed to any antinomianism of thought and belief as he is to any antinomianism of action and practice.

Even so, the striking thing about the Wesleyan witness is its preoccupation with the second kind of antinomianism and its insistence, accordingly, that good works are necessary to salvation, not right opinions. Although our active participation in God's love is outwardly expressed by how we think and what we believe as well as by how we act and what we do, the "outward salvation" with which Wesley is above all concerned is not orthodoxy but orthopraxis, or, as he himself puts it, "holiness of life and conversation."[31]

Very much the same bias toward praxis is also evident in process theology, especially as it has developed more recently. Contrary to popular stereotypes, even the "process theologies" that are only or primarily philosophical have typically demonstrated practical as well as speculative interests. But in the case of process theology in the proper sense of the word, its most influential expressions have increasingly evinced a concern with praxis that is quite pronounced. Most of them, to be sure, have a broadly political character that goes beyond anything that can be explicitly found in Wesley's witness. But if this is due in some degree to process philosophy, whose ethical theory assigns special importance to structures of social and cultural order, it is due in even greater degree to the formative influence of modern historical consciousness, in which

---

30. Sugden, *Wesley's Standard Sermons*, 2:129-46.
31. Cragg, *An Earnest Appeal to Men of Reason and Religion*, 68.

Wesley scarcely shared. For this reason, the pertinent question is how Wesley's own bias toward praxis could be expressed today by anyone fully sharing in this consciousness if not in terms validated by a specifically "political" or "liberation" type of theology.[32] But, then, if the answer to this question is the one I am suggesting, there must clearly be a close affinity between any adequate contemporary expression of the Wesleyan witness and the same bias toward praxis in process theology.

6. If a broadly political concern with forming and transforming structures is distinctive of modern theologies, process theology among them, the same is true of the concern to overcome homocentrism in Christian witness and theology. In this case, however, process theology has taken the lead, not only in being among the first to draw attention to homocentrism as a theological problem, but most especially in the relative adequacy of its proposals for a possible solution.

There is no mystery about the reason for such relative adequacy. Because the process philosophy in whose terms it critically reflects on the Christian witness is in every way antidualistic, in its ethics as well as in its metaphysics, process theology is able to offer an understanding of self and the world in relation to God in which the differences in kind between any one ultimate subject of predication and any other are all relative rather than absolute. In some of its expressions, this understanding takes the form of a panpsychic or psychicalist metaphysics, for which not only the self but any other thing comparably concrete and singular is an instance, or an individual sequence of instances, of mind or sentience in a completely generalized sense of the words. But even in such expressions of process theology as voice serious reservations about this or any other form of categorial metaphysics, there is no basis for dualism either metaphysical or ethical; for one can say even in strictly transcendental terms that anything concretely and singularly real in the full sense of the words is an instance of real, internal relatedness to others and, therefore, of intrinsic and not merely instrumental good. Consequently, all expressions of process theology are able, as

---

32. Runyon, *Sanctification and Liberation*; Schubert M. Ogden, "The Concept of a Theology of Liberation: Must Christian Theology Today Be So Conceived?" in Brian Mahan and L. Dale Richesin, eds., *The Challenge of Liberation Theology: A First World Response* (Maryknoll, N.Y.: Orbis Books, 1981), 127-40.

hardly any other kind of theology seems to be, to overcome homo-centrism both metaphysically and ethically. Without in the least questioning the important relative differences between the level of becoming occupied by the self and its fellow selves and all lower, less conscious levels of becoming, they can nevertheless stress the relativity of the differences and urge an indefinite extension of the scope of the second commandment. Because anything concrete and singular is insofar intrinsically good, and is fully accepted as such by God, the neighbors we are to love as ourselves include not only all our fellow selves but also all the others at every level of becoming who can in any way be affected by our own acceptance and action.

But, surely, if there is any point where process theology is different from the Wesleyan witness, it is here. Beyond any question, Wesley everywhere takes for granted an understanding of self and the world that is homocentric when viewed from the standpoint of process theology. One reason for this, presumably, is that he could still assume a cosmology as well as a natural history of life and humankind that was in many respects prescientific. And yet it is also clear, I think, that his explicit metaphysics is sufficiently classical at this point, as at most others, to accept the traditional dualism between matter and spirit—so much so, in fact, that he can subtly confuse our only truly ultimate end in God with our unique enjoyment of this end as spiritual beings.[33]

But if recognizing this serves to remind us that there are indeed differences as well as affinities between the Wesleyan witness and process theology, we may still need to look closely if we are not to exaggerate the differences. All thinkers, Whitehead suggests, enjoy insights beyond the limits of the systems that we are accustomed to associate with their names. And so it is, in my opinion, with at least some of the things Wesley has to say on this very point. This is particularly so if one reads a passage such as the following against the background of orthodox eschatology with its teaching of the final annihilation of all things other than spirits in the *consummatio saeculi:*

---

33. Cf. Schubert M. Ogden, "Why Did God Make Me? A Free-Church Answer," in Hans Küng and Jürgen Moltmann, eds., *Why Did God Make Me?* (New York: Seabury Press, 1978), 67-73.

Perhaps we may go a step farther still. Is not matter itself, as well as spirit, in one sense eternal? Not indeed *a parte ante*, as some senseless philosophers, both ancient and modern, have dreamed. . . . But although nothing beside the great God can have existed from ever-lasting–none else can be eternal, *a parte ante*; yet there is no absurd-ity in supposing that all creatures are eternal *a parte post*. All matter indeed is continually changing, and that into ten thousand forms; but that it is changeable, does in no wise imply that it is perishable. The substance may remain one and the same, though under innu-merable different forms. It is very possible any portion of matter may be resolved into the atoms of which it was originally composed: But what reason have we to believe that one of the atoms ever was, or ever will be, annihilated? It never can, unless by the uncontrol-lable power of its almighty Creator. And is it probable that ever He will exert this power in unmaking any of the things that he hath made? In this also, God is not "a son of man that he should repent." . . . [The elements] will be only dissolved not destroyed; they will melt, but they will not perish. Though they lose their present form, yet not a particle of them will ever lose its existence; but every atom of them will remain, under one form or other, to all eternity.[34]

I shall not repeat the kind of question I asked earlier so as to sug-gest that one could do justice today to Wesley's clear intention only by breaking with all homocentrism as sharply as process theology does. But I do wish to claim that even here there is more than sheer difference and that, when this passage is considered together with the other evidence and argument of this paper, there can be no question about the affinities between process theology and the Wesleyan witness. With whatever differences, they are sufficiently many and sufficiently close that not only those of us who do process theology as Wesleyan Christians, but anyone else con-cerned with "Wesleyan theology and the next century" cannot afford to ignore them.

---

34. Thomas Jackson, ed. *The Works of John Wesley* (Grand Rapids: Zondervan, 1958-59), 6:191-92.

CHAPTER TWO

COMING HOME:
WESLEY, WHITEHEAD, AND WOMEN[1]

MARJORIE HEWITT SUCHOCKI

Long before I became a United Methodist I wondered at the "coincidence"—how was it that so many prominent process theologians were United Methodists? Recently I was asked that question, together with another—are there particular affinities between feminism and the Methodist tradition? My interest in the questions is more than academic since I myself am a process theologian and a feminist who chose to become a United Methodist three years ago. My affirmative answer to these questions stems from a growing sense of having "come home" as a relatively new member of this good tradition. My participation in these lectures gives me the privileged opportunity to reflect publicly on the reasons for my affirmation. Additionally, I suggest that process and feminist modes of thought might well be owned by this tradition as peculiarly suited to Methodism. It may be that they provide new ways to give expression to fundamental Wesleyan positions on experience, Christian perfection, and theological pluralism.

My initial decision to become a United Methodist was pragmatic—a not unlikely Methodist trait! I was invited to become dean of Wesley Theological Seminary. Granted, they had never had a woman dean before, nor a lay dean before, nor a non-United Methodist dean before, but there it was: I was invited to be dean. As I considered the invitation, I also considered The United Methodist Church. Familiar with the tradition through my education at Claremont, I decided that, if I were to be dean, at least two of the oddities in my selection were not candidates for change. I expect always to be a woman and a layperson. But as for denomination,

---

1. This essay originally appeared in *The Drew Gateway* 57.3 (Fall 1987): 31-43 and is reprinted here with permission.

I preferred to be dean of this seminary working from within its denominational structure rather than from outside of that structure, and so I determined to unite with this United Methodist tradition.

All well and good—but there exists a laudable tradition of "pastors' schools" in this denomination, and the West Virginians not only invited me to teach, they also determined the topic: John Wesley's doctrine of Christian perfection! And as I studied that small gem, *A Plain Account of Christian Perfection*,[2] my excitement grew and my pragmatic choice began its transformation to a much deeper acknowledgment: in becoming United Methodist, I had come home to a doctrinal core which resonated with my already well defined process-feminist self. Shortly thereafter I encountered Albert Outler's now famous interpretation of Wesley's criteria for theology, the quadrilateral, and my transformation into a card-carrying United Methodist was complete: I have come home.

To explore the affinities between process, feminism, and the Wesley tradition, let us look first to the inclusion of experience within the quadrilateral. This prepares the way to consider the doctrine of Christian perfection, which in turn yields insights into a basis for theological pluralism. Experience, perfection, and pluralism are the strong connecting links between Wesley, Whitehead, and women.

EXPERIENCE

The explication of the quadrilateral as both the source and the norm for Christian theology is given in *An Interim Report to the General Conference* by The Theological Study Commission (Doctrine and Doctrinal Standards) in 1970, chaired by Albert C. Outler. The report both begins and concludes with reference to the "four-element compound of interdependent norms,"[3] described as "first scripture itself; then the historical interpretation of scripture which we call 'tradition'; then individual experience and finally, reason."[4]

---

2. *A Plain Account of Christian Perfection, Works* (Jackson) 11:366-446.

3. *An Interim Report to the General Conference*, The Theological Study Commission (Doctrine and Doctrinal Standards), The United Methodist Church (1970), Albert C. Outler, chair, 7-8.

4. Ibid., 66.

To a process-feminist, the intriguing aspect of this criterion lies in its inclusion of experience, and the interpretation of experience which is implied. It refers, of course, not to experience-in-general, but to specifically religious experience, more narrowly defined as the assurance of salvation or perfection through one's encounter with the "quick and lively" word of the gospel. Lest one get carried away with the excesses of enthusiasm in the eighteenth century sense of the word, this norm of experience is held to the primal norm of the scriptures, and must be expressed according to all the rules of rational discourse. This reasonable expression is itself the cutting edge of the Christian tradition, which has been continuously evoked by the gospel mediated to us through the Scriptures. The reasonable formulation of the experience of salvation is therefore a continuing dialogue with earlier formulations, and all are held to the criterion of the fundamental witness given in the Scriptures. Thus the interpretation of individual experience is shaped by communal experience and communal norms.

A comparative study of the importance of experience as a norm in Methodism and in feminism has already been given in a number of essays included within *Wesleyan Theology Today: A Bicentennial Theological Consultation*.[5] Insofar as the Wesleyan criterion calls for personal appropriation of the gospel, this applies without distinction to male and female. Indeed, the source materials of early Methodism include copious journals by women who followed the discipline of recording their religious experience. The witness of women is used by Wesley himself—note, for example, his long proof of the reality of Christian perfection through its illustration in the letters and life of Jane Cooper.[6]

The recognition of the validity of women's as well as men's experience of God's grace leads easily into recognition of their experience of God's call, and the consequent importance of women as well as men in the early Methodist movement. Wesley, in any case, seems to have had considerably less trouble over the call to women to preach than did many of his successors, and the vitality of the experiential norm may well have been a strong contributing factor.

---

5. Theodore Runyon, ed., *Wesleyan Theology Today: A Bicentennial Theological Consultation* (Nashville: Kingswood Books, 1985).

6. *A Plain Account*, §24, *Works* (Jackson) 11:409-14.

There is yet another implication which follows from according normative status to experience, and this has to do with the effect of its inclusion within the "four-element compound of interdependent norms." While it is the case that scripture is accorded primacy, the very interdependence of the norms can raise the issue of how the understanding of scripture is affected by one's own personal experience. While scripture may shape the way experience is interpreted, it is invariably the case that like it or not, experience also shapes the way scripture is interpreted. One may indeed intend to subordinate experience to scripture, but one cannot eliminate the perspectival effect of experience. Nor, say feminists, *should* one attempt to eliminate the personal perspective—to the contrary, one should lift it up. Otherwise, it becomes a hidden norm that in fact distorts the texts, undercutting their so-called primacy through the suppressed but operative viewpoint of the interpreter, and, indeed, the author. Thus the inclusion of experience as a norm, even a subordinate norm, provides strong theological justification for the rigorous biblical criticism advocated by the feminist movement, and called the "hermeneutics of suspicion."

If the inclusion of experience as a norm renders Methodism a good home for a feminist, there are other aspects of this inclusion which are equally hospitable to a process theologian. The dimension of experience which connects particularly with process sensitivities is its aspect of transcendence over sheer sensory perception. Clearly, while the religious experience in question is usually mediated by a preached word, something more than hearing the word is entailed. Hearing the word may immediately evoke "quickening," which is an interaction with the word which troubles the individual, luring toward yet another mode of experience. This second mode is that of "assurance," or inwardly grasping God's own justifying or sanctifying acceptance of the self. While this assurance *may* be connected with the activity of hearing or reading, it may just as likely happen subsequently to these activities. Thus the experience is not immediately connected with sense perception; rather, Wesley calls it an "inward impression upon the soul," received through "spiritual senses."[7]

What is the source of this "assurance"? The critical point is that

---

7. Sermon 10, "The Witness of the Spirit, I," §I.7 and §II.9-11, *Works* 1:274, 282-83.

it is precisely *not* mediated through the senses, as ordinary knowledge was considered to be mediated. If it is arguable that Wesley is indebted to Locke for much of his own interpretation of the world, this aspect of experience appears to be Wesley's un-Lockeian epistemological innovation. There is a mode of knowing which goes beyond that which is mediated by the senses, and this personal, subjective mode is part and parcel of one's material for constructing theology. Granted, this mode of knowing must be subject to and interpreted through scripture, and expressed through commonly accepted rules of reason. These external norms guard against subjectivization, idiosyncratism, and enthusiasm. Nonetheless, the experience itself is not mediated by sensory substances nor accidents, and insofar as it is independent of these, it signals a transcendence and/or transformation of an epistemology governed solely by sense perception.

The importance of this for process theology is its analogy to Whitehead's epistemology, which is based upon an analysis of experience not limited by sensory perception. Just as Wesley's epistemology contrasts with knowledge mediated through sense perception, Whitehead's epistemology contrasts with the more sensory dependent Newtonian epistemology.

Newton's powerful interpretation of the way of the world is governed heavily by sense perception: there is the assumption that what we see reveals the ultimate nature of things. Kant's critique of reason and the subsequent work of science and philosophy which show the relativism of all our thought are directed precisely against thought which is governed normatively by sensory perception. There is no metaphysical necessity that knowledge shaped by the senses should be normative for understanding ultimate reality, let alone modes of reality which escape the parameters available to our senses. Like Newtonian physics, a sensory epistemology is pragmatically useful for yielding knowledge relative to human custom and practice, but it cannot by itself give reliable information beyond that small sphere.

Nonetheless, a sensory epistemology contains the seeds of its own transcendence, since a Newtonian description of the world suggests models for probing more deeply into the nature of reality. Those models, developed and used, serve to relativize the very notions of physics which gave them birth. The result is to take the initial starting point, the world of solid objects, and turn it into a secondary rather than primary mode of existence. The primary mode is not immediately accessible to sensory perception. Yet it is fundamental, and gives rise to the world of objects which subjects perceive and analyze.

The Newtonian way of interpreting the world and all reality became the means of its own relativization, giving way to relativity theory. This realm of thought indeed entails an epistemology, but one which is no longer quite so dependent upon the macro-world of sensory perception; its models, in fact, are not tinier images of the sensory world, but radically different organizations of behavior.

In the case of the physicist/philosopher, Alfred North Whitehead, his fundamental basis of knowledge was a particular analysis of nonsensory experience. While human experience certainly includes sense perception, experience is deeper and more extensive than the senses alone can probe, and is based fundamentally on the transmission of energy through relationships. Further, Whitehead's understanding of experience is that it is basic to all existence, human and nonhuman. Experience is comprised of inter-relationality, including the primacy of a relation to God. This latter is a directive lure, given to every mode of existence whatsoever, appropriated and interpreted (insofar as the word applies) according to the conditions of that mode.

While the data of experience are always interpreted data, they are nonetheless interpreted *data*. There is a necessary connection with the objective content now subjectively appropriated. Unlike Kant, the "thing-in-itself" is not locked in mystery outside the gate of sensory perception; rather, in a Whiteheadian world, experience *is* the direct transmission of energy from one experient to the other. While the senses mediate much of what we know, they are not as fundamental to what we know as was previously thought. Deeper than sensory perception and supporting sensory perception is the direct transmission of energy through relational experience.

Thus sensory perception cannot exhaust the richness of experience: there is more given than sensory perception can account for. The "more than" provides a basis for metaphysical understanding which is more fundamental than sensory perception. It becomes the realm of quantum physics in science, and of relational metaphysics in philosophy. It provides a metaphysical frame of reference for theological discourse which dares to make epistemological statements about the nature of God. While the statements are certainly perspectival, they are not exhaustively so. There is a genuine connection with the given data. Experience itself, formed through an interrelational transmission of energy, yields valid insights into the nature of reality. An existent God, in such a world, must be involved in a direct transmission of energy to every existent reality, giving a relatively objective basis to the subjectively appropriated experience—or "assurance."

It would be stretching things indeed to claim that Wesley is a precursor of process philosophy/theology, much less the new physics. However, it is not at all stretching things to suggest that insofar as Wesley includes experience which transcends sensory perception as a norm for the doing of theology, he is deeply compatible with process thought. To introduce the experience of "assurance" into theological discussion is to open the way beyond the impasse presented to us by the philosophical critiques of a knowledge understood to be bound by the limitations of sensory perception. The admission of experiential knowing, even within the interpretive boundaries of human culture, becomes an invitation to the metaphysical legitimacy of God-talk.

Further, once experience as a norm for theology is given credence, the door is opened for an understanding of general as well as religious experience. No experience is isolated; every experience exists through its interconnectedness with yet other experiences. In a relational world, every individual experience is one which is "trailing clouds of glory" in that it implies much about further modes of experience. The world is one of mutual implication, of fuzzy edges, of "if's . . . then's." In short, to name experience as a norm for theology, even when that experience is specifically narrowed to religious experience, is to lay the basis for a Christian natural theology. Is it any wonder, then, that a tradition which allows nonperceptual experience into the normative material for theology should generate a mode of theology that is based upon a fundamentally nonperceptual analysis of experience? I remind you again: most process theologians are United Methodists.

Yet another value of Wesley's use of experience as a norm for

theology rests with Wesley's unyielding emphasis upon the concrete. For too long theology has given its more sanctioned attention
to reason, tradition, and scripture, and wound up in realms of
abstraction which led the laity of the church—to whom theology
must belong—to consider theology a most profound if not obtuse
subject. To insist upon experience as a norm is to demand that the
practical results of theology be tested in the crucible of dailiness.
Wesley is once again our example, for his "plain accounts" for
"plain people" follow most seriously from his emphasis upon the
norm of experience. Both process theologians and feminist theologians—and those like myself who claim to be both—had best learn
from this master communicator what it means to test one's theology
through its applicability in the living experience of "plain people."

Thus the norm of experience in the Wesleyan quadrilateral
speaks to me as a process-feminist in many ways. With regard to
feminism, it manifests deep compatibility with the sensitivity that
women's modes of interpreting experience are as much grist for the
theological mill as are men's modes. To leave our perspectives out
is to have a truncated theology, only partially informed by
Christian religious experience. Also, the inclusion of experience as
norm logically entails that biblical criticism must proceed through
a hermeneutics of suspicion.

With regard to process thought, the norm of experience in its
particular Wesleyan form has an interesting compatibility with the
interpretation of existence formulated by Whitehead and utilized
by process theologians. Wesley's "witness of the Spirit" elicits an
"of course!" from process theologians attuned to the lure of God,
specifically suited to the conditions and possibilities for every reality at every moment. No wonder the Wesleyan tradition generates
process theologians! And no wonder the Methodist church was in
the forefront of the recognition that women as well as men should
be ordained! Experience as an admissible norm for theological
reflection is crucial to both.

CHRISTIAN PERFECTION

To move from a discussion of experience in the quadrilateral to
Christian perfection is not at all amiss when one considers that the

two critically normative aspects of experience for Wesley were first of all that quickening which led to apprehension of divine grace for justification, and secondly, that infusion of love which signaled the advent of sanctification toward Christian perfection. Just as the notion of "experience" in the Wesleyan tradition is by all means congruent with process-feminist perspectives, even so is a Wesleyan understanding of holiness.

It seems to my newly converted self that this doctrine of Christian perfection is the "sine qua non" of Methodism, and is its unique contribution to the contemporary ecumenical dialogue. I hope it is more than the zeal of the convert which leads me to say that Wesley's insight into perfection captures the essential point of the gospel, that God so loved the *world,* and intends the world's good. Wesley's awesome audacity is to dare to assume that God can accomplish the divine intention for creation within creation and through creation. That intention is simply that creation shall be a living image of God's own love.

As I study Wesley's small book, *A Plain Account of Christian Perfection*, plus the pertinent sermons, it seems to me that the doctrine is necessarily set against the broad background of a cosmic perspective. Midway in the book, Wesley answers the question, "How is Christ the end of the law for righteousness to everyone that believeth?"[8] In answer, Wesley has recourse to a doctrine of creation, through reference to Adam. He speaks of God's intent in creation that humanity shall "use to the glory of God all the powers with which [they were] created."[9] Clearly, throughout the book, the glory of God is simply the wholeness of love in its unifying, interconnective work. Love wills the well-being of the other, binding the creation together in what is finally the fully reflected image of God, who is boundless love. Thus God creates the world for the sake of the love which it may set forth in time, as the moving image of eternity.

Wesley speaks of the Adamic law, which is the enjoinment of love, of the Mosaic law, which is the codification of love, and of the failures attendant upon both. God has created the world for the sake of the perfection of love, but this divinely ordained destiny is

---

8. *A Plain Account*, §25, *Works* (Jackson) 11:414.
9. Ibid.

frustrated by radical human failure. The failure dulls human faculties, clouding human reason, so that Wesley states, "hence at present no [one] can at all times apprehend clearly, or judge truly. And where either the judgment or apprehension is wrong, it is impossible to reason justly. Therefore, it is as natural [to make a] mistake as to breathe; and [one] can no more live without the one than without the other. Consequently, no [one] is able to perform the service which the Adamic law requires."[10] Thus everyone's reason and affections are distorted through failure to adhere to God's creative plan. We will return later to implications of this interpretation for theological pluralism; presently we continue with the outline of the dynamics of perfection.

Wesley understands Christ to be the end of the law in that Christ is himself the restoration and fulfillment of creation. The law of faith then supplants the Adamic and Mosaic law of works, since faith in Christ incorporates us into the restored creation. God's destiny for creation is made once again possible through faith. But God's destiny is nothing other than that the creation shall be the living love of God, spread out in time and space, informing time and space, infusing time and space with the divine image.

In such a vision, justification is but a necessary prelude to the full drama of destiny, which is Christian perfection. Justification is for the sake of sanctification, clearing away the hindrances, in order that God's creative destiny for the world shall at last have full sway. Thus Christian perfection is at the very core of Christian theology and Christian experience; it is the fruit which proves the vitality of the tree. Not justification, but sanctification, is the focal point of creation. Justification is the means to this great end.

If sanctification has its roots in the doctrine of creation, it has its destiny in a doctrine of eschatology, or creation's final end. For the love which is manifest in the sanctified life is no penultimate reality, but is indeed the present participation in that which is eternal. The love of God shed abroad in our hearts takes place in time, sanctifying time for all eternity. It is both the infusion of eternity into time, and the preparation of time for eternity. Thus the love which is Christian perfection is God's creative destiny for the world, temporally and eternally.

---

10. Ibid., 415.

Christian perfection yields a love of God that necessarily spills over into love for the world. This is seen in Wesley's comment that "One of the principal rules of religion is, to lose no occasion of serving God. And since God is invisible to our eyes, we are to serve [God] in our neighbour: which [is received] as if done to [God] in person, standing visibly before us."[11] One can understand this statement in several senses. To serve the neighbor as if serving God has its deep roots in the gospel, notably Matthew 25. From the viewpoint of Christian perfection, the logic is simply that to love God is to love that which God loves, and "God so loved the world." To love God is inevitably to participate in God's own great love for the world, evoking service to the world as service to God.

A second perspective is incarnational. God is present to us through the neighbor. But if God is present through the neighbor, and one loves God, then one perforce loves the neighbor, also. To the question, "who is my neighbor?" the gospel answer remains the same: the one who is in need. Hence the one journeying on toward Christian perfection views the world as a parish not simply in the sense of preaching, but essentially in the sense of loving. Love is of all things active, creating a sensitivity to the needs of the world and an energy for their redress. "Scripture perfection is pure love, filling the heart, and governing all the words and actions."[12] If Christian perfection is the love of God which evokes a heart full of love for the world, then there are implications for the unity of all creation through the love of God. Wesley considers love a union with God: "Through my union with Thee, I am full of light, of holiness, and happiness. But if I were left to myself, I should be nothing but sin, darkness, hell."[13] If love unites with God, and the love of God shed abroad in our hearts leads us to love God in the neighbor, is there not union with the neighbor, too? The love of Christian perfection can be seen as a unitive force binding all creation together in interdependence, thus leading to the temporal completion of God's creative destiny in the world.

But we are to "continue on to perfection," since the realization of this love is a relative rather than absolute state. One could call it a

---

11. Ibid., Q. 48, *Works* (Jackson) 11:440.
12. Ibid., §19, *Works* (Jackson) 11:401.
13. Ibid., §25, Q. 10, *Works* (Jackson) 11:417.

processive condition, adapted to the situation of the believer, and always luring the believer on toward yet fuller realization of love. Christian perfection is, to quote Wesley, "hedged in by outward circumstances."[14] Physical and mental frailties persist, leading to mistakes of judgment and action, and the love of God experienced and expressed by the soul may be clouded to view. It would seem that the gracious God is one who meets our condition, fitting our call to that which we can bear, and then leading us yet further on. Therefore, the Christian perfection which is the destiny of the world is not one which is a static once-for-allness to be achieved by the Church, but is in fact to be historically appropriated, so that all of time becomes the moving image of God's eternal/everlasting love. Christian perfection is a fullness which is called to a self-surpassing fullness yet again, and in this process, the divine destiny is achieved. It depends upon God's grace, and human openness to God's gracious action within the heart.

If I have phrased these statements in terms too reminiscent of process theology, I hope you will not only forgive me, but note that there is considerable justification for so doing. In fact, just as I drew out the foundations for feminism and process modes of thought through the criterion of experience within the quadrilateral, I now will highlight those aspects of Christian perfection which are deeply significant for one steeped in process theology and feminism.

Beginning with the last point (the processive nature of love) the fundamental insight of process thought is indeed that God meets our condition, providing modes of redemption for us which are relevant to who and where we are. This is the process understanding of the gracious character of God: that God leads us to that which is really possible for us, and not to some unattainable ideal in—to repeat Karl Barth's (and Aristophanes') unforgettable image—some "cloud cuckooland." History is seriously incorporated into God's providence for the world, conditioning that providence to the particularities of creation in all its times and places. Process theologians express this through all the intricacies of our metaphysics, but we can look to Wesley and learn from his "plain account" a simpler, more powerful way to say it: God's work with us is in fact "hedged in by outward circumstances." The relativity of God's

---

14. Ibid., §19, *Works* (Jackson) 11:400.

relation to us is witnessed in Wesley, and in process thought as well. While other traditions point to the same insight, I have not seen it so emphatically given as in Wesley and his process progeny.

Further, a survey of the works of some of our chief process theologians—John B. Cobb Jr., Schubert Ogden, and Delwin Brown (each of whom is United Methodist) bespeaks a necessary connection between process thought and liberation theology. *Process Theology as Political Theology, Faith and Freedom*, and *To Set at Liberty* are among their respective works.[15] The peculiar stance of process contributions to liberation theology comes from a fundamental presupposition concerning the inescapable interdependence of the world: we exist in interconnection, and are linked one with the other toward the common good. This interdependence is the fundamental structure of the universe, and we are called to live in accordance with this interdependence, bringing it to creative expression. Hence necessarily we are called to works which look to the common good, redressing oppression with liberation and restructuring our systems and societies such that they shall be conducive to the common good of all. Such love is the very completion of creation through its active assent to its structure of being. It is a love to which we are called in all its modes of specificity in every moment of existence. This love is necessarily societal.

Process thought outlines the foundations for social action through a metaphysics of interdependence—but does not John Wesley indicate it more simply with his affirmation that God has created the world for the sake of the perfection of love, and that Christian perfection is absolutely central to Christian faith? The language is different; the insight is the same.

Some criticize Wesley's understanding of perfection by claiming that it was in fact so oriented to the individual that it failed to tend to social analysis—yet this may be an anachronistic criticism. Wesley's views most surely led to cottage industries for the economically deprived, to active concern about the prison system, and to the structure of a connectional community. A holiness based on love is social holiness; there is no other kind—it would be a contradiction

---

15. John B. Cobb Jr., *Process Theology as Political Theology* (Philadelphia: Westminster Press, 1982); Schubert M. Ogden, *Faith and Freedom* (Nashville: Abingdon Press, 1979); and Delwin Brown, *To Set at Liberty* (Maryknoll, N.Y.: Orbis Books, 1981).

in terms. But the way in which that social holiness develops will and must be conditioned by the place of its appropriation, even while it contains the seeds of transformation of that time and place. Thus the contemporary development of the doctrine of Christian perfection may well utilize tools of economic and social analysis. But within the Methodist tradition, it seems to me that we must recognize that our concerned praxis of liberation is a contemporary branch on the root and trunk of the tree of Christian perfection.

As for the incorporation of feminist insight into the conversation, feminist theology is of course a mode of liberation theology. We feminists stress a nonhierarchical view of the world, and develop an ethic of mutuality and interdependence. Every story is a story to be heard and every human being is a locus of social dignity. Is this not a variation on the theme that God has created the world for the sake of holiness, which is nothing but the fullness of love? If the inclusion of experience in Wesleyan theology speaks to the methodology of feminist theology, the inclusion of perfection speaks to goals of feminist theology. The language used is undeniably different, but the intent of a society bound together toward a progressive and inclusive good is characteristic of both feminist and Wesleyan theology.

Both process and feminist theologians would extend interconnected existence and the perfection which is the goal of creation to the nonhuman as well as to the human realm. We exist in an ecology-minded age. Both process and feminist theorists include interconnectedness and therefore responsibility for the whole world, human and nonhuman, in an ethic of love. It can be read as a contemporary extension of Wesley's doctrine of Christian perfection.

PLURALISM

One further compatibility between Wesley, Whitehead, and women is Wesley's remarkable acceptance of theological pluralism. In the passage quoted earlier, Wesley speaks of human reason as clouded over, so that "no [one] can at all times apprehend clearly, or judge truly . . . it is impossible to reason justly." [16] Reason, as well

---

16. *A Plain Account*, §25, Q. 1, *Works* (Jackson) 11:415.

as love, is "hedged in by outward circumstances." It is well known that Wesley insisted on two primary doctrines, justification and sanctification, with a diversity in theological opinion expected beyond this foundation. His understanding of the limitations of reason give good grounds for the subsequent pluralism, for if our reason is indeed beset by limitations, then the theologies spun by our reason are likewise fallible. Further, our reason inescapably reflects its roots in our experience, necessarily rendering reason perspectival. How, then, shall we insist that all theologies shall conform to our own version of true theology? Even with the fourfold criterion as our guide, diversities of interpretation must of necessity arise. Recognizing this, there is a built-in openness to pluralism in theology. Love, not doctrinal conformity, unites.

The connections I would like to draw here with reference to process theology are twofold. On one hand, of course, there is most assuredly a preference for pluralism within process thought. John B. Cobb Jr. extends this not only on the basis of the limitations of our culturally conditioned perspectives, but also on the basis that reality itself yields a plurality of metaphysical principles.[17] I myself have followed John, my mentor, in this position, albeit somewhat differently stated.[18] Process thought affirms and requires pluralism.

But the other connection I wish to make pertains to the pluralism within Methodism itself. Holding to the two great doctrines of justification and sanctification, it has nonetheless spawned a great diversity of views. Its early mode of using the Conference, and later, Commissions of the Conference, for theological purposes almost guaranteed this diversity, given the regional and professional diversities within and among the Conferences. Given this, should there not be celebration within Methodism of its own pluralism of theological views, spanning modes as diverse as the Good News Movement *and* process theology? My call to our United Methodist Church is that it own process thought as peculiarly one of its own, even though not exclusively its own. A positive answer is perhaps already given by the inclusion of the "Process

---

17. John B. Cobb Jr., "Buddhist Emptiness and the Christian God," *Journal of the American Academy of Religion* 45.1 (1977): 11-25.

18. Marjorie Hewitt Suchocki, *God-Christ-Church: A Practical Guide to Process Theology* (New York: Crossroad Publishing, 1982), 151-60.

Theology and Wesleyan Thought" section of the *Wesleyan Theology Today* Bicentennial papers. The same request and answer might be said with regard to feminist thought, even though the impetus toward this mode of theology is probably less indigenous to Wesleyan thought than is process theology.

I have drawn connections between Wesley and feminist/process modes of thought—or, to put it more alliteratively, among Wesley, Whitehead, and women. My purpose has been to explicate some of the reasons for my own "at-homeness" within United Methodism, but my purpose perhaps immodestly goes beyond that. These lectures in which we are engaged here at Drew University are for the purpose of exploring directions in Methodist doctrine, a task which is perennially before this great church. I suggest that even as the apostle Paul examined many gifts, but declared that the greatest of them was love, we United Methodists might likewise declare that there are many doctrines, but the greatest of them is love. This is the classic doctrine of Christian perfection—that for the sake of which God created and redeemed the world. As we look at directions in Methodist doctrine, should we not, like John Wesley, make this our fundamental core, spelling out its implications in relation to the gospel, tradition, and our own experience?

As and if we do, I suggest that it would be well to make the doctrine of Christian perfection intentionally central from a valued diversity of perspectives. This means that we should study the meaning of Christian perfection from many points of departure— Good News, process thought, black theology, liberation theology, feminist theology, and as many theologies as have and may emerge through this now United Methodist tradition. As we each develop contemporary formulations of Christian perfection, perhaps we can view them all after the fashion of the many facets of a perfectly cut diamond, rejoicing at its variegated beauty, and learning from each other concerning its wholeness. A doctrine of Christian perfection so honed in theory may yet woo us into openness to its experience. Embracing our own diversity in love will give an embodied witness to Christian perfection as our unique offering to the ecumenical dialogue.

Because of Wesley's inclusion of experience among the norms for theology, and because of his insistence on a practical and dynamic doctrine of Christian perfection, and because of his essential openness to pluralism in theological expression, I feel I have "come home" by uniting with this church, this tradition. But precisely because of these same doctrines, "coming home" is not a process of arriving, but a process of joining a band of pilgrim people who are continuing the journey. There is a personal/social perfection God makes possible for the world, a perfection of love, shaped to our times. We are home, and yet home is always before us, calling us in a plurality of ways to continue the process of deepening our experience and understanding of Christian perfection.

CHAPTER THREE

PROCESS AND SANCTIFICATION

BRYAN P. STONE

My understanding of Christian faith has been so influenced by both Wesleyan and process modes of thought that the possibility of the relation expressed in the title does not arise for me lightly or inconsequentially. I have come to believe that a process meta-physics has much to offer Wesleyan theology as the latter goes about its task of critical reflection on our Christian witness in the world. What is equally clear, however, is that in attempting to trace the outlines of a process theology of sanctification (the very pur-pose of this essay), there are considerable resources within the Wesleyan tradition to which process thought might readily be drawn and upon which process thought might creatively draw.

John Wesley brings to the theological roundtable an unswerving advocacy for, and optimism about, the possibilities of grace in transforming human life, both personally and socially. He did not wear blinders to the fallenness of human beings nor did he wink at the terrible evil of which we are capable. At the same time, his doc-trine of sanctification is tenacious, all-embracing, and radical. Likewise, while Wesley was overwhelmingly anthropocentric in his soteriology, one catches a glimpse of a sanctification that is ulti-mately cosmic in scope, aimed as it is at the restoration of all God's creation into "a more beautiful paradise than Adam ever saw."[1]

Wesley's understanding of God's grace as persuasive and rela-tional rather than coercive and static is one that resonates clearly with themes in process thought, as does his emphasis on love as the primary clue for understanding what it means to be created in God's image and what it means to be transformed, restored, and per-fected into that image. But Wesley's thought also issues a challenge

---

1. Sermon 64, "The New Creation," §16, *Works* 2:508.

to any theology, including process theology, that might be tempted to confine itself to developing neat intellectual systems while forgetting that the flower of Christian holiness cannot grow apart from the soil of charity toward, solidarity with, and justice for the poor. A process theology of sanctification can be little more than an interesting sideshow for a handful of theologians and philosophers if it fails to grasp Wesley's intimate connection between the sanctified life and a liberating response to poverty and suffering. The criterion of ministry with, and to, the poor serves, for Wesley, as a theological and ecclesiastical starting point, a means of grace, and a fundamental aim of Christian holiness.[2] However much a process metaphysics may do justice to this prior commitment or starting point, I hold that it cannot be derived from a process metaphysics (or any metaphysics, for that matter). It is derived from the life and teachings of Jesus of Nazareth.

While Wesley's vision, optimism, and theological method are important resources for the development of a contemporary theology of sanctification, he was of course a man of his time. The historical situation and the crises of practice (both religious and secular), to which his theology is a response, are not ours; neither are the scientific, philosophical, nor psychological presuppositions of his thinking the same as ours. A process theology that intends to appropriate Wesley's theology of sanctification two hundred years later has no easy task. Modern theories of personality, guilt, and alienation, as well as a heightened awareness of our complicity and even embeddedness in sinful and unjust systems challenge us to rethink not only the meaning but also the truth of the radical, holistic, and all-inclusive transformation that Wesley envisioned.

LOVE AS THE IMAGE OF GOD

Wesley often began his own reflections on the nature of sanctification with the biblical affirmation that we are created in the "image of God" (Gen. 1:27). This declaration might strike us as out-

---

2. See Theodore W. Jennings Jr., *Good News to the Poor: John Wesley's Evangelical Economics* (Nashville: Abingdon Press, 1990); and Theodore Runyon, ed., *Sanctification and Liberation: Liberation Theologies in Light of the Wesleyan Tradition* (Nashville: Abingdon Press, 1981).

rageous, even preposterous, confronted as we are with daily evidence that, as Wesley said, we appear to be more beastly than godly.[3] Although we as Christians, over the last twenty centuries, have generally been consistent in affirming our creation in God's image, we have not always agreed on what the image of God is, how far damaged or destroyed that image is through sin, or to what extent the image of God may be restored, if at all. What we mean by *sanctification*, however, depends largely upon our answers to all three of these questions.

One of the earliest shapers of Christian thought on these matters was Irenaeus (ca. 135–202), who distinguished the *image* of God from our *likeness* (or *similitude*) to God. To Irenaeus, the *image* of God was an endowment in humans of the capacity for relationship with God (Irenaeus tended to focus on human rationality). Our *likeness* to God, by contrast, is the proper functioning of this capacity expressed in a righteous relationship with God. According to Irenaeus, humans do not actually possess the image of God. Rather, the image of God is the direction in which we are to grow and mature.[4] The image of God, therefore, is dynamic, future-oriented, and relational rather than a static essence, nature, substance, or possession. For example, Irenaeus thought of Eden not as a perfect state from which Adam and Eve fell but as a condition of immaturity. The Fall brought about death, disease, and enslavement to Satan that impaired our innate abilities to attain a proper relationship with God and that interrupted our process of growth. We nonetheless retain God's image as a capacity that remains relatively intact, even if improperly ordered toward God. It is still possible to grow into the image of God—namely, Christlikeness (for Christ himself is the image of God)—but only with the assistance of grace.

Upon this Irenaean foundation is built much of the classical Christian vision of redemption that found its way into both Catholicism in the West and Orthodoxy in the East. In Orthodox thought, for example, we find the progressive realization of our similitude to God through "deification" *(theosis)*. Our humanity is healed and matured as we participate in the divine life through

---

3. Sermon 141, "The Image of God," §3, *Works* 4:292.
4. Justo González, *A History of Christian Thought* (Nashville: Abingdon Press, 1970) 1:162.

worship and sacraments.[5] Catholicism likewise begins with Irenaeus's distinction between image and likeness, and this becomes the foundation for the notion of "grace completing nature" as its fundamental model of redemption.[6]

The Protestant Reformers (though there are important differences among them) held that the consequences of the Fall were much more drastic than Irenaeus had suggested, destroying not only the similitude but also the image of God and utterly corrupting human nature. They rejected the notion that anything other than a "relic" of the image of God remained as an innate capacity, by which, either through cooperation with grace or completion by grace, the human being could move toward salvation. The affirmation of any such natural capacity in humans failed to take seriously the far-reaching effects of sin in all of human life, including our freedom, will, conscience, and reason. They attacked any reliance on human abilities in favor of a sole dependence upon God's grace. In this respect, they can be said to recover much of what Augustine originally taught about the virtual extinction of the image of God in the Fall. Augustine held that humans were originally created in a state of perfection (unlike Irenaeus's notion of "immaturity"), including both the image of and the likeness to God. He further stressed that under the conditions of sin, even the image of God is distorted and corrupted. Rather than a capacity for movement toward God, the image of God becomes a restlessness, or hunger, for God.[7] Both Calvin and Luther retained some role for the image of God in the maintenance of civil life, but they were adamant that the image of God was nonetheless utterly corrupted and that as far as our theological existence before God was concerned, we are all sinners in infinite need of grace.

---

5. Recently, there has been a significant movement in Wesleyan studies to trace Wesley's own indebtedness to this distinctively Eastern way of looking at salvation as primarily a therapeutic process rather than a legal transaction. See, for example, Randy L. Maddox, *Responsible Grace: John Wesley's Practical Theology* (Nashville: Kingswood Books, 1994); Steve McCormick, "Theosis in Chrysostom and Wesley: An Eastern Paradigm on Faith and Love," *Wesleyan Theological Journal* 26:1 (1991): 38-103; and Michael Christensen, "Theosis and Sanctification: John Wesley's Reformulation of a Patristic Doctrine," *Wesleyan Theological Journal* 31.2 (1996): 71-94.

6. Daniel Day Williams, *The Spirit and the Forms of Love* (Lanham, Md.: University Press of America, 1981), 131.

7. Ray S. Anderson, *On Being Human: Essays in Theological Anthropology* (Grand Rapids: William B. Eerdmans, 1982), 217.

Wesley's characteristic way of approaching this thorny issue provides a central point of contact with process theology. Because Wesley drew on insights from both the ancient Eastern tradition as well as the Reformers, he was able to arrive at something of a mediating position that challenges the presuppositions of both positions. Wesley emphasized that the God in whose image we are created is love (1 John 4:8). Thus humanity "was what God is"— love.[8] Speaking of the first created human, Wesley said: "Love filled the whole expansion of his soul; it possessed him without a rival. Every movement of his heart was love: it knew no other fervour. Love was his vital heat; it was the genial warmth that animated his whole frame."[9]

In Wesley's vision, this love, though properly directed toward God, includes and integrates the love of self, fellow human beings, and all other creatures.[10] As Daniel Day Williams notes, however, the human being is "a battlefield upon which many loves clash."[11] Our constitution in love (and, therefore, in the image of God) becomes disintegrated as we become preoccupied with some loves to the exclusion of others and as we turn in on ourselves, or as we love creation more than God. This disintegration of love is what we mean when we use the word "sin." So it is that, for Wesley (and, as we shall see, for process theology), sin is ultimately a failure to love. Conversely, what Wesley spoke of as a "perfection" of love may be understood as the reintegration of love and, in that sense, a vanquishing of sin.

In expressing his understanding of the image of God, Wesley quite naturally operated out of a literalistic view of Creation and Fall as distant prehistorical events. For example, he could write about an original "state"[12] and "the total loss of righteousness and true holiness which we sustained by the sin of our first parent."[13] Even so, Wesley's anthropology was surprisingly dynamic. Human beings are to be understood neither statically nor deterministically. He described our creation in God's image in terms of

---

8. Sermon 141, "The Image of God," §I.2, *Works* 4:294.
9. Ibid., 4:294-95.
10. Maddox, *Responsible Grace*, 68.
11. Williams, *The Spirit and the Forms of Love*, 130.
12. Sermon 60, "The General Deliverance," §I.1, *Works* 2:439-40.
13. Sermon 44, "Original Sin," §III.5, *Works* 2:185.

the triad of *understanding, will,* and *liberty.*[14] These qualities are not fixed substances or static essences. Instead, Wesley—as Irenaeus—viewed them as capacities for relationship. Their ultimate significance is in relation to love. The will, for example, is the fundamental orientation of the self in action toward others. It is synonymous with the "affections," those fundamental and orienting dispositions of the human person that "integrate the rational and emotional dimensions of human life into a holistic inclination toward particular choices or actions."[15] Ideally, the affections are oriented *freely* and with *understanding* toward God and neighbor, so that to be created in the image of God is to be created in a posture of openness to and inclusion of God and neighbor—in other words, love. With discipline and accountability, these affections can be habituated into holy "tempers," an eighteenth-century usage of the term referring to the more enduring inclinations of our hearts—our habits, behaviors, and commitments.

Instead of contrasting "image" with "likeness," Wesley typically used the language of "natural image" and "moral image." As with Irenaeus, the former is the basic constitution of human existence—our innate capacity for loving relationships. The latter refers to the proper orientation of our understanding, affections, and liberty in love. For Wesley, however, the image of God was more centrally located in one's heart and affections, whereas, for Irenaeus, it tended to be identified with conscience and rationality. Wesley held that while the natural image is corrupted in the Fall, and the moral image is thereby lost, the natural image is not lost altogether. Indeed, we could not even be so much as human without the natural image of God—the capacity for freely understanding and loving God and neighbor.

With the Reformers, Wesley believed that the effects of sin on the image of God were nonetheless pervasive. The affections are bent inward, liberty is choked, and the understanding is darkened. We are radically in need of grace. But here Wesley differed from those who believed that sinful depravity was such that there was nothing humans could do in the process of redemption. On the contrary, grace operates "preveniently" in every human life to liberate

14. Sermon 141, "The Image of God," §I, *Works* 4:293-95.
15. Maddox, *Responsible Grace,* 69.

the will so that we can respond to God's grace. While Wesley agreed with the Reformers that, apart from grace, human beings could do nothing in moving toward their own salvation, for him, there simply was no human who was lacking that grace! Wesley believed that grace was "free in all"[16] and quite apart from any merit or activity of human beings. Grace is "found, at least in some small degree, in every child" and "in every human heart."[17] Grace is not a foreign substance or power that is over us, against us, or outside of us that appears only as a remedy to sin. We could not exist apart from grace. In fact, we could not even sin if it were not for grace! Grace constitutes us as human beings and makes freedom possible. Wesley refused to deny human freedom in favor of grace or to pit human freedom against grace. Instead, he understood grace as that which creates freedom.

A process theology of sanctification is not likely to adopt much of the language of Wesley's psychology. Nonetheless, there are strong affinities between a process anthropology and the trajectory of Wesley's thinking on these matters. In the first place, for both Wesley and process thought, God's presence and power are not external to the world or to human experience. God is radically immanent within the world and an ever-present influence on us all. Furthermore, our decisions and actions are internal to God and genuinely make a difference in God's responses to us. Randy L. Maddox describes the relationship between God and humans for Wesley as "a *dance* in which God always takes the first step but we must participate responsively, lest the dance stumble or end."[18] To the extent that we can also see God's own dance steps as unsurpassingly appropriate responses to ours, that characterization would be equally fitting for process theology.

Another similarity between process theology and Wesley is that both begin with the category of love to describe our creation in God's image.[19] In doing so, however, process thought has incorporated important intellectual developments since the time of Wesley—developments such as evolutionary and ecological insights, depth perspectives in psychology, the entire modern discipline

16. Sermon 110, "Free Grace," §2, *Works* 3:544.
17. Sermon 129, "Heavenly Treasure in Earthen Vessels," §I.1, *Works* 4:163.
18. Maddox, *Responsible Grace*, 151.
19. See especially Williams, *The Spirit and the Forms of Love*.

of sociology, and wave-particle theory, relativity theory, and quantum theory in the realm of the physical sciences. The result is an anthropology that views humans nonatomistically (as social and relational beings), nonstatically (as beings in the process of becoming), and nondualistically (as holistic and organic beings and as unities of mind and body).

In thinking about the image of God as love, process theology abandons substantialist language such as "state," "essence," or "human nature," preferring instead the language of "event" or "occasion." Consistent with postmodern thought more generally, even the very notion of a substantial "self" or "soul" is one that is enormously problematic for process thought, if that refers to some underlying and unchanging "I" who does things and to whom things happen—in the words of Norman Pittenger, "like a clothesline upon which the Monday washing is hung."[20] For process thought, the experiences and relations enjoyed by the human person are internal to what it means to be a person. A process anthropology, then, places emphasis on how we are constructed as selves within our particular historical, cultural, and social matrices. Because who we are is always bound together with the welfare of others (including nonhuman others), process thought will be attracted to the social dimensions of Wesley's doctrine of sanctification but will want to push further with respect to both the understanding of human existence and sin presupposed by his doctrine and the nature and scope of the transformation to which his doctrine points.

A process theology of sanctification will also be drawn to Wesley's understanding of grace as creative of freedom and constitutive of what it means to be created in the image of God. For process thought, the becoming of every entity is influenced causally by its past. Indeed, an entity would be doomed merely to repeat the past—to play the role of a mere conduit of the past into the future—were it not for the creativity and freedom it invariably exercises and the presence of God as a lure toward novelty and harmony presented to that entity. Every moment of experience is a moment filled with possibility and hope.

If we speak of sanctification as a restoration of the image of God,

---

20. Norman Pittenger, *After Death: Life in God* (New York: Seabury Press, 1980), 16-17.

we do not mean the recovery of a past state of perfection. We mean rather a reorientation of our lives toward God and others in openness and inclusion, a reorientation of our lives toward the future in hope, and a reconstitution of our lives in freedom. Until we understand this, any description of sanctification using Wesley's language of "perfection" will be misunderstood, trapped as it often is in static and substantialist modes of thought (as it often was for Wesley himself) that leave us equivocating about the real possibilities of human transformation. As Gregory of Nyssa (ca. 330–394) taught long ago, when we are talking about Christian perfection, we are *not* talking about the perfection of a cube—a geometric perfection that has a beginning and end. We are instead talking about a participation in God that is without boundary or limit and in which dissatisfaction and change—far from being marks of imperfection (as with classical Greek philosophy)—are the marks of Christian virtue.[21] Sin is in fact a refusal to change and to grow, a failure to be discontent, and an attachment to past stages in life.

Before proceeding further in tracing the outlines of a process understanding of sanctification, it will be important to highlight one of the significant differences between a process theology's understanding of the image of God and that of Wesley (or the greater part of Christian theology, for that matter). That difference is found in the way we compare human experience with the experience of nonhumans in our world. Wesley, for example, said that what distinguished human beings from mere matter was "spirit," the capacity for self-motion. In fact, Wesley sometimes added "spirit" to his triad of qualities that constitute the image of God.[22] At least one reason why Wesley moved in this direction was that he refused to locate the primary difference between humans and animals in terms of rationality. Indeed, the more we know of animal intelligence, Wesley appears to be right on this point. Instead, the sticking point for Wesley was that humans, unlike animals, are "capable of God."

Process thought might well agree with Wesley that "self-motion" is central to what it means to be created in God's image (though process

---

21. Paul M. Bassett and William M. Greathouse, *Exploring Christian Holiness* (Kansas City, Mo.: Beacon Hill Press, 1985) 2:79-86.
22. Sermon 60, "The General Deliverance," §I.1, *Works* 2:438-39.

thought would more typically use the category of "creativity"). It could not, however, agree that this quality—or even freedom, for that matter—is what fundamentally distinguishes humans from nonhumans. Developments in the physical sciences over the last half-century call into question Wesley's confident presupposition that what he calls "matter" is "totally, essentially passive and inactive."[23]

In process thought, to be an actual entity (Whitehead's term for those basic, real units of process that comprise the world) is, in some fashion, to bear the image of God and thus to enjoy relations to other entities—to "experience,"[24] or take account of other entities with some degree of creativity and freedom. Hartshorne goes so far as to say, "Love, taken as all-surpassing in God, not zero in any actuality generalizes the classical belief that a creature, any creature, is an image, a manifestation, of the divine nature."[25] In rejecting the classic dualism of spirit and matter, a process theology of sanctification rejects the anthropocentrism implicit in most Christian theology (Wesley is no exception). Although human experience provides the model upon which Whitehead and Hartshorne built their metaphysics, a process theology of sanctification begins with the notion that all actual entities receive God's loving acceptance, lure, and empowerment. There are, of course, important differences between human animals and other animals or between a human being and an electron. But process theology does not find in these differences the starting point for understanding the image of God. A process perspective attempts to take seriously the organic relation between humans and other forms of existence as well as the interpenetration of the physical and the mental in all experience. Wesley clearly hoped for the redemption

---

23. Ibid.

24. Not all process thinkers agree with the Whiteheadian-Hartshornian usage of "feeling" and "experience" as metaphysical categories. For example, Schubert M. Ogden disagrees with panpsychicalism and holds that the term "experience" is at best analogical rather than literal when used of all actual occasions. See Ogden, "The Experience of God: Critical Reflections on Hartshorne's Theory of Analogy," in John B. Cobb Jr. and Franklin I. Gamwell, eds., *Existence and Actuality: Conversations with Charles Hartshorne* (Chicago: University of Chicago Press, 1984), 16-37; and Hartshorne's response to Ogden in that same work, 37-42, and in "Metaphysical and Empirical Aspects of the Idea of God," in Philip E. Devenish and George L. Goodwin, eds., *Witness and Existence: Essays in Honor of Schubert M. Ogden* (Chicago: University of Chicago Press, 1989), 177-89.

25. Hartshorne, "Metaphysical and Empirical Aspects," 187.

of all creation;[26] perhaps it could even be said that Wesley held to an ultimately cosmic understanding of sanctification. Process thought attempts to provide a metaphysics that can more adequately give expression to that hope.

Despite the fact that process thought might not use Wesley's language of *spirit, understanding, will,* and *liberty* to describe the image of God, it can adopt much of Wesley's basic outlook, especially insofar as these qualities are, for Wesley, ways of describing the human openness to God and others in love made possible by grace. Yet, the kind of anthropology upon which a process theology of sanctification is built is grounded in a more fundamental metaphysics of *imago dei.* In this view, all reality is an instance of the Whiteheadian process that Charles Hartshorne refers to as "creative synthesis." I suggest that by taking a closer look at three essential aspects of creative synthesis—*community, creativity,* and *freedom*—we can arrive at a distinctively process triad for speaking about the image of God and, at the same time, can do justice to important Wesleyan insights about the nature of sanctification.

COMMUNITY

It is difficult to read either of the opening creation narratives of Genesis without being impressed by the importance of our creation as social beings—beings in community. As the writer of Genesis states, "In the image of God he created them; male and female he created them" (1:27). In the second narrative, God creates Adam first and then says, "It is not good that the man should be alone" (2:18). In both cases, our sociality is an important way we reflect who God is and what God is like.

In a process vision, to be a person is to be involved in a constellation of relationships including not only God and our fellow human beings but also social institutions, political and economic structures, animal life, and the natural environment. Indeed, many of our most important relationships are those of which we are simply unaware. Virtually everything we do is tinged by others' influences,

---

26. See especially Sermon 60, "The General Deliverance," §III, *Works* 2:445-50; and Sermon 64, "The New Creation," *Works* 2:500-510.

and, to that degree, we are "dependent" on others—we include others into our own becoming.

While sociality is central to who we are as humans, the dominant intellectual traditions in the West have generally faltered in applying this concept to God (with disastrous results, I might add, for our own human endeavors at forming community). For process thought, however, all reality is social and, therefore, conditioned by and, in some sense, dependent on others. This applies even to God, who is not merely social and conditioned by others but is eminently so. As Hartshorne says, God is "super-relative" (or "sur-relative").[27] God experiences and is intimately related to each entity by accepting it into the divine life and offering it a relevant aim, or lure, for its own becoming.

For process thought, sociality is a universal category and therefore applies to any and every actuality. Hartshorne defines sociality as "the appeal of life for life, of experience for experience. It is 'shared experience,' the echo of one experience in another."[28] God then is a member of a society, as we all are. As the supreme social being, God rules the world society not from the outside as a dictator but by being related perfectly to every member, as "the supreme conserving and coordinating influence."[29] According to Hartshorne,

> this is not quite the traditional theological idea of God; though it is, I believe, the religious idea. For religion, as a concrete practical matter, as a way of life, has generally viewed God as having social relations with [humans], as sympathizing with [us] and gaining something through [our] achievements. God was interested in [humans], therefore could be "pleased" or "displeased," made more or less happy, by [our] success or failure, and could thus be "served" by human efforts.[30]

It must be emphasized, of course, that God's relativity is scope-unlimited and therefore exceeds our relativity in the same way that

---

27. Charles Hartshorne, *The Divine Relativity: A Social Conception of God* (New Haven, Conn.: Yale University Press, 1948).

28. Charles Hartshorne, *Reality as Social Process: Studies in Metaphysics and Religion* (Glencoe, Ill.: Free Press, 1953), 34.

29. Ibid., 40.

30. Ibid.

"all" exceeds "some." Hartshorne describes the difference between our relativity and God's relativity as follows: "God is relative, but what we may call the extent of his relativity is wholly independent of circumstances, wholly nonrelative."[31] Thus, while all actual entities have some degree of "absoluteness" or independence of relationships and some degree of "relativity," God is the one being in whom both "absoluteness" and "relativity" are maximal. Not only is all of reality conditioned by God, but also God is conditioned by all of reality.

The implications of this key insight are significant for understanding both God's holiness and our own sanctification. The classical Western tradition has generally rejected the notion that God could literally be conditioned by creaturely contingency on the basis that this would constitute an assault on divine majesty, holiness, and perfection.[32] In the end, however, both God's holiness and God's love are distorted by the one-sidedness of our intellectual heritage that favors independence over dependence, intervention over participation, coercion over persuasion, hierarchy over equality, and the ability to give over the capacity to receive.

History is cluttered with the tragic consequences of this unbalanced outlook in gender, racial, economic, and geopolitical relationships. It is undoubtedly true that God is often portrayed in scripture as a remote sky God who looks down on the earth from his residence above and who, from time to time, intervenes in human affairs. But process thinkers join feminist theologians in seeing in this vision of deity little more than a pale reflection of traditionally masculine social values, such as influencing others without being influenced in turn, manipulating from a distance, being "in control," and having a rugged independence. Both process and feminist theologies ask whether this male, interventionist deity is ultimately compatible with the vision of God we discover in the life and ministry of Jesus of Nazareth—a God of compassion and love, of dependable changeableness, and of enduring persuasiveness. Or

31. Hartshorne, *The Divine Relativity*, 82.

32. Paul Tillich, as a modern example, claims that the word "holiness" expresses "the impossibility of having a relation with [God] in the proper sense of the word" (*Systematic Theology* [Chicago: University of Chicago Press, 1951], 1:271).

as Whitehead once said, God is "the great companion—the fellow-sufferer who understands."[33]

For process theology, our love is inferior to God's love not because of its relativity but because of its limited relativity. As Hartshorne says:

> When Charles Wesley, who must have known something of religious values, wrote: "Father, thou art all compassion, Pure unbounded love thou art," he was not distinguishing God by denying relativity or passivity to him. Yet he was distinguishing God metaphysically. For all other beings limit their compassion at some point. They are sympathetic, passive, relative, in some directions, not in all. Their love is not pure, but mixed with indifference, hardness of heart, resistance to or incapacity for some relativities.[34]

For a process theology of sanctification, it is not independence, control, distance, or unilateral influence that define God's holiness or perfection. Since when, after all, is independence an absolute virtue—at all times a virtue? As Hartshorne says, the only independence in God that is worthy of worship is that God "will promote the highest cosmic good, come what may."[35] Holiness is not distance from the world but engagement in the world. As St. James says, "Religion that is pure and undefiled before God, the Father, is this: to care for orphans and widows in their distress, and to keep oneself unstained by the world" (1:27). Here is the subversive truth about holiness: To keep clean requires getting dirty. Wesley knew this and practiced it, even though we who have come after Wesley have not always done as well.

What then is the meaning of sanctification? A process theology takes its first clues for answering this question from God's own holiness defined in terms of the supreme sympathy, openness, and inclusiveness that we discover in Jesus of Nazareth. To look to Jesus as the author of our sanctification is to find ourselves con-

---

33. Alfred North Whitehead, *Process and Reality: An Essay in Cosmology,* corrected ed., ed. David Ray Griffin and Donald W. Sherburne (New York: Free Press, 1978), 351.

34. Hartshorne, *The Divine Relativity,* 36. Perhaps it will not prove fatal to the Wesleyan-process dialogue that Hartshorne here appears to have misquoted Charles Wesley, who originally wrote, "Jesu, thou art all compassion," rather than "Father, thou art all compassion" (See *Hymns,* #374, *Works* 7:545). Possibly Hartshorne had access to an altered version of the hymn.

35. Ibid., 44.

fronted with a twofold possibility: first, that we understand our-selves as objects of God's supremely sympathetic and all-inclusive love and, second, that we respond by structuring our lives in accordance with that love.

In the first place, to understand ourselves as the object of God's love and to know that, whatever else happens, our lives unfailingly contribute to the divine life gives to our existence a new meaning and abiding significance. This is but another way of saying that sanctification is grounded both theologically and experientially in our acceptance by God, or what Christians have called "justifica-tion." That is why, for Wesley, both justification and initial sanctifi-cation coincide in the single experience of "new birth." Sanctification certainly entails a lifelong process of transformation into Christlikeness, but it begins with, and is grounded in, the awareness of our acceptance by God. To understand ourselves as loved and included by God is the foundation of a sanctified life with tremendous implications for our understanding of freedom. As Schubert M. Ogden explains:

> Because God's love for us is completely boundless and is offered to any and every person who is willing to receive it, nothing whatever can separate one from life's ultimate meaning. For this reason, to accept God's love through faith is to be freed from oneself and everything else as in any way a necessary condition of a meaningful life. But for the very same reason, the acceptance of God's love through faith establishes one's freedom *for* all things as well as one's freedom *from* them. Because God's love is utterly boundless and embraces everything within its scope, anything whatever is of ulti-mate significance and thus the proper object of one's returning love for God.[36]

In the second place, as Ogden indicates, to know oneself to be the object of God's unconditional love is to be free to love others as God has loved us. This means that our love must also, insofar as possible, be fully sympathetic and without bounds. As Christ says, "Be perfect, therefore, as your heavenly Father is perfect" (Matt. 5:48). Certainly our relations are finite and our ability to sympa-thize with, and include, others is radically limited in comparison to

36. Schubert M. Ogden, *The Point of Christology* (San Francisco: Harper & Row, 1982), 123.

God. But if the perfection about which Jesus is speaking is not one that is static or quantitative, then we may rightly see in God's own holiness the measure of our sanctification so that the path by which mere sociality is translated into authentic Christian community is through an ever-expanding openness, sympathy, and inclusion.

It is precisely in this context that we may be better able to understand what has classically been referred to as "original sin" and sanctification as a victory over sin. Although process thought operates out of an evolutionary perspective that abandons the notion of a literal, prehistoric Fall, it can nonetheless affirm the notion that we are "fallen"[37] and, therefore, that our basic human condition is one of captivity to structures of indifference and exclusion. On these terms, original sin is not so much the sin of our ancestral parents as it is our embeddedness in sinful structures. As Cobb says, "We are free to constitute ourselves out of our world, but what the world is, out of which we constitute ourselves, is given. We transcend that world, so that we are responsible for what we make of ourselves, but in the transcending we are still chiefly shaped by what we transcend."[38]

If we may speak of original sin as groundedness in our causal past, this in no way excuses our refusal to respond positively to the divine lure. If sin is universal and social, it is nonetheless existential and willful. Each moment of creative synthesis involves a decision in which the actual entity is never entirely lacking freedom and creativity and in which the future is never a mere outworking of the causal past. God presents to each entity an "initial aim"—a set of relevant possibilities uniquely suited for intensity of experience and graded by God toward a maximum of beauty, harmony, and novelty. This aim is offered not only in terms of the entity's present actualization but also in terms of its contribution to future experiences. Apart from this aim life would be sheer chaos.[39] Sin is the rejection of the ideal possibility within this aim (not unlike the Greek word, *hamartia*, which means "missing the mark") and an

---

37. C. Robert Mesle, *Process Theology: A Basic Introduction* (St. Louis: Chalice Press, 1993), 107.

38. John B. Cobb Jr., *Process Theology as Political Theology* (Philadelphia: Westminster Press, 1982), 101.

39. John B. Cobb Jr., "Spiritual Discernment in a Whiteheadian Perspective," in Harry James Cargas and Bernard Lee, eds., *Religious Experience and Process Theology: The Pastoral Implications of a Major Modern Movement* (New York: Paulist Press, 1976), 358.

opting instead for lower intensities of experience with lesser value and beauty. Although we are responsible for that rejection, we live in a context where other entities have also failed to actualize the ideal possibility offered to them by God, thereby creating for us a context biased against our actualization of God's ideal possibility for our lives. In a process universe the decisions of other entities influence our own decisions. As Martin Luther King Jr. said, "I can never be what I ought to be until you are what you ought to be. You can never be what you ought to be until I am what I ought to be. This is the way the world is made. . . . This is the interrelated structure of reality."[40] We may think, then, of original sin as the combined context or nexus of low intensities of experience and obscurity that influence us negatively from responding ideally to the divine lure. In this sense, it would be nonsensical to hold that one could ever be free from original sin.

And yet we should not draw the conclusion that the forces from the past influencing our present decisions are entirely negative. The causal past is not to be equated with original sin for process theology. Just as original sin may be understood as structures of exclusion and indifference, so are we justified to avail ourselves of liberating structures of grace ("means of grace") which may become for us new causal influences in our lives for the divine lure rather than against it.

Wesley especially helps us never to underestimate the importance of the means of grace and to understand that the victory over sin, which we may rightly term sanctification, is clearly a communal victory. Although Wesley emphasized this corporate dimension to sanctification, it is unfortunately often obscured by the largely individualistic theological framework within which he worked.[41] However personal the process of sanctification may be, it is never entirely individualistic precisely because structures of grace are

---

40. Martin Luther King Jr., "I Have a Dream," in James M. Washington, ed., *A Testament of Hope: The Essential Writings of Martin Luther King Jr.* (San Francisco: Harper & Row, 1986), 210.

41. See José Míguez Bonino, "Wesley's Doctrine of Sanctification from a Liberationist Perspective," in Runyon, *Sanctification and Liberation*. Bonino sees Wesley's inherited theological framework of the *ordo salutis* as a "straightjacket that Wesley was unable to cast off (55). Says Bonino, "Wesley's anthropology seems to me incurably individualistic . . . For Wesley, society is not an anthropological concept, but simply a convenient arrangement for the growth of the individual. It is the individual soul that finally is saved, sanctified, perfected" (55).

always intrinsic to our ability to hear and respond to the divine lure. For that reason Wesley could say, " 'Holy solitaries' is a phrase no more consistent with the gospel than holy adulterers. The gospel of Christ knows of no religion, but social; no holiness but social holiness. 'Faith working by love' is the length and breadth and depth and height of Christian perfection."[42]

Holiness, then, may never properly be defined as a distancing of ourselves from the world, even in the name of "fleeing from sin." As Whitehead says, "The kingdom of heaven is not the isolation of good from evil. It is the overcoming of evil by good."[43] The path to holiness is through an ever-broader inclusion of the world and an ever-wider availing of ourselves to structures of grace.

CREATIVITY

Central to process theism is the belief that God, as creator, is prior to and a persuasive influence in the becoming of every actual entity. The emphasis in this process doctrine of creation, however, is not on temporal origins (though God is certainly prior to any and every world temporally speaking) but on the manner of creativity. Whitehead states the matter as follows:

God's role is not the combat of productive force with productive force, of destructive force with destructive force; it lies in the patient operation of the overpowering rationality of his conceptual harmonization. He does not create the world, he saves it: or, more accurately, he is the poet of the world, with tender patience leading it by his vision of truth, beauty, and goodness.[44]

Whitehead overstates the case here, for God does indeed create the world precisely *by* saving it and by leading it patiently toward God's vision.

But God is not the only creator. The biblical witness affirms that humans also create through work, sexuality, art, and play. In this very important respect we may say that we bear the image of God

42. *Hymns and Sacred Poems* (1739), Preface, §5, *Works* (Jackson) 14:321.
43. Alfred North Whitehead, *Religion in the Making* (New York: Macmillan, 1926), 155.
44. Whitehead, *Process and Reality*, 346.

as *creative*. Of course, even if we can affirm that both God and creatures create, there is still a radical asymmetry between the way God is creative of the world and the way the world is creative of God. God always creates and is creative of every actuality whatsoever. Creatures by contrast most certainly do create but might not have, since they might not have existed at all. Furthermore, the scope of contribution that creatures make is restricted. Because of the obvious limitations on our own ability to make a difference to others, we are creative of only *some* others. Nonetheless, as with sociality, creativity must be understood as a metaphysical principle.

A theistic philosophy must take "create" or "creator" as a universal category, rather than as applicable to God alone. It must distinguish supreme creativity from lesser forms and attribute some degree of creativity to all actuality. It must make of creativity a "transcendental," the very essence of reality as self-surpassing process.[45]

Some degree of creativity is to be found in every experience: *"to be is to create."*[46] Each actuality is an emergent synthesis in which the many influences of the past are internalized ("prehended") by the actuality and created into something new. In this sense, every individual is both creative of something else and self-creative, no matter what else the individual may be.

What then are the implications of this "image-of-God" creativity for how we go about thinking of sanctification? The apostle Paul says, "If anyone is in Christ, there is a new creation [or 'new world']: everything old has passed away; see, everything has become new!" (2 Cor. 5:17). A Wesleyan doctrine of sanctification highlights the possibility of transformation about which Paul is speaking and insists that this is not only a relative change in status before God (as accepted and forgiven) but also a real change brought about by the agency of the Holy Spirit. As Wesley said, the Holy Spirit is "the immediate cause of all holiness in us: enlightening our understandings, rectifying our wills and affections, renewing our natures, uniting our persons to Christ, assuring us of the adoption of sons, leading us in our actions, purifying and sanctifying our

45. Charles Hartshorne, *A Natural Theology for Our Time* (LaSalle, Ill.: Open Court Publishing, 1967), 26.

46. Charles Hartshorne, *Creative Synthesis and Philosophic Method* (LaSalle, Ill.: Open Court Publishing, 1970), 1.

souls and bodies to a full and eternal enjoyment of God."[47] Wesley did not, however, provide an adequate account of just how God the Holy Spirit goes about doing all this. Wesley typically used the helpful metaphor of "breath" and therefore the notion of "inspiration" to describe the agency of the Holy Spirit.[48] This highlights that the Holy Spirit is a mode of sharing, participation, and interpenetration between God and the human being. Wesley also helps us understand that the Holy Spirit's mode of activity is persuasive rather than coercive, responsive rather than static, and prevenient rather than erratic. Still, Wesley's thought presupposed a basic cosmological dualism that serves as an obstacle to a credible appropriation of his creative insights about the agency of the Holy Spirit in the process of sanctification.

The dualism to which I refer is the dualism between body and mind, matter and spirit, the natural and supernatural. The Newtonian universe was like a giant machine, mechanical and self-contained with no room in nature for purpose, mentality, or spirit (the latter were to be found instead in the subjective realm of mind).[49] The Holy Spirit, of course, was assigned to the realm of the supernatural and was understood as acting upon only the mind or spirit of humans. Process thought holds instead to a unity of experience that transcends this dualism (as well as the dualism of subject and object) and thereby makes possible a way of talking about the Spirit's creative, transforming power in all of life. To speak of the Holy Spirit is to speak not of an otherworldly phantom but of a living and present God who is creative and transformative in the life of all creatures. In a process vision, nature itself has elements of purpose, mind, and beauty. This is closer to the biblical vision of *shalom* whereby the creative advance toward the reign of God is not only a matter of the individual's spiritual existence before God but also a matter of the well-being of the wider community, of animals, and of the ecosphere as well. And it fits a model of Christian perfection construed eschatologically as a contribution to the reign of God (rather than anthropocentrically as one's own interior righteousness).

---

47. *A Letter to a Roman Catholic*, §8, *John Wesley*, 495.
48. Maddox, *Responsible Grace*, 121-22.
49. G. Palmer Pardington, "The Holy Ghost Is Dead—The Holy Spirit Lives," in Cargas and Lee, *Religious Experience and Process Theology*, 124.

On this view, the Holy Spirit is not "supernatural" if by that it is meant "a completely self-contained being existing outside and apart from the natural order."[50] We would do better to speak of the Holy Spirit not in terms of "supernatural assistance," but as God's power of creative, transforming love (grace) experienced in and through the natural structures of our world.[51] This is not to say that God fails to transcend the world, but this transcendence is a self-surpassing perfection of ever-expanding inclusion, or surrelativity, rather than a static perfection of completion or an exterior power that stands over and against the world. There is much in Wesley's theology that is open to this way of understanding the Holy Spirit, such as Wesley's sensitivity to the interrelation between emotional and physical well-being.[52] Wesley clearly believed that grace was supernatural. Because he also insisted that there is no person who is born in an "ungraced" or "natural" state, however, the distinction between natural and supernatural is academic. This does not mean that we need not seek to place ourselves in distinctive matrices of grace (the church) or to avail ourselves of distinctive means of grace (the sacraments and works of mercy and justice), but these forms of grace are not to be understood as the channels through which the natural receives the supernatural that is otherwise unavailable naturally. When nature is reconceived as constituted by grace, the whole idea of a realm of supernature defined over and against nature disappears. We are then free to understand the Holy Spirit as embodied in the natural structures of our world and, accordingly, to understand the world as literally making a difference to God, enriching God.[53]

Another dualism rejected by process thought is a debilitating opposition between the individual and community. To speak of the creativity of the Holy Spirit is to speak not only of the transformative presence of God in our personal lives but also of the influence that makes a sanctified community possible by eliciting the creativity of each member of the community "for building up the body

---

50. Ibid., 128.

51. Ibid., 128-29.

52. As Maddox notes, "He insisted that the mind can be disordered by the body, *and* the body can be disordered by the mind (i.e., distorted passions or tempers)" (*Responsible Grace*, 147).

53. Pardington, "The Holy Ghost Is Dead," 131.

of Christ" (Eph. 4:12). The Holy Spirit is "the bond of love" that moves us toward the creation of structures and traditions that mediate grace in community. At the same time, the Holy Spirit—as the lure of God toward novelty—is the very source of the "divine discontent"[54] that challenges injustice within every structure and breaks the deadly hold of tradition on our own creative becoming. The sanctifying power of the Holy Spirit is to be found in her call to us to move forward together into the future in hope. This means, of course, that "expectation" plays a central role in the experience of sanctification. Indeed, in his ministry Wesley urged his followers to expect God's future transformation in their lives, and it is this very expectation that ended up fostering growth.[55]

If sanctification may be interpreted, as we have already seen, as a reorientation of our lives toward God and others in openness and inclusion, perhaps it is now also possible to interpret sanctification as an openness to the divine lure and therefore to the future in expectation and hope. Unfortunately, in the traditions that have followed Wesley, sanctification has often been interpreted as adherence to an established morality with God presented as a sanction for this morality and experienced primarily in terms of demand and guilt. If, however, creativity is fundamental to what it means to be created in the image of God, and if God the Holy Spirit's mode of activity in our lives is as a lure toward novelty, then sanctification will not be merely a commitment to inherited values. It will also be a deepening, perhaps even challenging, of these values. As Cobb says:

> [The] conservative element of the Church's teaching has never stood alone. Jesus and the prophets have been the central Christian heroes, and their direction was to challenge rules and ideas that were established in the name, and with the sanction, of God. They experienced God as the one who stood beyond and before the achievements of the past, even the religious and ethical norms of the past, and who called people into a new reality. In the most radical way Jesus invited people to live from the reality of the Kingdom of God that was the Not-yet rather than in terms of the given.[56]

Lest this hope and expectation be interpreted as empty idealism or

---

54. Ibid., 123.
55. Maddox, *Responsible Grace*, 154.
56. Cobb, "Spiritual Discernment," 356.

a naïve fantasy, we would do well to remember that in a process vision, hope is far from idealistic; it is instead eminently realistic. Our creativity, both as self-creative and creative of God and others, gives to our lives and our activity a real causal significance. We may live in the confidence not only that what we do matters but also that things can be different. Situations of violence, despair, hunger, shame, or suffering do not merely have to be tolerated. The meaning of God for us, with which Jesus confronts us, is the possibility of novel relations both in terms of our own individual lives and in terms of the transformation of our world. Our activity counts for something and, insofar as we are creative of God, our lives can even be said to have eternal weight and immortal consequences. If we really do contribute to the divine life, and if, in God, nothing perishes but instead all that "comes to be is fully embraced by his love, where it is retained forever without any loss of vividness of intensity,"[57] then certainly we may speak of our actions as everlastingly significant. Of course, we may also speak confidently on these grounds about the difference that we make to others, a difference that raises our consciousness and responsibility in every historical project we undertake.

However much the holy life is a life of activity, confidence, hope, and expectation, it is also always a life of gratitude. To understand ourselves as created by God is to instill in our lives a proper sense of dependency, of recognizing the sheer gratuity of our existence, and of living in worship and thanks to God. Though Jesus points us toward the reign of God as something that requires human participation and causality, there is also a sense in which the reign of God is God's own creation and a state of affairs that we simply receive. While we may live in the confidence that our own finite creativity contributes in an authentic way to the reign of God, we are also to live humbly and gratefully in the assurance that this confidence is based upon God as the ultimate source of novelty for our creativity.

FREEDOM

Finally, the image of God may be characterized as an image of "freedom." For process thought, the coming to be of any entity

---

57. Schubert M. Ogden, "The Meaning of Christian Hope," in Cargas and Lee, *Religious Experience and Process Theology*, 199.

implies the influence of others as well as the freedom of the entity that is becoming. Freedom is essential to all experience and, as Hartshorne says, "we shall never understand life and the world until we see that the zero of freedom can only be the zero of experiencing, and even of reality."[58] Both Hartshorne and Whitehead hold that all entities at all levels of existence—cosmic, human, animal, cellular, atomic, and so on—experience and are therefore, and in some measure, free. Within the coming to be of every actual entity, the influence of others is always a factor that conditions, but never rules out, that entity's freedom. This is obviously true of our influence on God, but it is also true of God's influence on us. As Hartshorne says: "Since an object always influences, but cannot dictate, the awareness of itself, we influence God by our experiences but do not thereby deprive him of freedom in his response to us. This divine response, becoming our object, by the same principle in turn influences us, but here, too, without removing all freedom."[59] God influences every becoming while our influences are limited. Our particular influence upon God is real, even though slight, while God's influence on us is great, even though it does not override our freedom. Hartshorne understands God's "providence" in this way—not as a coercive power that dictates the course of events but as God's own presence in every becoming.

> Thus God can rule the world and order it, setting optimal limits for our free action, by presenting himself as essential object, so characterized as to weight the possibilities of response in the desired respect. This divine method of world control is called "persuasion" by Whitehead and is one of the greatest of all metaphysical discoveries.[60]

As we have already seen, one of the consequences of this view is that God the Creator may also be said to be created in some sense. In addition, no creature fails to create. This is true because *"freedom is self-creation."*[61]

---

58. Hartshorne, *Creative Synthesis*, 6.
59. Hartshorne, *The Divine Relativity*, 141.
60. Ibid., 142.
61. Hartshorne, *Creative Synthesis*, 9.

Given this strong doctrine of human freedom, process theologians are sometimes criticized for making God appear to be too weak or too passive. Interestingly, Wesley received similar criticisms in his own time for espousing a doctrine of the resistibility of grace. One of Wesley's concerns was that the power of grace and the sovereignty of God might be misunderstood as producing or implying the passivity of human beings. Wesley envisioned grace as supremely powerful without being coercive, and as unsurpassingly perfect without overwhelming us. Mildred Bangs Wynkoop captures Wesley's spirit when she writes, "The splendor of God's reality and promise casts contrary loves into the shade. God does not force His way into the heart; he excites the jaded hopes of [people] until the old, cheap loves look shoddy and corrupt."[62]

Wesley's argument for human freedom points out the faulty logic of those who hold that what we do could ever both matter to, and be determined by, God: "Shall the stone be rewarded for rising from the sling, or punished for falling down? Shall the cannon ball be rewarded for flying towards the sun, or punished for receding from it?"[63] Wesley insists that, rather than robbing God of "glory," the affirmation of human freedom and the resistibility of grace helps to establish the sincerity and integrity of God. In "working out our own salvation," God nevertheless has all the glory. This is because "the very power to 'work together with [us]' was from God. Therefore to [God] is all the glory."[64] Wesley, like process thought, was battling against a strain in Christian thought that clings to the notions of power as fundamentally coercive and perfection as fundamentally legal or static. This strain of thinking prefers, as Albert Outler says, "to measure God's sovereignty by his freedom *from* the world" rather than "his victorious involvement *in* [the world]."[65]

Both Wesley and process thought refuse to give in to a trade-off between grace and freedom but instead move toward a creative interface between the two. Cobb expresses the essence of Wesley's thought in this regard:

---

62. Mildred Bangs Wynkoop, *A Theology of Love: The Dynamic of Wesleyanism* (Kansas City, Mo.: Beacon Hill Press, 1972), 159.

63. *Predestination Calmly Considered*, §37, *John Wesley*, 442.

64. Ibid., 448.

65. "The Struggle with the Calvinists," *John Wesley*, 426.

The human response is not an autonomous human act set over against a prior act of grace; for it can only occur as it is made possible by grace. Grace is, or at least includes, the gift of freedom. Apart from grace there is no freedom and hence no possibility of a human act. But grace *does* generate human freedom. There is no act of grace that simply determines the total outcome. By making freedom possible, even the freedom to reject the gift of freedom, grace both establishes its own absolute priority and also insures that the exercise of human responsibility plays a role in the outcome. . . . Perhaps it is not surprising that as a Methodist I am led to reaffirm John Wesley's understanding of this doctrine rather than Calvin's.[66]

What we find in the Wesleyan-process position is a distinctively Christian humanism. God's will, initiative, and power are asserted emphatically, but not in a way that controls, negates, or overrides human freedom and autonomy. For Wesley, God is "willing that all [humans] should be saved yet not willing to force them thereto; willing that [humans] should be saved, yet not as trees or stones but as [humans], as reasonable creatures, endued with understanding to discern what is good, and liberty either to accept or refuse it."[67] As Wesley said, every part of God's wisdom is "suited to this end, to save [us] as [humans]: to set life and death before [us], and then persuade, (not force) [us] to choose life!"[68]

But what does this doctrine of freedom mean for a process theology of sanctification? In the first place, Wesley helps us understand that this grace-created freedom is not for its own sake but is for the sake of the liberation of others. Just as grace makes it possible for us to act, it also requires us to act and therefore has the characteristics of both gift and demand. In answer to the question "Does not [God's] working thus supersede the necessity of our working at all?" Wesley replies: "First, God works; therefore you *can* work. Secondly, God works; therefore you *must* work."[69] We have already seen that sanctification is premised upon our creation in the image of God as *social*. It is, accordingly, a reorientation of our lives toward God and others in openness and inclusion. We

---

66. John B. Cobb Jr., "The Adequacy of Process Metaphysics for Christian Theology" (unpublished paper, 1983), 4-5.

67. *Predestination Calmly Considered*, §52, *John Wesley*, 450.

68. Ibid.

69. Sermon 85, "On Working Out Our Own Salvation," §III.1-2, *Works* 3:206.

may therefore speak with Wesley of sanctification as our "perfection in love." We then see that sanctification is premised upon our creation in the image of God as *creative*. It may, accordingly, be understood as a reorientation of our lives toward the future in confidence, gratitude, and expectation. It would not be improper to speak of sanctification as our "perfection in hope." We are now in a position to see that sanctification is equally premised upon our creation in the image of God as *free* and may, accordingly, be viewed as a reconstitution of our lives in and for liberation.

The mere fact that grace preveniently constitutes us as free beings does not automatically mean that we will determine to live our lives freely or for the sake of the liberation of others. As Paul knew, it is possible to accept Christ's call to freedom and yet become enslaved again to the past, to triviality, to the law, or even to the self (Paul uses the word "flesh"). But Paul reminds us that it was "for freedom Christ has set us free" (Gal. 5:1). Sanctification begins with a liberating acceptance of God's acceptance of us and then requires a daily exercise of faith in God through liberating activity in the world. In this way, as Wesley knew, faith and activity are not opposed to one another (as the old faith-works debate wrongly supposes) but imply one another. This means that sanctification not only includes a passive moment and an active moment but also is a gradual (though not "automatic"[70]) process and, at the same time, is inaugurated and advanced in decisive moments of surrender, engagement, and commitment. Perhaps we may even speak of sanctification as our "perfection in faith." To recall Ogden's words, "To accept God's love through faith is to be freed from oneself and everything else as in any way a necessary condition of a meaningful life. But for the very same reason, the acceptance of God's love through faith establishes one's freedom *for* all things as well as one's freedom *from* them."[71]

The freedom for which Christ has set us free is no mere private transaction between the individual and God just as it is no escape or retreat. As Wesley says:

By salvation I mean, not barely (according to the vulgar notion) deliverance from hell, or going to heaven, but a present deliverance

---

70. Maddox, *Responsible Grace*, 152-53.
71. Ogden, *The Point of Christology*, 123.

from sin, a restoration of the soul to its primitive health, its original purity; a recovery of the divine nature; the renewal of our souls after the image of God in righteousness and true holiness, in justice, mercy, and truth. This implies all holy and heavenly tempers, and by consequence all holiness of conversation.[72]

Given what we know today of unconscious (or preconscious) motivations and the impact of deep political, economic, and social structures on our formation as persons, Wesley's vision can appear extreme, unrealistic, and possibly even unhealthy from a psychological point of view. His individualistic anthropology often exacerbates this problem as, for example, when he tends toward an understanding of sin as something within a person that can be extinguished or rooted out.[73] Still, a process theology of sanctification, guided by Wesley as a theological mentor, will be able to assert confidently that there is a work of grace that perfects faith, hope, and love and that is nothing short of a victory over all sin.

Such a sanctification will be measured not idealistically by some static norm or inherited past, but by the openness of our lives to God and others (including nonhuman others) and by the adequacy of our response to concrete suffering and need in the world as a way of returning our love to God in obedience and faith. Sanctification is not a test to be passed, a state to be entered, or an achievement to be gauged. It is a creative project of love in which we, as cocreators with God, are increasingly led to reflect the image of God discovered in Christ and offered to us by the power of the Holy Spirit as gift, as demand, and as lure.

---

72. *A Farther Appeal to Men of Reason and Religion*, §I.3, *Works* 11:106.
73. See especially *A Plain Account of Christian Perfection*, *Works* (Jackson) 11:366-446.

CHAPTER FOUR

HUMAN RESPONSIBILITY AND THE PRIMACY OF GRACE

JOHN B. COBB JR.

No topic was of greater concern to John Wesley than the relation of God's grace and human responsibility. No one was more committed than he to the primacy of grace. Yet he was distressed that some drew conclusions from this primacy that undercut human striving. Some of his most original work was clarifying this relationship in such a way as to encourage human effort to grow spiritually.

Whitehead's thinking was not shaped by these theological issues highlighted in the Reformation. Yet he too was concerned about human responsibility. The threat to which he responded was from those philosophers that taught that the present is wholly determined by the past. In Whitehead's account of how this is not so, he developed the notion of an aim derived from God so that, in his thinking as well, human responsibility and God were related. When one unpacks Whitehead's account of God's role and human decision, one somewhat surprisingly finds a doctrine remarkably similar to that of Wesley. Like Wesley, Whitehead affirms the primacy of God's activity in a way that gives a significant role to human responsibility.

Thus, Whitehead's doctrine and Wesley's doctrine are surprisingly similar despite the differences in the way they came into being. It is the thesis of this essay that the use of Whitehead's analysis can give greater clarity and rigor to this central Wesleyan doctrine. Connecting Whitehead and Wesley in this way can help Whiteheadians understand more fully the moral and spiritual implications of their metaphysics.

WESLEY'S DOCTRINE

The religious temperature of eighteenth-century England was rather low. Most people believed in God and supposed that they should lead moral lives. Some attended church. But there was no intensity or strong conviction in the belief of most.

In fact, there was widespread fear of what was called "enthusiasm." In its origin, the term refers to possession by God. Hence, it connoted claims of having received personal divine revelation or providential guidance. The enthusiasts of the eighteenth century were the Pentecostals and charismatics of today. Church leadership then and now has been clearer in its suspicion of this form of religion than about the positive alternative it wanted and still wants to offer.

Wesley denied that he was an enthusiast and that he encouraged enthusiasm among his followers. But his denial did not imply a lack of strong commitment or zealous effort to live in a truly Christian way. Furthermore, it did not mean that God is distant from the world. Like the enthusiasts, he taught that God's Spirit is present in the world, especially in human beings. He differed from the enthusiasts only in that he saw the working of the Spirit chiefly in the shaping of character and especially in the deepening of love for the neighbor and for God. He did not encourage its expression in extraordinary phenomena, and he based no claims to authority upon it.

One reason for the low temperature and fear of enthusiasm was the memory of the religious wars that devastated Europe in the first half of the seventeenth century. Intensity of religious feeling remained associated with intolerance of those who held different views. For Wesley, it was important to associate such intensity with deep commitment to tolerance.

A second reason for the low temperature and fear of enthusiasm was the conviction that reason was to be fully trusted. By trusting reason, science was reconstructing the whole worldview. By subjecting religious claims to reason, there was the possibility of moving toward harmony and agreement. For Wesley, it was important to show that precisely by following reason to the end, one discovered religious truths that were worthy of wholehearted commitment.

Wesley saw that as a result of the low temperature there was little effort to take the gospel to the common people. The parish system had developed much earlier when the population was overwhelmingly rural. Population movements had led to a situation in which many of the people were poorly served by any parish. Lives were seldom touched by the ministry of the church. From Wesley's point of view, nothing could be more important than bringing the gospel to them in an effective way. But he found little interest in this project even among many who were sincere Christians.

At this point, he encountered a third obstacle to the kind of fervor that seemed so important to him. Many of the most sincere and thoughtful Christians were strict Calvinists who understood their theology to imply that the question of who is saved is decided by God independently of human effort. Some argued that before the foundation of the earth, God had decided who would be saved and who would not. This worked against a passion for evangelism.

Furthermore, even when Calvinists did become evangelists, Wesley questioned the effects of their preaching. Telling ordinary people that whether they were saved or not depended entirely on God and that there was nothing they could do about it did not consistently lead to active response.

Defenders of the doctrine of predestination could rightly argue that many Calvinists were in fact zealous in their response to such preaching and that its rightful purpose was to avoid any possibility of pride and boasting on the part of the elect. Wesley was determined to formulate the faith in such a way that those who heard its proclamation would not be prideful or boastful in their acceptance but would nonetheless feel called to respond and understand the importance of that response.

The theoretical problem he encountered was a daunting one. Most Christians thought in terms of human beings as self-contained creatures of God with particular capacities and limits. There seemed to be two basic possibilities. One possibility was that these capacities enabled them to respond to God's offer of salvation in Jesus Christ. Those who adopted this view usually asserted that God's offer is made to all. The logical conclusion seemed to be that the difference between those who respond positively and those who respond negatively is made entirely by their free decision. One can conclude that those who respond positively in this way thereby earn their salvation, while those who respond negatively deserve their loss. Clearly, there is a danger of allowing for self-righteousness on the part of believers.

In reaction to this danger, others, such as the Calvinists mentioned above, have asserted that human decision is not the issue. The second possibility was that the only relevant decision is God's. Humans do not have the capacity to decide for God, but God has the capacity to decide for them. Those who know themselves to be saved by God have no basis for boasting. They can only give God thanks and praise. The logical conclusion seems to be that there is indeed nothing for human beings to do about this; so we can turn our attention to other matters and leave spiritual matters entirely to God.

Many have tried to find their way between these two extremes. For example, one can affirm that indeed the decision is God's entirely, but God makes the decision in light of our actions. These actions in no way gain salvation, but they become the basis for God's decision about whom to save. This restores the importance of human decisions without supposing that we can decide to accept or refuse God's offer of salvation. Nonetheless, it implies that we do have the capacity to take those actions that God has shown us lead to our being elected. Some of us take those actions; others of us do not. The grounds of boasting are not gone.

Another step is possible. One may argue that taking those actions that lead God to elect us is possible only by God's grace. But then the question arises, is that grace given to all or only to some? If it is given to all, but only some of us take advantage of this to act in the requisite way, then we are back to boasting. If it is given only to some, then the decision of who receives this grace remains with God, and our role is excluded.

Further refinements are surely possible. But as long as God's decision and human decisions are understood as mutually external, it seems impossible to overcome the either/or indicated above. Either the question of who is saved is decided unilaterally by God, or human decisions ultimately determine whom God saves.

Wesley changed the underlying assumptions of the dominant debate. For him, God and human beings are not externally related. God is internal to every human being. To speak of a human being apart from God's effective presence is to speak of an abstraction. Wesley called this abstraction "human nature."

Human nature, in his view, is as lacking in capabilities for good as Calvinists had affirmed. It is quite correct to say that human nature can make no decision that works for human salvation. But this abstraction is not the actual human being. The actual human being is partly constituted by God's presence.

God's presence is, of course, grace. It is the working of the Holy Spirit in every human heart. It is prevenient. That is, there is no point in human life before it enters in. It does not exist in a human being as a separate entity. It is integral to what a human being is.

What the Holy Spirit is doing within us at any given time depends on where we are in our journey. It first leads us toward justifying faith, and it works that faith in our hearts. It then leads us into sanctification, or the strengthening of our love for others and for God.

At the same time, this grace is not unilaterally controlling. What a human being actually decides is a joint product of grace and of human nature. Each individual is different, so that the success of grace in leading toward sanctification varies greatly. This success depends on actual decisions that the human being makes. But the human being who makes them is the unity of the working of grace and of human nature.

It is clear that in this view, the hearer of the gospel is called to respond and capable of response. But that does not mean that the response can be made apart from grace. If there is a positive response, this is the work of grace. But the grace that works this response is integral to the actual human person. It is not an external decision by God that ignores what the actual human being has become.

This formulation allows Wesley to make unqualified statements about God's love for all people and God's desire for all to be saved. For him, one of the horrors of the strict Calvinist doctrine of election is that God chooses not to save so many whom God could save. This picture of God clashes terribly with the gospel affirmation of God's universal love.

Wesley insisted that God not only desires the salvation of all but also actively works to that end. Apart from this working, there would be no salvation whatsoever. But God does not save human beings apart from their willingness and their efforts. In fact, God works within us to generate that willingness and those efforts and then saves us through them.

Although Wesley's reformulation of the relation of God and human beings changes the complexion of the issue, one cannot say that it solves the problem altogether. The Calvinist critic may persist with questions. If God works toward salvation in all people, yet many are not saved, what determines who is saved and who is not? Does this not involve the contribution of human nature? Granted that all movements toward salvation are made by the Holy Spirit acting within us, is it not the case that in some of us human nature is more cooperative—or at least less resistant—than in others? Does this not allow some room for comparing ourselves with others who have rejected salvation? Is there not some room for boasting?

The reply may well be that one who recognizes that her or his growth in grace is entirely the work of the Holy Spirit will celebrate salvation as the work of God and not engage in such comparative judgments. One may call the attention of another who has not come to faith by the working of the Holy Spirit and encourage her or him to allow that work to proceed. But testimony to the achievements of the Spirit within oneself is not for boasting but for the encouragement of others.

Whether this answer satisfies all the concerns that are brought by the critic remains an open question. We will return to this after considering Whitehead's account. It may be that developing Wesley's doctrine along lines suggested by Whitehead's ontology can remove the remaining grounds for boasting.

WHITEHEAD'S ONTOLOGY

Whitehead teaches that the world consists of events rather than of substances, a change of thinking of immense importance. But it does not mean that everything written by those who have not consciously and intentionally made this shift is invalid. By no means has the dominance of substance thinking prevented people from taking events seriously and developing ideas that make more sense when their ontological primacy is affirmed.

To a large extent, this is true of Wesley. In a general sense, we may claim him as a "process" thinker. For example, the spiritual condition of a person is to be determined by what is happening *now*. The fact that at some point in the past one made the decision for faith does not settle one's condition forever. Indeed, "condition" is too static a term. If one is not moving forward in the direction of becoming more loving, one is falling from grace. Salvation is a process rather than a condition. Developing Wesley's ideas more consistently in process terms need not violate his insights.

Whitehead introduces the primacy of events over substances chiefly in response to changes in the natural sciences, not in order to resolve theological issues. The notion that the world is made up of inert bits of matter that change only in their respective locations is difficult to square with twentieth-century physics. The atom has been broken up into entities that can be interpreted better as quantum events than as still tinier lumps of matter. Relativity theory has shown that matter is a form of energy, so that the passivity once associated with matter has been denied.

Whitehead proposes that we take seriously the notion of quanta of energy as comprising the unit-events, or "actual entities" of which the physical world is composed. These are organized into societies, some of which support other actual entities of a more complex nature, whereas others do not. For example, some are organized into living unicellular organisms, which have their own unique subjectivity, whereas others constitute grains of sand, which, presumably, do not have that subjectivity. The most remarkable societies are organized in such complex ways as to constitute human bodies that support unified occasions of human experience.

Since these human occasions are who we are as subjective beings, they are uniquely available for our reflection. Whitehead's speculation is that, through this reflection, we can form hypotheses about what all actual entities are like. These hypotheses can be tested for their conformation to evidence that we already have.

What we find in the occasions of our human experience is that they are influenced by the past. "Influence" here is to be taken quite strictly. The past flows into these occasions. They do not first exist in themselves and then receive this inflow. On the contrary, they become what they become by virtue of the process. In short, the past is constitutive of the present.

There has been little reflection about this relation of the past and present in the history of Western philosophy, but it is central to Whitehead's philosophy. Hence, I will belabor it a bit more. In order to grasp the relation, one should consider how one's personal past helps to constitute one's personal present. For example, if one is hearing the end of a musical phrase, what is the relation of that hearing to the hearing of earlier parts of the phrase? These earlier occasions of experience must still be operative in the present. It is not that one recalls them. On the contrary, without the active participation of earlier occasions in the present, the present would not hear the end of a musical phrase—only an isolated chord. Whitehead uses the word "prehension" to identify the way in which the past is incorporated into the present, or how the past flows into the present.

From the side of the past, this same relation can be called "causal efficacy." Through this analysis, Whitehead is able to restore the notion of causality to a rich meaning it has lacked in the dominant philosophical discussion since the time of Hume and Kant. These two philosophers pointed out that we can have no sense experience of causality; that is, we cannot see it, touch it, or hear it. And since they believed that all knowledge of the external world arises through the senses, we can have no knowledge of causality.

Hume said that by a causal relation we can only mean regularity of succession. Kant, recognizing the limitations of such a notion, declared that the idea of a necessary relationship is imposed on the data by the inescapably ordering activity of the mind. Whitehead, by contrast, taught that we have a direct experience of causality in the way our personal past and our bodies flow into our present experience. A cause is an element of the past that participates in constituting the present.

The hypothesis arising from this phenomenological analysis is that other parts of the past are also prehended in the present occasion of experience, or causally efficacious for it, even though these prehensions cannot be brought to conscious awareness. We speculate that the neuronal events in the brain are also influencing the present experience. The evidence supporting this comes from physiological psychology, which traces the transmission of events in the eye or ear through these neurones and shows that what we see and hear is a function of this transmission. This transmission is also understood in terms of prehensive relations. And of course the events in the eyes and ears are prehending events in their environment, such as waves of light and sound that are transmitting influences from greater distances. To some extent, everything that has ever happened is playing some role in constituting my experience in each successive moment. My experience is an instance of the many becoming one, and Whitehead proposes that we think of all unit-events as such instances.

This vision is like that of the most important of all movements of process thought, namely, Buddhism. Buddhists often speak of "dependent origination." The idea is that everything that comes into being does so in dependence on everything else. Nothing exists in and of itself. Everything is as it is because other things are as they are.

There is, however, a very important difference between Whitehead's philosophy and most Buddhist thought. As a child of the West, deeply influenced by the Bible, Whitehead considers crucial the question of whether there is any self-determination in this process. Buddhists have not thematically considered this issue.

The problem arises because if we simply suppose that the present is what it is by virtue of the way the past flows into it, then it seems that we have a fully deterministic system. If that is the final word, then much of our common sense is in error. Whereas we suppose that we have some responsibility for our actions, this system declares any form of self-determination to be illusory.

Whitehead believes that our fundamental common sense beliefs are not illusory. Indeed, he points out that much more than our sense of moral responsibility presupposes that we are not wholly determined by the past. Our notion that some formulations are more accurate than others presupposes an ability to judge that does not fit with a wholly deterministic system. Those who affirm determinism are implicitly denying it in their very formulation. The task of philosophy is not to explain away what we cannot but presuppose. It is to show how it can be true.

It will not do, however, simply to assert that we are free. We must return to the analysis of experience to see what is there, other than the inflowing of the past. What we find is purposeful decision.

We are aiming at something. Put quite generally, we might say that we aim at happiness or satisfaction partly in the immediate moment, partly in the wider future, partly for ourselves as individuals, partly for those others about whom we care. In order to achieve a measure of this goal, we make decisions, choosing some alternatives and rejecting others. Sometimes our choices seem good to us; sometimes, even as we make them, we are aware that they could be better.

The question is, how can this be possible? It does not seem that an occasion of experience can choose how the past informs it, since it comes into existence only through that influence. No one can choose not to be influenced by the past, and in a very fundamental sense it seems that it is the past that decides how to shape the present. If the present is not simply the outcome of the past, it must supplement the causal determinacy of the past in some way, and just how it supplements that determination cannot in turn be determined by the past.

For this to happen, there must be something else that is prehended in each occasion besides the past. This must be a source of alternatives to the simple reenactment of the past. And these alternatives must be given as attractive possibilities rather than as additional elements of strict determination. Such attractive possibilities can explain the "aim" character of our experience as well as open a space for decision.

In order to explain the possibility of both purposive decision in our experience and other more strictly metaphysical reasons that are not our concern here, Whitehead posits the reality of an ordered realm of possibility transcending all that has been actualized in the world. Because it is causally efficacious in the world, it must be a part of an actual entity. Whitehead names that actual entity God. He believes it to be the reality about which the theistic religious communities have spoken.

For Whitehead, God is causally efficacious in the world much as the past is. That is, God is prehended by every occasion, and that means that God participates in constituting every occasion. Whereas past entities function as determinants of features of the new occasion, God functions to urge the occasion to transcend its past and to make its own decision about how to do so.

WESLEY AND WHITEHEAD

There is one strong point of contact in the concerns of Wesley and Whitehead. For both, it is a matter of great importance to assert human responsibility. For Wesley, the threat to such responsibility arose from beliefs about human incapacity to do anything of any positive value. This was accompanied by the idea that God is the only actor in our salvation. Human beings are passive recipients. For Whitehead, the threat came from the assumption of much modern thought that the present is exhaustively explained by the past. The present, it is thought, is simply the vector resultant of the forces that impinge on it.

Given the different threats to which they were responding, it is remarkable that their solutions tended to converge. Wesley located God within the human person in the form of grace so that he could affirm the capacity of human beings for right decisions without attributing goodness to human nature as such. Whitehead located God within the human occasion so as to explain how that occasion can transcend its past and act purposively. The human person for Wesley and the human occasion of experience for Whitehead are jointly constituted by God and other factors. To speak of them apart from God's participation in their constitution is, in both cases, to speak of an abstraction.

For Wesley, it was very important to insist on the primacy of grace. It is only grace that brings about good. Human nature cannot do so. For Wesley, the reason for this emphasis was to thwart pride in human achievement and to remind all believers that it is God to whom they owe all good.

Whitehead was not moved by the same theological motives. He did not favor human pride, but he did not structure his metaphysics to avoid it. His reasoning aimed at coherence and consistency with the facts. Nonetheless, his conclusions were remarkably congruent with those of Wesley.

Apart from the effective presence of God in an occasion, that occasion simply reenacts the past. Just how it does so will be particular to its locus in the scheme of things, and in that sense the occasion will be new. But it will contribute nothing of its own. It will simply pass on what it has received.

In general, one should make no moral judgment about this. If it were not the case that much of the physical world faithfully transmits what it receives, chaos would reign. But all of this repetitiveness in the physical world functions to make creative novelty possible among living things and especially among animals. In humans, this possibility rises to the highest level. For humans to allow themselves simply to reenact the past is to act contrary to the deeper purposes of the universe. God's "lure" within them is to introduce creative novelties in the world. Their ability to do so is entirely the result of God's presence within them.

Very important to Wesley is the emphasis on the primacy of grace. That is, God's activity has a priority over human agency. The meaning of this relation is changed by affirming that God's activity is a participant in human agency. But the dependence of human agency on God is primary.

This point is clearer, in some ways, in Whitehead's teaching than in Wesley's. It is God's agency that calls human agency into being moment by moment. Apart from God's agency, there would be no human decision. The human decision—the joint result of God and the other factors making up the occasion of experience—is made possible and inevitable by God's initial and initiating action.

For both Wesley and Whitehead, the way God works in a human being moment by moment depends on the prior decisions of that person. For Wesley, God's work is particular to the stage of spiritual progression of the person. For Whitehead, it is particular to the exact situation of that occasion, the entirety of its past and how that impinges. The decisions in the personal past of that occasion have special importance. That is, if one has responded quite fully to God's call or lure in the past, then one can be offered wider possibilities in the present. If one has resisted the lure and chosen to conform more to well-established habits, then less is possible now.

Obviously there are differences with respect to what God makes possible within human beings. For Wesley, the emphasis is on justification and sanctification understood as the growth of love for neighbor and for God. For Whitehead, the emphasis is on creative novelty. But even here the difference is not as great as it may first appear. For Wesley, the love of a neighbor names the whole of genuine concern for the neighbor's well-being and expresses itself in seeking the realization of many forms of value in the neighbor's life. For Whitehead, morality is a function of the breadth of the future for which an occasion is concerned. For both, God is understood as love.

CAN WHITEHEAD HELP WESLEYANS?

At the end of the first section of this essay, the question remained whether Wesley's transformation of the context of the issue of the human role in salvation actually freed his doctrine of the risk of supporting the human tendency to pride and boasting. Along with all the emphasis on the primacy of grace, there still remained the implication that a believer's human nature has been more supportive of, or acquiescent in, the work of the Spirit than that of a nonbeliever. Is this problem in any way reduced by Whitehead?

The answer, I believe, is yes. The limitation of Wesley's answer comes from his somewhat substantialist talk about human nature. Everything in a person other than grace seems to be seen as a single entity with a particular character. This is not an important part of Wesley's thought, but since he does not refine his thinking here, it seems that the critic can charge Wesley with leaving him or her in a situation where human nature has some autonomous freedom to cooperate with grace or resist it. If one's choice in this respect determines whether grace will be effective, then it still seems that a human decision apart from grace plays a determinative role in salvation. This is certainly not what Wesley intends, and I have tried to present Wesley's solution in a more favorable and accurate light. But the quasi-substantial human nature that Wesley does not reject remains a problem.

Whitehead dissolves that human nature. God is one of the many that become one. Among the many that take part in bringing the new occasion into being, some are no doubt more beneficent than others. Some are persons whose love continues to enrich one's life. Others are ancient resentments that continue to cloud one's judgment. To speak of them collectively as good or evil is meaningless. God has been present in all of them, and in various ways they mediate God to the new occasion. Many of them have in varying degree missed the mark of what they might have become, some viciously so.

To reenact them and to transmit the result to the future would not be an evil thing except in comparison with what is possible. Because we can be more than the sum of our past, we should be. To fail to respond to new possibilities is to decay. To choose that decay is to sin.

Even if we dare to respond in some measure to the challenge of the present made real for us by God, this does not ensure perfection. Alongside God's ideal call are pulls and pressures from diverse elements in the past that lead toward decisions that miss the mark. Rarely do we overcome all those pressures and respond only to God's call. Although some of the influences from the past encourage us much more than others toward that response, none are free from some distortion. Accordingly, we may say that all past influences act collectively as an impediment in the way of perfection.

Now it is certainly the case that the nature of these other pressures and pulls from the past affect the degree to which we are responsive to God's call. In this sense, it is simply the case that we differ in the fullness of our response. But is this cause for pride or boasting? To a much greater extent, if we have been supported in responsiveness to grace, this is cause for gratitude. We can be, and should be, grateful to parents, friends, teachers, pastors, the community of the church, and whomever else has nurtured and encouraged us so as to make it easier for us to be open to the working of grace within us.

But one might still ask, is there not a danger that we will take pride in previous decisions made in our past that pave the way for more effective activity by grace within us? No doubt this is possible. But from a Whiteheadian point of view, an attitude of gratitude makes more sense. There is no substantial person underlying the sequence of occasions of experience that make up the person. When I think of good decisions made in my youth, it makes more sense to be grateful for them than to take pride in them. I am grateful not only to those who made them possible, especially to God as the one who made them possible ultimately and ontologically, but also to that boy who made choices that have worked out well for me since then. I, now, am not that boy, and it makes little sense for me, now, to take credit for those decisions. I can only hope that decisions I now make by God's grace will be helpful to those future occasions that continue my personal history through time.

In general, my point is that process thought undercuts the grounds for boasting quite radically. There is no persistent, substantial "I" who has done these good things in the past and can, therefore, take credit for them now. There is only a sequence of occasions of experience that have been more and less blessed by the particularities of their past but have all been called into being and to the best possible decision by God. Some have come closer to the mark than others. These have blessed subsequent occasions—those in my personal history and others as well. I am grateful to God, and to that earlier person, for these gifts.

Is Pride a Virtue?

There is another question that should be addressed. Is pride, after all, so strenuously to be avoided? Has the tradition been wrong to regard it as the heart of sin? Is not a healthy pride, on the contrary, to be encouraged and celebrated? Does not the lack of self-respect that is so widespread in our society do more damage than pride? Would it not be better for believers to take more credit for their spiritual growth instead of always attributing all that is good to God and only evil to themselves? Does not the call for humility lead to failure in realizing our capacities and in enjoying our accomplishments?

This challenge to traditional Christian teaching is a critical one, and it is sometimes directed toward Wesley and Whitehead as well. But the opposition to pride built into their positions does not entail the negative consequences of much of the tradition. In that tradition, God's grace is external to the person. Given that assumption, to suppose that apart from grace one does nothing but sin is, indeed, profoundly to disparage oneself, and can contribute to unhealthy feelings of self-contempt and dependence. This may helpfully check the arrogance of the unduly prideful, but it may also prevent the development of healthy self-acceptance and self-affirmation among persons with fragile egos.

For Wesley and Whitehead, by contrast, God's grace is an inherent contributor to the concrete person. That concrete person will find internal tensions, but these will not prevent wise and righteous decisions. We may develop considerable confidence in our capacities, since these capacities express God's creative working within us. Yet we will not think of ourselves as self-made persons. Our abilities and our fruitful use of them are not autonomous achievements. They come to us from others. Above all and ultimately they express God's work within us. The recognition that God is able to use us in the fulfillment of God's purposes in the world is not a reason for arrogance as much as for gratitude.

From this point of view, Christian humility has nothing to do with pretending to have fewer capacities or accomplishments than we actually have or disparaging our achievements. It belongs with an honest and accurate appraisal of such matters. Such an honest and accurate appraisal normally includes a recognition that we have often fallen short and sometimes even acted hurtfully out of anger and contempt. But it dwells no more on these failures than on successes.

Authentic humility is possible only where there is sufficient self-assurance so that we do not need to parade our strengths before others in order to gain their admiration. Neither do we need to conceal our failures from ourselves or from others. We accept ourselves as we are with successes and failures, strengths and weaknesses, and direct ourselves to the task at hand rather than to winning acceptance from others and from ourselves. Humility is, therefore, an expression of strength, not weakness.

Authentic Christian humility is possible only as our self-acceptance is a function of our assurance of God's acceptance of us rather than of our judgment that we have measured up. It has nothing to do with judging that we are better or worse than other people, although it frees us to make honest appraisals. A humble person may judge that he or she is the person best qualified to lead in an important movement, and that person may say so. Humility opens us to respond to God's call whether that call is to lead or to follow.

CHAPTER FIVE

SEEKING A RESPONSE-ABLE GOD:
THE WESLEYAN TRADITION AND PROCESS THEOLOGY

RANDY L. MADDOX

While its roots run back into the nineteenth century, process theology found its distinct identity and garnered significant influence during the second half of the twentieth century. One of the notable characteristics of this formative generation is the high percentage of advocates drawn from a Wesleyan background, including such major voices as Schubert M. Ogden, John B. Cobb Jr., Marjorie Hewitt Suchocki, and David Pailin.[1]

This prominence might appear to be accidental. There is little concern for Wesleyan precedents for process convictions reflected in any of their programmatic works. But this pattern must be put in context. Through a variety of influences, Wesley had been widely dismissed as a theological mentor among his ecclesiastical descendants by the beginning of the twentieth century. This dismissal has been significantly reversed only in the last couple of decades, as theologians in the broad Wesleyan tradition have begun to reconsider both his model of theological activity and his central theological convictions.[2] One result is that some of the process theologians noted above have recently reflected on the possible congruence of their distinctive commitments with their Wesleyan roots.[3]

1. Cf. Schubert M. Ogden, *The Reality of God and Other Essays* (New York: Harper & Row, 1963); John B. Cobb Jr., *A Christian Natural Theology: Based on the Thought of Alfred North Whitehead* (Philadelphia: Westminster Press, 1965); Cobb, *God and the World* (Philadelphia: Westminster Press, 1969); John B. Cobb Jr. and David Ray Griffin, *Process Theology: An Introductory Exposition* (Philadelphia: Westminster Press, 1976); Marjorie Hewitt Suchocki, *God-Christ-Church: A Practical Guide to Process Theology,* rev. ed. (New York: Crossroad Publishing, 1989); Suchocki, *The End of Evil: Process Eschatology in Historical Context* (Albany, N.Y.: State University of New York Press, 1988); and David Pailin, *God and the Processes of Reality* (London: Routledge, 1989).

2. See Randy L. Maddox, "Reclaiming an Inheritance: Wesley as Theologian in the History of Methodist Theology," in *Rethinking Wesley's Theology for Contemporary Methodism.* ed. Randy L. Maddox (Nashville: Kingswood Books, 1998), 213-26.

3. E.g., Schubert M. Ogden, "Process Theology and the Wesleyan Witness," *Perkins School*

These Wesleyan process theologians have consistently identified the most relevant congruence in convictions about the nature of God and of God's interaction with humanity. This is significant because these issues are central to the emphases of process theology. As one standard introduction frames it, the defining goal of process theology has been to articulate a compelling model of God as Creative-Responsive Love, as a preferable alternative to such long-standing models as Cosmic Moralist, Unchanging and Passionless Absolute, Controlling Power, and the like.[4] The purpose of this essay is to trace an analogous theological project running through the Wesleyan tradition, as one way to explain the number of formative advocates of process theology nurtured in this tradition.

WESLEY'S THEOLOGICAL ADVOCACY OF A RESPONSE-ABLE GOD

While Wesley's theological concern had a soteriological focus, this focus did not restrict his doctrinal sweep. Through the course of his ministry, he came to recognize the formative impact of a broadening range of Christian teaching.[5] One area that drew more attention over the years was the various aspects of the doctrine of God.[6] Wesley grew increasingly sensitive to how differences in this area were integral to some of the issues he faced among his people. A good example is the debate over predestination. Wesley became convinced that this was not primarily a disagreement over how much freedom humans possess or how to interpret particular verses of Scripture. At its core, it was instead a disagreement over the nature of God.

of Theology Journal 37.3 (1984): 18-33; Marjorie Hewitt Suchocki, "Coming Home: Wesley, Whitehead, and Women," Drew Gateway 57.3 (1987): 31-43; and John B. Cobb Jr., Grace and Responsibility: A Wesleyan Theology for Today (Nashville: Abingdon Press, 1995). [Note: Ogden and Suchocki are reprinted in this volume].

4. See Cobb and Griffin, Process Theology, 8-9, 41.

5. For a survey of the range of his doctrinal concern, see Randy L. Maddox, Responsible Grace: John Wesley's Practical Theology (Nashville: Kingswood Books, 1994).

6. While Wesley's early sermons focus on soteriology, his themes about the divine nature become common later; e.g., Sermon 54, "On Eternity," Works 2:358-72; Sermon 67, "On Divine Providence," Works 2:535-50; Sermon 68, "The Wisdom of God's Counsels," Works 2:552-66; Sermon 118, "On the Omnipresence of God," Works 4:40-47; and Sermon 120, "The Unity of the Divine Being," Works 4:61-71.

As in many other cases, Wesley's deepest concern about the Calvinist affirmation of unconditional election/reprobation was strikingly articulated in verse by his brother Charles (which John endorsed by publication in the *Arminian Magazine*):

> 'Tis thus, O God, they picture Thee,
> Thy Justice and Sincerity;
> Thy Truth which never can remove,
> Thy bowels of unbounded Love:
> Thy freedom of Redeeming Grace,
> "With-held from almost all the Race,
> Made for Apollyon to devour,
> In honour of thy Sovereign Power!"[7]

Note that the objection offered here is to the way that the Calvinists "picture" God. In their predestinarian opponents, the Wesley brothers saw a defining model of a *sovereign monarch.* In the heat of controversy, John put it less graciously as an omnipresent almighty tyrant.[8] By contrast, their more characteristic model of God was that of a *loving parent.*[9]

This difference in fundamental models or analogies for God was reflected in assumptions about divine/human interaction in salvation. In contrast with the Calvinist emphasis on protecting God's sovereign freedom in all interactions with humanity, Wesley was concerned throughout his ministry with articulating what I have termed a model of "responsible grace."[10] He strove to preserve the vital tension between two biblical truths that he viewed as co-definitive of Christianity: Without God's grace, we *cannot* be saved, but without our (grace-empowered, but uncoerced) participation, God's grace *will not* save. The God whose prevenient gracious empowerment makes us *response-able* is like a truly loving parent in also finally respecting the integrity of our *responsible* appropriation of that grace.

---

7. "Address to the Calvinists," stanza 3, *Arminian Magazine* 3 (1778): 383-84.

8. Sermon 110, "Free Grace," §28, *Works* 3:557.

9. Note John's claim that wise persons are those who recognize God as their Father, their friend, and the parent of all good (Sermon 33, "Sermon on the Mount XIII," §II.2, *Works* 1:692); and his suggestion of how to explain God to a child (Sermon 94, "On Family Religion," §III.7, *Works* 3:340-41).

10. See Maddox, *Responsible Grace*, 19.

There are obviously strong implications of Wesley's favored analogy of God and its related emphasis on "responsible grace" for doctrines detailing the human dimensions of salvation. The implications for doctrinal debates concerning the nature of God are no less strong. Wesley's increased engagement with standard topics in the doctrine of God in his later years reflects some attempt to think through these implications, in dialogue with alternative stances championed in his time. Implications for understanding God's moral attributes emerged most immediately—with Wesley stringently rejecting any conception of divine justice and mercy, or God's universal love and goodness, that rendered these compatible with unconditional reprobation.[11] The point most relevant to our present concern is that he also became uneasy with some conceptions of God's natural attributes that were commonly defended in Protestant and Roman Catholic scholastic theologies because he sensed that these conceptions did not do justice to the way that God actually relates to us in responsible grace. The general trajectory of his reaction to these conceptions was to lay greater stress on the genuinely *response-able* nature of God.

Immutability and Response-ability

A good place to begin in getting a sense of this trajectory in Wesley's thought is with the Christian confession that God is immutable, or unchanging. The biblical roots of this confession primarily stress God's faithfulness to covenant commitments. Over time, further implications were connected with the notion of immutability, partly through the influence of Platonic and Aristotelian assumptions about perfection and change. It came to be broadly assumed that there could be *no* type of change in God since change either would be for the worse, or (if for the better) would indicate that God had not been as perfect as God could be. It was emphasized in particular that God could not "suffer" change—in the sense of being subjected to undesired change by an external agent. Given that several emotions are "suffered" in precisely this sense, many came to argue that the immutable God had no emotions, or at least no "passions," as they called those emo-

11. Cf. Sermon 110, "Free Grace," §§24-25, *Works* 3:554-56; and *Predestination Calmly Considered*, esp. §§36-43, *John Wesley*, 441-45.

tions that are suffered in response to things beyond our initiative and full control. Even those who allowed that God had affections or emotions tended to argue that God experienced no fluctuation or change of these in response to creaturely events. While God might timelessly grieve over the loss of innocent victims, they urged that God does not uniquely grieve at the time of and in response to the loss of any particular innocent victim.

While conclusions like this might seem to run counter to Christian sensibilities, they have been considered by many to be essential to protecting God's perfection and sovereignty.[12] Wesley was sensitive to these concerns but was also convinced that Scripture portrayed a God who took individual interest in us. This conviction is hinted at in his argument that the scriptural claim that God experiences joy at a person's conversion is an appropriate "representation."[13] It is more evident in his defense of the possibility of persons culpably falling from grace, against the charge that this made God changeable. His basic argument was that a God who did not take into account the changing response of humanity would cease to be unchangeably just and gracious![14] A God of truly responsible grace must respond to each of us in our unique situations.

This emphasis raises the question of whether Wesley shared the hesitance found in many scholastic theologies to assign emotions to God. The evidence is a little mixed. He could affirm Article I of his Anglican tradition, which maintained that, as a spirit, the living God had no "body, parts, or passions."[15] Yet he also defended the scriptural ascription of passions to God, as long as this was understood analogically.[16] Most important, he identified the affections as one of those analogues of God's being that we share as creatures graciously created in the Image of God.[17] "Affections" was Wesley's common term for those positive emotions that are the

---

12. For a very thoughtful presentation of this case, see Thomas G. Weinandy, *Does God Suffer? A Christian Theology of God and Suffering* (Notre Dame, Ind.: University of Notre Dame Press, 2000). A helpful articulation of the alternative is Paul S. Fiddes, *The Creative Suffering of God* (Oxford: Clarendon Press, 1988).

13. *NT Notes*, Luke 15:7.

14. *Serious Thoughts upon the Perseverance of the Saints*, §14, *Works* (Jackson) 10:289-90.

15. He refers to this article in Sermon 120, "The Unity of the Divine Being," §8, *Works* 4:63.

16. See *NT Notes*, Rom. 5:9; and *A Letter to William Law* (6 January 1756), §II.2, *Letters* (Telford) 3:346.

17. Cf. Sermon 45, "The New Birth," §I.1, *Works* 2:188.

empowering and inclining source of our actions, with love being the prime example. Thus, when he described love as God's "reigning attribute, the attribute that sheds an amiable glory on all [God's] other perfections," he was making emotion central to his conception of God.[18] This helps to explain why someone deleted the phrase denying passions to God from Article I of the edited version of the Anglican Articles that Wesley prepared for the newly independent American Methodists when they organized into a church.[19] Far from being "above" responsive emotions, Wesley affirmed a God who epitomized the proper response-ability of the emotions.

Omnipotence and Response-ability

How did Wesley square this affirmation of God's responsiveness with the notion of God's omnipotence or sovereign power? He could define God's omnipotence, in fairly traditional terms, as the exclusion of any bounds to God's power. Whenever he developed this point, however, it became clear that his distinctive concern was that God's power not be defined in any way that would undercut the integrity of responsible grace.

Wesley discerned such a mistaken conception of divine power in the claims of his predestinarian opponents that they preserved the glory of God better than he did. Their obvious assumption was that one could ascribe the full glory of salvation to God only if God effected salvation unilaterally, rather than responsively seeking some human concurrence. Wesley countered that affirming a place for God awaiting our uncoerced response to the divine initiative did not detract from God's glory, provided that it was God's grace that enabled us to respond. Moreover, he contended that the biblical notion of the "glory of God" does not refer primarily to God's power but to the manifestation of all God's attributes, especially justice and love.[20]

Wesley also stressed the relationship of God's power with God's

---

18. *NT Notes*, 1 John 4:8; and *Predestination Calmly Considered*, §43, *John Wesley*, 445.

19. It appears that Wesley left the phrase in when editing Anglican Article I, but it was gone by the time the Articles were circulated in America. It is not clear who removed it, but perhaps it was Thomas Coke. Cf. Ted A. Campbell, "The Mystery of the First Article of Religion, and the Mystery of Divine Passibility," *OXFORDnotes* 4.1 (24 May 1996): 5.

20. *Predestination Calmly Considered*, §§47-50, *John Wesley*, 447-49.

wisdom. As he once put it, if God were to abolish sin and evil by overriding human freedom, this "would imply no wisdom at all, but barely a stroke of omnipotence. Whereas all the manifold wisdom of God (as well as all his power and goodness) is displayed in governing [humans] as [human]; not as a stock or a stone, but as an intelligent and free spirit."[21] For Wesley, it was as important that God be response-able in dealing with humanity as it was that God be omnipotent!

Indeed he reshaped the very conception of God's omnipotence in light of this conviction. A distinction between God's work as Creator and as Governor was central to his case. Wesley allowed that it may be permissible to speak of God working alone and irresistibly when creating and sustaining nonpersonal nature, but not when governing human life—for this would eliminate human responsibility.[22] As Governor, God enables human obedience but will not force it. Wesley reminded his followers:

> You know how God wrought in *your own* soul when he first enabled you to say, "The life I now live, I live by faith in the Son of God, who loved me, and gave himself for me." He did not take away your understanding, but enlightened and strengthened it. He did not destroy any of your affections; rather they were more vigorous than before. Least of all did he take away your liberty, your power of choosing good or evil; he did not *force* you; but being *assisted* by his grace you . . . *chose* the better part.[23]

Perhaps the best way to capture Wesley's conviction here is to say that he construed God's power, or sovereignty, fundamentally in terms of *empowerment*, rather than control or *overpowerment*. This is not to weaken God's power but to determine its character! As Wesley was fond of saying, God works "strongly and sweetly" in matters of human life and salvation.[24] But this means that God also works responsively. Thus, Wesley would insist that while God's empowering grace is always prevenient to any action on our part, "God does not continue to act upon the soul unless the soul re-acts

---

21. Sermon 67, "On Divine Providence," §15, *Works* 2:541.
22. *Thoughts upon God's Sovereignty, Works* (Jackson) 10:361-63.
23. Sermon 63, "The General Spread of the Gospel," §11, *Works* 2:489.
24. *NT Notes*, Rom. 8:28; Sermon 66, "The Signs of the Times," §II.9, *Works* 2:530; and Sermon 118, "On the Omnipresence of God," §II.1, *Works* 4:43.

upon God. . . . He will not continue to breathe into our soul unless our soul breathes toward him again."[25]

Temporality and Response-ability

As attractive as it sounds, the type of responsive interaction with individuals that Wesley was ascribing to God in this 1748 sermon must eventually explain how this is possible for God—since God's relationship to time differs from that of humanity. But how does it differ? What do we mean when we identify eternality as one of the distinctive attributes of the divine nature? This question has been the focus of long-standing dispute. The dispute grows out of the mingling of two different streams of reflection upon God's nature in early Christian tradition. The biblical roots of our tradition tend to describe eternity as "unending duration," reflecting a relative comfort with analogical use of human experience (such as our experience of duration) to portray God. The Greco-Roman roots of our tradition tend to equate eternity with "atemporality," reflecting a tendency to see the divine nature as the opposite of everything that we experience in creaturely existence as limitations (such as some aspects of being temporal).

Early Christian theologians were broadly drawn to the emphasis on atemporality. In its strongest form, this meant adopting Plato's model of eternal realities and portraying God's existence as the antithesis of temporal succession—a tenseless, unchanging Now (*nunc stans* in Latin). On these terms, God embraces and knows all of time in a unity that dissolves the succession of temporal events. Despite the difficulty of squaring this with biblical accounts of God's activity, influential theologians such as Augustine adopted the *nunc stans* model of eternity, leading it to become dominant in scholastic theologies. A subtle but significant variant of this model is evident in some of these theologies. On this variant, God exists "above" time, still embracing and knowing all of time, but in a way that (proponents of this view believe) preserves the succession of temporal reality.[26] In other words, the biblical notion of duration is introduced, but the atemporal emphasis is retained as most funda-

---

25. Sermon 19, "The Great Privilege of those that are Born of God," §III.3, *Works* 1:442.
26. See the analysis and recommendation of this variant in Wolfhart Pannenberg, *Systematic Theology*, trans. Geoffrey Bromiley (Grand Rapids: William B. Eerdmans, 1991) 1:403-409.

mental.[27] Almost no one prior to the eighteenth century ventured to go further to champion a model of God as fundamentally *temporal*—that is, as existing in the ongoing passage of time as we do, though without beginning or end. The clearest advocate was Socinius, and God's temporality was included among the teachings for which he was condemned by both Protestant and Catholic scholastics.

Where did Wesley's convictions about God's responsive interaction lead him in assessing these three alternative models? There is little evidence of initial reticence about the *nunc stans* model that he would have imbibed in his Anglican training. Indeed, when controversy broke out between Wesleyan and Calvinist Methodists over predestination in the 1750s, Wesley readily appealed to the notion of God's existing in the Eternal Now to explain that our eternal election was based not on divine decree but on God's timeless knowledge of our actual response to the gracious offer of salvation.[28] At least indirect endorsements of this model can be found into the mid-1780s.[29]

But there is also evidence that in his later years, Wesley began to sense that the classic *nunc stans* model did not fit well his emphasis on God's response-ability: If all "moments" of time are experienced by God as simultaneously *now*, how could God sense and respond to specific transitions in our lives? Concern to address this lack of fit would explain the increasing use in Wesley's later sermons of language to describe God's relation to time that resonates more with the "above time" variation of the typical scholastic model. An early example is a 1773 sermon that distilled the main themes of his prior controversial writings on predestination. In this sermon, Wesley again invoked the notion of an Eternal Now, but his extended description of how God relates to time picks up some duration themes. While God sees all things in one view, Wesley

---

27. See the critique of the coherence of this view as traditionally formulated and a proposed refinement (drawing on John Duns Scotus) of conceiving God instead as "relatively timeless" in Alan G. Padgett, *God, Eternity, and the Nature of Time* (New York: St. Martin's Press, 1992); or Padgett, "God the Lord of Time," in *God and Time: Four Views*, ed. Greg Ganssle (Downer's Grove, Ill.: InterVarsity Press, forthcoming).

28. Cf. *Predestination Calmly Considered*, §18, *John Wesley*, 433. See also from the same time period Wesley's comments on Rom. 1:28 and 1 Peter 1:2 in *NT Notes*.

29. See particularly two articles he extracted and reprinted in the *Arminian Magazine*: [Author not given], "On the Eternity of God," *AM* 3 (1780): 33-41; and Extracted from a late Author, "Of God's Immensity," *AM* 9 (1786): 22-25.

stresses that what God sees runs "from everlasting to everlasting," presenting the full span of "whatever was, is, or will be to the end of time."[30] This emphasis is even stronger in sermons after 1785, as the elder Wesley chooses to define God's eternal existence not with reference to an Eternal Now but with more classically biblical language of "everlastingness" or "boundless duration."[31] He was clearly seeking a theological account that did justice to his conviction that God interacts responsively with humanity in our temporal setting.

Prescience and Response-ability?

One of the shared aspects of the *nunc stans* model and the model emphasizing God as "above time" was the assumption that God eternally knows not only what stands to us as past and present, but also what stands to us as future. The classic way of affirming this was to say that God—as omniscient—has *pre*science or *fore*knowledge of all future events, although immediately added was the fact that this is at best an analogical expression (since nothing is truly "future" to God). Whatever the precision of the claim, there is a deeper question about its implications. Those in the Christian family that affirm unconditional election have often appealed to God's infallible foreknowledge as demonstrating the eternal *certainty* of our final states, and argued that this means our choices concerning salvation could have been no different than they actually were. This implication would obviously have been unacceptable to Wesley, considering his concern to maintain the integrity of our response to God's interactive, gracious work.

If one agreed that foreknowledge of our future choices truly undercuts the contingency of those choices, the most obvious way to preserve the integrity of moral choices would be to deny (as Socinius did) that God can have foreknowledge. Somewhat more modest is the model advanced by one of Wesley's prominent contemporaries, Andrew Ramsay. This model proposes that while God exists "above time" and is thus able to know the future, God vol-

---

30. Sermon 58, "On Predestination," §5, *Works* 2:417. See also §15 (2:420), which contains the reference to the Eternal Now.

31. See Sermon 54, "On Eternity," §1, *Works* 2:358; Sermon 118, "On the Omnipresence of God," §I.2, *Works* 4:42; and Sermon 120, "The Unity of the Divine Being," §2, *Works* 4:61.

untarily chooses not to exercise this ability in order to preserve human freedom. When Wesley first encountered this proposal in the 1750s, he summarily rejected it on exegetical grounds. While he showed some openness to Ramsay's proposal late in his life, Wesley generally assumed that the biblical claim that God's works were known unto God from eternity (Acts 15:18) required affirming divine prescience of all future events, even if there were difficulties understanding how this is consistent with human freedom.[32]

Actually, Wesley had long been aware of a model for explaining the consistency of divine foreknowledge with human freedom. His mother had recommended it early in his student years. This model holds that the certainty of divine prescience is one of *recognition* (like in human perception), not one of *causation*. As Susanna put it, there is no more reason to suppose "that the prescience of God is the cause that so many finally perish, than that our knowing the sun will rise tomorrow is the cause of its rise."[33] As William Wollaston put it in a book that Wesley read a little later at Oxford: "The truth is, God foresees, or rather sees the actions of free agents, because they *will be*; not that they will be, because He *foresees* them."[34]

Wesley invoked this model (sometimes called "simple fore-knowledge") in his famous 1739 sermon "Free Grace," the opening volley of his debate with George Whitefield and the Calvinist Methodists. He argued that biblical claims about eternal election simply reflect God's ability as one "above time" to see from the beginning each individual's final response to the gracious—but resistible—offer of salvation.[35] While Whitefield was not convinced, others found this argument persuasive.[36] Thus it recurred

---

32. Cf. Andrew Ramsay, *The Philosophical Principles of Natural and Revealed Religion* (Glasgow: Robert Foulis, 1748), 142-74. Wesley's initial reaction is evident in *Letter to Dr. John Robertson* (24 September 1753), Works 26:517. Related responses can be found in *NT Notes* Acts 15:8; and *A Letter to Richard Locke* (14 September 1770), *Letters* (Telford) 5:199. But these must be balanced by the fact that the elder Wesley published an excerpt of pages 161-74 of Ramsay as "Of the Foreknowledge of God, extracted from a late author," *AM 8* (1785): 27-29, 88-90, 146-48.

33. *A Letter from Mrs. Susanna Wesley* (18 August 1725), Works 25:180.

34. William Wollaston, *The Religion of Nature Delineated* (London: Samuel Palmer, 1724), 102. Wesley read Wollaston in 1733.

35. See Sermon 110, "Free Grace," §§20, 29, Works 3:552-53, 558-59.

36. Whitefield responded with a 1740 public letter titled *Free Grace Indeed?* that can be

in every major subsequent work where Wesley challenged the notion of unconditional election.[37] It was also utilized by John Fletcher, Wesley's close associate who offered an extended apologetic for the Wesleyan position in debates with the Calvinists.[38] On the weight of such warrant it was established as the standard Wesleyan/Methodist position on divine foreknowledge by Wesley's death in 1791. Although we will find some of his nineteenth-century heirs debating the point, Wesley clearly judged this "simple foreknowledge" model to be consistent with both the integrity of our human choices and the response-able nature of God.

DEFENDING AND EXTENDING WESLEY'S TRAJECTORY IN NINETEENTH-CENTURY METHODISM

Wesley's mature pastoral/theological reflections on the divine attributes just considered are sufficient for demonstrating his willingness to revise certain scholastic conceptions in order to nurture among his people a sense of God's responsive gracious interaction with humanity. One might expect that his immediate heirs would push such revisions and nuances even further, citing Wesley's

---

found in *George Whitefield's Journals*, ed. Iain Murray (London: Banner of Truth, 1960), 571-88 (see p. 586). For an immediate defense of Wesley against Whitefield by an Anglican in the North American colonies see, John Checkley, *Dialogues between a minister and an honest country-man. . . . To which is annexed, Divine prescience consistent with human liberty; or Mr. Wesley's opinion of election and reprobation, prov'd to be not so absurd as represented in a late letter . . .* (Philadelphia: Andrew Bradford, Jacob Duche, William Parsons, and Evan Morgan, 1741), 29-39.

37. *Predestination Calmly Considered*, §18, *John Wesley*, 433; Sermon 58, "On Predestination," §5, *Works* 2:417; and Sermon 59, "God's Love to Fallen Man," §3, *Works* 2:424. It is also found in works he reprinted in the *AM*: Thomas Goad, "A Discourse Concerning the Necessity and Contingency of Events in the World, in Respect of God's Eternal Decrees," *AM* 1 (1778): 250-64, 289-302 (see pp. 262, 301); and "Treatise on Election and Reprobation, extracted from a Late Author," *AM* 2 (1779): 161ff. I do not see Wesley showing reticence about this position as possibly compatibilist, as suggested in Walter Lamoyne Parr Jr., "John Wesley's *Thoughts upon Necessity* in his Search for the Middle Verity" (University of Aberdeen Ph.D. thesis, 1994), 255-60, 276-79.

38. It is surprising how little Fletcher deals with the specific topic of foreknowledge, but when he does, he insists that foreknowledge does not have a causative effect. Cf. *Third Part of an Equal Check*, Section VI, in *The Works of the Reverend John Fletcher, Late Vicar of Madeley* (New York: Carlton and Porter, 1835) 2:176-83; and *An Answer to the Rev. Mr. Toplady's "Vindication of the Decrees,"* Section VIII, *Works* 2:462-67.

precedent as warrant. Instead, their energies were almost immediately consumed in resisting the pressure to return to reigning scholastic conceptions.

Part of the reason that Wesley felt free to differ from Roman Catholic and Protestant scholastic theologies was his self-conscious Anglican identity. There are lines of inheritance from both Protestant and Roman Catholic scholastic theologies in the Anglican standards of doctrine, but one of the significant ways these standards differed from the continental model was in form. The Anglican church returned to the early church model of relying on first-order forms such as liturgy, creed, and catechetical sermons as standards of doctrine. The closer connection of these forms to the daily worship and life of the church served to nuance and enrich some of the abstract conceptions of the divine attributes that had made their way into scholastic theological debate.

It is against this background that we can appreciate the theological impact of the rapid "de-Anglicanization" of Methodism. This process began when American Methodists formed The Methodist Episcopal Church following the Revolutionary War. After Wesley's death, British Methodists quickly formalized their own independent existence and worked to define themselves against their Anglican mother. This threw Methodists in both settings into primary dialogue with churches rooted in continental Protestantism, and they soon realized that their inherited (Anglican) forms of theological expression were not considered "real" theology in these circles. Their response was not to question the primacy of the continental forms but to focus their energies on developing the scholastic theology for Methodism that Wesley had lamentably failed to provide.[39] In the process, they inevitably had to explain places where Wesley had diverged from scholastic conceptions of the nature of God. And to the degree that they were concerned to defend their status as orthodox Protestants, there was pressure to reconsider these divergences.

---

39. For a detailed discussion of this transition, focusing on the American Methodists, see Randy L. Maddox, "An Untapped Inheritance: American Methodism and Wesley's Practical Theology," in *Doctrines and Discipline: Methodist Theology and Practice*, ed. Dennis M. Campbell, et al. (Nashville: Abingdon Press, 1999), 19-52, 292-309.

Conservative Precedent of Nineteenth-Century British Methodism

The growing impact of such pressure is evident in nineteenth-century British Methodism. The generation that overlapped Wesley's death continued to rely on forms of theological expression aimed at instructing the entire community, particularly sermon collections and general Bible commentaries. The most widely recognized of this generation was Adam Clarke, but Clarke was also the center of much controversy in Methodist circles precisely because he challenged some traditional theological conceptions in his multi-volume commentary.[40] Most relevant to our investigation is a controversy sparked by Clarke's comment on the reference to God's "fore-ordained knowledge" in Acts 2. True to his Wesleyan roots, Clarke sought to understand this phrase in a way that did not equate it with unconditional election. His main strategy was to invoke the now-standard model of God existing above time and thereby observing (rather than causing) our future choices and actions. But then Clarke ventured a step further—on analogy with Wesley's argument that omnipotence did not require that God actually control all that God could control. Clarke proposed that "God, although omniscient, is not obliged, in consequence of this, *to know all that he can know.*"[41]

In other words, Clarke embraced more overtly than the elder Wesley the proposal of Andrew Ramsay that we should understand God as *voluntarily* renouncing prescience of at least some future events in order to preserve human responsibility. But when Clarke "extended" Wesley's trajectory on this point, official British Methodism was not willing to follow. The Book Committee refused the initial draft of his commentary in 1799, citing in part the publication underway of Thomas Coke's six-volume commentary. When Conference then issued Joseph Benson's commentary in 1809 as a second official work, the ignored Clarke reluctantly agreed

---

40. For a detailed account of the actions described in this paragraph, see Ian Sellers, *Adam Clarke, Controversialist: Wesleyanism and the Historic Faith in the Age of Bunting* (St. Columb Major: Wesley Historical Society, 1976). This work was drawn to my attention by Martin Astell.

41. See Adam Clarke, *The New Testament . . . with a Commentary and Critical Notes* (New York: Waugh and Mason, 1834), comment on Acts 2:47. See also his description of God as above time in his comment on Luke 1:34.

to move ahead with an independent press. As he prepared to issue a revised version in 1830, Clarke checked once more with the Book Steward; told that he would have to remove all "objectionable" passages, he again settled for an independent press. Even Samuel Dunn's compendium of excerpts on various doctrinal topics from Clarke's writings (prepared shortly after his death) was released outside Conference auspices, despite the fact that Dunn had carefully omitted the controversial proposals.[42]

The effort to distance themselves from Clarke reflects a key agenda of British Methodist leaders in these early decades, which was to gain the theological respect of their dialogue partners in the other dissenting traditions. They soon sensed that a prerequisite to this goal was having a comprehensive and carefully organized survey of Methodist belief and practice that engaged the long tradition of Christian theological debate, defended any controversial Methodist claims, and provided rational grounding for the whole—that is, a Methodist "scholastic theology." Richard Watson published his *Theological Institutes* as the pioneering work in this genre in 1823, and it remained the standard British Methodist theology text for over half a century.[43] It has frequently been noted that Watson seldom quotes Wesley in this work. While this is true, it is largely because of Watson's recognition that his non-Methodist critics would not consider Wesley to serve as a significant warrant because he was not a "serious" theologian. Careful reading reveals Watson's actual concern in articulating and defending Wesley's stance on several debated issues, including those related to the doctrine of God that we have been considering.

For example, in his discussion of immutability (1:435-37) Watson echoed Wesley's defense of the biblical claim of God "repenting," arguing that a God that fails to take into account the changing response of humanity would not be truly unchangeable in righteousness and love. He likewise faithfully affirmed the ascription of passions or affections to God. Concerning the topic of omnipotence, Watson reiterated the claim that God's power is self-limited

---

42. Cf. Samuel Dunn, *Christian Theology: By Adam Clarke, LL.D., F.A.S.* (New York: T. Mason and G. Lane, 1840), 69-70, 74.

43. Richard Watson, *Theological Institutes; Or, A View of the Evidences, Doctrines, Morals and Institutions of Christianity*, 3 vols. (London: Mason, 1823). Page references in the following two paragraphs refer to this edition.

by God's nature, particularly by God's wisdom and goodness in wanting to deal with humans as responsible agents (1:403, 3:174-77). Reflecting his more scholastic sensitivities, Watson took up the question of God's relationship to time and enlarged upon the hints in Wesley's late sermons (1:395-99). He spelled out the objections to the *nunc stans* model and then defended at some length the biblical language of God's "eternal duration." He clearly took this language to imply a model of God as "above time," able to recognize succession in events without being confined to the present.

Watson's discussion of foreknowledge is particularly interesting (1:416-27). He joined Wesley in defending the simple foreknowledge model, insisting that God's foreknowledge had "no influence upon either the freedom or the certainty of actions, for this plain reason, that it is *knowledge* and not *influence*" (1:422). The main opponents against which Watson directed his argument were not the predestinarians but those that were ready to deny divine prescience in order to protect human freedom. Watson first considered Andrew Ramsay's suggestion that God voluntarily renounces prescience (he tactfully did not mention Clarke's similar proposal). He rejected this possibility because it was contradictory and contended that the phrase "knowledge of God" refers not only to God's capacity to acquire knowledge but also to God's actually comprehending all things that are and that can be (1:418). He then turned to the stronger claim of Socinius that knowledge of future contingent events is metaphysically impossible even for the omniscient (temporal) God, since these events do not yet exist as something to be known. Watson's immediate rejoinder to this claim was to cite biblical prophecies that he assumed involved God's certain knowledge of future contingent events (1:418-20). But he added that "the great fallacy of this argument is its assumption that certain prescience of a moral action destroys its contingent nature, for this supposes that contingency and certainty are the opposites of each other when the real opposite of contingent is not certainty but necessity" (1:421). In other words, he saw in Socinius the mirror position of the predestinarians, both based on the same mistaken assumption.

On balance, while Watson adopted the form and tone of scholastic theology, he used these tools to clarify and defend places where

Wesley had challenged or revised scholastic conceptions of God's nature. But the longer that British Methodist theologians worked within the scholastic genre, the more pressure there was to minimize the ways that Wesley had pushed the edges.

This can be illustrated by the most thoroughgoing scholastic theology produced in British Methodism: William Burt Pope's *A Compendium of Christian Theology*, published in 1880.[44] Pope consistently affirmed as much of the traditional conception of the divine attributes as he could, without conceding the crucial Wesleyan conviction. His discussion of immutability, for example, focused on denying any development in God; there was little mention of the debated topic of whether God had passions, though Pope finally insisted that we must understand the attribute in a way that allows God to interact with us "personally" (1:302-304). Likewise, Pope adopted the traditional framing of omnipotence as an application of divine freedom but then used this to defend God's "freedom" to self-limit omnipotence in order to allow a measure of freedom to humans (1:311-13). And he directed discussion of omniscience with somewhat greater ease to the simple foreknowledge model, stressing how this avoided unconditional election (1:315-19).

Pope's discussion of God's relation to time is the most interesting. Without listing Watson by name (or discussing Wesley's later sermons), he criticized those who dismissed the model of the Eternal Now in favor of assigning duration to God. He endorsed the scholastic claim that the divine essence in itself must be absolutely unconditioned. Thus, it can experience no succession of time. But then he argued that in dealing with creation, God must behold, direct, and control all things as under the law to time (1:297-99). He summarized this balance a little later: "Instead of saying with the Schoolmen that to God there is only an eternal now, it were better to say that to God as absolute essence there is the eternal now, and also to God as related to the creature there is the process of succession" (1:317). Anticipating the question of how both claims can be true, he appealed to mystery.[45] What remains no

---

44. Page references in this and the next paragraphs are to William Burt Pope, *A Compendium of Christian Theology*, 2nd ed. (London: Wesleyan Conference Office, 1880).

45. Pope, *Compendium*, 1:299. Actually, the position that Pope is groping for seems much like the notion of God as "relatively timeless" developed by Alan G. Padgett (see note 27 above).

mystery is the fact that the basic Wesleyan conviction of God's response-able nature served as the limit of Pope's concessions to scholastic tradition.

The Tentative Independence of Early American Methodist Theology

The "primitivist" strain in American Methodism allowed, in theory, greater independence from both Wesley and scholastic theology than is evident in the British precedent. This strain reflected the optimistic assumption that pilgrimage to the New World had provided freedom from the tyranny of *all* past tradition and the opportunity to reinstitute the beliefs and practice of the New Testament church. Thus, we get a methodology like that affirmed by Asa Shinn in *An Essay on the Plan of Salvation*, one of the first theological monographs by an American Methodist:

> Each one is bound under a sacred obligation, to go to the Bible for [one's] system of divinity, and so far as any is governed by a regard to any human creed, in the formation of [one's] religious opinions, so far [one] is deficient in the very principle of Christian faith; and pays that homage to human authority that is due only to the Divine.[46]

In retrospect, the naivete of this mandate is palpable; American Methodists constantly drew upon traditional theological proposals in their interpretation of Scripture. At the same time, they were somewhat less reticent about championing marginal or nonmajority proposals. In particular, it appears that a number of early American preachers embraced Adam Clarke's notion of God voluntarily laying aside prescience.[47] The most striking case was that of Billy Hibbard Sr., an early circuit rider, who published in his *Memoirs* an extended argument that God does not foreknow future contingent events.[48] Hibbard had long puzzled over how to relate Divine prescience to human freedom and had said he found no help

---

46. Asa Shinn, *An Essay on the Plan of Salvation* (Baltimore: Neal, Wills and Cole, 1813), 230.

47. Cf. the examples cited censoriously in James Anderson, *Strictures on Arminian Methodism* (Lancaster, Ohio: J. R. Dixon, 1844), 18-19.

48. Page references in the next three paragraphs refer to Billy Hibbard, *Memoirs of the Life and Travels of B. Hibbard*, 2nd ed. (New York: for the author, 1843), 369-414. Note that this section was not present in Hibbard's 1825 first edition of *Memoirs*.

in the authors he had read on the topic until he came across an extract on foreknowledge with which he fully agreed in "Mr. Wesley's American (sic) Magazine, ninth volume." Fortunately, Hibbard reprints (an abridgment of) the extract before commenting on it. Thereby it can be verified that he was actually reading the extract of Ramsay that Wesley published in volume eight of the *Arminian Magazine*.[49]

The stated goal of the extract was to find a medium between the extremes of fatalism (God's prescience renders all future events necessary) and Socinianism (God is not able to foresee or foretell any of the actions of free agents). But it does not present the "simple foreknowledge" alternative that had become standard in Methodism. Instead it asserts that God knows everything past and present (as well as all logical truths) with certainty but perceives future events only as *possible*. Against the fatalists, this view emphasizes that God knows *all* possible future combinations of physical and moral causes and prepares for all contingencies, both of which, it argues, are "far more perfect than foreseeing infallibly of only one sort of events, and excluding all the others, by an omnipotent, irresistible power" (374). Against the Socinians, it insists that God is theoretically *able* to foresee, foreordain, and execute whatever God pleases, but God "neither foresees nor foreordains as infallibly future, what he leaves to the free choice of intellectual agents, because this is repugnant and contradictory" (376). In other words, it develops the model of a voluntary surrender of prescience like that tentatively advanced by Clarke.

Hibbard appended to this first extract another of unidentified origin that argued that any notion of prescience—even a notion with God "above time"—leads necessarily to unconditional predestination (376-86). Taking his own voice, Hibbard offered an extended endorsement of this necessary connection (405-12). On that basis, he argued that affirming divine prescience made God the author of sinning, contradicting both the divine perfection and human moral agency (387-90). This led him to charge (with reference to Richard Watson) that "the advocates of eternal prescience, apart from predestination, are far more inconsistent than

---

49. Compare Hibbard, *Memoirs*, 373-76 to *AM* 8 (1785): 27-29, 88-90, 146-48 (cf. note 32 above).

their predestinarian Brethren . . . and I call upon them as ingenious and honest men, either to reject their notion of a certain prescience of a contingent event, or to renounce the doctrine of human liberty."[50] The alternative that Hibbard recommended paralleled the first extract. He put it colloquially as this, "God knows just what he has a mind to know, and what he has not a mind to know, he lets alone" (413).

The most striking thing about Hibbard's discussion was the extent (particularly in comparison with Clarke) to which he developed this model of self-limited foreknowledge. For example, in its defense he cited scriptural claims about God's grief over human decisions to sin (395). And responding to the use of biblical prophecies as proof of prescience, he argued that prophecies were just expressions of God's intention to accomplish something in the future that was within God's power and nature to do but that would not include determining future contingent actions (404). Despite the vigor of his argument, Hibbard did not succeed in convincing leading voices in contemporary American Methodism of the superiority of his model.

The reality was that through most of the nineteenth century, formal teaching on the doctrine of God among American Methodists—whatever their independence in other areas—echoed that of their British counterpart. Across the range of the splintering American family, they readily assigned Watson's *Institutes* as the main theological text on the course of study for prospective elders.[51] Discussion of these topics in their denominational journals defended the stance that Watson had expounded, particularly the "simple foreknowledge" model of God as a rebuttal to predestination.[52]

---

50. Hibbard, *Memoirs*, 412. The references to Watson are on pp. 400-403. Ironically, Hibbard also targets Clarke in this critique (see p. 405), even though he is actually defending a position that Clarke had tentatively suggested. Perhaps Hibbard had only read the collection of excerpts from Clarke's writings, which omit this suggestion.

51. Watson was on the course of study for The Methodist Episcopal Church from 1833–92; The Methodist Protestant Church, 1830–1920; The African Methodist Episcopal Church, 1844–92; The African Methodist Episcopal Church Zion, 1872–1900; The Methodist Episcopal Church South, 1878–1906; and The Colored (Christian) Methodist Episcopal Church, 1872–1920.

52. E.g., Anonymous [Joshua Soule?], "Thoughts on the Foreknowledge of God," *MQR* 3 (1820): 11-14, 49-53; La Roy Sunderland, "Unoriginated Decrees," *Methodist Quarterly Review* 16 (1833): 322-40; S [Abel Stephens?], "God's Determinant Counsel and Foreknowledge," *MQR* 21 (1839): 39-61, esp. 41; and Henry Bidleman Bascom, "The Divine Prescience Not Inconsistent with Free Agency of Man," *Methodist Quarterly Review of the MECS* 1 (1847) 161-75.

And when American authors began producing their own survey texts, the early generations drew their discussion of the divine attributes direct from Watson.[53] Even on the conservative side, someone as concerned to demonstrate continuity with classical Christian tradition as Thomas Summers retained the major points about God's response-able nature that had been made by Wesley and passed along in slightly refined form in Watson.[54]

Solidifying the Progressive Strand in American Methodist Theology, 1875–1900

Throughout the nineteenth century, those who exercised the teaching office in American Methodism steadfastly rejected the equation of official Methodist teaching with the occasional suggestion of individual Methodists that the only way to avoid predestination was to deny that God had foreknowledge of future contingent events.[55] For most of the century, this rejection required little elaboration because the suggestions were either tentative (such as Clarke's suggestions) or from persons of marginal theological influence (such as Hibbard). Near the end of the century, this situation changed dramatically, owing largely to the impact of one writer—Lorenzo Dow McCabe.

McCabe taught philosophy for more than thirty years at Ohio Wesleyan University. Like his namesake (Lorenzo Dow, the flamboyant circuit rider), McCabe was not afraid to challenge conventional Methodist stances when he was convinced that challenging was what truth required. In 1878, he published through the MEC publishing house a vigorous philosophical and theological critique of the "simple foreknowledge" model of God.[56] In this work, he

---

53. E.g., Amos Binney, *Theological Compend* (New York: Carlton and Lanahan, 1840), 53; Thomas Neely Ralston, *Elements of Divinity* (Louisville: E. Stevenson for the Methodist Episcopal Church, South, 1851), 23-26; and Samuel Wakefield, *A Complete System of Christian Theology* (Pittsburgh: J. L. Read and Son, 1869), 145-59.

54. See Thomas O. Summers, *Systematic Theology*, 2 vols. (Nashville: Publishing House of the MECS, 1888), on eternity (1:75-80), immutability (1:80-82), omnipotence (1:84), and omniscience (1:85-90).

55. E.g., Daniel D. Whedon, *The Freedom of the Will* (New York: Carlton and Porter, 1864), 273-74; and Thomas O. Summers's rejection of the suggestion that Clarke speaks for all Methodists (*Systematic Theology* 1:88). On the status of editors like Whedon and Summers as exercising the teaching office, see Russell E. Richey, "The Legacy of Francis Asbury: The Teaching Office in Episcopal Methodism," *Quarterly Review* 15 (1995): 145-74.

56. Lorenzo Dow McCabe, *The Foreknowledge of God, and Cognate Themes in Theology and Philosophy* (Cincinnati: Hitchcock and Walden, 1878). Page references in this and the following three paragraphs are to this book.

specifically rejected the contentions of Wesley, Watson, and Whedon that this model provided a logically defensible way of allowing divine prescience while preserving human accountability (cf. 21, 161, 310-15). Moreover, he argued that the basic assumption of Clarke's alternative model—that God *could* foreknow future contingent actions but chooses not to—was also fallacious (218-19). What both models failed to realize, McCabe insisted, was that there could be certain knowledge of only past facts, logical necessities, and future actions, which are totally determined by present causal factors. Truly contingent future actions can be anticipated only as possibilities but not fore*known* as existing facts.

The conventional Methodist response to McCabe would be to allow that this is true for human knowledge, since we are temporal creatures, but to deny that God exists "in the present" like we do. However, this is where McCabe disagreed most fundamentally with earlier Wesleyan tradition. He charged that Wesley should have gone further in reversing the scholastic emphasis on God's atemporal nature, an emphasis that Wesley recognized was hard to align with the biblical accounts of God's engaging temporal human beings in a truly responsive manner (223-24). McCabe was convinced that the only way to achieve Wesley's underlying concern of affirming God's response-able nature was to affirm that God experiences succession in a way that is not fundamentally different from how we experience it. He put it rhetorically: "Has God no attraction for what is new? Has he no capability of the delightful experiences of wonder and surprise and variety? We ought never to lose sight of what God has explicitly revealed of himself when he declares that we were made in his own image and likeness" (174).

This quotation makes clear that McCabe assumed that the God revealed in Scripture and Christian life was more appropriately conceived in terms of the model of a "person" than that of an "Unmoved Mover." To speak of God as a "person," related meaningfully to a contingent world, demanded in McCabe's view that temporality itself was a primary, not a secondary experience, of God (259ff.). But how does God's experience of temporality differ from our own? McCabe was ambiguous on this point. In one setting, he described God's eternal existence as simply duration without beginning or end (382-83). Elsewhere, he seemed to suggest that God was atemporal before creation and freely adopted the self-limitation of entering into temporality as part of the decision to create a universe with true temporality, novelty, and freedom (cf. 204-205, 387).[57]

Regardless of the way McCabe's account of divine eternity is sorted out, it is clear that he viewed his temporal conception of God as particularly appropriate to the biblical accounts of a God that experiences states of feeling and is open to change (see 272ff., 313). But how did it fit with the notion of God as omniscient? Anticipating charges that he unduly limited God's knowledge, McCabe emphasized that God would know all the interrelated contingent possibilities of the future—which is infinitely more than knowing only the possibilities that will be realized (250). This anticipatory knowledge would allow God to be prepared for providential action. Moreover, since God would be able to discern relative probabilities, this would account for some of the biblical prophecies (153ff.). Yet McCabe agreed that other prophecies, like that of Peter's triple denial, seemed too specific to account for in this way. He assumed that in these few cases God must have overridden human liberty to fulfill the prophecy, but added that, as a result, the persons involved would not be morally accountable for their acts (88-92)!

As this last proposal suggests, McCabe was still thinking through many dimensions of his overall model of God and foreknowledge. In 1882, he published a second book titled *Divine Nescience of Future Contingencies A Necessity*, which he described as an introduction to the first work.[58] In this follow-up, he identified his main target as "the Augustinian conception of God that has captured most theology to present which so far elevates the conception of God to a universal infinite that it logically annihilates him in his concrete personality." McCabe's alternative goal was an account of God—rooted in facts of religious experience and scriptural testimony—that portrayed God as capable of relating fully to the contingencies of personal life and historical change (17-18). At

---

57. This suggestion would come close to the position defended by William Craig in Ganssle, ed., *God and Time*.

58. Lorenzo Dow McCabe, *Divine Nescience of Future Contingencies a Necessity, Being an Introduction to "The Foreknowledge of God, and Cognate Themes"* (New York: Phillips and Hunt, 1882). (Note: Nescience is the opposite of prescience).

the heart of this account was the argument that divine prescience of future contingent actions was logically and metaphysically impossible. While there was considerable overlap with the first book, a few items of interest emerge in this study. For example, McCabe devoted more attention to practical implications of his model for such central religious issues as prayer and theodicy. He developed the logical point that if future contingents do not yet exist, then it is not a restriction of omniscience to deny God's knowledge of them (191). And he returned to the issue of prophecy, this time highlighting how the numerous conditional prophecies in scripture fit his model (76).

As one would expect, McCabe's ambitious revisionary proposal generated significant response. Much of the initial response was negative. Two concerns came up repeatedly. One was the charge that McCabe was playing into the hands of those Calvinists who rejected the Methodist affirmation of human freedom because he granted their assumption that divine prescience necessarily eliminates authentic human freedom.[59] In response, McCabe argued that predestinarian Calvinism would have been discredited long ago if misguided Arminians had not continued to defend the doctrine of divine prescience.[60] The second common claim advanced against McCabe's proposal was that the many scriptural prophecies of specific future contingent events compel us to affirm divine prescience, despite the theological quandaries this might pose. It was not difficult for those stressing this concern to demonstrate the inadequacy of McCabe's scattered attempts to account for the range of apparent prophetic material in scripture.[61] Unfortunately, they did not engage the more extended discussion of this topic in Joel Hayes's *The Foreknowledge of God*, a book published through the Southern Methodist Publishing House about a decade

---

59. See particularly the first published review of *Foreknowledge of God* by "GH" [likely Gilbert Haven] in *MQR* 61 (1879): 162-66. Other short negative evaluations of McCabe in this influential journal include George Steele, "Dr. McCabe on the Divine Prescience," *MQR* 74 (1892): 963-65; W. W. W. Wilson, "Prescience or Nescience—Which?" *MQR* 76 (1894): 639; and Austin H. Herrick, "An Objection to Divine Nescience," *MQR* 76 (1894): 639.

60. See Lorenzo Dow McCabe, "Prescience of Future Contingencies Impossible," *MQR* 74 (1892): 760-73, esp. 773.

61. Note how central this issue is to the evaluations of McCabe in Loring C. Webster, *The End from the Beginning; or, Divine Prescience vs. Divine Nescience of Future Contingencies* (Cincinnati: Cranston and Curts, 1895), esp. 308-30; and Randolph S. Foster, *God: Nature and Attributes* (New York: Eaton and Mains, 1897), 200ff.

after McCabe's books were published. Hayes's book argues for the same basic model of God's temporal nature and knowledge.[62]

Given that the "simple foreknowledge" model of God had dominated official teaching for nearly a century, the most interesting aspect of the reaction to McCabe's revisionist proposal was the emerging openness it encountered among influential voices in Northern Methodism. John F. Hurst (president of Drew Theological Seminary and soon to be elected an MEC bishop) provided the cautiously supportive introduction to McCabe's first volume.[63] Daniel D. Whedon (prominent editor of the *Methodist Quarterly Review*) protested any suggestion that McCabe verged on heresy, arguing that while he did not believe McCabe's proposed revision was necessary, it deserved a tolerant hearing.[64] Even Randolph S. Foster (a MEC bishop), who offered an extended defense of William Burt Pope's model of foreknowledge over that of McCabe, prefaced his arguments with a description of McCabe as an "orthodox of the orthodox of Arminian faith" whose books deserved careful reading. Significantly, Foster allowed to McCabe that prescience of contingent events was not absolutely necessary for God's just and perfect administration of the universe.[65]

In retrospect, the most significant nineteenth-century engagement with McCabe's proposal was that of John Miley (longtime professor of theology at Drew) in his *Systematic Theology*, published in 1892.[66] Miley's discussion of omniscience included a direct dialogue with McCabe (1:180-85). In this dialogue, Miley argued in favor of prescience, based mainly on the apparent evidence of

---

62. Joel S. Hayes, *The Foreknowledge of God; or, the Omniscience of God Consistent with His Own Holiness and Man's Free Agency* (Nashville: MECS Publishing House, 1890). Over half of the book (187-397) is devoted to discussing both scriptures that Hayes believed supported his model and that appeared to undercut it. Among his contributions to points made by McCabe was recognition that many supposed specific prophecies were evident only by selective hindsight (272) and insistence that God promised future providential action without implying that God rigidly controlled all the variables leading up to that action (218).

63. J. F. Hurst, "Introduction," in McCabe, *Foreknowledge of God*, 7-15.

64. See Whedon's review of *Divine Nescience* in *MQR* 65 (1883): 176-77; and McCabe's claim that Whedon only reluctantly published "GH's" earlier negative review of *Foreknowledge* (*Divine Nescience*, 290). Remember that Whedon accepted the "simple foreknowledge" model, which held there was no necessary conflict between foreknowledge and freedom.

65. See Foster, *God*, 181 and 187 (on Foster's preference for Pope see 18-20). Cf. McCabe's report of Foster's compliments on his first book, in *Divine Nescience*, 290.

66. John Miley, *Systematic Theology*, 2 vols. (New York: Hunt and Eaton, 1892–94).

biblical prophecy, but added that accepting divine nescience would not undermine any vital Methodist doctrines. He said that rather, "the chief perceivable result would be to free the system from the perplexity for freedom which arises with the divine prescience" (1:185). Turning his focus from human freedom to the biblical accounts of God experiencing changing feelings and acting providentially in our world, Miley conceded that both types of accounts are more comprehensible if we reject divine prescience than if we assume it (1:189-92). Going further, he insisted that "if the ministries of providence in the free agency of God, with all the emotional activities of such ministries, be not consistent or possible with his foreknowledge, then foreknowledge cannot be true" (1:192). But he stopped just short of actually embracing this conclusion, suggesting that such inconsistency had not yet been decisively proved.

It might not be surprising that some readers sensed an implicit endorsement of McCabe behind Miley's carefully stated qualifications.[67] At the very least, Miley clearly placed McCabe's position within the boundaries of legitimate alternative theological "opinions" for Methodists. This placement was significant because Miley's *Systematic Theology* served as the assigned text in the course of study for pastoral ministry in the MEC from 1892 to 1908. Thereby it provided more impetus than had previously existed for those in training to consider moving beyond simply *defending* the revisions that Wesley himself had made in certain scholastic assumptions about God; they could join McCabe in *extending* the trajectory of these revisions by affirming God's fully "temporal" nature. One evidence that it was having this effect can be seen in the 1899 volume of the *Methodist Quarterly Review*. In an early issue, Milton Terry, a theologian at Garrett Theological Seminary, published an editorial essay criticizing Clarke and McCabe for rejecting prescience and opening the door to the notion that God can "grow." This essay quickly drew two rejoinders from MEC pastors that defended McCabe and quizzed Terry about why the notion of God having new experiences was objectionable.[68]

---

67. Note, for example, the defense of McCabe by appeal to Miley in H. C. Buss, "Prescience of Future Contingencies," *MQR* 75 (1893): 968.

68. See Milton Terry, "Nescience and God," *MQR* 81 (1899): 112-13; J. Wallace Webb, "Nescience of God," *MQR* 81 (1899): 464-65; J. S. Breckinridge, "Nescience of God," *MQR* 81 (1899): 622-25; and Milton Terry, "Nescience of God," *MQR* 81 (1899): 628-29.

THE PROGRESSIVE WESLEYAN TRAJECTORY THROUGH THE MID-TWENTIETH CENTURY

There have been many Methodists and Wesleyans from Terry's time to the present that would echo his objection to the notion of a God that has truly new experiences or "grows" in any sense. By contrast, process theologians champion this notion. Given the role that Lorenzo Dow McCabe played in creating room in American Methodist circles for serious consideration of a model of God as truly temporal, contemporary Wesleyan process theologians can very appropriately look to him as one of the significant forerunners of their stance.[69] The task that remains for our consideration is to briefly trace how this type of progressive *extension* of Wesley's original trajectory found a growing place through the mid-twentieth century in Methodism, creating a receptiveness to explicit process theology as it emerged.

The Progressive Spirit in British Methodist Theology

British Methodist theology maintained a fairly uniform conservative stance through the nineteenth century by ignoring or resisting most of the emerging intellectual challenges in biblical and historical studies as well as in the natural sciences. With the turn of the century came a striking new spirit and approach—a willingness to question old certainties and become more forward-looking. This new spirit was particularly evident in the British Methodists who emerged as prominent biblical scholars, striving to engage the canonical materials more on their own terms than through ill-fitting traditional assumptions. British Methodist doctrinal theologians, though few in number, embodied a similar concern.

J. Scott Lidgett was the pioneer of this group and can serve as representative. He is most noted for his advocacy of reclaiming the doctrine of God's fatherhood in *The Fatherhood of God in Christian Truth and Life*.[70] In Lidgett's framing, this doctrine had

---

69. Cf. the appreciative study of McCabe in William McGuire King, "God's Nescience of Future Contingents: A Nineteenth-Century Theory," *Process Studies* 9 (Fall 1979): 105-15.

70. See J. Scott Lidgett, *The Fatherhood of God in Christian Truth and Life* (Edinburgh: T. & T. Clark, 1902). Page numbers in this paragraph refer to this book.

nothing to do with God's gender. On the contrary, it was an affirmation that we must conceive of the creation of humankind as

> the calling into existence by God, *out of His own life*, of beings at once kindred with Himself, and having a distinct individuality of their own. . . . [this creation] is motivated by the love of God; introduces them into a world, a home, of love, which environs their whole life; and has, at its end, that fellowship of mutual giving and receiving, that most intimate communion, which can only be between those who are spiritually akin (288).

Lidgett contended that this sense of the Fatherhood of God, while clearly taught in Scripture, was obscured in later Christian tradition by an alternative emphasis on the abstract ideal of Divine Sovereignty. He traced this alternative emphasis back to the influence of Platonism on Christian reflection (164-66) and stressed Augustine's role in helping this model of God as sovereign become dominant in medieval theology (180-200). He then lauded how this dominant model had been called into question in the recent years, specifically praising early Methodism for its contribution to recovering the stress on Divine Fatherhood (267-70).

The concept of God as existing in the Eternal Now was one aspect of the previously dominant model that Lidgett identified as needing revision. But his 1902 book provides little sense of his alternative. For this we must turn to a series of essays published in *Contemporary Review* in the 1930s.[71] The most relevant is a 1938 essay where Lidgett affirmed that time must have reality for God, "because it is the condition of His progressive self-giving to and through the process of His world" (109). Lidgett was interacting with Alfred North Whitehead's new book *Modes of Thought* in this essay, and specifically praised Whitehead for his interpretation of reality in terms of universal process (112). He clearly felt some sympathy for the emerging process model of a temporal God. It could allow a more response-able God, as long as God was actually *able* to respond. In this latter connection, Lidgett had reservations about Whitehead's insistence that God always interacts with us in the mode of persuasion, but never more actively. Lidgett considered

---

71. These essays collected in J. Scott Lidgett, *God and the World: Essays in Christian Theism* (London: Epworth, 1943).

this to be an overreaction to the distorted emphasis on God's coercive sovereignty that developed in Christianity with the displacement of the biblical theme of Divine Fatherhood. This led him to argue that the new Reformation that Whitehead desired should be brought about "not by dismissing God from Creative Sovereignty over the world, but by exploring more deeply and setting forth more fully His fatherhood" (19).

Although there was some distance yet to cover, the sympathy expressed for themes in Whitehead by a person of Lidgett's stature in the 1930s solidified the trajectory within which explicit process theology could emerge in the 1980s.[72] This emergence was delayed mainly by the priority British Methodists gave to biblical and social/political theologies over philosophical theology. It is one thing to identify problems with models of God on exegetical or other grounds; it is another to construct detailed alternatives. The only ones likely to invest time in the second activity are those who consider the metaphysical enterprise central to the theological task.

Developments in American Methodist Theology

This reality is reflected as well in a branching within progressive (or "liberal") American Methodist theology in the first half of the twentieth century. One branch of this stream limited itself in principle to *descriptive accounts* of Christian experience.[73] These accounts rarely addressed (one way or the other) such traditional debates as God's relation to time.[74] The other branch characterized such empirical work as merely preliminary to the rational task of constructing a metaphysical account of Christian belief. This branch was dominated by Boston Personalism, the most influential "school" in American Methodist theology during this period, and it is in this school that most accounts locate the immediate precedents to process theology in Methodism.

The founder of Boston Personalism was Borden Parker Bowne.

---

72. E.g., David Pailin, *Groundwork of Philosophy of Religion* (London: Epworth Press, 1986); and Pailin, *God and the Processes of Reality*.

73. This would be the "empirical theology" epitomized by Harris Franklin Rall. For his method, see Rall, "Theology, Empirical and Christian," in *Contemporary American Theology*, ed. Vergilius Ferm (New York: Round Table, 1933) 2:245-73.

74. Cf. Harris Franklin Rall, *The Meaning of God* (Nashville: Cokesbury, 1925); *What Can I Believe* (Chicago: Commission on Men's Work, Board of Education, MEC, 1933); and *A Faith for Today* (New York: Abingdon Press, 1936), 88ff.

Bowne championed a type of neo-Kantian idealism (which he named "personalism") as the metaphysic most appropriate to Christian faith and most adequate by modern standards.[75] He gave particular prominence to elaborating the concept of God as the ultimate "person," as an alternative to the scholastic model. One might assume that this led Bowne to share McCabe's stress on God's temporality, but his Kantian commitments pushed instead for God's transcendence of the particularities of the temporal order. The most he was willing to propose was a position like that of William Pope, in which God is atemporal in essential nature but able to engage the created order temporally.[76]

It was Francis John McConnell that introduced a stress on God's truly temporal nature into the typical themes of Boston Personalism. His 1924 book titled *Is God Limited?* repeatedly charged the scholastic tradition with limiting God inappropriately by imposing abstract metaphysical principles on God. A model of God accepting such "self-limits" as restricting omnipotence and omniscience—in the interest of responsive interaction with humanity—was championed in contrast as providing a greater richness and fullness in the divine life. In the midst of his argument, McConnell revealed that he had been a student of McCabe in college and was sympathetic with McCabe's philosophical critique of divine prescience.[77] However, he based his own arguments more on the importance of defining the divine attributes in a way that is faithful to the revelation of God given in Christ.[78] In keeping with this emphasis he strongly defended the legitimacy of assigning "feelings" to God, including the ability for God to "suffer." He even showed some willingness to talk of God as open to growth or development, as long as it was clear that this is in areas other than God's basic moral nature.[79]

---

75. Bowne's major philosophical works include: *Metaphysics: A Study in First Principles* (New York: Harper and Brothers, 1882); *Philosophy of Theism* (New York: Harper and Brothers, 1887; revised as *Theism* [New York: American Book Co., 1902]); and *Personalism* (Boston: Houghton Mifflin, 1908).

76. Compare Bowne, *Theism*, 184-85; to Bowne, *Metaphysics*, 190. See also the discussion of Bowne's ambivalence on this topic in Edgar Sheffield Brightman, "A Temporalist View of God," *Journal of Religion* 12 (1932): 545-55, esp. 551-52; and Rufus Burrow Jr., *Personalism: A Critical Introduction* (St. Louis: Chalice Press, 1999), 142-48.

77. See Francis John McConnell, *Is God Limited?* (New York: Abingdon Press, 1924), 123-24.

78. This is central to his follow-up book: McConnell, *The Christlike God: A Survey of the Divine Attributes from the Christian Point of View* (New York: Abingdon Press, 1927).

79. See respectively McConnell, *Is God Limited?* 283-93; and *The Christlike God*, 73-86.

SEEKING A RESPONSE-ABLE GOD

The advocacy of a limited God was taken up by Edgar Sheffield Brightman, probably the most prominent of the Boston Personalists. While the theme was the same, Brightman's focal agenda differed significantly from that of McConnell. What challenged the traditional conception of God for him were the findings of modern science and the problem of suffering (such as his wife's painful death from cancer), not its lack of fit with scripture or spirituality.[80] He was ultimately less concerned with defending God's response-ability in relating to humanity than with insulating God from responsibility for natural evil. This led him to propose that God is actually finite—being eternally confronted by a "Given" that is not self-imposed (God did not create it) and can never be wholly eliminated even if it can be increasingly subdued. It is this Given that is responsible for evils; God is responsible for challenging them and enabling us to do so as well.[81]

While most of Brightman's colleagues and students were less than comfortable with his notion of the Given, he ensconced firmly within Boston Personalism an appreciation for a God who is truly temporal, and can "grow" in some sense. Brightman was aware of parallels between these themes and the emerging metaphysical system of Whitehead. Others would soon turn to this system as a preferred metaphysical framework for their Methodist-honed convictions.

CONCLUSION: A CHARACTERISTICALLY WESLEYAN CONCERN ABOUT CLASSIC PROCESS THEOLOGY?

This essay has focused on one trajectory in the Wesleyan theological tradition that cultivated a receptivity to the themes and concerns of process theology. There are surely others that played a role. Likewise, there are several areas where one could identify points of

80. See the evaluation of the influences on and agenda of Brightman's works in Rufus Burrow Jr., *Personalism*, 160-64; and John H. Lavely, "Edgar Sheffield Brightman: Good-and-Evil and the Finite-Infinite God," in *The Boston Personalist Tradition in Philosophy, Social Ethics, and Theology*, ed. Paul Deats and Carol Robb (Macon, Ga: Mercer University Press, 1986), 121-46.

81. See the progressive development of this notion in Edgar Sheffield Brightman, *The Problem of God* (New York: Abingdon Press, 1930); *The Finding of God* (New York: Abingdon Press, 1931), esp. 115-93; *A Philosophy of Religion* (Englewood Cliffs, N.J.: Prentice-Hall, 1940), 305-41; and *Person and Reality: An Introduction to Metaphysics* (New York: Ronald Press, 1958), 323-42.

tension between characteristically Wesleyan theological emphases and the emphases of classic process theology. I will close by noting the area most continuous with the history we have been tracing.

While the long-standing Wesleyan commitment to God's *response*-ability resonates strongly with the process emphasis on God's temporal, creative, and persuasive nature, it should be no surprise that this same commitment renders many Wesleyans less happy with the apparent restriction of God's role in the ongoing process of the whole of reality to only that of "lure."[82] Is such a God still truly response-able? Where is the basis for solid eschatological hope within this restriction? Is there not a place for the wise God to engage us more actively than this, without resorting to coercion?

Some contemporary Wesleyans are convinced that clarifying and nuancing process theology can provide adequate answers to questions like these.[83] Others believe that an "adequate" model of a truly temporal God requires more significant revising of classic process metaphysics.[84] And still others are inclined to elaborate and reaffirm mediating positions like those worked out by Watson or Pope.[85] For Wesley, the decision would be made in favor of the approach that best captures the balance of the biblical God—a God that works "strongly and sweetly."

---

82. See, for example, Michael L. Peterson, "Orthodox Christianity, Wesleyanism, and Process Theology," *Wesleyan Theological Journal* 15.2 (1980): 45-58.

83. E.g., Tyron L. Inbody, *The Transforming God: An Interpretation of Suffering and Evil* (Louisville: Westminster John Knox Press, 1997).

84. Cf. *Searching for an Adequate God: A Dialogue between Process and Free Will Theists*, ed. John B. Cobb Jr. and Clark H. Pinnock (Grand Rapids: William B. Eerdmans, 2000).

85. A good example is Alan G. Padgett (see note 45 above).

CHAPTER SIX

A TRINITARIAN ALTERNATIVE TO PROCESS THEISM

SAMUEL M. POWELL

At least one motivation behind the present volume arises out of the observation that there are remarkable similarities between Wesleyan theology and process theism, similarities that have not been found between process theism and other members of the Christian family. For example, it is instructive to compare this book with *Process Theology*, edited by Ronald H. Nash.[1] The latter, an anthology of essays by leading evangelicals, is, like this book, an engagement with process theism. Unlike the present volume, however, the essays of *Process Theology* adopt a uniformly negative tone toward process theism, and no representatives of process thought are allotted space in the anthology. The present volume approaches process theism in a different way. Prominent exponents of process theism are represented here; most of the essays in this volume are favorable to, and supportive of, process theism. The assumption is that there is an affinity between the two systems that warrants further exploration. At the very least, it appears that Wesleyan theologians are more amenable to process theism than are theologians of some other traditions.

What is the basis of the ostensible similarities between Wesleyan theology and process theism? I suggest that the basis is John Wesley's own theology as it has been construed in a certain, admittedly long-standing and popular way.[2] This way of construing Wesley's theology focuses on his soteriological concern and regards

---

1. Ronald H. Nash, ed., *Process Theology* (Grand Rapids: Baker Book House, 1987).

2. As is well known, interpreting Wesley can be quite problematic because his thought is eclectic, occasional, and resists easy systematizing. The last two centuries have witnessed a succession of Wesley interpretations: Wesley the evangelist, Wesley the theologian of religious experience, Wesley the Protestant Reformer, Wesley the ecumenical leader, and so on. Obviously, Wesley can be viewed in more than one way. The role of ideological factors cannot be ruled out in any of these interpretations.

it as the center of his thought. This is not a far-fetched interpretation, for John Wesley himself emphasized the importance and centrality of the doctrines related to salvation. A review of the Standard Sermons will confirm this. Not surprisingly, recent books on Wesley's theology have focused on these doctrines.[3]

In spite of the basis of these similarities, the use of process theism by Wesleyans brings some debits to the theological account that outweigh the acknowledged credits. I propose that the center of Wesley's theology is broader than just soteriology and, specifically, that it includes the doctrine of the Trinity. Moreover, I will argue that the doctrine of the Trinity is one of Wesley's most heartfelt doctrinal commitments and that process theism has not yet produced (and, in fact, cannot produce) a satisfactory account of the Trinity. Consequently, process theism must be judged an inadequate tool for Wesleyan theology.

ACCOUNTING FOR THE AFFINITY BETWEEN PROCESS THEISM AND WESLEYAN THEOLOGY

One of the greatest obstacles to accepting the thesis that process theism is unsuitable for Wesleyan thought is that many contemporary American Wesleyans are favorably disposed toward certain aspects of process theism. This disposition, however, is readily comprehensible. Wesleyans are attracted to process theism because it offers a metaphysics that supports their interest in the idea of God as person and, in this way, as similar to human beings. Because process theism affirms a fundamental similarity between God and humans and portrays God as a single, personal being, it is natural for Wesleyans to be attracted to it.[4] Of course, neither Wesleyans nor process theists claim that God and humans are

---

3. See, for example, Theodore Runyon, *The New Creation: John Wesley's Theology Today* (Nashville: Abingdon Press, 1998); and Kenneth J. Collins, *The Scripture Way of Salvation: The Heart of John Wesley's Theology* (Nashville: Abingdon Press, 1997).

4. Of course, process theists would want to extend the range of this judgment so that not only God and humans but also God and all actualities are alike in an important respect. Furthermore, not all Wesleyans would immediately adopt the entire metaphysical apparatus by which process theists understand this essential likeness between God and humans. However, for the sake of convenience, I will restrict myself to similarity between God and humans.

alike in every sense or that there are no important differences between them. Both acknowledge the real and important differences. Nonetheless, both affirm a fundamental analogy between God and humans on the basis of shared characteristics. Wesleyans have historically used the category of person to denote these characteristics.

The theological problem with the use of "person" to describe God and to establish a similarity between God and humanity is that it diminishes the possibility of trinitarian thought. It is difficult to think of God as the Trinity to the extent that God is represented as a person. The Wesleyan tradition exhibits just such an effect. As the concept of person grows in importance, the doctrine of the Trinity becomes increasingly puzzling. Accordingly, it is appropriate to trace the rise of personalist thinking in Wesleyanism.

But where is one to begin in this search? John Wesley himself did not expressly represent God in terms of an essential similarity to humanity or in terms of the concept of person. Sustained Wesleyan interest in God's personality first occurred in the development of Wesleyan theology in the nineteenth century. Nonetheless, it is appropriate to begin with Wesley himself, since the ultimate cause of Wesleyan interest in personality lies in the soteriological focus of his theology.

The soteriological focus includes those doctrines that pertain to repentance, grace, faith, assurance, justification, sanctification, and related matters. That these doctrines constitute the center of Wesley's theology is the judgment of leading historians. As Albert C. Outler says, "Its heart and center was 'the gospel': a call to repentance, faith, justification, regeneration, and 'holy living'. . . . Soteriology is the intense focus of more than half his sermons."[5] In another essay, Outler says that Wesley's "axial theme, which organizes all else in his thought, is grace, and the focus of all his thinking about grace is on the order of *salvation*."[6] And according to Frank Baker, Wesley wanted "to understand the fundamental problems of the human condition, and the finer points of Christian

---

5. Albert C. Outler, "John Wesley: Folk Theologian," in Thomas C. Oden and Leicester R. Longden, eds., *The Wesleyan Theological Heritage: Essays of Albert C. Outler* (Grand Rapids: Francis Asbury, 1991), 115.

6. Albert C. Outler, "A New Future for Wesley Studies: An Agenda for 'Phase III,'" in *The Wesleyan Theological Heritage*, 139-40.

living . . . armed with all the theological sophistication of a specialist in the ways of God with men, and man's way to God—practical divinity. He was content not to understand the mysteries of speculative theology."[7] Note in these resumes of Wesley's theology the absence of the doctrine of the Trinity. Of course, Wesley would never have thought of denying the doctrine, and one may reasonably assume that, as an Anglican priest, he would have affirmed it. But the point is that the Trinity does not seem to have been a central part of his message. The implication is that it has only a loose or remote relation to soteriology.

What is clear then is that John Wesley's practical divinity, understood in one particular way, steered later Methodist theologians in certain directions but away from others—toward philosophical ideas consistent with Wesley's view of salvation, particularly as it diverged from Calvinist views, but away from doctrines such as the Trinity that seemed to function as mere background to soteriology and were consequently idle. After all, in the polemical situation of American theology in the nineteenth century, there was no sense arguing over a doctrine such as the Trinity that Wesleyans shared with their main competitors, the Calvinists. It was much more efficient to focus on the points of divergence. As a result, Wesleyans came to be nearly obsessed with such anthropological issues as freedom and responsibility. In turn, these anthropological ideas generated an interest in the idea of personality. These were the theological hot topics of the day.

The Wesleyan fascination with freedom is illustrated in Daniel D. Whedon's *The Freedom of the Will*. Here he defined freedom in moral and personalist terms as the ability to do other than what one has done.[8] This definition is in contrast to that of Augustine, for whom freedom not only is the power to choose but also is actually doing what is good. Augustine's definition of freedom is more theological in nature; Whedon's is more philosophical and ethical. The moral and personalist character of Whedon's view is seen in the fact that the arguments he adduced for freedom are taken from humanity's psychological and moral nature: "The doctrine of the

---

7. Frank Baker, "Practical Divinity—John Wesley's Doctrinal Agenda for Methodism," *Wesleyan Theological Journal* 22.1 (1987): 13.

8. Daniel D. Whedon, *The Freedom of the Will as a Basis of Human Responsibility and a Divine Government* (New York: Carlton & Porter, 1864), 25.

freedom of the human Will, therefore, is an axiom of the intellect affirmed by the common consciousness of all mankind. It is an inborn self-knowledge."[9] Far from freedom being something that humans receive by means of grace, freedom, for Whedon, is a necessary component of human nature. He also argued for freedom on the basis of human responsibility: "No agent can be morally obligatory, rewardable, or punishable—unless there be in the agent adequate power for [an] other act than the act in question."[10] Finally, Whedon clearly saw that this emphasis on freedom implied that both God and humanity must be understood to be persons: "The *necessary* CONDITION to the *possible existence of a true Divine Government is the Volitional* FREEDOM, *both of the infinite and the finite Person.*"[11] Note that for Whedon, the personality of God is deduced from soteriological demands for freedom. This logic is in keeping with the view that soteriology is the heart of Wesley's theology. In the debate with the Calvinists in which freedom was the disputed concept, the personality of God was invoked to guarantee human freedom. The concept of the Trinity, not able to perform such a feat, fell by the wayside.

Not surprisingly, subsequent Wesleyans followed suit. John Miley defined God as "an eternal personal Being, of absolute knowledge, power, and goodness."[12] But this definition possesses importance for understanding humans as well because "in all the range of being, finite and infinite, personal attributes are the highest."[13] Humans are like God in their common possession of personality. God differs from humanity as the infinite from the finite, a point that Miley underlined in his discussion of the image of God:

> The spiritual nature was itself of the original likeness of man to God. Ontologically, spirit is like spirit, though one be finite and the other infinite. . . . Again we are face to face with the profound distinction between the finite and the infinite; but such distinction does not preclude a profound truth of likeness. . . . Personality is the central truth of man's original likeness to God. As a person he was thoroughly differentiated from all lower orders of existence, and in the highest sense lifted up into the image of God.[14]

9. Ibid., 369.
10. Ibid., 377.
11. Ibid., 436.
12. John Miley, *Systematic Theology* (New York: Hunt and Eaton, 1894) 1:60.
13. Ibid., 1:149.
14. Ibid., 1:407.

Humans are to be regarded as essentially like God because, like God, they are persons. This separates them "thoroughly" from all lower forms of existence. Humans are finite persons; God is the infinite person.

This trend toward the use of moral and personalist categories continued into the twentieth century in the thought of Albert C. Knudson. Knudson took note of the fact that the concept of person had only lately been applied to the being of God, the more traditional use lying in its reference to the trinitarian persons. He attributed this oddity to the fact that, in the early church and under the influence of Platonic thought, being was conceived as essence, not as person.[15] Prior to the eighteenth century, he observed, "God was [conceived as] personal, but he was not personal to the very core of his being." Fortunately, according to Knudson, in more recent times "the expression, the personality of *God*, is now commonly accepted as a proper formulation of" the doctrine of God.[16] The cause of this happy change was twofold. First, with the impact of science, there came to be an emphasis on "the unity of the world and the consequent unity of its underlying cause." Second, modern philosophy introduced "a new insight into the metaphysics of personality . . . [as being] the key to ultimate reality and identical with it."[17] Knudson also declared that "the body is not an analytically necessary factor of our mental life. . . . Personality as such does not necessarily imply corporeality. In its essence personality is, then, psychical and spiritual."[18] This is an important claim, for it establishes a metaphysical gulf between essentially corporeal beings and personal beings. It seems obvious that in this scheme, humans stand on the same side on which God stands. Knudson could thus consistently assert that "personality and goodness are characteristics that God shares with men, but absoluteness sets him apart from all creaturely existence."[19] As with Miley, there is an affirmation of the thesis that God and humans are significantly alike, differing only as the infinite differs from the finite. The fundamental

---

15. Albert C. Knudson, *The Doctrine of God* (New York: Abingdon-Cokesbury Press, 1930), 286-87.
16. Ibid., 289.
17. Ibid., 290-91.
18. Ibid., 293.
19. Ibid., 242.

meta-physical divide is not between Creator and creation but between the nonpersonal and the personal. Where Knudson advanced beyond Miley was in developing the concept of personality in a more relational direction: "Personality is also social. It implies reciprocal intercourse with other persons. . . . [As personal, God] is a Being who knows us and loves us and whom we can trust. This communion is ethical, not metaphysical."[20]

The effect of this development from Wesley to Knudson was, on the whole, negative for the doctrine of the Trinity. Of course, no one in the Wesleyan tradition denied the doctrine; but the Trinity seems to have played no significant role in Wesleyan thinking. It was effectively relegated to the status of heirloom, something to be admired but not used. The reason for this deleterious effect on the doctrine was that an emphasis on personality, with its psychological overtones, would inevitably result in regarding God as either a single personality or three persons, each with its own subjectivity. The latter was never an option, of course, since it is equivalent to tritheism. The former view became the dominant one. But if God is a single personality, then the doctrine of the Trinity becomes a puzzle about numbers: How can three be one? Although the needs of Christology prevented the doctrine of the Trinity from becoming a mere museum piece, Wesleyans did not try very hard to think in a trinitarian way.[21] Knudson, for one, in spite of asserting the importance of the Trinity, was reduced to regarding the doctrine as something that "dramatize[s] the divine love in a way that appeals to the imagination and that makes it an effective symbol of the divine grace."[22] Faced with the modern concept of person as a center of subjectivity and with the resulting threat of tritheism, Knudson could only take refuge in the concept of mystery: "In some respects [it] transcends both the limits of reason and the demands of faith. . . . So far as its underlying motives are concerned we affirm them as confidently as ever. . . . [But] we are not convinced that the traditional Trinitarian theory has pointed out the only way in which the highest values in the Christian idea of God can be conserved."[23] God as person had eclipsed God the Trinity.[24]

20. Ibid., 297-98.
21. Cf. Sam Powell, "The Doctrine of the Trinity in 19th Century American Wesleyanism 1850–1900," *Wesleyan Theological Journal* 18.2 (1983): 33-46.
22. Knudson, *The Doctrine of God*, 428.
23. Ibid., 422-23.
24. That personhood is a central concept for Wesleyans can be seen from the fact that it

In conclusion, by the mid-twentieth century, Wesleyans had progressively moved toward a theology resting on a fundamental analogy between God and humanity and had increasingly defined the relation between them in moral, personal, and relational terms. Consequently, it is not difficult to see why some Wesleyans have come to embrace process theism. Throughout their history, they have consistently adopted philosophical and theological ideas that support the cardinal values of freedom, responsibility, and personhood. Process theism supports these affirmations as well. As a result, process theism has proved attractive to Wesleyans, even if some of its tenets are unacceptable to some Wesleyans on other grounds.[25]

However, even though many Wesleyans are attracted to process theism, the question of whether it is the best conceptuality available for Wesleyans must be considered. There is no simple answer. On the one hand, it is obvious that the recent Wesleyan embrace of process theism is consistent with Wesleyan theology when the latter is construed in a certain way, namely, when the center of Wesley's thought is represented as the doctrine of salvation and understood in relational and personalist terms. On the other hand, there may be a way of construing Wesley's theology that differs from the prevailing view, makes better sense of Wesley's theology, and is inconsistent with process theism. If this way does exist, then the task is to show that Wesley's thought may plausibly be regarded as having a center different from the center it is commonly supposed to have and then to show how the resulting picture of Wesleyan theology differs from the way in which Wesleyan theology has been developing in the last two centuries. Since it is impos-

provides the basis not only for the affirmation of process theism, as argued in this essay, but also for a critique of process theism. See Michael L. Peterson, "Orthodox Christianity, Wesleyanism, and Process Theology," *Wesleyan Theological Journal* 15.2 (1980), who asserts that within process theology, God cannot be considered either a definite being or a person (50). Further, even human personhood is compromised, as the process view reduces the person to a series of events and thus eliminates any important sense of personal continuity (51).

25. The importance of freedom as a ground for contemporary Wesleyan interest in process theism can be seen in the following essays: John Culp, "A Dialog with the Process Theology of John B. Cobb Jr.," *Wesleyan Theological Journal* 15.2 (1980): 38-39; Sheila Greeve Davaney, "Feminism, Process Thought, and the Wesleyan Tradition," in Theodore Runyon, ed., *Wesleyan Theology Today: A Bicentennial Theological Consultation* (Nashville: Kingswood Books, 1985), 108; Ignacio Castuera, "Wesley, Process and Liberation Theologies: A Test Case," in *Wesleyan Theology Today*, 100; and Paul A. Mickey, "Process Theology and Wesleyan Thought: An Evangelical Perspective," in *Wesleyan Theology Today*, 81.

sible in the space of an essay to set forth such an alternate center with all its ramifications, I will focus on one aspect—the doctrine of the Trinity. Three issues are relevant to this focus: the fact that John Wesley affirmed the doctrine of the Trinity, the reason for his affirmation, and the reason why it forms so little of his actual preaching and writing.

WESLEY AND THE TRINITY

That Wesley affirmed the doctrine of the Trinity is evident. He regarded the Trinity as a matter of revelation, even if he demurred to proceed beyond the bare fact: "I believe this *fact* . . . that God is Three and One. But the *manner, how*, I do not comprehend. . . . I believe just so much as God has revealed and no more. But this, the *manner*, he has not revealed."[26]

Why did Wesley affirm the doctrine? Here it is important to note that he did more than merely believe the doctrine to be true. He also regarded it as a highly significant doctrine:

What God has been pleased to reveal upon this head is far from being a point of indifference, is a truth of the last importance. It enters into the very heart of Christianity. . . . Unless these three are one, how can "all men honour the Son, even as they honour the Father"? . . . But the thing which I here particularly mean is this: the knowledge of the Three-One God is interwoven with all true Christian faith. . . . But I know not how anyone can be a Christian believer till . . . "the Spirit of God witnesses with his spirit that he is a child of God"—that is, in effect, till God the Holy Ghost witnesses that God the Father has accepted him through the merits of God the Son—and having this witness he honours the Son and the blessed Spirit "even as he honours the Father."[27]

Note that the importance of this doctrine lies not in the mere fact that it is revealed or that it supports other doctrines but in its place amid the doctrines of salvation that are commonly thought to be the heart of his theology. The doctrine of the Trinity grounds the

---

26. Sermon 55, "On the Trinity," §15, *Works* 2:384.
27. Ibid., §17, 2:384-85.

fact that Christians worship Jesus. More important, the believer's experience of salvation involves the three trinitarian persons in their interrelatedness. Wesley's doctrine of salvation is a trinitarian doctrine. Of course, he did not capitalize on this point with the thoroughness that may be wished. Nonetheless, Wesley saw the closest connection between the doctrine of the Trinity and the doctrines to which he devoted his energies.[28]

Further support for the thesis that the doctrine of the Trinity is a doctrine of salvation is found in its prominence in the Wesleyan hymns. According to Barry E. Bryant, for the Wesleys

> the hymn had a greater purpose than simply an aesthetic or emotive appeal. From the very beginning . . . their hymns had a didactic character to them. . . . When *A Collection of Hymns for a People Called Methodist* finally appeared in 1780, John ambitiously . . . called it a little body of experimental and practical divinity. It was finally admitted into the "Wesley canon" as one of the standard books on Wesleyan doctrine. . . . The Wesleys' hymns were intended to be metrical theology and should be read as such.[29]

This suggests that in the search for Wesley's doctrine of salvation, hymns as well as sermons should be considered. If so, then the doctrine of the Trinity is not excluded from the doctrines of salvation by the mere fact that only one sermon on the Trinity appears in the Bicentennial Edition of John Wesley's sermons. The considerable number of hymns on the Trinity must also be weighed. This is especially the case in light of the following statement by Wesley: "If anything is wanting [with respect to the doctrine of the Trinity], it is the application, lest it should appear to be a mere speculative doctrine, which has no influence on our hearts or lives; but this is abundantly supplied by my brother's *Hymns*."[30] Taken at face value, this statement suggests that Wesley indeed regarded the doctrine of the Trinity as an intrinsically practical doctrine, with an application to salvation as shown by the hymns of Charles Wesley.

28. For other scholarly testimony to the centrality of the Trinity to Wesley's soteriology, see Geoffrey Wainwright, "Why Wesley Was a Trinitarian," *The Drew Gateway* 59 (1990): 33-36; and Thomas Wright Pillow, "John Wesley's Doctrine of the Trinity," *The Cumberland Seminarian* 24 (1986): 3-7.

29. Barry E. Bryant, "Trinity and Hymnody: The Doctrine of the Trinity in the Hymns of Charles Wesley," *Wesleyan Theological Journal* 25.2 (1990): 64.

30. *A Letter to Mary Bishop* (17 April 1776), *Letters* (Telford) 6:213.

How then can one account for the fact that in the sermons and other public documents Wesley seemingly had so little use for the doctrine? I suggest that the answer lies in grasping Wesley's understanding of his role in eighteenth-century church life. Although Wesley, early in his adult life, considered the academic life and seemed suited to it, he consciously turned away from it in order to pursue his calling as a reformer of Christianity in Britain. His theology, as reflected in the sermons, focused on the doctrine of salvation because that was, in his view, the pressing need of the day. He refrained from extensive comment on the doctrine of the Trinity, not because he regarded it as unimportant, but because his calling lay in the reformation of Christian practice.

Further, given his well-known veneration for the early church's doctrines and customs and for the Church of England, he could presuppose the doctrine's truth as well-established. He could also assume that the definitive defense of the doctrine had already been delivered by patristic and Church of England divines. This strategy of focusing on matters at hand and presupposing the validity of tradition left him free to emphasize the doctrines that had fallen by the wayside—doctrines such as faith, repentance, and assurance.[31] Based on this interpretation, Wesley is regarded as a theologian who eschewed the form of systematic or creedal theology and instead focused on the situations of his day. This explains both the shape of Wesley's theology (its eclectic and occasional character) and its deeply traditional convictions. Doctrines such as the Trinity, for Wesley, were not mere relics of tradition to be venerated because they were traditional; they were instead an integral part of his theology, even though he did not feel required to address them in any depth.

Consequently, it is a mistake to regard soteriology alone as the intrinsic core of Wesley's theology. Its prominence in his writings is due to historical conditions. In different circumstances, he might well have emphasized different doctrines. Accordingly, there is a

---

31. Bryant argues that part of John and Charles Wesley's purpose in publishing the trinitarian hymns was to resist Arian and Unitarian tendencies of their day ("Trinity and Hymnody," 65-66). See Henry D. Rack, "Early Methodist Visions of the Trinity," *Proceedings of the Wesleyan Historical Society* 46 (1987): 65-67, for a brief review of anti-trinitarian thought in eighteenth-century Britain and its possible influence on Methodist experiences of the Trinity.

distinction between the manifest center (those doctrines that simply occur often in his writings) and the real center (those doctrines that form the core of his thinking, whether frequently expressed in writing or not) of his theology. This is why merely repeating the theology of the Standard Sermons cannot be sufficient today. In doing so, we could easily miss the body of theology that lies presupposed in everything Wesley said and did. As Albert Outler stated, "The Methodist theological complex has never been a stable entity by itself—and was never meant to be. In Wesley's own time, it was contained and sustained by the doctrinal and liturgical context of the Church of England. . . . Outside such an atmosphere Methodism has had perennial problems of theological identity that have encouraged an eclectic drift."[32] Accordingly, the mere fact that process theism shares a number of concerns with Wesleyan theology as it developed does not in itself constitute a Wesleyan recommendation of process theism, for Wesleyan theology in its historical development may well have omitted matters of great importance to both Wesley and the Christian faith. I submit that the doctrine of the Trinity is one such doctrine that both process theism and Wesleyan theology have passed over lightly with regrettable consequences.

INTERLUDE

At this point a question arises: Are the process and trinitarian views of God really in conflict? Can one not be both a process theist and a trinitarian theologian? If so, then the alternate interpretation of Wesley I have suggested above will not be necessary, and its critique of process theism will have lost its force. In order to answer these questions, a brief engagement with process trinitarian thought is required.

Process trinitarian thought may be divided into two overlapping phases. In the first phase, various process theists attempted to correlate the trinitarian persons with Alfred North Whitehead's description of God. In the second and current phase, process theists

---

32. Albert C. Outler, "Methodism's Theological Heritage: A Study in Perspective," in *The Wesleyan Theological Heritage*, 207.

have set this task aside and seek to use other aspects of process thought in order to expound the doctrine of the Trinity. I turn first to the earlier phase, selecting for attention only a small sampling of the available efforts.

John B. Cobb Jr.'s *Christ in a Pluralistic Age* attempts a correlation of the trinitarian persons with God's nature as understood by process theists. Briefly put, the Father represents God in all aspects, the Son represents the primordial nature of God, and the Spirit corresponds to the consequent nature of God.[33] Cobb recognized that the basic problem in this attempt at correlation is trying to fit a trinitarian doctrine onto a bipolar metaphysics. Accordingly, he appealed to early Christian liturgy and art to support his claim that the early church thought of Son and Spirit as modes of God's activities.[34] Although imaginatively accomplished and not without some support from the early church, Cobb's attempt here is implausible. He has to step outside the mainstream of trinitarian thought in order to find a Christian warrant for his interpretation. Furthermore, his portrayal implies that the Son and Spirit are aspects of God's nature. It is difficult to avoid the conclusion that they are merely names for some feature of God or abstractions from the concrete reality of God.

Lewis S. Ford, in *The Lure of God*, agreed with Cobb that the Father refers to God as an actuality and that the Son refers to the primordial nature of God.[35] However, he balked at identifying the Spirit with the consequent nature of God, for this aspect of God is that by which the world is immanent in God. Whereas in trinitarian theology, the Spirit is that by which God is immanent in the world. In Whiteheadian terms, Ford identified the Spirit as associated with "our experience of successive divine aims." Whereas the Son/Logos is the content of the aims, the Spirit pertains to *how* those aims are given. We affirm that God is Spirit because we experience God as responsive to us and as dynamically related to us. Because God is Spirit and not simply Logos, the aims of God for the world are continuously adjusted in light of God's experiences.[36]

---

33. John B. Cobb Jr., *Christ in a Pluralistic Age* (Philadelphia: Westminster Press, 1975), 261-62.

34. Ibid., 259-60.

35. Lewis S. Ford, *The Lure of God: A Biblical Background for Process Theism* (Philadelphia: Fortress Press, 1978), 101-3.

36. Ibid., 103.

Ford's nuanced view of the Spirit is an advance over that of Cobb. However, the apparent suggestion that it is by the Spirit that God is immanent in the world is too simple, for the Son likewise is an avenue of God's immanence in Christian theology. Furthermore, he does not escape the criticism that Son and Spirit are essentially either names for some aspect of God or abstractions from the concrete reality of God.

This sampling of efforts to correlate the doctrine of the Trinity with the Whiteheadian analysis of God reveals a basic problem. It is the problem of trying to fit a square peg into a round hole. The common procedure of these efforts is to take the developed doctrine of the Trinity and attempt to state it in a different conceptual scheme in which God is understood as a single entity with a bipolar nature. Inevitably, one or more of the trinitarian persons becomes an abstraction or a mere name.

The limitations of this approach have become evident to process theists. For example, Cobb has recently written that process theism provides a "binity that is real both ontologically in terms of the nature of God and experientially in terms of how God is known by human beings." Furthermore, he asserts that "this binitarian doctrine is more important than trinitarian doctrine."[37] This is because the Trinity "is, emphatically, not the only way to make theologically significant distinctions in God. . . . We can analyze our doctrine of God into three elements as has been traditionally done, or into two. We could also use a fourfold distinction as one text in Whitehead suggests. . . . We could . . . add a fifth name for what unites all these. My point . . . is only . . . to relativize the three of God. The absolutization of this threeness is not biblical."[38] The doctrine of the Trinity then is one analysis of God, but has no special claim to truth. It is simply one analysis alongside other possible ways of thinking about God.

It should be noted that it is not only process theists who wish to relativize the Trinity. Some Wesleyans have joined the act. Paul A. Mickey, for example, claims that "the theological function of a high doctrine of the Trinity is the best way available in traditional theological categories to express their [i.e., evangelicals] conception of

37. John B. Cobb Jr., "The Relativization of the Trinity," in Joseph A. Bracken and Marjorie Hewitt Suchocki, eds., *Trinity in Process: A Relational Theology of God* (New York: Continuum, 1997), 12.
38. Ibid., 20-21.

God as a social and temporal being."[39] In Mickey's view, Wesleyan evangelicals are really trying to express a belief in God's sociality and temporality. In order to do so they draw upon traditional theological categories and thus arrive at the doctrine of the Trinity. The reason they do not simply use words such as sociality and temporality, instead of obfuscating the discussion by using traditional categories, is not stated by Mickey. At any rate, he finds in the doctrine of the Trinity the same affirmation that we find in process theism's view of God as temporal and relational.

The problem here is that Mickey makes the same mistake the process theists make, namely, assuming that the doctrine of the Trinity is a faltering, sputtering attempt to say something about God in vastly inadequate language. Process theists propose to use more adept language to express this content. Perhaps theologians would do better to assume that what the doctrine is trying to say about God is what it does in fact say. At any rate, it is clear from the history of Christian thought that the doctrine of the Trinity is not about God's social and temporal nature. It is about Jesus Christ, God the Father, and the Holy Spirit. Attempts at fitting a process view of God onto the doctrine of the Trinity remain unconvincing.

Lewis S. Ford has recently abandoned the attempt to correlate the trinitarian persons with the bipolar concept of God for a different reason. He currently believes that the attempt to relate the persons of the Trinity to God's metaphysical and necessary nature is mistaken. Instead, he proposes to discuss the Trinity in terms of God's contingent relation to the world.[40] In this way, justice may be done to the role of the historical Jesus in the Trinity: "Trinitarian formulations that apply to necessary metaphysical conditions cannot help but be too abstract to do justice to the concrete particularity of Christian affirmations concerning Jesus' life, death, and resurrection."[41]

In order to avoid this problem, Ford constructs the doctrine of the Trinity from "the root experiences of the Christian faith,"[42] principal among which is "the way we are reconciled with God through Christ."[43] However, he believes that these root experiences

---

39. Mickey, "Process Theology and Wesleyan Thought," 83.
40. Lewis S. Ford, "Contingent Trinitarianism," in *Trinity in Process*, 42.
41. Ibid., 51.
42. Ibid., 53.
43. Ibid., 54.

of the early Christians were immediately misinterpreted because these Christians labored under the notion that God was immutable. In short, what happened was that early Christians experienced salvation by God through Christ. The character of God was changed for them. Previously the savior of Israel, God was now experienced as the savior of the world. However, their assumptions of immutability prevented them from acknowledging such a change in God. Accordingly, they interpreted their experience of salvation by God through Christ as salvation by Christ. Jesus Christ came to be represented as standing alongside God. In this way, the problems of Christology and the Trinity arose.[44]

It is important to note that Ford means that God's own immediate purposes actually did change in some way through the interaction God had with Jesus: "Jesus' filial obedience to God's will could easily have evoked a responsive intensification of divine purposing" in relation to Jesus.[45] Through Jesus, something new became true of God. However, the disciples, with their assumptions of God's immutability, could not conceive of such a change in God. As a result, when on the third day after the crucifixion and "the concerns, aims, and personality traits that had characterized their beloved master were now experienced as characterizing the living God," they had to represent Jesus as a resurrected being distinct from God because they could not conceive of God becoming in some sense like Jesus.[46] Today, however, under the guidance of process theism, it is possible to see the truth: God became "Christ." That is, God took on a certain Jesus-like quality that did not previously characterize God. But this change in God was, so to speak, hypostatized and represented as the resurrected Jesus. In this way, an acceptance of God's contingent and changeable nature allows Christians today to maintain "strict monotheism"[47] by conceiving "the *Personae* as the various images of the invisible God."[48]

This brief review suggests that the doctrine of the Trinity cannot be naturally or easily reconciled with process theism. One bit of evidence for this is that process theists have not come to a consen-

---

44. Ibid., 57-58.
45. Ibid., 58.
46. Ibid., 60.
47. Ibid.
48. Ibid., 62.

sus about such a reconciliation. There is no single and obviously correct exposition of the doctrine of the Trinity on the basis of process metaphysics. The main problem with any such reconciliation is that the doctrine of the Trinity and process theology's view of God were developed for two quite different reasons. The doctrine of the Trinity arose out of Christological and soteriological concerns; process theism arose out of certain needs associated with Whitehead's metaphysics. While attempts may be made in good faith to accommodate the doctrine of the Trinity to process theism, these attempts will always remain somewhat contrived. With good reason, Lewis Ford has recently seen the folly of trying to merge a doctrine of the Trinity rooted in history with a metaphysical view of God.

However, Ford's own attempt at expounding the Trinity by means of the notion of contingency also falls short. He argues that early Christians came to think of the crucified Jesus as resurrected and as a distinct heavenly being alongside God the Father because they presupposed God's immutability. This argument assumes that the Christians were compelled to interpret their experience of God under pressure from their metaphysical presuppositions. They experienced God as changed, but they could not intellectually accept this experience and so came to represent Jesus as resurrected. The resurrection is thus an image of the change in God's character. The implication of this argument is that the Christians would not have represented Jesus as a heavenly being apart from their commitment to immutability, but only that metaphysical commitment could override their Jewish monotheism.

There is a far more plausible way of regarding the matter. As demonstrated by Jewish views about God's wisdom, especially as developed in the Hellenistic period, Jewish monotheism was much more flexible than Ford imagines. Jews seem to have been able to grant the reality of wisdom as both divine and in some sense distinct from God without giving up monotheism. Jewish Christians in this same intellectual milieu would have had no problem in positing a heavenly reality alongside God the Father. What was distinctive about early Christianity was not its positing this heavenly entity alongside God but its identification of this entity with Jesus of Nazareth. In short, we do not need to invoke an alleged allegiance to divine immutability in order to explain how

Christians came to predicate a resurrected and distinct existence for Jesus Christ. Their Jewish milieu already provided them with a conceptuality for regarding the divine as both one and, in some sense, plural. Ford has erred because he has sought to interpret the doctrine of the Trinity on the basis of an unsuitable view of God and contingency.

I argue, therefore, that process theism both lacks an adequate doctrine of the Trinity and, in fact, probably cannot develop one. As the previous quotations from Cobb show, process theism is in the end no more committed to a trinity in God than to a binity or a quaternity. Process theism is committed, first of all, to a theology founded on the distinction between the necessary and contingent aspects of God. Accommodation of a doctrine such as the Trinity will always be a secondary matter. But how then can some persuasively argue that there is a natural affinity between process theism and Wesleyan theology? Because Wesleyan theology, from Daniel D. Whedon and John Miley to the era of Albert Knudson, has become a theology of the single personality of God. Since most process theists also represent God as a single subjective being and since there is agreement with Wesleyan thought on other issues such as freedom, the argument for their essential harmony becomes plausible.

In conclusion, there truly is a conflict between the trinitarian view of God and that of process theism. Of course, this fact in itself does not argue for the truth of the doctrine of the Trinity. But it does frame the pressing question: Which view of God best does justice to all of Wesley's legitimate doctrinal commitments? Keeping in mind that Wesley's doctrinal commitments were not only to the soteriological doctrines that dominate the Standard Sermons but also to the central affirmations of the Christian faith, I believe that the conclusion is inescapable that only a trinitarian view of God is both Wesleyan and Christian.

TRINITARIAN ONTOLOGY AS AN ALTERNATIVE TO PROCESS THEISM

More is needed than merely asserting that the doctrine of the Trinity is both Wesleyan and Christian. To their credit, process theists have argued in the public arena for the adequacy and coherence of their views. A trinitarian doctrine of God must do the same. I agree with Lewis S. Ford and other process theists that the place to begin is with the experience of Jesus' followers, although I recognize that this experience was incorporated into New Testament writings that were thoroughly worked and reworked in the process of tradition. So, the New Testament writings are the actual point of departure. My disagreement with process theists lies not in their starting point but in the metaphysics they use to interpret early Christian experience.

In particular, it seems to me that certain fundamental principles of process theism are problematic for expounding the Christian doctrine of God—in particular the notion of applicability and the related method of generalization. The applicability of a principle means that the principle refers to and elucidates some aspect of experience. By the method of generalization, one seeks to know whether the same principle refers to and can elucidate other aspects of experience as well. The ultimate goal of metaphysics is what Whitehead called a "synoptic vision" of reality.[49] However, the problem with applicability and generalization lies in the supposition that the goal is to discover general truths about reality, metaphysical principles that are universally valid. On the one hand, this is a worthy goal and potentially fruitful. On the other hand, the implication of this view is that there is a set of principles that all reality exhibits. It is this implication that I find troubling. It is one thing to seek coherence of knowledge. As Whitehead stated, "No entity can be conceived in complete abstraction from the system of the universe."[50] It is another thing to suppose that, therefore, "every proposition refers to a universe exhibiting some general systematic metaphysical character."[51] In other words, while it is true that we cannot conceive of things in abstraction from their relations to other things, this truth does not imply that all reality exhibits a "general systematic metaphysical character." The implication is especially tenuous when it is suggested that the (or at least one) general systematic metaphysical principle that characterizes

---

49. Alfred North Whitehead, *Process and Reality: An Essay in Cosmology*, corrected ed., ed. David Ray Griffin and Donald W. Sherburne (New York: Free Press, 1978), 4-5.
50. Ibid., 3.
51. Ibid., 11.

all reality is what Whitehead variously called the principle of relativity and the reformed subjectivist principle. According to this principle, every instance of being has reference to some process of becoming.[52] In other words, the process of becoming is the ultimate metaphysical truth of reality.[53]

What is problematic about this metaphysics is that it posits one fundamental form of entity, which Whitehead called the actual entity. To be sure, Whitehead acknowledged a kind of plurality in the universe. He enumerated several categories of existence: actual entities, prehensions, nexus, subjective forms, eternal objects, propositions, multiplicities, and contrasts.[54] But two of these categories, actual entities and eternal objects, are considered "fundamental," the others being "how all entities of the two fundamental types are in community with each other."[55] In fact, according to the "ontological principle," actual entities, with respect to being, are absolutely fundamental.[56] In the words of the reformed subjectivist principle, "Apart from the experiences of subjects there is nothing."[57] Consequently, the fundamental stuff of reality is experiential: "Each actual entity is conceived as an act of experience arising out of data. It is a process of 'feeling' the many data."[58]

Like Wesleyan personalism, process theism raises the category of subjectivity to the level of the metaphysical ultimate. Admittedly, process theists extend this subjectivity to all entities, whereas Wesleyan personalists have thought almost exclusively in terms of God and humans. Nonetheless, the similarity is patent. But this understanding of reality does not, in my opinion, take into sufficient account the plurality found in reality. Although Whitehead allowed for eight distinct categories of existence, his is still not a pluralistic ontology, for seven of the eight have reality only in actual entities. I suggest that a truly adequate ontology must be based on a firmer sense of the plurality of types of being and must not reduce the plurality to actual entities and ingredients of actual entities.

---

52. Ibid., 166.
53. Ibid., 21, "'Creativity' is the universal of universals characterizing ultimate matter of fact."
54. Ibid., 22.
55. Ibid., 25.
56. Ibid., 24.
57. Ibid., 167.
58. Ibid., 40.

But why is it in the interest of a trinitarian theology to argue for such a pluralistic ontology? Because doing so preserves two matters of importance to the Christian tradition. First, it maintains an important insight of the Nicene-Constantinopolitan doctrine of God. Second, it maintains God's essential difference from all other beings.

As to the first, one of the conclusions that one may draw from the patristic doctrine of the Trinity is that God's sort of being differs dramatically from all others of which we know. This conclusion is derived from the notion that the one essence of God subsists in three persons. Although it is possible to understand this notion as implying that the essence is related to the persons as a species is related to an individual, the mainstream of patristic writers rejected this interpretation. It fails because no member of a species is everything that the species is, whereas, according to the doctrine of the Trinity, each person is the complete divine essence. It also fails because species are abstractions; they are the traits that all members of the species have in common. But in the doctrine of the Trinity, the divine essence is not an abstraction; instead, it *subsists* in the persons. The doctrine of the Trinity compels us to consider God as the being who exists in three ways, contrary to other beings in our experience who exist in only one way. In the Trinity, the one being exists equally and fully in three persons. In other sorts of being, each being exists in only one.

As to the second matter of importance, it is an aspect of the Christian faith that God differs from human beings and from all other sorts of beings. In the past, this difference has been expressed in a variety of ways, from the distinction between time and eternity to the Barthian concept of God as wholly other. However the difference is expressed, the Christian theologian is obligated to suitably expound this difference and not minimize it. But it is just here where not only process theism but also Wesleyan theology falls short, for both regard God as being essentially similar to humans. In Wesleyan thought, both God and humans have been regarded as persons, differing only as the infinite differs from the finite. No doubt this is a substantial difference, but it is essentially a quantitative difference, not a qualitative difference. In this view, God, like humans, is a person; admittedly, God is a greater person, everlasting, and without human limitations. Nonetheless, it is evident that Wesleyans, in the interests of defending the values of creaturely freedom and responsibility, have developed a doctrine of God that regards God as an enlarged version of the human moral agent. In the same way, process theism regards both God and all other actualities as temporal series of concrescing feelings. God differs from other entities because only God is everlasting, because God, through envisaging the eternal objects, has an influence on the universal process that other entities do not have, and because God's experience of the world is universal in a sense in which that of other entities is not. But God's difference from other entities is still represented in quantitative terms. God is like other entities, but more than them. I regard this and the related Wesleyan view as seriously mistaken. God's essential difference must be maintained. Otherwise, Wesleyan theology tends to become a religious humanism in which humanity stands with God on the side of personal beings while separated from the rest of nonpersonal creation.

My argument should not be taken as implying that the Nicene formulation of the doctrine of the Trinity is above improvement. Terminology such as essence and person may not be fully suitable today. The modern period has witnessed numerous attempts at conceiving the Trinity in a more adequate way. In particular, a Hegelian meditation on the Trinity may open some promising paths.

According to Hegel, the trinitarian persons are to be thought of as different ways in which Spirit is. Specifically, the Father is Spirit in the realm of thought. Here, Spirit is the object of cognition, or something to be considered rationally. For Hegel, this form of Spirit is enshrined in the creedal doctrine of the Trinity. The Son is Spirit in the mode of sensuous immediacy. Here, Spirit is apprehended by us as something immediately given and visually apparent. For Hegel, this form of Spirit was Jesus of Nazareth, God in the flesh. Finally, the Holy Spirit is Spirit in the mode of community. Here, Spirit is given to us neither as the content of thought nor as the object of perception, but as certainty of the truth. What Hegel is pointing to is the belief that God has historically been revealed to us in these three ways. Not only has God been revealed to us in three ways, but also God *is* in these three ways. Each of these ways is truly God.

Hegel's philosophy is so sufficiently out-of-date that merely taking over his understanding of the Trinity is out of the question. However, if we compare the Nicene doctrine with the general direction of Hegel's trinitarian thought, a potentially fruitful way is opened for thinking about the Trinity. This way starts with a pluralistic ontology. This means allowing that things in the universe may have modes of being that differ from one another. This introduces a Platonic strain into our thought, for it was Plato who held that a complete inventory of reality must include at least three or four basic sorts of being: matter, form, soul, and (perhaps) the receptacle of becoming. Armed with this assumption, we can meditate upon the Christian doctrine of God along the lines indicated by the Nicene Creed and by Hegel; we take as a premise that God has a distinctive sort of being, of which the doctrine of the Trinity is the exposition; and we can conclude that the doctrine of the Trinity is first of all about the man Jesus Christ, the God whom he called Father, and the Holy Spirit given to us as the Spirit of Jesus. It is not a theory about eternal relations in the divine nature or about how three can be one. It is about the three ways in which God is revealed to us: as the historical individual Jesus, as the God whom Jesus obeyed and to whom he prayed, and as the Spirit by which we live eschatologically in a future that is already present. But it is not just about the revelation of God, as though this revelation were different from God's own being, and as though behind this revelation there were a mysterious divine being that is not and cannot be revealed. Instead, the doctrine of the Trinity states that this man Jesus Christ, in his life and death and resurrection, is God and that God's life is enacted in this man's life—not that Jesus had a divine consciousness, as though the Logos had simply appeared in human guise. This very human life is God's life, but in an historical form. This form is one mode of God's existence.

The doctrine of the Trinity also states that God is the Father, a thesis that has never been controversial. But it states that the Father is not simply God, as though the Father exhausts the divine being, but a mode of God's being, no more and no less important than God's mode of being in Jesus. In this view, the Father is not *a* being who sends Jesus but is instead that form of divine being whereby God is both hidden and revealed, present and absent. God is revealed in the world, revealed by Jesus Christ, revealed through our experiences, but at the same time hidden by all this, concealed by that which is revelatory. In all things, God is present while at the same time distant, unapproachable yet present, light and darkness at once.

The doctrine of the Trinity also states that God is the Holy Spirit. This does not mean simply God, as though we could make a simple equation of God and spirit, so that it would be obvious that God is a spirit and that the Spirit is God. God is not *a* spirit, as though spirit were the sort of thing that could be numerically counted and individualized. Rather, the Spirit is a mode of God's existence, one very different from the mode of being that is Jesus and the other mode of being that is the Father. Of this mode it is difficult to say much, because the Spirit is that mode of God's being by which we are enabled to say anything at all about God. The Spirit is that grace given to us whereby we are lifted into the awful and awesome presence of God and by which we live in God's future already now. It is by the Spirit that we know God, just as it is by light that we see physical things; consequently, we do not know the Spirit, just as we do not see light.

Unlike human being, which has one mode of existence, although admittedly a complex one, God has these three modes. Of course, this brief sketch leaves many questions unanswered: What of the eternal Trinity? How should the incarnation be conceived? In what sense, if at all, are the trinitarian persons to be regarded as personal beings in the modern sense? How can we know that this Trinity actually exists and is not merely a projection of fideistic Christian belief?

These questions, which have never ceased to perplex theologians, cannot be answered in this essay. Nonetheless, the trinitarian theology I am proposing possesses strengths that, I believe, tip the balance toward trinitarian thought and away from process theism. First, this trinitarian theology arises out of the New Testament writings. How well it does so may be debated, but I believe it corresponds to the teachings of the New Testament at least as well as do the tenets of process theism. Second, it preserves Wesley's commitment to the traditional Christian faith, although not without some modern updating. Third, it maintains the distinction between God and other beings and recognizes the uniqueness of the divine being. Finally, it can accommodate the traditional Wesleyan concern for human responsiveness and responsibility at least as well as process theism can. In fact, it may be more adept than process theism at preserving freedom to the extent that it regards freedom not as an intrinsic property of human nature but instead as something attained only in and through the Holy Spirit.

In summary, Wesleyan theology should be a trinitarian theology. Although the movement away from trinitarian thought and toward personalist thought is understandable, that movement must be regarded as a mistake. Consequently, the Wesleyan theological attraction to process theism must also be regarded as a mistake.

CHAPTER SEVEN

RECONCEPTIONS OF DIVINE POWER IN JOHN WESLEY, PANENTHEISM, AND TRINITARIAN THEOLOGY

TYRON L. INBODY

Subtle differences on this issue [of how God interacts with humanity] are what distinguish the various Christian theological traditions. E.g., is our major concern protecting God's sovereign freedom in all human interaction, or is it the validation of the call for humans to become truly Christlike?[1]

THE CRISIS IN THEISM IN LATE MODERNITY

The meaning of divine sovereignty has been one of the most controversial ideas in biblical religion and Christian theology. This controversy was implicit in John Wesley's debate with Calvinism in the eighteenth century, and it has taken center stage in the last half of the twentieth century with the emergence of panentheism and reconceptions of the doctrine of the Trinity. These reconceptions recognize to what extent the meaning of divine sovereignty has been determined by the assumptions of classical theism. Any serious challenge to the theistic concept of God will imply a significant revision in the meaning of sovereignty.

Theism is under attack today, not only from outside the Christian community, but also from inside. From outside, the theistic concept of God is dismissed as a mistaken or unnecessary principle of interpretation, an illusion of experience or perception, or a key concept in an ideology of oppression. From inside, the theistic God increasingly is dismissed as not being the biblical or Christian God at all. These internal critiques come from at least five different sources.

---

1. Randy L. Maddox, "The Recovery of Theology as a Practical Discipline," *Theological Studies* 51 (1990): 672.

First, although British and North American philosophers of religion and theologians continue to debate the truth or falsity of theism, few Continental theologians in the 150 years since Kant, either in the liberal or neoorthodox tradition, would consider themselves theists or even take their bearings from theism.[2] Second, in North American philosophy of religion and theology, a major gulf exists between the American Philosophical Association and the Society of Christian Philosophers on the one hand, where critique and defense of classical theism guide the debate, and the Philosophy of Religion and the Theology and Religious Reflection sections of the American Academy of Religion on the other, where the question of the status of any God-language at all, not simply theistic, sets the agenda. Third, most postliberal theologians in North America tend to see theism as a distinct product of modernity. Because modernity is waning (and properly so because of its hegemonic and demonic characteristics), theism is exiting along with it and is being replaced by a concept of God formulated more on the basis of Wittgensteinian language usage, phenomenology of experience, or postmodern narrative theory.[3] Fourth, many of Barth's successors on the Continent, such as Jürgen Moltmann, Johann Baptist Metz, and Dorothee Soelle, have been highly critical of theism on biblical, theological, and political grounds. Finally, an entire range of ideology critiques based on the postmodern hermeneutics of suspicion (including deconstructionism, poststructuralism, historicism, feminism, and Black and Latin American liberation theologies) have focused on the ideological, exploitive, and repressive character and consequences of theism.

---

2. See John B. Cobb Jr.'s discussion in Stephen T. Davis, ed., *Encountering Evil: Live Options in Theodicy* (Atlanta: John Knox Press, 1981), 172-73. When I use the term "theism" alone in this essay I refer to "classical theism": the concept of God including the classical attributes of aseity, creator *ex nihilo*, immutability, apatheia, omnipotence, omniscience, and so forth. When I refer to "neo-classical theism," I refer to process concepts of God based on the philosophy of Whitehead and Hartshorne. All of the concepts of God I discuss in this chapter—classical, neo-classical, and trinitarian—are theistic in the monotheistic sense (in distinction from polytheistic, henotheistic, tritheistic, or deistic). But I mean to distinguish between "classical" and "neo-classical" forms of theism and, at times, use the term theism alone to refer to the former meaning of the concept of God.

3. See, for example, Theodore W. Jennings, *Beyond Theism: A Grammar of God-Language* (New York: Oxford University Press, 1985); William Placher, *Unapologetic Theology: A Christian Voice in a Pluralistic Conversation* (Louisville: Westminster John Knox Press, 1989) and *Narratives of a Vulnerable God: Christ, Theology, and Scripture* (Louisville: Westminster John Knox Press, 1994); and Stanley Hauerwas and L. Gregory Jones, eds., *Why Narrative: Readings in Narrative Theology* (Grand Rapids: William B. Eerdmans, 1989), esp. "Introduction: Why Narrative?"

What is common to all five of these critiques and also an impetus for the reconception of God by biblical hermeneuticians, philosophers of religion, and systematic theologians is the way theism has denied (predestination) or minimized (election) human freedom in favor of divine power and causality, thereby undercutting human responsibility to be agents of history. In our late modern period, however, two somewhat different but related themes are common to the "ideology critique" of theism. The first is that theism is a major source of violence in human history, and the second is that the idea of monotheism is a totalizing concept and therefore is exclusive, repressive, and destructive not so much of human agency but of "difference" and "otherness."

There are responses to these critiques, of course, that cannot be easily dismissed. First, many Christians experience theism, including divine sovereignty, as liberative instead of repressive. The most powerful example is the experience of the African American church, in which notions of divine sovereignty, including omnipotence, continue to be used comfortably, confidently, and as the grounds of hope in the midst of despair. This suggests that if such concepts are ideological, then they are not an ideology of repression but instead an ideology of hope. Second, some Western theologians argue that monotheism is not a principle of exclusion but precisely the opposite, a principle of transcendence that functions as a principle of prophetic criticism of all finite loyalties and the inclusion of all under one God. Specifically, because the monotheistic God is wholly transcendent, the concept of God serves as a principle of relativity of all finite reality and as the inclusion, instead of exclusion, of all within or under the transcending One.[4]

It is not my purpose in this essay to try to resolve this fundamental debate about whether monotheism is a totalizing principle of negation of the many or, instead, a critical principle that relativizes all finite being. My purpose, rather, is to argue that the theistic concept of God needs to be rethought today and that this classical concept of God—and particularly the notion of divine power it entails—is both a conceptual and a pragmatic liability for our late modern conceptions of community, plurality, shared power,

---

4. See, for example, H. Richard Niebuhr, *Radical Monotheism and Western Culture* (New York: Harper & Brothers, 1960), especially chap. 2.

and justice. Divine sovereignty has been thought about in a variety of ways, such as God's universal control, God's universal sustaining power, God's reign among the faithful, the human implementation of God's will, the ultimacy of the Good, or God's persistent and tender love.[5] I will argue that John Wesley suggests some significant moves away from the classical concept of sovereignty and that he can be brought into our conversation about this issue (despite the fact that it is beyond the horizon of Wesley's thought) through his conceptualization of divine sovereignty in terms of justice and mercy instead of omnipotence.

WESLEY'S NOTIONS OF THE TRINITY AND DIVINE SOVEREIGNTY

On Saturday I wrote *Thoughts upon God's Sovereignty*. To a cool man I think the whole matter will appear to rest on a single point: As *Creator* he could not but act according to his own sovereign will, But as *Governor* he acts, not as a mere Sovereign, but according to justice and mercy.[6]

As Wesleyans, we must acknowledge there are no explicit grounds in the thought of John Wesley on which to argue that we have a ready-made alternative to modern theism. Indeed, with respect to the doctrine of God, Wesley was very much a product of eighteenth-century Anglican theology. He was orthodox in his doctrine of the Trinity, and he was traditional in his thinking about the attributes of God as formulated within the theistic tradition. Wesley did not have any grave doubts about the truth of the doctrinal tradition. He simply assumed the truth of the Anglican doctrinal consensus of his day as embodied in the first five Edwardian *Homilies*, as well as the doctrine of the Trinity in specific, hewed out by Bishop John Pearson in *An Exposition of the Creed* (1659).[7] The locus of his concerns about any doctrine, however, was "practical,"

5. David A. Pailin, "On the Significance of the Sovereignty of God," *Theology Today* 53 (1996): 35-46.
6. *Journal* (11 June 1777), *Works* 23:55.
7. Outler, *John Wesley*, 122, 373.

not speculative or comprehensive. As Outler said, "his single, sufficient motive in theologizing was to reinforce the spiritual and ethical concerns of his societies in particular and the Church in general."[8]

Nonetheless, there are features of Wesley's thinking that serve to "destabilize" eighteenth-century theism and to plant seeds for a revision of the concept of God's sovereignty. I will highlight three of those features. First, Wesley contributed to a destabilization of the classical theistic understanding of divine power and sovereignty. This is true in his controversy with rationalistic Anglicans such as Richard Hooker, George Bull, and Thomas Sherlock, but even more so in his controversy with the Calvinists because of what he saw as the danger of antinomianism implicit in their doctrine of predestination. Wesley, of course, always agreed with the Calvinists on the doctrine of justification by grace through faith and the necessity of grace as undergirding and empowering any human decision. Nonetheless, through his preoccupation with sanctification, Wesley reflected and contributed to the development of the modern notion of freedom, in which human agency and decision must be part of what he meant by divine sovereignty.[9] This theme is apparent especially in his soteriology[10] and in his eschatology.[11] Even more important for our current discussion and for the reconception of both theism and trinity is that his controversy with Calvinism refocuses the discussion from God's freedom *from* the world to God's freedom *in* the world.[12]

Second, although Wesley's doctrine of the Trinity was orthodox for its day, his focus on soteriology, instead of theology proper, had the effect of interpreting the orthodox doctrine of the Trinity in light of the economy of salvation instead of speculation about the inner being of God. There are very few references to the doctrine of the Trinity in Wesley's writings and only one extended discussion

---

8. Ibid., 27.

9. For a discussion of the classical versus the modern notions of human freedom and divine causality, see Langdon Gilkey, *Reaping the Whirlwind: A Christian Interpretation of History* (New York: Seabury Press, 1981), chap. 7, especially 168-70.

10. See, for example, his important sermon on the idea of salvation, Sermon 85, "On Working Out Our Own Salvation," *Works* 3:199-209.

11. See, for example, Sermon 62, "The End of Christ's Coming," *Works* 2:471-84; and Sermon 63, "The General Spread of the Gospel," *Works* 2:485-99.

12. Outler, *John Wesley*, 426. This becomes especially clear in Sermon 58, "On Predestination," *Works* 2:413-21.

of it.[13] What is significant about this discussion is that he understands the importance of the doctrine to be for the piety of the believer; he has no interest in and sees no importance in the doctrine as an explanation of the being or inner life of God. His explication is strictly of the "economic" Trinity as it relates to salvation. To be sure, Wesley insists on maintaining the trinitarian formula ("the direct words" of Scripture) and the truth of the doctrine but also believes that the doctrine of the Trinity is more important than other doctrines only because of its "close connection with vital religion."[14]

Furthermore, it is the formula itself that is significant for piety, not any explanation ("right opinion") of it. No essentialist doctrine of the Trinity is ever offered, let alone explained, by Wesley: "I insist upon no explication at all."[15] He believes nothing about the "manner" of the Trinity or the incarnation.[16] The Trinity as such is a "mystery" that cannot be comprehended. However, the Christian is required to believe it as a "fact" (the mystery lies in the manner, not the "fact" of the three in one) because the "Three and One" God is the heart of Christianity and vital piety. Again, the Trinity is of interest to him only in relation to the economy of salvation. Specifically, God the Holy Spirit witnesses that God the Father has accepted us through Jesus Christ, God the Son.[17] Once one locates the identity of God in an economic instead of an essentialist "doctrine of God," he or she shifts from speculation about the inner life of God. Not only that, he or she lays an entirely different foundation for talking about the attributes of God, including divine power and sovereignty. Indeed, to the extent that Wesley ties the being of God to justice and mercy instead of transcendence and sovereignty, he has refocused the meaning and significance of the trinitarian God.

Wesley maintains many of the classical attributes of God that reflect the theism of his day. In his sermon "The Unity of the Divine

---

13. Sermon 55, "On the Trinity," *Works* 2:373-86.
14. Ibid., §2, 2:376.
15. Ibid., §3, 2:377.
16. Ibid., §14, 2:383.
17. Ibid., §17, 2:385, "But I know not how anyone can be a Christian believer . . . till God the Holy Ghost witnesses that God the Father has accepted him through the merits of God the Son—and having this witness he honors the Son and the blessed Spirit 'even as he honors the Father.' "

Being," the list of attributes is thoroughly theistic: eternal, omnipresent, all-perfect, omnipotent, omniscient, holy, spirit, and creator. Omnipotence is retained as an attribute of God and further defined here by phrases such as "no more bounds to his power," "doth whatsoever pleaseth him," and "all things possible." It is noteworthy, however, that when Wesley gets to the end of the sermon, where true religion as the right tempers of gratitude and benevolence toward God and humanity is front and center, his interpretation of the classical attributes of theism shifts to two metaphors that imply significantly different understandings of divine power: "We have the fullest evidence that the eternal, omnipresent, almighty, all-wise Spirit, as he created all things, so he continually *superintends* whatever he has created. He *governs* all, not only to the bounds of creation, but through the utmost extent of space. . . . We know that as all nature, so all religion and all happiness depend on him."[18] Indeed, the metaphor of governor is central to his essay on the meaning of the term power. In the latter part of the essay, God is presented as the source of all human power and God's sovereignty is presented in relation to God's role as "Governor of the world,"[19] not as the determiner of all things.

Perhaps the most stunning and potentially revolutionary thinking about the Trinity proposed by Wesley, however, is an idea that stands at the center of the contemporary reconception of the Trinity as a social and relational reality, and is suggested in hymn 7 in his *Collection of Hymns*. Wesley begins by claiming that the beasts are "strangers to the life divine," and that the human beings, "on whom he favours showers," are "creatures capable of God." Then stanza three proposes this potentially rich image:

> You, whom he ordained to be
> Transcripts of the Trinity;
> You, whom he in life doth hold,
> You, for whom himself was sold,
> You, on whom he still doth wait,
> Whom he would again create;
> Made by him, and purchased, why,
> Why will you for ever die? [20]

18. Sermon 120, "The Unity of the Divine Being," §21, *Works* 4:69 (italics added).
19. *Thoughts Concerning the Origin of Power*, §20, *Works* (Jackson) 11:52.
20. *Works* 7:88.

At one level, the phrase "Transcripts of the Trinity" implies nothing more than the image of God, the presence of noble powers, and the capacity for a relationship with God. But the image of transcript implies much more. It implies that relationship is not simply a capacity of the human creature; since humans *are* "transcripts" of God, relationship is constitutive of the divine life itself. Indeed, because creatures are in the image of God, the divine relationship within the Trinity is "transcribed" into the relational capacity of this particular creature.

Such an image suggests not only a radically dynamic alternative to the monistic God of theism but also a claim about the divine identity and life itself. As we shall see below, insofar as the economic doctrine of the Trinity tells us something about the inner life of God, Wesley's image of the social and relational creature as a "transcript of the Trinity" implies a concept of God that he never explored. Such a move takes us into the more speculative realm of the inner life of God beyond Wesley's interest but where much recent trinitarian doctrine of God has moved. Because Wesley did not see the necessity of such a move for the life of vital piety, he did not proceed this way. It has become more apparent to us today that it is important to move into a radical reconception of God—both the God of theism and the triune God—precisely for reasons of vital piety. This is especially true if vital piety is conceived as the love of God and of neighbor in terms of social, communal, and just relationships.

Third, his explicit discussion of divine sovereignty contains notions and themes that render it somewhat different from the theism of his day, in its both Calvinistic and deistic forms. Although Wesley was hardly a late-twentieth-century thinker on this problem in systematic theology, his thought carries seeds for the late modern reconception of God that are beginning to flower in panentheism and trinitarian theology. Wesley directly addressed the meaning of divine providence in several places. In many respects, his discussion was directly in line with classical statements about providence and sovereignty. He implied that God creates out of absolute sovereignty and that God sustains and preserves the creation. God sees and knows all interrelations of all creatures. In *Thoughts upon God's Sovereignty*, he began by describing God as a

Creator wholly independent of creatures.[21] However, the power of the creator is not omnipotence (as determiner of all things or "omnicausality") but the power to set the reality, the conditions, and the limits for free human decisions.[22]

Furthermore, omnipotence does not appear in this essay as a concept with which to describe God's sovereignty. Sovereignty can be defined only in relation to the other divine attributes: "You will never speak of the sovereignty of God, but in conjunction with his other attributes. For Scripture nowhere speaks of this single attribute, as separate from the rest. Much less does it anywhere speak of the sovereignty of God as singly disposing the eternal states of men. No, no; in this awful work, God proceeds according to the known rules of his justice and mercy; but never assigns his sovereignty as the cause why any man is punished with everlasting destruction."[23] Indeed, Wesley even argues for some affinity between the power of the creator and the creature, and, in so doing, he supplements—if he does not subordinate—the idea of God the *creator* with God the *governor* of the world.

> Only we are sure the difference cannot be so great, as to necessitate one to be good, or the other to be evil; to force one into everlasting glory, or the other into everlasting burnings. This cannot be, because it would suppose the character of God as a Creator, to interfere with God as a Governor; wherein he does not, cannot possibly, act according to his own mere sovereign will; but, as he has expressly told us, according to the invariable rules both of justice and mercy. . . . Whenever, therefore, God acts as a Governor, as a rewarder, or punisher, he no longer acts as a mere Sovereign, by his own sole will and pleasure; but as an impartial Judge, guided in all things by invariable justice.[24]

To be sure, Wesley has not replaced the classical notion of sovereignty in this tract; it is present as a trump card, so to speak, that he does not play. God *may* act as (omnipotent) "sovereign" on particular occasions, but this is not Wesley's focus while discussing divine sovereignty within Wesley's framework of divine governance

---

21. *Thoughts upon God's Sovereignty*, Works (Jackson) 10:361.
22. Ibid., 362-63.
23. *Predestination Calmly Considered*, §29, Works (Jackson) 10:220.
24. *Thoughts upon God's Sovereignty*, Works (Jackson) 10:362.

and moral justice. Indeed, Wesley simply sets the two notions side by side and does not use one to interpret the other: "Let then these two ideas of God the Creator, the sovereign Creator, and God the Governor, the just Governor, be always kept apart."[25] Wesley never considers a rejection of some of the theistic themes he retains as a result of his conjunction of creator and governor; each apparently has some role to play in vital piety. But the focus of the meaning of sovereignty is shifted from theistic notions of omnipotence and providence to the more social and political notions of governance, in which shared power is required.

Likewise, in his sermon "On Divine Providence," Wesley implies a rejection of the classical idea when he contrasts divine wisdom with omnipotence and moves again to his metaphor of governance as the way to understand the divine sovereignty. In this sermon, Wesley rejects the idea of omnipotence as a description of divine sovereignty, in part because the idea would imply that humans would be "as incapable of virtue as stones," and because the heart of vital piety thereby would be cut. Providence does not refer to the omnipotence of God as sheer power but to the power of God to govern wisely and to bring the creation to its true purpose. God cannot contradict Godself by abolishing sin and pain out of the world with a whisk broom:

> But were it to be done it would imply no wisdom at all, but barely a stroke of omnipotence. Whereas all the manifold wisdom of God (as well as all his power and goodness) is displayed in governing man as man; not as a stock or a stone, but as an intelligent and free spirit, capable of choosing either good or evil. Herein appears the depth of the wisdom of God in his adorable providence! In governing men so as not to destroy either their understanding, will, or liberty! He commands all things both in heaven and earth to assist man in attaining the end of his being, in working out his own salvation—so far as it can be done without compulsion, without overruling his liberty. An attentive inquirer may easily discern, the whole frame of divine providence is so constituted as to afford man every possible help, in order to his doing good and eschewing evil, which can be done without turning man into a machine, without making him incapable of virtue or vice, reward or punishment.[26]

25. Ibid., 363.
26. Sermon 67, "On Divine Providence," §15, *Works* 2:541.

It is God's "superintending providence"[27] that describes the divine sovereignty as "a general in contradistinction to a particular providence."[28]

Wesley's descriptions of the freedom, power, predestination,[29] and the sovereignty of God retain much of the distinctive language of theism and are still "monarchical" in many respects. Nonetheless, through the particular metaphors he uses and through his elaboration of these metaphors (in what he explicitly denies and in what he does not discuss in any detail from classical theology), Wesley implies a different view of God's sovereign power than theism represents. God's freedom, power, and sovereignty are more *in* and *for* the world instead of *from* and *toward* the world. His focus and his metaphorical language destabilize not only eighteenth-century theism with its "omnis" but also all essentialist speculation about the inner being of God apart from the world and apart from soteriology.

All three of these themes point toward a more social concept of God and God's power, in the sense that the identity and power of God include human agency and history and that the meaning of the identity and power of God is social or communal in nature. Once sociality and plurality are introduced into our thinking about God, the impulse and the structure of theistic thinking are destabilized. Wesley contributed to the destabilization of theism in his time—a time that was clearly one of theism's strongest periods of development and commitment in Western Europe and North America. As I shall argue, this destabilization and reconstruction of

---

27. Ibid., §16, 2:542.

28. Ibid., §20, 2:545. Also revealing of Wesley's understanding of sovereignty are three stories he tells in illustrating what he means by "a remarkable scene of Providence." Two stories deal with abused women who are rescued from their plight by a mysterious confluence of circumstance, and the third tells of a prank leading to saving a man's life. Cf. "God's Eyes Are Over All the Earth," "A Remarkable Providence," and "A Providential Event," *Works* (Jackson) 11:496-501.

29. Sermon 58, "On Predestination," *Works* 2:413-21. Wesley maintains a sort of predestinarian doctrine of his own founded on his idea of divine foreknowledge. Predestination refers not to an abstract chain of causes and effects within a doctrine of creation or foreordination as the inauguration of the doctrine of salvation but to God's prescience of our human decision, a knowledge based on the classical notion that there is no before or after in God (past, present, and future "being present to him at once" [417]). Predestination is God's eternal and faithful decree that whoever believes in him will be saved (418). Wesley reads the doctrine in reverse and says, "He knew, he saw them as believers, and as such predestined them to salvation, according to his eternal decree. . . . Thus we see the whole process of the work of God from the end to the beginning" (420).

the concept of God in both philosophy of religion and systematic theology has begun to come to fruition in the late modern period.

RECONSTRUCTING THE DOCTRINE OF GOD IN CONTEMPORARY THEOLOGY

> The power of God is best understood as solidarity. The Trinity is a model of the very being of God as solidarity. It is a perspective on the being of God which is directly counter to the uses of monotheism as a legitimation of the violence of the One against the All.[30]

The roots of the destabilization of classical theism—the shifting of focus in the doctrine of the Trinity to soteriology from speculation about the being of God, and the suggesting of metaphors for thinking of God's power along more historical, social, and communal lines—are all present in John Wesley's implicit challenge to several features of eighteenth-century theism and trinitarianism. Something revolutionary happens to the doctrine of God when, in Wesley's kind of language, we recognize that God cannot deny God's own character or being, since the law of justice and mercy is within God's being.[31] Classical theism, with its twin notions of divine impassibility and omnipotence, is repudiated because it is contrary to the Christian revelation about the identity and character of God and because the doctrine of God gets reinterpreted along more social and communal notions of person and power.

More thoroughgoing reconstructions of the doctrine of God beyond Wesley have occurred in two developments in theology during the last half-century. First, although it is true that there have been other revisions of classical theism, one of the most significant

---

30. Susan Brooks Thistlethwaite, "I Am Become Death: God in the Nuclear Age," in *Lift Every Voice: Constructing Christian Theologies from the Underside*, ed. Susan Brooks Thistlethwaite and Mary Potter Engel (New York: Harper & Row, 1990), 106.

31. See, for example, *Thoughts upon God's Sovereignty, Works* (Jackson) 10:361-63: "This [unconditional election] cannot be, because it would suppose the character of God as a Creator, to interfere with God as a Governor; wherein he does not, cannot possibly, act according to his own mere sovereign will; but, as he has expressly told us, according to the invariable rules both of justice and mercy. Let then these two ideas of God the Creator, the sovereign Creator, and God the Governor, the just Governor, be always kept apart. Let us distinguish them from each other, with the utmost care. So shall we give God the full glory of his sovereign grace, without impeaching his inviolable justice."

is the North American reconception of theism along the lines of panentheism. The second major reconception is the North American, British, European, Latin American, and Asian reinterpretation of the doctrine of the Trinity. What is common in, and most characteristic of, these two developments is that God's identity, nature, and power are interpreted through social and communal categories. The theological effect of these developments is to counter theism with a different understanding of God. The political effect is to undercut the autonomous, self-possessive individualism of the West by locating sociality, community, equality, shared power, solidarity, justice, and responsibility within the divine life itself. When God, who is the object of devotion and loyalty, is thought of in temporal and social categories instead of the autonomous, self-sufficient, self-contained, and nontemporal categories of theism, the nature and goal of the historical, social, and communal life of both the Creator and of the creature gets reshaped as well. This change in the doctrine of God is nothing short of a politically revolutionary development in the way God, society, and individual are to be conceived in our late modern Christian world.

Theism in North America has been challenged and reconceived for the last half-century by panentheism, the doctrine that all is in God and God is in all. Panentheism stands in direct contrast to a theism that depicts the world as external to God. Theism is "monopolar" in the sense that God is thought of in terms of the Greek prejudice against time and change, as a perfect (nontemporal) being who exists in aseity beyond the world. The world as finite is wholly dependent upon God, but God is in every respect (essentially) independent of the world. Theism affirms that the perfection of God consists of God's absoluteness (nonrelativity), immutability or impassibility *(apatheia)*, eternality (unconditionedness), and complete independence from the world. Panentheism, by contrast, thinks of God in a "dipolar" fashion. Although true perfection involves an element or "pole" of absoluteness, immutability, eternality, and independence, perfection also involves relationality, mutability or responsiveness, temporality, and dependence. God as "dipolar" includes the world. This means that God is essentially related to the world, affected by the world, and dependent on what happens in the world for the *fullness* of

God's being. A dipolar concept of God, panentheists argue, reconstructs theism along the lines of the biblical God who loves and knows the world, acts in it and is acted upon by it, and shares the world's joys and sorrows. Aseity, immutability, and impassibility are denied, as both the radical difference and the radical interdependence of God and the world are maintained as essential to the full reality of God.[32]

What is crucial in this reconstruction of theism is maintaining faithfulness to the biblical understanding of God and to the dynamic intra-relationality of God's own self in the doctrine of the Trinity. That, in itself, is reason enough for Wesleyans to reject theism and to subscribe to a more synergistic view of God and the world.[33] But there is another reason. Theism in the West has assumed another set of very nonbiblical and nontrinitarian notions inherited from the Greek metaphysics of substance: that what is really real must be absolute, eternal, wholly independent of the finite world, and unaffected by time. Theism is the doctrine of the totally self-sufficient God—the God whose inner life cannot in any *essential* way be related to other than God's own self. Theism is therefore left with the question of how a totally self-contained and self-sufficient reality can relate to anything outside of itself in any way except in a purely formal way. What panentheism does is offer a social definition of all reality, including God. Each "actual occasion" and "society of occasions," including God, is constituted by its relationships; no event or society of occasions exists as an autonomous agency. Relationships are constitutive of all reality, including the divine reality. All reality is social or communal; all beings exist in and as communities of interacting occasions of experience.

This means that not only identity is social but also power is social.

---

32. For a classic statement of panentheism from the point of view of the philosophy of religion, see Charles Hartshorne, *The Divine Relativity: A Social Conception of God* (New Haven, Conn.: Yale University Press, 1948); from the point of view of theology, see John B. Cobb Jr., *A Christian Natural Theology: Based on the Thought of Alfred North Whitehead* (Philadelphia: Westminster Press, 1965).

33. For a discussion of the relation of panentheism to Wesleyan theology, see Theodore Runyon, ed., *Wesleyan Theology Today: A Bicentennial Theological Consultation* (Nashville: Kingswood Books, 1985). Part II of this volume contains essays by Paul A. Mickey, Carl Bangs, Ignacio Castuera, Sheila Greeve Davaney, and especially Schubert M. Ogden, "Process Theology and Wesleyan Witness," 65-75 (reprinted above as chap. 1 of this volume).

Unilateral power is an abstraction, for power by its very definition implies the capacity of one agent to have some mutual effect upon another agent.[34] The idea of power as a social concept includes divine power as well as creaturely power. In this way of thinking, omnipotence, defined in theism as the capacity to cause and effect an event unilaterally, is not merely denied but judged to be nonsense. The notion that all power could exist within one agent simply does not make sense. Omnipotence, or absolute power, may still be applied appropriately to God, but it now means "the ideal limit of the power of persuasion."[35] Hartshorne puts this another way: "[God's] power is absolutely maximal, the greatest possible, but even the greatest possible power is still one power among others, is not the only power."[36] Sovereignty, moreover, means that although much happens contrary to the will of God and despite the fact that God's guidance is frequently thwarted, "yet God is not, for that reason, finally defeated. He constantly readjusts his aim to the partial successes and partial failures of the past so that some new possibility of achievement always lies ahead. The effectiveness of God's providential concern depends upon the receptivity and responsiveness of man, yet the outcome is not simply the product of human effort."[37]

The panentheistic doctrine of the relational God rejects also the theistic notion of divine impassibility.[38] If reality is social, if every agent is constituted by its relationships, and if power is the capacity of one agent to affect another and be affected, then every agent, including God, must be subject to effects of the decisions of other agents. God, no less than creatures, is affected by creaturely decisions and activity. The concepts of immutability and impassibility

34. See, for example, Bernard Loomer, "Two Kinds of Power," *Criterion* 15 (Winter 1976): 12-29; and Schubert M. Ogden, "Evil and Belief in God: The Distinctive Relevance of a 'Process Theology,'" *Perkins Journal* 31 (Summer 1978): 32-33.
35. John B. Cobb Jr., quoted in Randy Ramal, "John Cobb and Schubert Ogden on Process Thought," *Process Perspectives* 22.1 (Spring 1999): 17.
36. Hartshorne, *The Divine Relativity*, 138.
37. Cobb, *Christian Natural Theology*, 251.
38. Ted A. Campbell has noted the difference between the first Anglican Article of Religion and the first United Methodist Article of Religion on the question of the passibility of God. The Anglican Article reads, "There is but one living and true God, everlasting, without body, parts, or passions," whereas the United Methodist Article drops the claim that God is "without passions," refusing to affirm divine impassibility and in doing so opens the possibility of thinking of God as embracing passions. Cf. Ted Campbell, "The Mystery of the First Article of Religion, and the Mystery of Divine Passibility," *OXFORDnotes* 4:1 (May 24 1996): 5.

as defined by the doctrine of the *apatheia* of God must be replaced by doctrines of the divine passion and compassion for the world.

The other thoroughgoing reconception of the doctrine of God along social or communal lines in contemporary theology is trinitarian theology.[39] Although the doctrine of the Trinity can be interpreted within a theistic framework by retaining such ideas as immutability, *apatheia*, and omnipotence, the doctrine of the triune God can also be interpreted as a radically different perspective on divine relationality, affectability, vulnerability, and shared power. For instance, if the Trinity is interpreted as the relationship between the three persons within the Godhead, the Godhead may still be ascribed these three qualities in relation to the world. However, when Christology, soteriology, and pneumatology become definitive of the doctrine of God, as they clearly have in much trinitarian theology since Karl Barth, the concepts of divine immutability and divine power get radically revised.

The concept of the triune God, especially as it bears upon the problems of suffering, mercy, and justice within the divine sovereignty, has considerable affinity with process theology's concept of the relational God and its criticism of theism: "The distinctive contribution of Christianity was not monotheism, but a trinitarian understanding of God which recognized differences in the work of God in history, and also maintained the unity of God."[40] The concept of the power of God is consistently described by the gospel

---

39. Many examples can be given to show how widespread this "revolution" in the understanding of God has become in recent Christian theology. On the Continent, Karl Barth's *Church Dogmatics*, Karl Rahner's *The Trinity*, Eberhard Jüngel's *The Doctrine of the Trinity: God's Being Is in Becoming*, Jürgen Moltmann's *The Crucified God*, Wolfhart Pannenberg's *Systematic Theology*, and Dorothee Soelle's *Suffering* stand out. Among liberation theologians, especially Latin American and feminist, Leonardo Boff's *Trinity and Society*, Elizabeth Johnson's *She Who Is: The Mystery of God in Feminist Theological Discourse*, and Catherine LaCugna's *God with Us: The Trinity and Christian Life* have been significant. Similarly, the theme has appeared in the theologies of many Asian Christians: from Japan, Jung Lee's *God Suffers for Us* and his *Trinity in Asian Perspective*, Kazoh Kitamori's *Theology of the Pain of God*, C S. Song's *The Compassionate God*, and Kosuke Koyama's *Mount Fuji and Mount Sinai*; and from the Korean American perspective, Andrew Sung Park's *The Wounded Heart of God* all speak of the suffering God. From a North American narrative perspective, we may note William Placher's *Narratives of a Vulnerable God: Christ, Theology, and Scripture*, in addition to Ted Peters's *God as Trinity: Relationality and Temporality in Divine Life*, Arthur McGill's *Suffering: A Test of Theological Method*, Douglas Hall's *God and Human Suffering*, Geddes MacGregor's *He Who Lets Us Be*, and S. Paul Schilling's *God and Human Anguish*.

40. Barbara Brown Zikmund, "The Trinity and Women's Experience," *The Christian Century* (15 April 1987): 355. See also, Catherine Mowry LaCugna, "The Practical Trinity," *The Christian Century* (15-22 July 1992): 678-82; LaCugna, *God For Us: The Trinity and Christian*

narratives and by trinitarian doctrine in terms of the life, crucifixion, and resurrection of Jesus Christ. The triune God is the relational God who knows the suffering and transformation of the world within God's own life: "The crucial point is that a trinitarian understanding of divine providence and the reality of evil is marked not by a pagan notion of God as sheer almightiness but by the power of love at work in the ministry, cross, and resurrection of Jesus."[41] The kind of power that is characteristic of the triune God is not immutability and omnipotence but the power of suffering, liberating, reconciling, and transforming love.

The concept of the relationality of God, contrary to what some panentheists claim, is not unique to panentheistic concepts of God. It is a common idea shared by trinitarian and process theologians.[42] There are, to be sure, vast differences between theologians who work out of dogmatic trinitarian framework and those who work from the philosophical perspective of neoclassical theism.[43] These theologians differ on methodology, on the sources and norms for their claims, and on their interpretation of many of the classic loci of Christian doctrine. When it comes to the question of the nature of God's power, however, these different approaches are much closer together in their understanding of God than are modern trinitarian theologies and classical theism. Here, contemporary theology has taken some of Wesley's language about the relation of

---

Life (San Francisco: HarperSanFrancisco, 1993); LaCugna, "The Baptismal Formula, Feminist Objections, and Trinitarian Theology," *Journal of Ecumenical Studies* (Spring 1989): 235-50; Patricia Wilson-Kastner, *Faith, Feminism, and the Christ* (Philadelphia: Fortress Press, 1983): 131-37; and Thistlethwaite, *Lift Every Voice.*

41. Daniel Migliore, *Faith Seeking Understanding: An Introduction to Christian Theology* (Grand Rapids: William B. Eerdmans, 1991), 115-16.

42. This thesis is shared also by Ted Peters. "What process theists . . . have in common with the Barthian legacy is exploration of the temporal character of God and process character and relational character of the divine reality. . . . The process school has no patent on such ideas, however. They are now the common property of nearly all participants to the current trinitarian discussion." *God as Trinity: Relationality and Temporality in Divine Life* (Louisville: Westminster John Knox Press, 1993), 122. For a discussion of the idea of the Trinity by process theologians, see Joseph A. Bracken and Marjorie Hewitt Suchocki, eds., *Trinity in Process: A Relational Theology of God* (New York: Continuum, 1996).

43. For an outstanding discussion of the differences and affinities between process and trinitarian theologians on the concept of the suffering of God, see Paul S. Fiddes, *The Creative Suffering of God* (Oxford: Clarendon Press, 1988). Fiddes argues for the superiority of trinitarian theology in understanding the suffering and transforming power of God, for the superiority of the self-limiting instead of the ontologically limited God, specifically, "in the *desire* of God and the response of creation rather than in any ultimate process of creativity" (262).

Creator and Governor, moved beyond his eighteenth-century horizon of thought, and made the focus on soteriology definitive of the very idea of God.

A revised concept of theism and the Trinity is crucial to any reconception of divine sovereignty: "The concept of the Trinity has become a weapon in the contemporary war against classical metaphysics—that is, against the classical philosopher's deity that is *a se*, immutable and unrelated to the world."[44] Although this has been a very complex and widespread development throughout the Christian world in the last half-century[45] and one that cannot be recounted in this essay, I will highlight three features of recent trinitarian thinking that undercut theism and have direct consequences for our reflection on the nature of God and the relation of God to the world, especially the meaning of divine sovereignty.

First, the separation between the economic and immanent (or essentialist) doctrines of the Trinity has collapsed. With that collapse the radical separation between the being of God and the being of the world disappears. "Rahner's rule" has become the byword for almost all trinitarian thinking today: "The *basic thesis* which establishes this connection between the treatises and presents the Trinity *as* a mystery of salvation (in reality and not merely as a doctrine) might be formulated as follows: *The 'economic' Trinity is the 'immanent' Trinity and the 'immanent' Trinity is the 'economic' Trinity.*"[46] Traditional formulations of the Trinity are concerned with immanent (essential or ontological) relations between the "persons" of the Godhead, and they seem to assume that this eternal relationship would continue unabated, even if the creation had not come into existence. When, however, God is defined and described as the God of the gospel, as the God in God's revelation of Godself in the economy of salvation (surely the major theme of Wesleyan theology if any can be identified), then the temporal creation is incorporated into the very identity of the three "persons" that characterizes the trinitarian life of God. God is what God does in the economy of salvation. When we see that the God of Jesus Christ is inextricably and passionately involved in the affairs of

44. Peters, *God as Trinity*, 81.
45. For an excellent summary of this development, see Peters, especially chap. 3.
46. Karl Rahner, *The Trinity* (New York: Herder and Herder, 1970), 21-22.

human history, we see that this involvement is not only reflective of but also constitutive of the life of God proper. God is actually and internally just the way we experience God to be in relation to us—namely, Father, Son, and Holy Spirit.

Second, if there is a correspondence between the inner life of God as three equal persons in mutual relationship and power and God's relationship to the creation in mutuality, solidarity, vulnerability, suffering, and transforming power, then God, who is a community of equal, irreducibly diverse, and mutually interdependent persons, defines "person" by interdependence and interrelationships. Sociality thereby is made central for the identity of any "person." Almost all contemporary trinitarian theologians agree that the term "person" in the doctrine of the Trinity does not mean what "person" meant in the Enlightenment, namely, an individual and independent center of identity and power. Rather, person is defined as person-in-relation, in that relations are constitutive of each person's being, and that notion of interpersonal personhood is constitutive of the inner life of God and God's relation to the world. The divine personhood as community is the model for the human person and community. Thus God is not a single person existing in total isolation but a social or communal reality of internal relationships identified as such by the doctrine of the Trinity. In the trinitarian doctrine of God, the ultimate unity is itself communal in nature, in and through an irreducible diversity. God is now understood not as a simple unity but as a plurality in community. Furthermore, God is understood not as independent but in solidarity with the creation. In such a view, diversity, plurality, shared power, and equality are not merely human values or virtues but go to the very heart of the meaning of God.

Third, by making Christology, especially soteriology, central to the triune identity of God, the theistic doctrines of *apatheia* and impassibility have given way to the compassion, vulnerability, and suffering of God.[47] By the third century, many Christian theologians

---

47. The suffering of the relational God has become so eminent in Christian theology that by mid century, Daniel Day Williams, in *What Present-Day Theologians Are Thinking* (New York: Harper & Brothers, 1952), could call it a "structural shift in the Christian mind." The theme was so well-established by the 1980s that Ronald Goetz complained in a 1986 issue of *The Christian Century* that the suffering of God has become "the new orthodoxy." Cf. Ronald Goetz, "The Suffering God: The Rise of a New Orthodoxy," *The Christian Century* (16 April 1986): 385-89.

had declared as heresy the doctrine of patripassianism (the belief that God the Father suffered). In the subsequent Christological controversy, theopaschitism was also condemned for arguing that God suffered in the death of Jesus Christ. Even some contemporary trinitarian theologians continue to hold that God cannot undergo the pain and anguish of the world, meaning either that God the Father could not know pain or, along with Athanasius, that Jesus Christ in his divine nature did not endure the agony of the cross. But most theologians argue that the doctrine of the Trinity introduces a dynamic principle of changeability and vulnerability into the immutability of the classical theistic God. As Marjorie Hewitt Suchocki has said,

> It is not sufficient to speak of the classical God as simply the immutable being containing all power, presence, and knowledge; the classical God must be dynamic as well. To account for this, the doctrine of the Trinity answered the tension between immutability and grace, suggesting a divine story that touched human history. ... In a sense, the doctrine of immutability guaranteed the qualities in God that contrasted with and answered the human problem of evil, and the doctrine of the Trinity guaranteed the ability to apply these qualities to human history.[48]

The God of Jesus Christ is inextricably and passionately involved in the affairs of the world, and that involvement is constitutive of the trinitarian life of God. It thereby becomes necessary to speak of the suffering of God, the God who is changed, and even the alienation and death of God. As Paul S. Fiddes says, "Today we must affirm that if Christ is one with God and one with humanity, he must be so as a whole person. God cannot be safeguarded from suffering by preserving an area of experience in Christ from contamination by change, suffering, ignorance, and death. This must be the case whether we think of the 'oneness' of Jesus with God as a matter of function (God's acting through Jesus) or as a matter of ontology (God's being one with Jesus)."[49] Divine perfection and divine power are radically reconceived in such a concept of God. Perfection

---

48. Marjorie Hewitt Suchocki, "God, Sexism, and Transformation," in Rebecca Chopp and Mark Taylor, eds., *Reconstructing Christian Theology* (Minneapolis: Fortress Press, 1994), 30-31.
49. Fiddes, *Creative Suffering of God*, 28.

is not the invulnerability of God to the world, its suffering, alienation, and death, but is the depth of identity with, and care for, the world. So also, power is not the capacity to unilaterally produce a cause and effect upon the world but the capacity to undergo the suffering of the world and to transform the world through the power of resurrection.

In summary and conclusion, there are significant differences between Wesley's soteriology, process theology, and modern trinitarian theology with respect to their conceptions of the nature of God's power and sovereignty.[50] Wesley only hints at what God, as Governor, implies about what we say about God, as Creator, and about the relation of justice and mercy to sovereignty. Also, the doctrine of God as triune is not typically found within the basic conceptuality of process theology.[51] It is impossible to take the process view of God in Whiteheadian and Hartshornian perspective as a restatement of trinitarian dogma. Rather, one can point out that some of the claims about the triune God are coherent with some of the claims of panentheism, especially in their common criticism of the classical theistic concept of God, of their notion of power as social, and of their reconception of divine sovereignty. Both trinitarian theology and panentheism go beyond Wesley in their reconception of the identity, or being, of God in social categories. Essentially, the categories of process theology provide one way of understanding God as the active, living, related, suffering, and loving God who is both the primary causative agency in the world and the chief recipient of what happens in the world. Contemporary

---

50. For a fuller discussion of the wide range of trinitarian thought today, and further comparisons and contrasts between panentheism and trinitarian thought, see my book, *The Transforming God: An Interpretation of Suffering and Evil* (Louisville: Westminster John Knox Press, 1997), chap. 8.

51. In addition to the Bracken and Suchocki book noted above, earlier process discussion of the trinity include Norman Pittenger, *God in Process* (London: SCM, 1967); Anthony J. Kelly, "Trinity and Process: Relevance of the Basic Christian Confession of God," *Theological Studies* 31 (1970): 393-414; Norman Pittenger, "Trinity and Process: Some Comments in Reply," *Theological Studies* 32 (1971): 290-96; Lewis S. Ford, "Process Trinitarianism," *Journal of the American Academy of Religion* 43 (1975): 199-213; John B. Cobb Jr., *Christ in a Pluralistic Age* (Philadelphia: Westminster Press, 1975); Norman Pittenger, *The Divine Triunity* (Philadelphia: Pilgrim, 1977); Schubert M. Ogden, "On the Trinity," *Theology* 83 (1980): 97-102; Joseph A. Bracken, "Process Philosophy and Trinitarian Theology II," *Process Studies* 11 (1981): 83-96; Marjorie Hewitt Suchocki, *God-Christ-Church: A Practical Guide to Process Theology* (New York: Crossroad Publishing, 1982); and Joseph A. Bracken, *The Triune Symbol: Persons, Process, and Community* (Lanham, Md.: University Press of America, 1985).

immanent and economic interpretations of the trinity, such as that of Moltmann, are other ways to reconstruct the Christian concept of God, ways rooted more in the liturgical and dogmatic language of the church than either classical or neoclassical metaphysics and theology.

What is noteworthy about contemporary discussions on the doctrine of God, however, is the gradual convergence of two theological developments at decisive points. Trinitarian theologians talk about God in ways that are much closer to panentheism than to classical theism, and some process theologians are increasingly interested in exploring the affinities between process and trinitarian language and relational concepts.

Despite their differences, panentheistic and trinitarian theologies speak with one voice in opposition to the theistic understanding of sovereignty in relation to the problems of suffering, human community, and justice. Their common strategy is to affirm a notion of divine power that is more biblical, more true to our experience, and more coherent with the centrality of the cross and resurrection of Jesus Christ than theism is. Within such a strategy, God "answers" our problem of sin, suffering, and injustice through God's own suffering and transformation of the world. These theologies speak of the suffering and transforming God whose will and power is the redemption of the sin, suffering, and evil of the world as opposed to the omnipotent God who wills and controls everything that happens in our lives. Undoubtedly, they come to this shared conclusion from different philosophical and theological points of view. Process theologians think that broader philosophical speculations based on the primary intuitions and claims of the Christian witness lead to this revision of the divine power in human affairs. Trinitarian theologians think of the Christian answer more in terms of the language of Christian liturgy and dogma, which also leads their theology to a radically different view of the redeeming power of God in the face of suffering and injustice. Yet, with one voice, they speak of a new Christian perspective on the problem of human community and shared power.

Their shared concept of God has revolutionary implications for our social context in which interrelationship, interdependence, community, diversity, plurality, equality, shared power, vulnerability, justice, and transformation are desperately needed if we are to survive and flourish as God's creatures. If a social conception of God—including notions of compassion, vulnerability, interdependence, and mutuality—has moved to the center of the doctrine of God in systematic theology, then these notions also become central to our understanding of the world, of history, of community, and of individuals.[52] Equality, interdependence, mutuality, justice, and self-giving compassion are neither simply a set of Christian virtues established for the religious life nor virtues derived from our contemporary interpretation of the world. These qualities are constitutive of the being and character of God, and, as structures of the divine reality, they must also be seen as constitutive of creaturely reality and normative for the life of faith and practice. Although Wesley did not go as far in his critique and reconstruction of theism as these current reconceptions go, he still provides, based on his soteriology, grounds for such a reconception and hints about how one might proceed in such a task. Process and trinitarian theologians have pushed beyond Wesley's horizon in reformulating theism, but the reconceptions of the theistic God along the lines of panentheism and trinitarian thinking are in line with the Wesleyan witness of Christian faith.

---

52. There is a divergence between trinitarians who believe God suffers because God is internally related to the world in Christ and is therefore affected by suffering and knows powerlessness and those who believe God suffers simply because God in God's trinitarian life knows mutuality and in God's freedom and power wills to emulate that inner relatedness with the world through the incarnation. This difference over "real relations" exists between the process theologians and most trinitarians and also among some trinitarians as well. In the cases of Jüngel and Moltmann, for example, their differences from classical theism are significant. But God's powerlessness (on the cross) is a self-willed powerlessness and reflects the relationship between the Father and the Son and not an internal (constitutive) relationship between God and the world. The world depends upon God for its being, but God in no way depends upon the world for the divine being.

CHAPTER EIGHT

A Process Wesleyan Theodicy:

Freedom, Embodiment, and the Almighty God

Thomas Jay Oord

A viable theodicy is indispensable for an intellectually and existentially adequate theology. In this essay, I offer a process Wesleyan theodicy that I believe is more adequate for Christian faith than other theodicies. I begin by briefly discussing the three main Christian responses to the problem of evil. In the second section, I focus upon creaturely freedom as a central component for why evil occurs despite God's perfect love and almightiness. At the heart of the theodicy I am proposing is a form of libertarianism that I call "essential free-will theism." I argue that this hypothesis accounts for why God does not prevent genuinely evil events from happening. In the third section, I contend that John Wesley's belief in God as a bodiless spirit serves as a crucial, but often overlooked, aspect of theodicy. God, the universal spirit without a wholly divine body, *is not* culpable for failing to prevent evil; creatures, which possess localized, nondivine bodies, *are* often culpable. I conclude by proposing a doctrine of divine power that, I believe, corresponds to the broad biblical witness regarding divine activity without jeopardizing notions crucial to a viable theodicy. This God is neither a wimp nor a deity culpable for evil. Instead, as both Wesleyans and process theists agree, God's name and nature is love.

CONTEMPORARY THEODICIES

In recent decades, process theism has become more widely known for its answer to the problem of evil.[1] An illustration of this

---

1. For technical presentations of a process theodicy, see David Ray Griffin's works, *God, Power, and Evil: A Process Theodicy* (Philadelphia: Westminster Press, 1976) and *Evil Revisited: Responses and Reconsiderations* (Albany, N.Y.: State University of New York Press, 1991). For less

increased recognition is John Hick's discussion of theodicy in his widely read *Philosophy of Religion*; Hick does not even mention process theodicy as a plausible hypothesis in the first and second editions of this text, but by the third edition, he is treating it as one of the "three main Christian responses to the problem of evil."[2] As this might suggest, one reason that process theodicy is becoming more widely known is that many people find the alternative theodicies unsatisfactory. Although a full exposition of these alternatives and their inadequacies is beyond the scope of this essay, a brief addressing of some inadequacies of the other two theodicies that Hick classifies among "main Christian responses" will begin this essay.

Augustinian Theodicy

The most dominant theodicy in the Christian tradition finds its original formulation in St. Augustine. Central to this theodicy is an argument from aesthetics, according to which all pain, suffering, and horror in the created order contribute to the ultimate beauty of the whole. Augustine believed, in other words, that every event that occurs in history, when viewed from the divine standpoint, contributes to the good. Everything that happens, whether perceived by us as good or as evil, is ultimately *supposed* to happen because God is the ultimate cause of all things. The implication of this scheme, besides its implicit denial of creaturely freedom, is that nothing is genuinely evil because God, who is omnibenevolent and omnipotent, can cause only what is good and beautiful. Augustine's conviction in this regard is illustrated in his prayer: "To Thee there is no such thing as evil."[3] The problem of evil is "solved" by denying evil.

Augustinian theodicy has been relentlessly criticized since the

technical presentations of process theodicies, see Tyron L. Inbody, *The Transforming God: An Interpretation of Suffering and Evil* (Louisville: Westminster John Knox Press, 1997) and Burton Z. Cooper, *Why God?* (Atlanta: John Knox Press, 1988). An excellent bibliography on theodicy is offered by Barry L. Whitney entitled *Theodicy: An Annotated Bibliography on the Problem of Evil, 1960–1991* (Bowling Green, Ohio: The Philosophy Documentation Center, 1998).

2. John Hick, *Philosophy of Religion*, 3rd ed. (Englewood Cliffs, N.J.: Prentice-Hall, 1983), 41. David Ray Griffin makes this same point but compares Hick's *Evil and the God of Love* (New York: Harper & Row, 1966) to the third edition of *Philosophy of Religion*.

3. Augustine, *Confessions* in *Basic Writings of St. Augustine*, ed. W. J. Oates, 2 vols. (New York: Random, 1948), 1:8, 13.

seventeenth century. Among the various criticisms leveled against it, one of the strongest revolves around its denial of evil. Recently, David Ray Griffin has offered helpful categories for clarifying some issues involved in this criticism. Griffin distinguishes *genuinely* evil events from those that are only *apparently* evil. He defines a genuinely evil event as one "that would retain its evilness when viewed from an all-inclusive perspective."[4] It is an event, all things considered, without which the universe would have been better.[5] An event producing ill-being that could have been avoided if individuals had chosen a better possible action deserves the label "genuine evil." Such occurrences are different in kind from events that are only apparently evil. Apparent evils, when considered for what they contribute to the overall state of affairs, *do* bring about greater well-being (or are at least neutral).[6] The qualification of evil as "genuine" is meant to highlight a difference between those acts that are truly evil and those acts that, despite their pain and wreckage, ultimately make the world a better place than it otherwise could have been.

Griffin further contributes to the issues pertaining to the problem of evil by noting that we all acknowledge, at least in our actions, that some events are genuinely evil. While some may verbally deny that anything occurs without which, all things considered, the universe would have been better, their own sense of guilt or regret betrays that denial.[7] All persons reveal by their actions (including emotions and attitudes) that they *truly* believe that not everything that occurs is for the best. If everyone supposes that genuinely evil events happen, a theodicy denying genuine evil is inadequate to the extent that it asks us to believe something contrary to the way we all inevitably live.

Of course, one could affirm that all humans inevitably act out their

---

4. Griffin, *Evil Revisited*, 3.

5. Griffin, *God, Power, and Evil*, 22. This can be stated in reverse as well. We all inevitably presuppose in practice that some things would have made the universe worse than it might have been had these things not occurred.

6. Griffin discusses the differences between genuine and only apparent (*prima facie*) evil in *Evil Revisited*, 79-80, among other places.

7. Griffin calls this fact a "hard-core commonsense notion" because it is universally presupposed in practice even if some would deny it verbally (*Evil Revisited*, 3, 180). For a more extensive discussion of what Griffin means by hard-core commonsense notions, see *Unsnarling the World-Knot: Consciousness, Freedom, and the Mind-Body Problem* (Berkeley: University of California Press, 1998), 34-41.

belief that genuine evils occur, yet nothing is truly evil from the divine standpoint. This option finally amounts to no theodicy at all, however, for it admits that what is truly good or loving is mysterious and utterly incomprehensible to us. If what God calls "good" we call "evil," then our calling God good or loving is ultimately nonsensical. To say "God is good" or "God is love" while also asserting that God's love and goodness are nonsensical is to agree with Augustine that God is "we know not what." In the end, appealing to an unknown God or claiming that God's ways are utterly incomprehensible solves the problem of evil by all but verbally acknowledging that God does not exist.

Irenaean-Hick Theodicy

A common objection to calling some events genuinely evil is the truth that sometimes pain and suffering serve the ultimate good by increasing overall well-being. The fact that some painful events bring about greater good lies at the core of John Hick's Irenaean-inspired theodicy, a second main Christian response to the problem of evil. Following the basic notions of Irenaeus, Hick argues that God allows the conflicts of life for human growth into moral self-consciousness and personal responsibility. God purposefully created an imperfect world in order for humans to mature, through the exercise of freedom, toward what Irenaeus called "likeness" to God. Even natural evils are integral to that growth because they serve as one aspect of a meaningful environment meant for constructing mature character. This alternative is commonly called a "soul-making" theodicy because it is based upon the notion that developing one's "soul" is the good that God prizes most.[8] It should be noted that the notion of divine power in this theory is essentially the same as the notion embraced by Augustine, except that those espousing the soul-making theodicy typically also believe that God provides freedom to humans and is self-limited out of respect for that freedom.

Various criticisms of the soul-making theodicy reveal its inadequacies. First, the actual extent of suffering, both human and nonhuman, seems much, much greater than is needed for building

---

8. See Hick, *Evil and the God of Love.*

character. Second, when confronted by specific atrocities like the Oklahoma City bombing or the Jewish holocaust, it is extremely difficult to imagine that these immense horrors are truly more effective in building character than if other possible events had taken place. Third, and related to the first two, the competence of the God who is supposedly omnipotent is placed into question. Could not such a Creator, whose power is not limited by anything other than what is logically possible and what lies in accordance with the divine nature, have done much better than this? Finally, one wonders about the pain that animals suffer. If animal suffering, whether in the present or in the past millions of years, plays no part in building the character of humans, why would a perfectly loving God allow it?[9]

Perhaps the most powerful criticism of the soul-making theodicy, however, emerges when considering the issue of genuine evil. If God has allowed all past pain and agony in order to produce what is the greatest good—human character—then there have not been any painful or destructive events that have made the universe, all things considered, worse than it might have otherwise been. In other words, there has never been any event that is genuinely evil. Or, as Hick admits, "What now threatens us as final evil will prove to have been interim evil out of which good will in the end have been brought."[10]

Hick's denial of genuine evil makes unnecessary the redemptive themes at the core of Christian theology. Christianity presupposes genuine evil because, if nothing occurs that makes the world a worse place than it might have otherwise been, salvation is ultimately unnecessary. Jesus' actions to secure salvation would be ultimately superfluous because what God prizes most—character development through endurance of suffering—could have been accomplished without incarnation and atonement. In fact, according to the soul-making scheme, it would have been a genuine evil had God initially created *ex nihilo* a painless paradise because such a place would not have provided the pain and suffering necessary for the soul-making deity desires most.

9. These and other criticisms of Hick's theodicy are found in the work of Griffin and Inbody noted above, as well as in C. Robert Mesle, *John Hick's Theodicy: A Process Humanist Critique* (New York: St. Martin's Press, 1991).

10. Hick, *Evil and the God of Love*, 399-400. For criticisms of Hick on this specific point, see Mesle, *John Hick's Theodicy*, chap. 4, and Griffin, *God, Power, and Evil*, chap. 13.

Because the Irenaean-Hick theodicy ultimately denies that any painful event is genuinely evil, it offers a less than satisfactory solution to the problem of evil. While it is true that some painful events ultimately make us better, our actions reveal our common belief that not every painful event engenders growth. Some events are genuinely evil. While we might be able to imagine that some small measure of good has emerged from the Oklahoma City bombing, for instance, few if any would suppose that this good outweighs the good that would have been enjoyed had this tragedy never occurred. The harsh sentences given the perpetrators of this evil attest to this common belief. As I said of Augustine's thought, any theodicy denying the reality of genuine evil cannot be adequate because it asks us to believe something (that no event is genuinely evil) that contradicts what we all inevitably presuppose in our practice.

Process Theodicy

Having addressed why the other main Christian responses to the problem of evil are inadequate, I turn to briefly address process theodicy. It is generally recognized that process theodicy involves a reconception of divine power. Process theodicist David Ray Griffin states, "My solution dissolves the problem of evil by denying the doctrine of omnipotence fundamental to it."[11] This denial of classical omnipotence and, subsequently, reconception of divine power is required because of the inadequate formulations of divine power offered in most theologies. Instead of speaking of omnipotence, Griffin argues that God's power is perfect. However, the perfect power ascribed to divinity does not make God culpable for genuine evil because other creatures possess power of their own that cannot be superseded.[12] God's inability to supersede creaturely power is an inability based upon metaphysical laws, not divine self-limitation.

With this sketch of the three main Christian responses to the problem of evil in mind, I turn to propose elements for a process Wesleyan theodicy.

---

11. David Ray Griffin, "Creation out of Chaos and the Problem of Evil," in Stephen T. Davis, ed., *Encountering Evil: Live Options in Theodicy* (Atlanta: John Knox Press, 1980), 105.
12. See Griffin, *God, Power and Evil*, 265-74.

FREEDOM IN PROCESS WESLEYAN THEODICY

The process Wesleyan theodicy I propose, while essentially in harmony with Griffin's process proposal, begins tackling the problem of evil from a different starting point. Instead of beginning by reconceiving divine power, I begin by reconceiving creaturely freedom—although my reconception of the latter has implications for the former.

I call the form of libertarianism at the heart of this process Wesleyan theodicy "essential free-will theism." Essential free-will theism postulates that all existing individuals essentially possess a measure of freedom that cannot be entirely withdrawn or overridden by others. Because all actual individuals are essentially free, no one can be entirely controlled (i.e., unilaterally determined) by some outside force. A degree of freedom is metaphysically necessary for all actual individuals.

In contrast to freedom implying that creatures are free to choose to do absolutely anything, self-determination in essential free-will theism is best understood as entailing what might be called "limited" freedom. Personal freedom is limited because others who have previously exercised freedom necessarily exert influence. With process theists, I speculate that at least two factors destine all individuals: (1) the past, which includes the free actions of God and other individuals and the possibilities for action offered by God (i.e., efficient and [non-Aristotelian] formal causation), and (2) the freedom each individual expresses in response to the past (i.e., final causation in the sense of self-determination). On the one hand, essential free-will theism denies that anyone can be *entirely* controlled by something else (which includes elements in one's environment or genetics); on the other hand, it denies that anyone chooses from a limitless number of options. Freedom is essential to individuals, but this freedom is limited to what is genuinely possible given the circumstances in which one is compelled to choose.[13]

The essential free-will theism of this process Wesleyan theodicy is a cousin to another form of free-will theism: what I call "accidental

---

13. The use of "compel" in this sentence is meant to reflect the form of causation, which is similar to Aristotle's notion of "material cause" that Whitehead called "creativity" and identified as the power of ongoing process.

free-will theism." This form of libertarianism entails the belief that God *unilaterally* granted freedom to individuals at creation and/or *unilaterally* grants freedom in the present. God *could* withdraw or override creaturely powers but has chosen to regulate divine power in conformity to divine love. In short, God is self-limited. In accidental free-will theism, creatures are free in the sense that their choices cannot be completely determined by *almost* any other influence, which would include human, nonhuman, genetic, and environmental influences. The "almost" is included because, in this scheme, God is capable of—and occasionally *does*—control circumstances entirely so that the divine will is carried out. Because God can occasionally withdraw or override the freedom provided to others, self-determination in this classic free-will theism is ultimately accidental, rather than essential, to nondivine individuals. It should be admitted that Wesley's own hypotheses regarding creaturely freedom probably fit most comfortably in the accidental free-will hypothesis.[14]

While my essential free-will theism agrees with accidental free-will theism in many ways, it also differs in a crucial way: It does not make allowance for an occasional withdrawal or overriding of creaturely freedom by God, or even the possibility thereof. In essential free-will theism, all individuals, both divine and nondivine, necessarily exercise a degree of self-determination that cannot be thwarted. God is the individual who exercises the greatest degree of influence and self-determination, but even God cannot unilaterally determine others because all actual individuals are essentially free.[15] Just as the principles of logic commit us to affirm or deny to God various activities as logically possible or impossible, I suggest that the hypothesis that freedom is essential to all individuals is a principle of metaphysics committing us to affirm or deny to God various activities as metaphysically possible or impossible. For God to withdraw or override essential creaturely freedom is a metaphysical impossibility.

The process Wesleyan theodicy I propose embraces essential free-

---

14. See *Thoughts upon Necessity*, §III.8, §IV.4-5, *John Wesley*, 485, 490-91.

15. Charles Hartshorne's words serve as a succinct summary of this position: "God's influence upon others is not decisive to the last degree of determination" (Hartshorne, "Whitehead's Idea of God," in Paul Arthur Schilpp, ed., *The Philosophy of Alfred North Whitehead*, 2nd ed. [New York: Tudor Publishing, 1951], 527).

will theism because this form of libertarianism evades the charge that God is culpable for not having prevented genuinely evil events from occurring. While both forms of libertarianism enjoy the luxury of claiming that the genuine evils of the world result from the misuse of creaturely freedom, accidental free-will theism cannot finally avoid the issues surrounding the question of why God chooses not to prevent genuinely evil events since it assumes that God is capable of doing so. After all, the God of accidental free-will theism is capable of withdrawing or overriding the freedom of those who perpetrate evil. Because the God of accidental free-will theism fails to override or withdraw the freedom of such perpetrators, attributing perfect love to this God seems implausible.

The God of essential free-will theism, by contrast, is not culpable for failing to prevent the genuine evil of the world because, as its core hypothesis states, the freedom exercised by evil's perpetrators cannot be overridden or withdrawn by anyone. To say it another way, because self-determination is essential for all individuals, neither the most relatively insignificant creature nor the most significant Creator of us all can prevent individuals from exercising the freedom they essentially possess. This hypothesis offers an explanation for why God does not override or withdraw freedom from those who perpetrate genuine evil, thus providing an essential component of a theodicy that affirms with Wesley the primacy of divine love.

Contending that God is absolved from culpability for genuine evil because creatures are essentially free does not also require one to suppose these creatures as completely autonomous in relation to God. In other words, essential free-will theism is not a form of Pelagianism. Instead, I contend that creatures cannot exist unless God acts preveniently—initiating each moment—in order to make existence possible. God is a necessary, creative agent who acts first to establish the existence of, and divine relationship with, creatures. In this sense, divine action makes freedom possible for others as God continually graces creation with the divine creative presence. Without prior divine action, our free decisions are impossible. It is crucial to note, however, that claiming that God makes creaturely freedom possible does not contradict the essential free-will hypothesis that God can neither withdraw nor override creaturely freedom. God is a necessary but not sufficient cause for self-causation. In other words, I speculate that freedom is essential to creatures, while also speculating that God acts first as Creator and Sustainer in the moment-by-moment existence of every individual.

It should be clearer now why this aspect of the process Wesleyan theodicy I propose agrees essentially with Griffin's process theodicy, despite its different starting point. The hypothesis that all individuals are essentially free has implications for how divine power can be conceived. While most doctrines of divine power speculate that God *essentially* possesses all power (or at least could at some time), process theodicy and the essential free-will theism of this process Wesleyan theodicy speculate that a degree of power is necessary for all individuals, both creaturely and divine.

The hypothesis that God does not essentially possess all power does not require one to endorse an inherently deficient vision of the Supreme Being. I contend that divine power in this scheme is uniquely excellent in quality and scope while in no way inferior to any coherently conceivable power.[16] Charles Hartshorne's words regarding the relationship between the freedom creatures essentially possess and divine power are noteworthy: "It has become customary to say that we must limit divine power to save human freedom and to avoid making deity responsible for evil. But to speak of limiting a concept seems to imply that the concept, without the limitation, makes sense. The notion of a cosmic power that determines all decisions fails to make sense."[17] Because more should be said regarding divine power than is appropriate here, I will wait until the fourth section of this essay to discuss it more fully.

EMBODIMENT ISSUES IN THEODICY

The hypothesis that individuals essentially possess a degree of freedom that others cannot entirely override or withdraw is central to this process Wesleyan theodicy. However, it does not go far enough in clearing God from the charge that deity fails to prevent

---

16. On this point, see Charles Hartshorne, *Omnipotence and Other Theological Mistakes* (Albany, N.Y.: State University of New York Press, 1984), 26.

17. Hartshorne, *The Divine Relativity: A Social Conception of God* (New Haven, Conn.: Yale University Press, 1948), 138.

genuine evils. After all, if creatures can be convicted for failing to prevent evils even though they, like God, are unable to override or withdraw the freedom of others, one wonders if God is also indictable for the same crime. Something more than essential free-will theism is required in order to account for why creatures can be culpable for not having prevented genuine evil, while God is not. To meet this requirement, a much less developed aspect of theodicy must be addressed: the question of God's "composition." I believe that Wesley's thought can be especially helpful here. In this section, I address the question of God's composition by considering the implications of divine disembodiment and creaturely embodiment for theodicy.

The importance of how we conceive God's composition and what this importance means concerning divinity's prevention of evil can be illustrated when considering events related to the Oklahoma City bombing. In April of 1995, one hundred and sixty-eight people were killed—including nineteen children—and more than five hundred others were injured in this tragedy. This event was the most deadly episode of terrorism on U.S. soil that Americans have ever witnessed.

Three years after the disaster, Michael Fortier joined Timothy McVeigh and Terry Nichols as those convicted for this evil act of terror. Unlike the others, however, Fortier was indirectly responsible for the tragedy. He was convicted for knowing about the plot to bomb the Oklahoma City federal building but failing to do something to prevent the completion of that plot. Even his attorney acknowledged that Fortier was "terribly wrong" for not alerting authorities about the plans for destruction.[18] Fortier was sentenced to twelve years in prison. This conviction and sentence reminds us that those who have an opportunity to prevent genuine evil the magnitude of the Oklahoma City bombing are required to do so.

According to my essential free-will hypothesis, Michael Fortier could not control any situation entirely by overriding or withdrawing the freedom of others. Yet, he was justly convicted for failing to prevent this heinous act of terrorism. Does this mean that God, who is also unable to override or withdraw others' freedom, is vulnerable to indictment for the same crime? If Fortier's conviction

---

18. "Fortier Gets 12 Years in Deadly Bombing," *Los Angeles Times* (28 May 1998): 1, 14.

was justified, and I believe it was, would God's conviction also be justified? If God can be convicted for failing to prevent genuine evil, can we really call God "love"? These questions reveal why claiming that each individual is essentially free does not go far enough in explaining how God can be perfectly loving and almighty even though genuine evils occur.

Wesley's emphasis upon God as an omnipresent, bodiless spirit answers the question of God's culpability in this case and provides a key element in this process Wesleyan theodicy. Wesley says plainly at the end of his life what is implied in many of his earlier sermons: "God is a Spirit; not having such a body . . . as men have. It was the opinion both of the ancient Jews and the ancient Christians that he alone is a pure spirit."[19] Wesley's words correspond well with the most direct reference to God's composition found in scripture. The writer of John's Gospel says, "God is spirit" (4:24).[20] According to Wolfhart Pannenberg, the Johannine statements "God is spirit" and "God is love" (1 John 4:8, 16) are the Bible's only "clear-cut saying[s] about God's [essential nature]."[21] These biblical statements are also crucial for this process Wesleyan theodicy.

Wesley has much to say about the omnipresence of the Spirit. For instance, he declares that "the great God, the eternal, the almighty Spirit, is . . . unbounded in his presence. . . . In condescension, indeed, to our weak understanding, he is said to 'dwell in heaven'; but strictly speaking the heaven of heavens cannot contain him, but he is in every part of his dominion. The universal God dwelleth in universal space."[22]

Continuing in the same sermon and advancing notions espoused by free-will theists, Wesley says:

---

19. Sermon 120, "The Unity of the Divine Being," §8, *Works* 4:62.

20. The biblical authors use the word "spirit" in a variety of ways. In fact, William F. Arndt and F. Wilbur Gingrich note at least eight main uses of the word, not counting the various nuances within each of the eight (*A Greek-English Lexicon of the New Testament and Other Early Christian Literature*, 2nd ed. [Chicago: University of Chicago Press, 1979], 674-78). A few of its meanings include reference to God as an individual (e.g., the "Holy Spirit" [Matt. 28:19] or "Spirit of the Lord" [Luke 4:18]); reference to the mind or governing entity of an individual ("the spirit is willing but the flesh is weak" [Matt. 26:41, Mark 14:38]); reference to an attitude or mood (Luke 1:17; 1 Cor. 4:21); and reference to what might be called ghosts or demons (Mark 1:23; 5:2-8; Luke 4:33; 8:29; 9:39-42).

21. Wolfhart Pannenberg, *Systematic Theology*, trans. Geoffrey W. Bromiley (Grand Rapids: William B. Eerdmans, 1991) 1:395-96.

22. Sermon 118, "On the Omnipresence of God," §I.2, *Works* 4:42.

God acts in heaven, in earth, and under the earth, throughout the whole compass of his creation; by sustaining all things, without which everything would in an instant sink into its primitive nothing; by governing all, every moment superintending everything that he has made; strongly and sweetly influencing all, and yet without destroying the liberty of his rational creatures.[23]

The point of divine disembodiment and ubiquity with regard to theodicy is that God, as the universal, bodiless Spirit, does not exert force in the same way that localized, embodied individuals do. While Michael Fortier possesses a body over which his influence is decisive to the degree that we can hold him accountable for failing to exercise the bodily functions that would have "blown the whistle" on the bombing plot, God does not possess such a body. Fortier is genuinely subject to indictment for failing to use his bodily parts (mouth, hands, and so on) to prevent this genuine evil. Deity is not indictable because God has no divine body. Embodied creatures are able to exert direct bodily impact on others because they have bodies, rather than simply relating to others soul to soul. God's direct influence upon all things is analogous to a mind influencing another mind without mediating bodies between them. Because of God's spirit-ness, deity is not culpable for failing to prevent genuine evil, yet embodied creatures like Michael Fortier can be.

It is crucial to note that claiming God is a spirit does *not* mean we must fall victim to the spirit/body metaphysical dualism that has plagued philosophy and theology for centuries. In other words, this does not mean that we must separate God (and our own spirits) and the actualities that make up our physical bodies into different ontological categories. Process metaphysics offers conceptual tools by which we can speak of God as a spirit with a physical dimension.[24] The divine Spirit has an element of physicality analogous, in many ways, to the physicality a human mind possesses. Just as a human mind possesses a physical dimension that cannot be observed, although it exerts influence upon bodily members, so God as spirit possesses a physical dimension undetectable by sensory perception yet exerting influence upon all. Despite not processing

---

23. Ibid., §II.1, *Works* 4:42.
24. On this, see Griffin, *Unsnarling the World-Knot*, 204-6.

a body consisting of hands, feet, and the like with which to manipulate, God as spirit does possess the capacity to affect others.

It should be noted that Wesley does not emphasize God's inability as spirit to exert bodily impact. However, many of his statements, in addition to his denial that God possesses a body, support the notion. For instance, he compares the human spirit with the divine spirit and speaks of the existence of a bodiless God undetectable by our five senses.[25] He writes: "By which of your senses do you perceive your soul? Surely you do not deny either the existence or the presence of this! And yet it is not the object of your sight, or of any of your other senses. Suffice it then to consider that God is a spirit, as is your soul also."[26]

Wesley also compares the relationship between our spirit and body to God's relationship with the universe:

> Perhaps what the ancient philosopher speaks of the soul in regard to its residence in the body, that it is *tota in toto, et tota in qualibet parte,* might in some sense be spoken of the omnipresent Spirit in regard to the universe—that he is not only "all in the whole, but all in every part."[27]

Similarly, he states that "God is in all things, and that we are to see the Creator in the glass of every creature; that we should use and look upon nothing as separate from God . . . who by his intimate presence holds them all in being, who pervades and actuates the whole created frame, and is in a true sense the soul of the universe."[28]

The notions that (1) God is related to the universe as its soul and (2) this relationship is analogous, in some ways, to the relationship human souls have with human bodies offer helpful means by which to talk about God and the world. These notions are advanced convincingly by Grace Jantzen in *God's World, God's Body,*

---

25. For a discussion of how a postmodern Wesleyan philosophy is helpful when accounting for creaturely perception of the divine, see Thomas Jay Oord, "A Postmodern Wesleyan Philosophy and David Ray Griffin's Postmodern Vision," *Wesleyan Theological Journal* 35.1 (2000): 216-44.

26. Sermon 118, "On the Omnipresence of God," §II.8, *Works* 4:45.

27. Sermon 67, "On Divine Providence," §10, *Works* 2:538.

28. Sermon 23, "Upon our Lord's Sermon on the Mount, III," §I.11, *Works* 1:516-17.

although process theists and Wesleyans, with their emphasis upon the primacy of divine love, would probably want to make some qualifications regarding the finer points of her theses.[29]

Charles Hartshorne's God/world-mind/body analogy sets forth many of these crucial qualifications.[30] One can speak, as Hartshorne does, about God's interactive relations with the world as analogous to the way creaturely minds interactively relate to creaturely bodies.

The God/world-mind/body analogy has its limitations however. It does not adequately account for various questions related to theodicy. For instance, while creaturely bodies may possess creaturely souls, the universe is not a wholly *divine* body housing the divine Spirit. Both process theists and Wesleyans reject such pantheism. More specifically, the degree of control a human mind has over its bodily members is often greater than the control the divine Spirit has over the world's creatures. One reason for this difference in degree is that the human mind influences bodily members whose complexity and freedom is far less than the complexity and freedom of many creatures—humans in particular—that God is influencing. Another reason for this difference is that the genesis of each creaturely mind corresponds, at least roughly, with the genesis of each creaturely body. While it may be that there has always been some world or another to which the divine Spirit relates, our particular world apparently did have a cosmological beginning. The codevelopment of creaturely minds and bodies—subsequent to their roughly concurrent commencement—would ensure historical habits of mutuality differing from the habits of mutuality an everlasting Spirit would enjoy with a developing cosmos in any

29. Grace Jantzen, *God's World, God's Body* (Philadelphia: Westminster Press, 1984).

30. Hartshorne states that "the body is simply that much of the world with which the mind, or personal society, has effective immediate interactions of mutual inheritance, and over which its influence is dominant. Such is God's relation to all of the world, and therefore all of it is his body. This has none of the degrading effects that giving God a body is supposed to have; indeed, it is only a way of saying that God's social relations with all things are uniquely adequate, that he really and fully loves all of them, and that they all, however inadequately or unconsciously, love him." Hartshorne continues, saying that it is *not* true, "that the lesser organisms within a mind's organism are absolutely controlled by that mind, deprived of all decisions of their own, or that what the parts of the body decide for themselves the dominant mind decides for itself. Hence creaturely freedom and God's nonresponsibility for evil are compatible with the view that God is the personality of the cosmic body, the totality of societies inferior to that personal-order society which is the mind and life of God" ("Whitehead's Idea of God," 549-50).

particular cosmic epoch. Consequently, while holding humans accountable for their evil bodily actions is proper, the "Soul of the universe" cannot be held accountable for the evil actions of essentially free creatures that partially comprise this Soul's worldly body.

In sum, God as spirit does not possess a wholly divine body by which to exert bodily impact, although deity does affect all things as the ubiquitous Spirit. Because God does not possess a divine body, deity is not culpable for failing to prevent genuine evils that could have been deterred had someone lovingly exercised their own body parts.

THE ALMIGHTY GOD

Having suggested hypotheses for why God is not culpable for evil, I conclude this essay by outlining a doctrine of divine power meant to be adequate for theodicy while also corresponding with the broad biblical witness regarding God's almighty activity. I believe the doctrine of divine power I offer is more robust than perhaps many thought possible without jeopardizing the process Wesleyan theodicy I have proposed. I also believe this doctrine serves as one element in rendering the God spoken of here as a deity worthy of worship.

A few words regarding my appropriation of the word "almighty" with regard to God are in order. In the previous sections, I have made various qualifications regarding divine power in order to offer elements of what I believe is a more satisfying theodicy. I suggested that all actual individuals are essentially free, and that no one, not even God, can withdraw or override that freedom. I also argued that, because deity is a bodiless spirit, God is unable to exert direct bodily impact with a divine body, although embodied creatures exert impact upon others with creaturely bodies. In addition to these hypotheses, I follow most theologians by claiming that God cannot do the logically impossible, and I follow most Wesleyans and process theists by claiming that divine power is never exerted in ways antithetical to God's name and nature, which is love.

I do not believe that these qualifications require me to refrain from referring to God as "almighty" when designating divine power. What *is* required, however, is a basic notion of what one means by "almighty." I mean by this word that (1) God's influence is greater than all others (mightier than all) and (2) God exerts this influence upon every actuality in the universe by empowering all through prevenient grace (might upon all).

The notions that God is the mightiest and that God exerts power upon all are found many places in the biblical witness.[31] The psalmist witnesses to this divine power: "Mightier than the thunder of the great waters, mightier than the breakers of the sea—the Lord on high is mighty" (93:4 NIV). Paul witnesses to the power of God upon all when he proclaims that "the God who made the world and everything in it" is also the one in whom "we live and move and have our being" (Acts 17:24, 28). Peter Geach has noted that "almighty" is the most common designation for God's power rendered by biblical translators and that the Bible speaks only of God as "almighty" but never of divine power in the sense of classical omnipotence.[32]

With these qualifications regarding the meaning of God's influence and the meaning of "almighty" in mind, I turn now to discuss hypotheses regarding the nature of divine power. I contend that God's exertion of force includes both persuasion and *indirect* bodily impact upon others, but God does not withdraw or override the freedom that all actual individuals essentially possess.

Persuasion and Coercion

There is little doubt that a major reason some Christians have not readily embraced process theology is that its doctrine of divine power, as they interpret it, is unsatisfying to them.[33] Some would

31. This does not mean that there are no biblical passages that appear to support conceptions of omnipotence that I reject. For instance, Matthew 19:26 (NIV) says that "with God all things are possible." In this and other instances, however, what is actually being emphasized is God's ability to grant salvation. In addition, the writers of Hebrews and 2 Timothy tell us that some actions *are* impossible for God (Heb. 6:18, 2 Tim. 2:13).

32. Peter Geach, "Omnipotence and Almightiness," *Philosophy* 48 (1973) reprinted in Louis P. Pojman, ed., *Philosophy of Religion: An Anthology* (Belmont, Calif.: Wadsworth, 1987), 248-57.

33. For essays written primarily from an evangelical perspective that generally oppose process theology, see Ronald H. Nash, ed., *Process Theology* (Grand Rapids: Baker Book House, 1987). Among the derogatory labels the book's essayists give the God conceived by process theists are "stunted," "lame," and "puny godling."

even characterize the God described by process thought as a "wimp," unworthy of worship. When Whitehead says that "the power of God is the worship He inspires,"[34] they assume that this could not possibly be the God described in Scripture: the God who exerts power even on those who refuse to worship him.

The charge that the process God is too weak arises out of Whitehead's assertion that the Galilean origin of Christianity does not depend upon the premise that God is a ruling Caesar.[35] Whitehead laments the unfortunate fact that a concept of a divine despot and a slavish universe has been interwoven in Christian theology.[36] His conviction is that "the divine element in the world is to be conceived as a persuasive agency and not as a coercive agency."[37] Following Whitehead's lead, process theologians and philosophers often use the language of persuasion (versus coercion) in qualifying what they mean by divine power.

Of course, one need not be a process theist to agree with Whitehead's emphasis upon divine persuasion. For instance, evangelical theologian Clark H. Pinnock claims that love is God's primary perfection and that "it is love's way not to overpower but to be gentle and persuade."[38] Many also agree with Whitehead when he recognizes that an obvious feature of Jesus' life is his service to and suffering with, rather than power over, others. What seems to be unsatisfying to some, however, is that identifying divine power exclusively with persuasion does not account for the biblical God whose actions are sometimes something other than genial and gentle, timid and tame, meek and mild.

Many problems arising in the contemporary discussion of divine power result from misunderstandings regarding what participants in that discussion mean when they use the word "persuasion."[39] After

34. Alfred North Whitehead, *Science and the Modern World* (New York: Free Press, 1925), 192.

35. Whitehead, *Process and Reality: An Essay in Cosmology*, corrected ed., David Ray Griffin and Donald W. Sherburne, eds. (New York: Free Press, 1978), 343.

36. Whitehead, *Adventures of Ideas* (New York: Macmillan, 1933), 26.

37. Ibid., 166.

38. Clark H. Pinnock, *Flame of Love: A Theology of the Holy Spirit* (Downers Grove, Ill.: InterVarsity Press, 1996), 158. See also his essay "Systematic Theology," in Clark H. Pinnock, et al., eds., *The Openness of God: A Biblical Challenge to the Traditional Understanding of God* (Downers Grove, Ill.: InterVarsity Press, 1994), 101-125.

39. For examples of the problems that arise when individuals understand these terms differently, see Griffin, *Evil Revisited*.

all, the word has diverse meanings. What makes Whitehead's use of the word "persuasion" notable is the *metaphysical* sense in which he uses this word. In this metaphysical sense, persuasion refers to influence upon another that does not override the other's self-determination. It has nothing to do with gentleness, timidity, or meekness. Whitehead equates the metaphysical sense of coercion, by contrast, with influence that *does* override the self-determination of others (i.e., unilateral determination). In the metaphysical sense, coercion and persuasion are absolutely different because coercion refers to one cause as sufficient while persuasion refers to actions resulting from the exercise of a degree of self-determination by the actor.

Unlike Whitehead, many of those in contemporary discussion use the words "persuasion" and "coercion" in their psychological senses. In these senses, persuasion and coercion are different in degree but not in kind. One can coerce another, in the psychological sense of the word, yet the other can retain a degree of self-determination. For instance, one might say that one is coerced into making a decision because the options available do not seem attractive or because one option is much, much more attractive. In the psychological sense, then, the difference between persuasion and coercion is relative.

Given the essential free-will theism that abides at the heart of this process Wesleyan theodicy, it is not surprising that I affirm process theology's notion that God's *direct* influence upon others is, in the metaphysical sense, persuasive and not coercive. However, within this kind of divine power there are differences in the way influence is felt. Sometimes persuasive power is that power that attracts or lures another to choose among options of similar attractiveness. When we choose among options of similar attractiveness, we might say that we are "generally persuaded" to choose one option over others that are almost as attractive. Sometimes, however, persuasive power is the power exerted whereby one option is *far* more attractive when compared to others. In our usual way of speaking, we might say that one option is "extremely persuasive." A salesman is extremely persuasive if he presents a product in such a way that the customer believes he would be foolish not to purchase it. A bully at school can be extremely persuasive when she picks up a scrawny kindergartner and yells at her, "Tell me I'm the best or I'll smash your nose!" Although both the customer and the kindergartner might conclude that they have but one option given their circumstances, other options *are* available. The customer could refuse to purchase the product and risk living life less fully; the kindergartner could refuse to pay a compliment and risk getting a bloody nose. Each is genuinely free to choose an option other than the one that he or she finds extremely persuasive.

The power exerted by God is sometimes generally persuasive and sometimes extremely persuasive. Sometimes, because the options are similarly attractive, God acts to persuade us gently to choose one option over others. Other times, when one option is far more attractive given the alternatives, God's actions are extremely persuasive. In either case, God's persuasive power is always based upon genuine love and the concern to achieve what is best given what is possible. Moreover, the essential free-will theist would argue, the self-determination of the one persuaded is not jeopardized in either case. Perhaps the most common form of these types of persuasion found in Scripture are recorded in various covenants God makes with creatures.

But there are certain instances of divine activity recorded in the Bible that one might doubt can be accounted for in terms of God acting as generally persuasive or even extremely persuasive. An instance that seems to require more than divine persuasion is recorded by the Chronicler: "If my people who are called by my name humble themselves, pray, seek my face, and turn from their wicked ways, then I will hear from heaven, and will forgive their sin and heal their land. . . . But if you turn aside . . . and go and serve other gods . . . then I will pluck you up from the land that I have given you" (2 Chron. 7:14-20).[40] Can God fulfill these promises through persuasive power alone, even when that influence is extremely persuasive? It does not seem likely. These pledges seem to require that God possess either the ability to withdraw or over-

---

40. I refer to this particular covenant attributed to God to illustrate the need for my hypothesis that God exercises indirect bodily impact. I do this despite the historical circumstances surrounding this covenant that place into question its historical context. The fact that this passage was written after the events described by its author does not negate the fact that it serves to illustrate the notion of divine power for which I argue. Furthermore, one is not required to believe that God desired that the Babylonians act upon Israel in the precise way they acted.

ride creaturely freedom or the ability to exercise members of a wholly divine body. In the case of divine "plucking," God seems to need either the capacity for unilateral determination or the ability to scoop up the Israelites with a divine hand and transport them to some far-off land. I have denied that God can do either. To account for divine activity in this case, I turn to a second aspect of God's almighty power.

God's Indirect Bodily Impact

A second means by which God exercises almighty power is what I call "*indirect* bodily impact." I define God's indirect bodily impact as the ability of deity to persuade individuals with local physical bodies to exert *direct* bodily impact upon others. This means that God has the capacity to impact others without possessing a local-ized body consisting of hands, feet, claws, wings, fins, and the like. In understanding that divine *indirect* bodily impact occurs when God persuades nondivine individuals to act with their own bodies, we understand how God can "pluck."

Illustrations of God's indirect bodily impact occur throughout Scripture. They come in the form of God "calling" individuals, groups, or nations to exercise bodily force upon others. Such impact may include the laying on of hands for healing (James 5:14), the feeding of the hungry (Matt. 25:37), the giving of a holy kiss (1 Thess. 5:26). It might also include excluding one from the church (1 Cor. 5:1-5), cleansing the temple (Matt. 21:12, 13), opposition to unjust and oppressive government or clergy (Exod. 7–13), and even the use of the sword (Matt. 10:34).

Of course, believing that God exerts indirect bodily impact upon others does not require believing that every event credited to God in Scripture is correctly credited. For instance, although biblical writers often claim that God called upon Israel to act as God's hands and feet, this does not also require belief that God com-manded the Israelites to exercise *all* the destructive actions described in Scripture, such as bashing babies' heads against the rocks. Just as individuals and groups misinterpret the call of God today, the Israelites surely misinterpreted that call in the past. Given that, we must remember that God's perfect love is the offer-ing of what is best given the circumstances. Drastic times may call for drastic measures, and the best possible measures—given the circumstances—may be something other than pleasant. Sometimes choices are between bad and worse; God's call, however, is always a perfectly loving call for the best given the circumstances.

Some may object to identifying God's use of indirect bodily impact as God's *own* power because this force relies upon God's persuading others to act. In one sense, this objection is correct. The impact of a localized creaturely body upon others is not a direct expression of God's almightiness. There is, however, another sense in which we can call the bodily impact of localized bodies expressions of divine almighty power. If creatures respond with their bodies to God's call to act in various ways, their bodily response expresses the will of God. When creatures use their own bodies in conformity to divine desires, we may rightfully speak of them as the "hands" and "feet" of the almighty God.

To illustrate why we should speak of divine activity as involving indirect bodily impact, I offer examples of two individuals that we recognize as powerful because of their indirect bodily impact. A negative example of indirect bodily impact is seen in the power of Adolf Hitler. Hitler was extremely persuasive in getting fellow Germans to use their own bodies to impact others, and this persuasiveness leads us to acknowledge him as one of the most powerful persons of his time. We regard him as powerful despite the fact that this power was most often exhibited through Hitler's indirect bodily impact. A contrasting positive example of indirect bodily impact is found in Mother Teresa of Calcutta. While it is true that Mother Teresa used her own bodily members in loving activity, her power is expressed even more greatly in the bodily impact of others who followed her example and teachings. In other words, Mother Teresa's power, like Hitler's, finds its greatest expression in her indirect bodily impact upon others. For this reason, this saint should be regarded as one of the most powerful persons of her time.

Besides the fact that Adolf Hitler and Mother Teresa both possess bodies while God does not, the extent to which their power can be said to be analogous to God's breaks down at a crucial point: Neither of these individuals are, like God, necessary causes in the existence of every individual in the universe. Their influence is necessarily localized and short-lived, whereas God's is universal and everlasting. Expressions of their power through indirect bodily impact are necessarily limited by their creaturely constitutions, while God's expressions of power through indirect bodily impact are able to extend beyond such boundaries. Their limitations remind us of why God alone should be considered almighty. Despite the inadequacies of the analogy, both Adolf Hitler and Mother Teresa serve as examples for why it is legitimate to speak of divine almighty power as including God's indirect bodily impact.

Despite God's being able to persuade others, whether gently or strongly, it is crucial to recognize that sometimes, perhaps more often than not, creatures fail to respond appropriately to God's call to exert direct bodily impact. That God's call is often ignored is evidenced throughout the Bible and in the lives of individuals throughout history. The prophets often pointed to the fact that Israel thwarted God's intentions for well-being by their disobedience. God's plan that all should repent (2 Pet. 3:9) has also not been realized. It is possible, then, that those whom God is attempting to persuade to exert bodily impact as divine hands and feet will fail to respond appropriately, thus thwarting God's plans. This possibility helps us understand how God can be loving and yet not culpable for the evil of our world. It is vital to a viable theodicy.

There may be individuals (saints), however, who respond positively to the call of God. These individuals may be especially revelatory of divine love. In other words, some creatures may respond appropriately as God's hands and feet and, therefore, be agents of God's power upon others. In this synergism, love flows freely. When saints are persuaded to exercise direct bodily impact, it may legitimately be said that they "fulfill the law of Christ" (Gal. 6:2).

One should also note that my hypothesis suggesting that God can persuade and exert indirect bodily impact upon all actualities (from atoms, to cells, to donkeys, to humans) provides a way to account for many miraculous events attributed to God in Scripture. Because this hypothesis provides a means by which to account for these events, I believe it fulfills an important Christian theological requirement: that miracles attributed to God in the Bible be taken seriously as evidence of divine causation.[41] Once again, this does require one to believe that every miracle attributed to God is correctly attributed. The point is that the God described here can be accurately considered the primary agent effecting those miracles Christians should legitimately consider authentic, and that God occasions such miracles through the use of both gentle and strong persuasion and through indirect bodily impact.

Finally, I submit that the conception of the God who persuades and exerts indirect bodily impact is a God worthy of awe; this is *not* the God who is a wimp unworthy of worship. Besides being the Creator of the universe, this God exercises power upon creatures that refuse to worship their Creator. Sometimes, because love demands it, God's exercise of power is something other than gentle. However, in God, the ultimate harmony of love and power dwell in such a way that this deity is worthy of worship. The almighty God of grace is worthy of being loved with all of one's heart, soul, mind, and strength. The speculation that God is a disembodied Spirit who can do all that is logically and metaphysically possible through persuasion and indirect bodily impact is potentially more satisfying to those who want to account for the strong God of love depicted in scripture. This conception also meets the requirement that God's power be conceived in a way that prevents indicting God as culpable for the evil in our world. In this process Wesleyan theodicy, then, the divine Spirit can be conceived as almighty and perfectly loving and yet not culpable for failing to prevent the genuine evils occasioned by essentially free creatures.

---

41. William Hasker is one who also believes that biblical miracles need to be accounted for in a doctrine of divine causation ("A Philosophical Perspective," in *The Openness of God*, 139-40).

CHAPTER NINE

CREATION OUT OF NOTHING? OR IS *NEXT* TO NOTHING ENOUGH?

MICHAEL E. LODAHL

Probably the most frequent and most heated criticism leveled at process theologians from more traditional perspectives is that, by and large, these thinkers reject the ancient doctrine of *creatio ex nihilo*. The question I shall explore in this essay is: Can John Wesley's theology contribute a fresh or conciliatory word to this controversy?

If we proceed on the assumption that Wesley can be properly characterized as a representative of mainstream Christian tradition, then it may be instructive to consider whether there is anything distinctive in Wesley's understanding of God that might cast a different hue on the question of whether or not God created (and perhaps, in some fashion, continues to create) the world out of nothing—and why the answer to that question might be deemed important. The defining purposes of this essay then are: (1) to understand what is at stake in the traditional doctrine of *creatio ex nihilo*; (2) to learn why most process theologians find this doctrine inadequate; and (3) to seek some grounds for conversation and mutual criticism between Wesley's theology and the process theological model for the doctrine of creation.

WHY CREATIO EX NIHILO?

Literally, *creatio ex nihilo* simply means "creation out of nothing." But is this really so simple a phrase? More to the point: Do we understand what "nothing" means? The philosopher Peter van Inwagen carefully reminds us that "nothing" is a strange and unique word and virtually indefinable except as a tautology: "To say that there is nothing is to say that there isn't *anything*, not even a vast emptiness. If there were a vast emptiness, there would be no material objects—no atoms or elementary particles or anything made of them—but there would nevertheless be something: the vast emptiness."[1] To claim, then, that God has created the universe *out of nothing* appears, at first glance, to be at least paradoxical, if not sheer nonsense. Nothing, after all, is not some "thing" out of which other things can be generated. From "nothing," no thing can come: "And how can 'nothing' serve as the basis of an explanation? If nothing exists then nothing is going on."[2]

Van Inwagen's observations on "nothing" may help to point us in an important direction: It is likely that the doctrine of *creatio ex nihilo* has never properly been intended to be an explanation. Perhaps it is best understood as only a certain kind of *negation*. "Nothing," as we have already suggested, is not the name of some thing. It is nothing other than utter *lack*. We might surmise that the doctrine of *creatio ex nihilo* is not an attempt to describe (let alone to explain) how God creates. Perhaps, like so many other doctrines in Christian tradition, its function is not so much positive as it is negative, not so much what it affirms as what it denies, not so much to offer a certain content of belief as to eliminate an unacceptable alternative. If this is correct, then its purpose is not really to affirm something about the initial conditions of creation (which are utterly unimaginable to us) but to deny the idea that there might conceivably be some element or power that is ultimately outside of God's purview. Stated in positive terms, *creatio ex nihilo* claims that God, *as God*, occupies a unique ontological status as sovereign Creator and that there is no other power, reality, or material that exists alongside God apart from God's willing it to be. It is a logical necessity that God creates *ex nihilo* precisely because there is no thing that exists apart from God's creative will and power. The contemporary Lutheran theologian Philip Hefner champions this understanding of *creatio ex nihilo* when he writes that the doctrine exemplifies "the only relationship between the world and God that is consistent with what Christians and Jews believe about God," wherein "the universe and our planet within it are totally dependent upon God for its origin and perseverance."[3]

---

1. Peter van Inwagen, *Metaphysics* (Boulder: Westview Press, 1993), 72.
2. Ibid., 71.
3. Philip Hefner, "The Evolution of the Created Co-Creator," in *Cosmos as Creation: Theology and Science in Consonance*, ed. Ted Peters (Nashville: Abingdon Press, 1989), 226.

There are, however, Christians and Jews who find Hefner's claim debatable and who would ask why *creatio ex nihilo* should be assumed to be "the only game in town" when it comes to thinking about God's relationship to the world. It certainly cannot be so assumed on biblical grounds. Process theologians are not alone in raising questions about the biblical sanction for the idea of creation out of nothing. The Hebrew construction in the opening phrase of Genesis 1 is now famous for its ambiguity; it even seems likely that the opening of our Bible is saying something like, "When God began creating heaven and earth, the earth was without form and void, with darkness over the face of the deep [waters] and a wind from God sweeping over the surface of the waters." In his penetrating study *Creation and the Persistence of Evil*, Jon D. Levenson has argued that the dominant and recurring image for creation in the Hebraic tradition is that God has sufficiently overcome the powers of the abyss to provide for a relatively ordered cosmos. In his words,

> Two and a half millennia of Western theology have made it easy to forget that throughout the ancient Near Eastern world, including Israel, the point of creation is not the production of matter out of nothing, but rather the emergence of a stable community in a benevolent and life-sustaining order. The defeat by YHWH of the forces that have interrupted that order is intrinsically an act of creation. The fact that order is being restored rather than instituted was not a difference of great consequence in ancient Hebrew culture. To call upon the arm of YHWH to awake as in "days of old" is to acknowledge that those adversarial forces were not annihilated in perpetuity in primordial times. Rising anew, they have escaped their appointed bounds and thus flung a challenge at their divine vanquisher.[4]

Let us grant Levenson his argument that, at least in ancient Hebrew thinking about God and the world, there is something of an unfinished struggle that continues to threaten the stability of natural, communal, and individual existence. The mythological elements of that struggle may be muted considerably in Genesis 1,

---

4. Jon D. Levenson, *Creation and the Persistence of Evil* (San Francisco: Harper & Row, 1988), 12.

but they are less hidden in many other passages (e.g., Ps. 74:12-17, Isa. 27:1, 51:9-11). Levenson admits that subsequent developments in Jewish religious thought, particularly in Isaiah, appear to be deeply critical of the notion of God having to struggle with resistant chaotic powers, even offering instead "a confession that moves dramatically toward the doctrine of *creatio ex nihilo*."[5] On the whole, however, this observation simply underscores the fact that there are uncertainties, ambiguities, and tensions in the history of Israel's thinking about creation.

If the Hebrew Bible is, at best, ambiguous on the issue of *ex nihilo*, the Christian Testament's testimony is equally indistinct even if one argues that the evidence is implicitly present. A traditionally favored text is Romans 4:17 where Paul describes God as the One "who gives life to the dead and calls into existence the things that do not exist." This is obviously a creation passage, but it is not particularly obvious that the creative activity described is *ex nihilo*. In fact, since Paul is offering Jesus' resurrection from the dead as the decisive exemplification of God's creative activity, a creation from nothing is precisely *not* what is suggested. God does not "create" the resurrected Christ *ex nihilo*, for the resurrection is indeed the glorious—if exceedingly mysterious—reanimating of the crucified Jesus who indeed bears his wounds even in the resurrection state. Even less does another text traditionally used to support *ex nihilo*, Hebrews 11:3, actually deliver the doctrinal goods: "By faith we understand that the worlds were prepared by the word of God, so that what is seen was made out of things which are not visible." Of course, we do not want to force texts into dealing with metaphysical issues that were presumably very far removed from their authors' minds, but "things which are not visible" is a far cry from "nothing." In fact, many scholars freely admit that the only unambiguous textual support for *creatio ex nihilo* may be in the Apocrypha—2 Maccabees 7:28.

The fact of the matter is that the doctrine of *creatio ex nihilo* is not grounded primarily in Jewish or Christian holy writ but in theological and religious necessity. For example, Lutheran theologian Ted Peters offers what might be styled an "evangelical" argument for the doctrine that is not dependent upon specific Bible passages

---

5. Ibid., 127.

per se but on what he sees to be the overall portrait of God and God's saving activity in the gospel of Christ. In his systematic theology, *God—The World's Future*, Peters states that the seeds of *ex nihilo* lie in the biblical concepts of "historical time, the unrepeatability of events, the eschatological power of creating new things, and the gospel of salvation."[6] It was in the church's early struggles with dualism and pantheism, Peters and many others maintain, that these seeds sprouted. Conceding the ambiguities in the opening of Genesis, Peters argues that "such textual ambiguity is insufficient grounds for returning to an affirmation of some sort of eternal material chaos and abandoning *ex nihilo*."[7] For Peters, the doctrine of creation is ultimately grounded in soteriology. The only Power that can ultimately deliver us, and indeed the world, is the Power that has created the world: "If the God of salvation is truly Lord of all, then this God must also be the source of all."[8] If there is some element or aspect of our universe that exists not because God calls it into being but *just because*, then there is something of which God is not truly God. This idea is theologically repugnant, at least from a traditional perspective, because it implies a dualism of "God and something else" and thus severely compromises the divine uniqueness and sovereignty; similarly, it is religiously repugnant because it means that our worship of God is directed toward a power that is less than ultimate.

These positive implications allowed, there is a somewhat insidious implication of *creatio ex nihilo* that should be brought to light and expunged: The doctrine often seems to imply that God works like a magician who pronounces "Presto!" and pulls a rabbit (i.e., the world) out of his or her top hat (i.e., nothing). In this picture, the creation of the universe appears perfunctory and arbitrary with little, if any real, investment or care on the Creator's part—a picture that lends itself to a devaluing of the world and our lives in it. It is safe to say that this is not, and cannot be, what Christians (or Jews or Muslims) mean by creation out of nothing. The particularly Christian conviction that God has created by the Word—the Word that became flesh in the person of Jesus of Nazareth—belies

---

6. Ted Peters, *God—the World's Future: Systematic Theology for a New Era*, 2nd ed. (Minneapolis: Fortress Press, 2000), 136.

7. Ibid., 138.

8. Ibid., 136.

any hint of arbitrariness or caprice in God's act of creation, suggesting instead that creation is the deliberate expression of divine love revealed at Gethsemane and Golgotha. In this case, perhaps *creatio ex nihilo* might be well-complemented by *creatio ex amore*: God creates out of (and as an expression of) self-giving, creative love. Mark William Worthing seems to be suggesting as much when he writes:

> A creation out of *absolute* nothingness is an impossibility; a creation out of God's own "substance" leads to a pantheistic deification of the physical world. *Creatio ex nihilo*, therefore, signifies the theological recognition that God created a universe distinct from the divine being, not out of any preexisting matter or principle, but out of nothing other than the fullness of God's own being.[9]

Worthing is clearly not espousing pantheism. He is, however, correctly indicating that if creation is not a matter of arbitrary finger-snapping but rather an activity that is *true of*, and *true to*, who God is, then it must truly *proceed from* (or "out of") *God*. If "the fullness of God's own being" (to employ Worthing's phrase) is indeed the love revealed in the ministry of Jesus Christ (1 John 3:16, 4:8), then *creatio ex nihilo* must be complemented (if not challenged, or even corrected) by *creatio ex amore*. Worthing further writes, "Nothing comes out of nothing—but out of nothing other than the fullness of God's own being was created a life producing universe that is contingent on God in each moment and each aspect of its existence."[10] Indeed, I will argue subsequently that such an observation is germane to the Wesleyan theological tradition's understanding of God, and may provide a halting step or two in the direction of the process theologians.

THE PROCESS ALTERNATIVE TO CREATIO EX NIHILO

In his 1927–28 Gifford Lectures at Edinburgh, the grand patron of process thought, Alfred North Whitehead, put it straightforwardly:

---

9. Mark William Worthing, *God, Creation and Contemporary Physics* (Minneapolis: Fortress Press, 1996), 75.
10. Ibid., 110.

"It is as true to say that God creates the World, as that the World creates God."[11] Of course, he had much more to say on the subject, but this simple statement not only gets to the heart of the process cosmology but also provides a clear signpost for the suspicions of orthodoxy. What, after all, does it mean to say that "the World creates God"? Even if we concede, however hesitantly, that the world makes its own contributions to God's own growing wealth of experience and therefore in some way to God's *being God*, would we be thereby constrained to say that "the World creates God"? Need we say that the God-world relationship is as reciprocal as Whitehead implied?

For Whitehead and for most process theologians after him, to say that "the World creates God" means that there is *necessarily* a world *of some kind* that exists apart from God and independently of God's will or desire. Both God and the world, Whitehead continued, "are in the grip of the ultimate metaphysical ground, the creative advance into novelty."[12] No matter how Whitehead's language might be soft-pedaled, even the most sympathetic reading cannot ease the jolt that most traditionally religious people feel when they try to imagine God "in the grip" of something or anything else— especially when that grip allegedly belongs to "the ultimate metaphysical ground"! Is not *that* "ultimate metaphysical ground" what we have meant by *God*?

What could be more ultimate than God? Two of his early theological interpreters, Henry Nelson Wieman and Bernard Meland, cogently described Whitehead's position in this way:

> God clings to this process of creativity. He is to be found as an order in this process. He does not make this process go. He is not the power back of it. Why does this process keep going on and on and on without end? For no reason at all. It keeps on going and always will because it is the ultimate nature of things to go and go and go. Whatever meaning and value is brought forth out of this process is due to God, but the process itself is not due to God. Rather, if one is to speak in such terms, God is due to it.[13]

---

11. Alfred North Whitehead, *Process and Reality: An Essay in Cosmology,* corrected ed., ed. David Ray Griffin and Donald W. Sherburne (New York: Free Press, 1978), 348.
12. Ibid., 349.
13. Henry Nelson Wieman and Bernard Eugene Meland, *American Philosophies of Religion* (New York: Willett, Clark and Co., 1936), 231.

Despite the initially shocking implications of notions such as these, one of the most attractive aspects of this cosmology for process theists has been well-rehearsed over the years: It offers a solution to the problem of evil. In the process view, God is doing the best that God can do to lure the elements of the world toward greater beauty and richer harmony; but since those elements are ultimately *not* God's creation, God cannot be blamed if they do not behave as God would like. God does the best that God can do, given what God is given to work with from one moment to the next. Yes, God, throughout our aeon, has called and lured the world into greater levels of complexity and thus of beauty; hence, God is responsible, in an important sense, for the sort of world in which we live. God *could* have left the elements of our universe at the level of the barest puffs of existence, perhaps something roughly comparable to what we now call subatomic particles. (I suspect, however, that even at that "level," we are dealing with a considerable degree of organization and complexity.) If God had done that, of course, there would certainly be nothing of the pain and struggle of our world. But neither would there be creatures such as we who undergo those pains or, contrarily, who enjoy love, beauty, goodness, art, and the like. Apparently God deems a world of such richness of experience to be worth the cost.

What God *could not* have, according to the Whiteheadian position, is no world of any kind, for whether or not there is something other than God is not up to God. We might say that the dominant process notion about God's relation to the world is, at best, that God has created it out of *next to* nothing.[14] It is creation "from scratch." That is, to be sure, an impressive bit of creative power, but it still leaves us with an unacceptable dualism. John B. Cobb Jr., in his work *A Christian Natural Theology*, wrote that "in every moment there is given to God a world that has in part determined its own form and that is free to reject in part the new possibilities of ideal realization he offers it."[15] The key point here is that this is true of *every moment* precisely because there has always been such a world.

---

14. Clark M. Williamson has given perhaps the most persuasive argument for this interpretation of God's creative activity in his *A Guest in the House of Israel: Post-Holocaust Church Theology* (Louisville: Westminster John Knox Press, 1993), 220-24.

15. John B. Cobb Jr., *A Christian Natural Theology: Based on the Thought of Alfred North Whitehead* (Philadelphia: Westminster Press, 1965), 205.

And more important, the relation between God and the world is not a relation that God has called into being, that God particularly wills, or for which God can give an account. It is a relation that simply *is*.

Again, an important reason why this is attractive to many process thinkers is that to relieve God of omnipotence in this way also relieves God of omniresponsibility for the pain and suffering of our world. It may be easier to appreciate the power of this position by making a move similar to that made in the first section of this essay: We might suggest that it is not so much what Whitehead and his followers *affirm* about God and the world that is important, as it is what they *deny*. They deny *creatio ex nihilo* because to affirm it would be, presumably, to affirm that God possesses the sort of power that could readily and immediately—"at the drop of a hat," as it were—change and recreate the world such that it would have no more pain, suffering, evil, or heartache. (This is, admittedly, the gist of the eschatological hopes of virtually all theistic traditions.) If God is indeed able to exercise such power, it seems that we are at a loss to know why God has not exercised it more effectively to this point.

This is a dilemma upon the horns of which it is not difficult to be impaled. A God who is, *like the world*, "in the grip" of certain metaphysical constraints but nonetheless labors ceaselessly to call that world forward into harmony, beauty, and zest plays the role of a tragic hero or perhaps a tragic lover. Such a God might not be the sort of God we have traditionally imagined God to be—or to *have to be* in order to be what we have meant by "God"—but might well be the sort of God we could admire. But is admiration enough? Perhaps such a God could move us more deeply; perhaps this is a deity that one might be compelled to "root for," to be attracted to, or even to join energies and efforts with. Those compelling words of William James come to mind:

> Suppose that the world's author put the case to you before creation, saying: "I am going to make a world not certain to be saved, a world the perfection of which shall be conditional merely, the condition being that each several agent does its own 'level best.' I offer you the chance of taking part in such a world. Its safety, you see, is unwarranted. It is a real adventure, with real danger, yet it may win through. It is a social scheme of co-operative work genuinely to be

done. Will you join the procession? Will you trust yourself and trust the other agents enough to face the risk?"[16]

The adventuresome soul resounds its "Yes!" to such a dare. James's own theological assumptions aside, for Whitehead, the winsome, glint-eyed deity who makes us this zestful offer actually has no other choice than such a world. Indeed, for Whitehead, it is *the principle* of creativity itself that, in a manner of speaking, offers such a dare—to God! Such a god seems a bit too small, to put the matter mildly, for most religious tastes. The traditional critique is that even if one might be moved to admire such a deity, one would not likely bow one's knee in awe or worship. Yes, such an understanding of deity can exonerate God of the charge of cruelty, for in this scenario God cannot help the hard and brute fact that both he and the world are exemplifications of creativity, "the ultimate metaphysical ground." But the flip side of that consolation is this: God is no longer thought to be truly the Creator of the world but, in fact, a part of the world. We find ourselves in a world in which the one we call God is also a member, a being among other beings in a larger ontological environment. Which horn of this dilemma is less pointed?

Perhaps a function of Western religious conditioning, the idea of God many of us bear seems unavoidably linked to what philosophers sometimes call "the cosmological questions." Why is there a cosmos? Where did the world come from? Why is there something, rather than nothing at all? These are questions that Whitehead was apparently neither prepared nor willing to answer. Aquinas, in his arguments for God, would seem to have said it well for the bulk of Western theists over the centuries: "It is necessary to arrive at a first mover, moved by no other; . . . it is necessary to admit a first efficient cause . . . we cannot but admit the existence of some being having of itself its own necessity, and not receiving it from another, but rather causing in others their necessity. This all men speak of as God."[17] To paraphrase the Angelic Doctor: *This is what we mean by God.* But it is evident that this is not what Whitehead meant by God. Whitehead's vision of the God-world relation does not intend

---

16. William James, *Pragmatism* (Indianapolis: Hackett Publishing, 1981), 130.
17. St. Thomas Aquinas, *The Summa Theologica*, ed. Anton C. Pegis, *Introduction to St. Thomas Aquinas* (New York: Modern Library, 1945), 25, 26.

at all to address the cosmological question. This may indeed somewhat help with the problem of evil by exonerating God, but one must wonder if, in the long run, it is a bit of cold comfort. For the same cosmology that would exonerate God of evil in our world would also offer us a God who cannot truly promise human creatures, to say nothing of the world, an ultimate deliverance.

Similarly, the metaphysical issue of unitary explanation is also at stake in this discussion. Put simply: Can we accept a religious cosmology that imagines God to be one instance of creative advance, albeit a very important one, among other countless instances? Does not the mind—at least the Western, theistic mind—earnestly yearn for the beauty and simplicity of some unitary and unifying source? If so, then Whitehead's vision of deity is indeed insufficient. As Wieman and Meland observed over sixty years ago, "Perhaps it makes more sense [in Whitehead's system] to say there are three kinds of ultimate reality—this process [of creativity], God and the eternal forms or possibilities which come into existence and pass out of existence."[18] *Three* kinds? *One* "kind of ultimate reality" is just the right amount for most human minds! Even only *two*—God and "next to nothing"—is too much.

Allow this illustration. Occasionally philosophers utilize a category they identify as "brute fact." For example, John Hick has suggested that people who refuse to take seriously the cosmological question ("Why is there a world?" or "Why is there anything at all?") appear to be willing to consider the world to be "a mere unintelligible brute fact," that is, *it just is, period.* As Hick has written in his introductory work on the philosophy of religion, "Apart from the emotional coloring suggested by the phrase [a mere unintelligible brute fact], this is precisely what the skeptic believes [the universe] to be; and to exclude this possibility at the outset is merely to beg the question at issue."[19] By contrast, the traditional theist believes that the universe is *not* a "brute fact," for it can be "explained" as the creation of God. What is often overlooked, and indeed what Hick overlooks in this particular treatment of the issue, is that for the believer, a brute fact yet remains: Now the

---

18. Wieman and Meland, 231.
19. John Hick, *Philosophy of Religion*, 3rd ed. (Englewood Cliffs, N.J.: Prentice-Hall, 1983), 21.

dubious honor is reserved for God. Granted, "brute fact" is not a particularly endearing or widely used label for God, but most theists would undoubtedly accept its implications: There is no explanation for God; there is nothing "behind" or "before" God; *God simply is and one cannot ask why*. Hence, according to the logic of traditional theism, either the world itself or the world's Creator is a "brute fact" that we cannot explain or for which give an account.

What makes Whitehead's cosmology so unusual is that it postulates two "brute facts," God *and* the world. This is twice as many brute facts as most people, at least of the Western mind, are able or willing to concede. Whether because of intuition, the structure of human thought, or cultural conditioning may be difficult to say, but it seems that we seek some unitary and unifying ground of thought, existence, and experience. Process thought appears not to offer such a ground; or if it does, it is in the principle of creativity itself. For Whitehead and most of his followers, if there is such a ground then it is not in God—and this will never do, either theologically or religiously. From the perspective of the church's traditional reading of Scripture, such a view is an obvious compromise of divine holiness and is thus equivalent to idolatry.

To be fair, it should be noted that some process theologians have offered cautious suggestions regarding the nature of God's relationship to the world that nudge the Whiteheadian tradition at least a little toward *creatio ex nihilo*. For example, Charles Hartshorne has written that "the total concrete cause of *this* world is . . . God"—but, to be sure, it is "God as having actually created and now possessing all previous worlds." Since "all previous worlds" have contributed a rich variety of experiences to God's becoming, and thus in fact are *in* God and *intimately* part of who and what God is, Hartshorne is even willing to say that "God creates us 'out of nothing' precisely because

> God as supremely relative is "the valuation of the world" (Whitehead), wholly containing it as datum of His valuative act. Thus the other-than-ourselves-now which creates us, as of now, is God and in addition to God, nothing. Our past, which . . . is required material for our present self-creation, is already included in God's receptive valuation, just as our new present is about to be, or is in process of being, included. God then is the *whole* creative source.[20]

---

20. Charles Hartshorne, *The Logic of Perfection* (LaSalle, Ill.: Open Court Publishing, 1962), 273-74.

This is not exactly a traditional rendering (to put it mildly) of *creatio ex nihilo*, but it is a way of describing God's ongoing creative and recreative activity that takes seriously God's eminently social character vis-à-vis the world. Hartshorne may indeed help us think more clearly about the relationship between God's creative activity as *ex nihilo* and as *continua*—as an ongoing and dynamic process in concert with creaturely vitality and creativity. If nothing else, it appears that Hartshorne (at least in this passage) takes a step toward wedding what Whitehead has put asunder: the metaphysical principle of creativity and God's own being/becoming.

Similarly, over three decades ago, John B. Cobb Jr. observed in his *Christian Natural Theology* that for Whitehead "the role of the creator is to provide form for a reality given to him." Cobb proceeded to argue, however, that "the role of the creator in Whitehead must be more drastic . . . than Whitehead recognized,"[21] and did so on the grounds of Whitehead's own metaphysic. It was "characteristic of Whitehead" to dismiss the cosmological question ("Why is there a world?"), but Cobb admirably and rightly pushes it anyway:

> Whitehead . . . was convinced that the process is everlasting. Creativity will always take new forms, but it will always continue to be unchangingly creative. My point is only that the notion of creativity in itself provides no grounds for this faith. . . . If the question as to why things are at all is raised in the Whiteheadian context, the answer must be in terms of the decisions of actual entities. We have already seen that the decisive element in the initiation of each actual occasion is the granting to that occasion of an initial aim. Since Whitehead attributes this function to God, it seems that, to a greater degree than Whitehead intended, God must be conceived as being the reason that entities occur at all as well as determining the limits within which they can achieve their own forms.[22]

Cobb here makes an even larger stride than Hartshorne toward a more traditional understanding of God's role as Creator of the world. Like Hartshorne, however, Cobb maintains the God-world relation as an everlasting and mutually creative dynamic. One is

---

21. Cobb, *Christian Natural Theology*, 206-7.
22. Ibid., 211.

reminded again of Whitehead's jarring aphorism, "It is as true to say that God creates the World, as that the World creates God." Cobb continues:

> It is no objection to my mind that if that which has the power to give existence requires also that it receive existence, then we are involved in an infinite regress. I assume that we are indeed involved in an infinite regress. Each divine occasion . . . must receive its being from its predecessors, and I can imagine no beginning of such a series.[23]

There are other process theologians, or theologians deeply influenced by process modes of thought, who have been far more adamant in questioning Whitehead's understanding of God's creative role. Thinkers such as Robert Neville, Langdon Gilkey, and Thomas Hosinski, while largely sympathetic to the Whiteheadian project, have raised pointed questions regarding Whitehead's sundering of creativity from God.[24] They wonder if there is not a way to speak of God's continually interactive and persuasive presence in the world, *and* of the world's own real powers and vitalities, without surrendering the traditional doctrine of *creatio ex nihilo*. It is time for us now to turn to John Wesley as a potential resource in this issue.

A WESLEYAN RENDERING OF CREATIO EX NIHILO

Let there be no mistake about it: Wesley did not write extensively on the doctrine of creation *per se*, but when he did write about it, it was clear that he assumed the doctrine of *creatio ex nihilo*. Furthermore, he understood this doctrine to imply that all of creation hangs every moment upon the continuing, sustaining, creative grace of God. He probably said it no more plainly than in his sermon "Spiritual Worship":

23. Ibid., 212.
24. See, for example, Robert C. Neville, *Creativity and God: A Challenge to Process Theology*, new ed. (Albany N.Y.: State University of New York Press, 1995); Langdon Gilkey, *Reaping the Whirlwind: A Christian Interpretation of History* (New York: Seabury Press, 1981); and Thomas E. Hosinski, *Stubborn Fact and Creative Advance: An Introduction to the Metaphysics of Alfred North Whitehead* (Lanham, Md.: Rowman and Littlefield, 1993). Hosinski's is generally the least known of these but is also the most sympathetic to the Whiteheadian vision. All the more noteworthy, then, that on the question of "Whitehead's separation of creativity from God," Hosinski writes that "Christian theology might need to revise Whitehead's philosophy," 244.

He "beareth," upholdeth, sustaineth, "all" created "things by the word of his power," by the same powerful word which brought them out of nothing. As this was absolutely necessary for the beginning of their existence, it is equally so for the continuance of it: were his almighty influence withdrawn they could not subsist a moment longer. Hold up a stone in the air; the moment you withdraw your hand it naturally falls to the ground. In like manner, were he to withdraw his hand for a moment the creation would fall into nothing.[25]

Similarly, in his sermonic treatment of the doctrine of divine omnipresence, Wesley avers quaintly that, apart from God's continuously sustaining presence throughout the universe, "everything would in an instant sink into its primitive nothing."[26] Such scraps of evidence could be multiplied, but the point should be clear: If Wesley has a fresh word for the debate over *ex nihilo*, then it will not be an explicit word. Rather, it will have to be unearthed as a word-concept that resides implicitly in the "depth grammar" of Wesley's overall vision of the nature and mode of God's activity in the world.

One word that would decidedly *not* appear to hold much promise in this regard is "almighty." This term may, however, provide an important starting point insofar as Wesley did use it in the extended quotation above; he wrote of the "almighty influence" that continuously sustains "all created things." Furthermore, the term is of potential significance because John Cobb, reading Wesley through a process lens in his work *Grace and Responsibility: A Wesleyan Theology for Today*, explores the use of the term "almighty" in a well-known Wesleyan hymn. Arguing compellingly that the Wesley brothers celebrated the "centrality of divine love . . . most powerfully in the hymns of early Methodism,"[27] Cobb points out that the Wesleyan understanding of God is never simply in terms of sheer sovereignty or unrestrained power. Rather, at the heart of this theological vision is not *power as such* but the *empowering of love*. Cobb proceeds to illustrate this by engaging in some careful

---

25. Sermon 77, "Spiritual Worship," §I.3, *Works* 3:91. It is noteworthy that Wesley was speaking in this passage specifically of *Christ* as 'the true God,' the only Cause, the sole Creator of all things."

26. Sermon 118, "On the Omnipresence of God," §II.1 *Works* 4:42.

27. John B. Cobb Jr., *Grace and Responsibility: A Wesleyan Theology for Today* (Nashville: Abingdon Press, 1995), 58.

hermeneutical work on one of their undisputed classics, "Love Divine, All Loves Excelling." He points out that in the Wesleys' careful wording, the second verse does not address God as "Almighty," as in "Come, Almighty, to deliver." Rather, the Wesleys prayed that "Love divine" would "Come, almighty *to deliver*" us from bondage to sin (emphasis added). Cobb writes:

> Addressing God simply as "Almighty" would not be Wesleyan. In this context it would be asking the Omnipotent One to take one form of action, namely, deliverance, when divine power might be used in other ways. The Wesleys did not think of divine power in this abstract sense. . . . Hence, in this hymn, Divine Love is characterized as "almighty to deliver." Divine Love is the only power there is for deliverance. The focus in this hymn is on God's love of us and our dependence on that love's indwelling us.[28]

Cobb is right; there is no question that the preaching, liturgy, and theology of the Wesleys, and of the Wesleyan tradition after them, have revolved around that central affirmation that "God is love" (1 John 4:8, 16). If one must choose between addressing God as "Love Divine" and "Almighty," then there should be no question, no agonizing, for a Christian believer of the Wesleyan stream. The question, of course, is precisely whether one must choose. Let us not assume yet that we must; instead, let us pursue this term "almighty" further.

In his sermon "Spiritual Worship," Wesley could refer to God in Christ's "almighty influence" in the sustaining of the entire universe; might we follow Cobb's lead and suggest that God who is Love is not only "almighty to deliver" but also "almighty to influence"? This raises a fascinating possibility: To "influence" literally means to "flow into," and Cobb himself has interpreted Wesley as believing that "with respect to living things, their capacity to move is itself due to the way in which God flows into them, thereby causing them to become agents."[29] This divine influencing, or "flowing

---

28. Ibid., 59.
29. Ibid., 51. The perceptive reader will recognize that Cobb is here describing what is generally known, especially (though not exclusively) in Wesleyan circles, as the doctrine of "prevenient grace." Here, the doctrine is being broadened (as it certainly ought to be) to encompass not only human beings but also all of God's creation. I have attempted elsewhere to describe this broadening of prevenient grace under the category of "creative grace" and sug-

into," is not almighty in the sense that it absolutely determines either the nature or the activity of God's creatures. Such a notion would clearly go against the grain of Wesley's understanding of God's ways in the world or, at least, of God's ways with human creatures. We may even detect Wesley interpreting Scripture in this very direction near the end of his sermon "On the Omnipresence of God." There he exhorts his readers, "Never forget [God's] comprehensive word to the great father of the faithful, 'I am the Almighty' (rather, *the All-sufficient*) 'God; walk before me, and be thou perfect!'"[30] Wesley here interprets "almighty" explicitly not in terms of sheer unlimited power but in terms of divine sufficiency, as God's empowering of the human to "walk perfectly" (i.e., in love) in God's presence.

The divine influence is, then, an *empowering* of the creature to "move itself," to exercise the agency appropriate to its capacities. God's inflowing *is* almighty, however, at least in the sense that God is not limited in influencing the world in precisely this way; in Wesley's own words, "There is no point of space, whether within or without the bounds of creation, where God is not"[31]—and thus no place, no creature, no event, where God is not the Inflowing Presence.

We could, in fact, continue to say that God is omnipotent, recognizing that the very nature of this divine potency—self-giving love—is to be everlastingly outpoured and flowing into "the other," into creation. Thus, Love Divine who is omnipotent does not "have" all the power, for that power is by nature freely outpoured to the world as its empowering *to be*. As Cobb writes of the hymn under consideration, "The whole hymn follows from understanding God as Love that pours itself into human beings"[32] and—we surely could add with Cobb's thorough approval—into all that exists. In this way, a Wesleyan understanding of the nature of God would move a step toward the process theological claim that God *cannot* exercise coercive power—not, however, because of an ultimate

---

gested its ecological implications. See "All of Creation is Groaning: Is There a Distinctively Wesleyan Contribution to an Environmental Ethic?" *The Center for Theology and the Natural Sciences Bulletin* 18.2 (Spring, 1998).

30. Sermon 118, "On the Omnipresence of God," §III.6, *Works* 4:47.
31. Ibid., §I.1, *Works* 4:42.
32. Cobb, *Grace and Responsibility*, 58.

metaphysical structure of reality to which even God is necessarily subject, for this compromises too much of a traditional understanding of God's role as Creator. But a Wesleyan understanding of creation would postulate that God *cannot* exercise coercive power precisely because it would be contrary to God's character of self-emptying, compassionate Love to do so. Similarly, the exercise of such coercive power would be contrary to God's purpose in creating responsible agents who can respond to, and grow in, that love. God cannot force us, or the world, to go the way of Love Divine because it would not be consistent with Love Divine to do so. "God acts . . . throughout the whole compass of his creation," Wesley preached, "by . . . strongly and sweetly *influencing* all, and yet *without destroying the liberty of his rational creatures.*"[33]

If this Inflowing Presence that is none other than "Love Divine, all loves excelling" is everywhere present and active—if there is *no place,* "no point of space," as Wesley put it, where God is not—then there is equally *no time* where God is not this Inflowing Presence of Love. Here we find ourselves hedging toward the likelihood of an everlasting creation not entirely unlike the model espoused by process theologians. There are, in fact, a pair of implications in the doctrine of creation that virtually *demand* the idea of an everlasting creation.

First, as Augustine argued so cogently long ago in his *Confessions,* time is an aspect of God's creation, and, therefore, we cannot ask what God was doing before the creation of the world because there *is* no such "before"—the notion of "before" logically depending entirely upon the idea and experience of time as succession of events. In fact, Augustine's observation implies that there has "always" been a creation, since our idea of "always" also partakes of the category of time. We might adapt the Athanasian cry and say it this way: There is no time when the world is not, for where the world is, there also is time. Creation, therefore, *always is.*

Essentially the same point is implied in the Christian—perhaps particularly Wesleyan—conviction that God is love. If God's eternal character is the self-giving love revealed in the cross of Jesus (1 John 3:16), and, furthermore, if God is not *incidentally* Creator—creating not arbitrarily but as the expression of divine creative and

---

33. Sermon 118, "On the Omnipresence of God," §II.1, *Works* 4:42-3 (italics added).

recreative love—then presumably there was no time when God was not this sort of God. The creator God did not pop up out of a hat any more than the world did. The age-old conundrum of why God began to create when God did, and not sooner—or why then, and not some other time—is thus revealed for the false problem that it is.

Wesley himself betrayed an awareness of this "problem" (but not its "solution") when he wrote in his sermon "The Unity of the Divine Being" that "at that point of duration which the infinite wisdom of God saw to be most proper, for reasons which lie hid in the abyss of his own understanding, not to be fathomed by any finite mind, God 'called into being all that is', created the heavens and the earth."[34] If Wesley had understood the notion of God as Creator more consistently with his own "depth grammar" about God as the Inflowing Presence of Love Divine, then perhaps he could have understood creation less as *ex nihilo* and more as *ex amore*. If, in other words, it is the very nature of God to be the outflow of self-giving, other-receiving, empowering Love, then it makes theological sense to speculate that God is indeed everlastingly creating. Although Hartshorne's metaphysical assumptions are decidedly different from the Wesleyan theological convictions we are probing at this point, his questions are no less pertinent: "Ah, is it the idea of a beginning which you worship? Do you exalt God's power by deciding that He has created only a finitude of past time? Whence this passion for limiting God by explicit negations?"[35] As many theologians from at least as far back as Aquinas have observed that there is no inherent logical reason why *creatio ex nihilo* automatically or necessarily excludes *creatio continua*, the notion of an everlasting activity of creation by God in which God is always lovingly creating by "almighty influence," that is, laboring redemptively with "the world that is given to [God] in that moment,"[36] a world that is also, of course, God's continuing creation. Presbyterian theologian Daniel L. Migliore helps us to make this loosely "Wesleyan" point:

> In [a] sense . . . creation may be called "necessary" that is, in the sense that God creates in total consistency with God's nature. Creation fittingly expresses the true character of God, who is love. . . .

---

34. Sermon 120, *"The Unity of the Divine Being,"* §8, *Works* 4:63.
35. Hartshorne, *The Logic of Perfection*, 123.
36. John B. Cobb Jr., *God and the World* (Philadelphia: Westminster Press, 1969), 91.

> To speak of God as the creator is to speak of a beneficent, generous God, whose love and will-to-community are freely, consistently, and fittingly displayed in the act of creation. . . . In the act of creation, God already manifests the self-communicating, other-affirming, community-forming love that defines God's eternal triune reality and that is decisively disclosed in the ministry and sacrificial death of Jesus Christ. God is love, and this eternal love of the triune God constitutes, in Jonathan Edwards' words, a "disposition to abundant communication."[37]

If God has never been other than a "disposition to abundant communication," then there has *never been when time was not*; for time is an aspect of creation, and such a God as we are here attempting to describe has "always" been a loving Creator, been everlastingly creating, and "always" labored with a world by the almighty inflowing of divine love. Hence, both the nature of creation as timeful and, more important, the nature of God as creative, abundant, and fecund love strongly imply the theological concept of an everlasting and continuing creation. While such a notion may play havoc with our sequentially ordered minds,[38] it should also help Christians, and especially Christians of the Wesleyan theological tradition, to "create some space" of their own for appreciating the process notion that God has always had some world with which God labors—some world which "comes" to God, as it were, as a "given." We must add, however, that it is precisely at this point that the traditional safeguard of *creatio ex nihilo* is critical as a check to the Whiteheadian idea of a world, for which God finally and ultimately cannot account, as though it were ultimately an alien "other" outside the divine purview.

Finally, and perhaps most important, it is not the case that a Wesleyan insistence upon *ex nihilo* is indicative of a religious fascination with sheer power; it is not (or at least should not be) a result of worshiping sheer almightiness as though that were in itself a religious value. Rather, as we keep in mind Wesley's foremost theological concern—how it is that *God saves and sanctifies us—ex nihilo*

---

37. Daniel L. Migliore, *Faith Seeking Understanding: An Introduction to Christian Theology* (Grand Rapids: Eerdmans, 1991), 85.

38. I confess to having more difficulty imagining "an infinite regress" (though I can affirm it logically and theologically) than does Cobb; cf. above, footnote 22.

becomes important on soteriological grounds, as indeed we have already seen in the work of Peters. Wesleyanism, it seems, would generally follow the soteriologic of some of the church's most important and influential early thinkers, such as Irenaeus and Athanasius, who taught that the only power that can truly save a fallen creation is the power of our *Creator*, Maker of heaven and earth. Thus, while Cobb is correct in arguing that in their hymn "Love Divine, All Loves Excelling" the Wesleys characterize God as "almighty to deliver," the argument of the early church theologians is that the only one sufficiently mighty to deliver is one who is almighty to *create all things*. Furthermore, unless God creates all things *ex nihilo*, there is an unaccountable power in reality that God in fact may not be almighty to deliver—or from which God may finally be unable to deliver us. In fact, in Whitehead's own words, such a God is "in the grip" (or at least in a serious grappling match) with that unaccountable power. For this reason, the Wesleyan tradition shall always, I predict, insist upon *creatio ex nihilo* and is on good grounds for doing so. If the power to deliver is not also the power to create, then the saving of creation is uncertain on metaphysical grounds. Hence, the power of God's saving and sanctifying grace should be rooted theologically in God's power to create that which God redeems. This conviction reflects the Wesleyan insistence upon the priority of grace.

Of course, while a Wesleyan understanding of salvation must always begin with the priority of grace, it never simply ends there. Wesley consistently understood divine grace to be evocative grace, alluring grace, a grace that calls us but does not coerce us or negate our creaturely realities and vitalities. Thus, once again, *ex amore* begins to overshadow, or at least to provide a counterbalance for, *ex nihilo*. If God's labors to "renew us in love" through Christ by the Spirit always take seriously our cooperation with, and contribution to, sanctifying grace, then God does not recreate us into the divine image instantaneously or *ex nihilo*. Rather, the nature of God's activity is to work redeemingly with real human beings as they truly exist in this world "moment by moment." In fact, as far as Scripture testifies, it would seem that new creation inevitably emerges from the "old" by the inflowing power of God. The apostle Paul in Romans 8, for example, describes the creation we inhabit as yearning for divine liberation[39] and describes the eschatological "adoption" of God's children as specifically involving "the redemption of our [present] bodies" (Rom. 8:23). One could accordingly argue the other side of Peters' "evangelical" exposition of *ex nihilo* along these lines: What we know through experience of God's creative and recreative activity is that God works with the material that is available. This understanding of grace, wherein God gently and lovingly works *with* us, not *above* or *in spite of* us, assuredly bears some consonance with a Whiteheadian cosmology, wherein the same can be said for how God works with the world.[40] Such an ideal reflects the Wesleyan insistence upon the responsibility of the creatures to the initiatives of grace.

And if we are right in these speculations about God's nature as everlastingly creative, in-flowing love, then we surmise that God has labored everlastingly and always with *some kind* or *another* of creaturely responses to grace, with the world's capacities to respond always depending greatly upon the responses of those who have gone before. This much sounds "process." However, if there has been, and everlastingly will be, a world of creaturely response, it is not because such a world exists of its own necessity but because "Love Divine, all loves excelling" freely and abundantly creates *ex amore*. This much sounds "Wesleyan." May faithful thinkers of both streams be graced to pray with the congregation of Israel, "O give thanks to the God of gods . . . who spread[s] out the earth on the waters, for his steadfast love endures forever" (Ps. 136:2, 4). World without end, Amen, Amen.

---

39. For Wesley's stimulating and challenging sermonic treatment of this passage from Romans 8, see Sermon 60, "The General Deliverance," *Works* 2:436-50.

40. This was summed up nicely once by Cobb in personal conversation: "There is a natural consonance between Whitehead and Wesley: They're both Arminian!" The anachronism was intentionally ironic.

CHAPTER TEN

A WESLEYAN CONTRIBUTION TO CONTEMPORARY EPISTEMOLOGICAL DISCUSSIONS

JOHN CULP

Lurking beneath most ethical debates is the question of how one gains knowledge. Passionately held views about where life begins or ends and questions about sexual morality all presuppose critically important views on how we come to know and the sources of that knowledge. Thus, the question about knowledge—epistemology—plays a crucial, though often unrecognized role in the contemporary world.

Most of us begin with a sense that our ideas represent objects and correspond to reality. We assume, for example, that science, as a set of ideas, describes the physical world. However, the growing recognition of the different ideas that we hold about reality, about our commitments to a set of ideas in the face of counterevidence, and about the influence of ideas upon the description of objects, raises questions as to whether ideas provide genuine knowledge of objects. The technical epistemological discussion that has taken place over the last six centuries offers a complex and sophisticated treatment of the relationship between ideas and objects and between the person who knows and the reality that is known. Three major perspectives arising out of this discussion are classical foundationalism, postmodernism, and Reformed epistemology. A brief description of each perspective, followed by an examination of Wesley's thought, will allow us to identify possible contributions that the Wesleyan theological tradition can make to contemporary epistemology.

CONTEMPORARY EPISTEMOLOGICAL OPTIONS

The earliest forms of classical (or modern) foundationalism based knowledge primarily upon sense experience. This form of foundationalism is best described as sensation-based. According to Alvin Plantinga, sensation-based foundationalism holds three basic principles. The first principle is that foundational beliefs provide the support for all other beliefs. Foundational beliefs are themselves inferred from what is either self-evident to the mind or evident to the senses. The concept of being evident to the senses was eventually refined to the concept of incorrigibility.[1] A sensation is incorrigible when it cannot be questioned because there is no way for someone else to identify a different sensation in that situation.

The second principle of sensation-based foundationalism is that beliefs should be held with different degrees of certainty. Only those beliefs that are based upon self-evident ideas or incorrigible sensations are certain. Others must be held tentatively.

The third principle is that some beliefs are more central than others to one's entire epistemological structure because these beliefs support other beliefs.[2] Certainty regarding the basis for knowledge characterizes the truth. Reliance on the self-evident or incorrigible beliefs as a basis for other beliefs severely limits what can be known; incorrigibility limits truth only to what an individual knows. Consequently, many beliefs about human experience in ethics and religion lost their status as "self-evident" in the modern period.[3] The only acceptable basis for public beliefs was physical sensation directly correlated with objects. But the connection between the idea and the object is not self-evident; it must be assumed. Therefore, knowing depends upon the belief that certain sensations cause certain ideas, or that ideas can be inferred from sensations. The belief that the senses themselves, when carefully controlled, provide knowledge about some types of objects becomes the basis for knowledge.

Postmodern epistemology responds to this severe limitation to knowledge. Because of the variety of responses to the modern period that are called "postmodern," I will use the phrase "socially constituted knowledge" to identify more precisely this second per-

---

1. Alvin Plantinga, "Reason and Belief in God," in *Faith and Rationality: Reason and Belief in God*, ed. Alvin Plantinga and Nicholas Wolterstorff (Notre Dame, Ind.: University of Notre Dame Press, 1983), 58.

2. Ibid., 50.

3. This is the basis for the evidentialism in sense-based foundationalism that Plantinga and Wolterstorff discuss in their essays in *Faith and Rationality*.

spective on how we come to know reality. A socially constituted understanding of knowledge rejects the major components of sensation-based knowledge. It rejects the argument that knowledge is structured hierarchically based upon foundations, and it denies any secure epistemological foundation. A socially constituted understanding of knowledge gives up the modern claim to have achieved certainty by means of an absolute basis for knowledge.[4] Thus, it rejects claims to universal absolutes.[5]

Socially constituted epistemologies do attempt to develop a constructive understanding of knowledge by claiming that knowledge is social in nature, involving relationships rather than isolated realities.[6] Furthermore, such epistemologies claim that knowledge is constructed rather than discovered[7] and practical rather than certain.[8] The standards for evaluating these claims do not exist independently of communities; instead, they express the values of specific communities.[9] While these epistemologies often face the charge of relativism, socially constituted understandings of nature do seek intersubjective agreement.[10] Furthermore, they anticipate that ongoing critical reflection and modification of the communal standards of rationality provide for correction even though there can be no certainty that is based upon a reality known outside of the community's way of knowing.[11]

Seeking to determine the relationship between the idea and reality is an inappropriate goal for this perspective. Instead, human meaning is found through acknowledging the social nature of knowledge and then utilizing that insight to construct more satisfying communities than were previously available. Because there is no metaphysical or ontological reality that can provide a basis for knowledge, sensation-based foundationalism unnecessarily limits the possibilities for constructing meaning.

---

4. Richard Rorty, "Solidarity or Objectivity," in *Post-Analytic Philosophy*, ed. John Rajcheman and Cornel West (New York: Columbia University Press, 1985), 5.

5. Richard J. Bernstein, *Beyond Objectivism and Relativism: Science, Hermeneutics, and Praxis* (Philadelphia: University of Pennsylvania Press, 1983), 27, 61, 75.

6. Ibid., 24.

7. Rorty, "Solidarity or Objectivity," 10.

8. Bernstein, *Beyond Objectivism and Relativism*, 63.

9. Ibid., 27, 55; and Rorty, "Solidarity or Objectivity," 6.

10. Rorty, "Solidarity or Objectivity," 5.

11. Bernstein, *Beyond Objectivism and Relativism*, 223; and Rorty, "Solidarity or Objectivity," 16.

The absence of any criteria for selecting among different claims to knowledge poses a problem for socially constructed epistemologies. Richard J. Bernstein acknowledges this absence of criteria prior to judgment but claims that this is the way things are. While Bernstein makes the important point that this situation points toward human fallibility and need not result in skepticism,[12] he fails to provide any guidelines for evaluating diverse claims to knowledge. Recognizing the limits of every community often leads some members of a community to seek to transcend the limits of that community. That desire to transcend needs some direction in order to be open to options that are novel to the particular community and that also are effective in the development of those options. As important as community and the creation of knowledge are, there appears to be more involved in claims to knowledge—and efforts to evaluate those claims—than mere community consensus.

Reformed epistemology provides the third perspective on the relationship between ideas and objects. The label "belief foundationalism" best describes this distinctive approach because of its emphasis upon belief and the formation of belief. Belief foundationalism developed in response to the Enlightenment utilization of sensation-based foundationalism in order to challenge the validity of belief in God or appeals to either a self-evident or impossible-to-challenge basis for belief in God. This Enlightenment approach led to the conclusion that belief in God required a rational justification based on other beliefs.[13] Some, such as John Locke, thought it was possible to give a rational justification for belief in God. But sensation-based foundationalism, especially in David Hume, concluded that such a justification was impossible. In fact, beliefs in areas such as morality and religion came to be considered unjustified in principle because they lacked a basis in sensation. Belief foundationalism responds to this evaluation by pointing out the diversity of beliefs involved in human knowing and by claiming that belief in God is itself a foundational belief rather than a belief requiring rational justification. This perspective fits with the Reformed tradition's rejection of argumentation on behalf of belief in God.[14] Human

---

12. Bernstein, *Beyond Objectivism and Relativism*, 68-69.
13. Nicholas Wolterstorff, introduction to *Faith and Rationality*, 5-6.
14. Ibid., 8.

arguments based on sensations are incapable of providing knowledge of God because (1) God transcends human rationality and (2) human sin obstructs such knowledge. Belief in God is the starting point for knowledge of God.

Belief foundationalists, while primarily concerned to defend the rationality of belief in God, point out that belief is also crucial in sensation-based knowledge. One must first believe in the reliability of the specific sensations in order to accept the input of the sense as providing knowledge. At this point, belief foundationalism finds the thought of Thomas Reid helpful. Reid held that it was a natural phenomenon that certain sensations were invariably connected with the conception and belief about certain objects. This phenomenon did not provide a law of nature, but it did indicate the importance of mind in providing true beliefs. According to Reid, all who believed in God and all who did not believe in God assumed the reliability of their faculties.[15] Drawing upon Reid, belief foundationalists contend that God created each individual with belief forming faculties. These human dispositions to believe lead to the development of certain types of beliefs in certain types of situations.[16] In some types of situations the beliefs formed will be beliefs about physical objects. In other types of situations the beliefs formed will be beliefs about God. These faculties may develop over time, rather than being fully functioning at birth.[17]

Understanding belief in God as foundational, or as a basic belief, does not mean that belief in God is arbitrary and nonrational. Belief foundationalists claim that belief in God is rational because of the way in which this belief is developed, rather than because of the nature of the belief itself.[18] Plantinga offers two requirements for determining whether a person is justified in holding a belief within a specific situation. These requirements are (1) that the person not violate epistemic duties with regard to developing, retaining, or rejecting a belief,[19] and (2) that accepting the belief will not

---

15. Derek R. Brookes, introduction to *An Inquiry into the Human Mind: On the Principles of Common Sense* (University Park: Pennsylvania State University Press, 1997), xx-xxiii.

16. Plantinga, "Reason and Belief," 90.

17. Wolterstorff, "Can Belief in God Be Rational If It Has No Foundations?" in *Faith and Rationality*, 149-50.

18. Ibid., 156.

19. Plantinga, "Reason and Belief," 31-32.

render the person's way of knowing invalid.[20] A belief should be given up only if there is evidence that the belief was developed in an unreliable manner.[21] The community of those who hold a belief establishes the criteria for what is acceptable evidence.[22]

WESLEY'S UNDERSTANDING OF KNOWING AND KNOWING GOD

John Wesley lived during the epistemological debates of the seventeenth and eighteenth centuries. He knew of Isaac Newton, Locke, Hume, and Reid. Although he did not participate directly in the debates, he thought it important to inform the ordinary people in his movement of the central issues.[23] An examination of Wesley's specific ideas about knowing (especially knowing God) and the implications of his general theological orientation can provide resources for contemporary reflection on how we know.

Despite the fact that modern distinctions between philosophy and theology challenge the validity of any theological considerations in the discussion about knowing, it is significant that recent epistemological positions have consciously drawn upon theological traditions. Reformed epistemology has become an important participant in these discussions through the efforts of Alvin Plantinga, Nicholas Wolterstorff, and others working out the implications of Reformed theology. Nancey Murphy and George F. R. Ellis have developed an alternative approach to understanding knowledge as socially constituted by bringing an Anabaptist/Quaker theological tradition to bear on the problems of ethical knowledge.[24] Their emphasis upon the role of community in the knowledge of ethical principles broadens postmodern ideas about knowledge beyond the concern for scientific and political knowledge.

John Wesley's specific ideas about knowing express his view that

---

20. Ibid., 79.
21. Wolterstorff, "Can Belief in God Be Rational," 171.
22. Plantinga, "Reason and Belief," 76-77.
23. See, for example, Wesley's *Remarks upon Mr. Locke's "Essay on Human Understanding,"* *Works* (Jackson) 13:455-64.
24. See Nancey Murphy and George F. R. Ellis, *On the Moral Nature of the Universe: Theology, Cosmology, and Ethics* (Minneapolis: Fortress Press, 1996).

knowledge is based upon perception, that special senses give knowledge of God, that perception is generally reliable, and that knowledge is characterized by probability. Wesley was a confirmed empiricist in his explicit statements regarding human knowledge of any kind. His use of the phrase *Nihil est in intellectu quod non fuit prius in sensu* (there is nothing in the understanding, which was not first perceived by some of the senses) clearly expressed his position that experience was the basis for knowledge.[25]

For Wesley, knowledge involved moving from the apprehension of something through the senses to judgment about what was apprehended. Judgment then compared those realities conceived by the mind in order to determine their agreements and differences. Based on these comparisons, a person was able to evaluate judgments in order to certify knowledge.[26]

Wesley demonstrated his commitment to an experiential basis for knowledge in his writing and practical advice to people. When he abridged what others had written in order to provide practical advice, his decisions of what to include and exclude were based on experience.[27] This was true in the case of theological issues as well. For example, Wesley's experience of freedom was a vital support for his commitment to the freedom of the human will.[28]

Wesley clearly opposed basing knowledge upon innate ideas.[29] He did not accept that humans were born, or created, with ideas that enabled them to know and live. Furthermore, he did not think that God presented an individual with ideas that made it possible to know the world. God played a crucial role in Wesley's understanding of knowledge, but that role was to create humans with the capabilities to sense reality.[30] Wesley gave an explicitly theological reason for rejecting innate ideas rather than affirming Locke's rejection of innate ideas based upon the difficulty of demonstrating their universality. His rejection of innate ideas owed more to English

---

25. Wesley uses this phrase in two sermons: Sermon 117, "On the Discoveries of Faith," §1, *Works* 4:29; and Sermon 119, "Walking by Sight and Walking by Faith," §7, *Works* 4:51.

26. Sermon 70, "The Case of Reason Impartially Considered," §I.2, *Works* 2:590.

27. See, for example, *Advice with Respect to Health. Extracted from a Late Author,* "Preface," §§7-8, *Works* (Jackson) 14:258.

28. *Thoughts upon Necessity*, §IV.3, *John Wesley*, 488-89.

29. Sermon 69, "The Imperfection of Human Knowledge," §I.4, *Works* 2:570-71; *Remarks upon Mr. Locke's "Essay on Human Understanding,"* *Works* (Jackson) 13:455; and Sermon 117, "On the Discoveries of Faith," §1, *Works* 4:29.

30. Sermon 69, "The Imperfection of Human Knowledge," §3, *Works* 2:569.

Aristotelians at Oxford than to Locke.[31] Wesley rejected innate ideas because such ideas would have been affected by original sin; they would have been unreliable even if they had existed.

The nature and role of ideas in knowing is an important issue in epistemology, even for those who reject the concept of innate ideas. Wesley's own awareness of this issue is demonstrated in his comments on the discussion about ideas and especially in his response to Reid's criticism of Locke.[32] Reid had criticized Locke's assumptions that the mind receives images only through the senses and that sensations are only ideas and therefore unrelated to matter.[33] Locke's distinction between ideas and objects made possible a skepticism about the accuracy of the ideas as representations of the object. Reid solved this problem by rejecting ideas and proposing beliefs—created by God in the knower—as the connection between the mind and the object.[34] Wesley defended Locke against Reid's criticism of Locke's use of ideas in knowing.[35] In the context of defending the assertion that humans are morally responsible, Wesley explicitly discussed the issue of the knowledge of color. Reid had challenged Locke by saying that it was impossible to know that a body had color because there are no qualities, such as color, in a body.[36] Wesley considered color the result of light rays, rather than an illusion. The fact that individuals did not call their sensation "color" indicated that color existed distinct from sensation. Humans denied the knowledge of color because they confused the perception with the thing perceived.[37] Wesley was not an idealist, though, because he rejected the view that simple ideas coexisted in substance. For Wesley, ideas existed only in the mind.[38]

31. Rex Dale Matthews, "'Religion and Reason Joined': A Study in the Theology of John Wesley," (Th.D. Dissertation, Harvard Divinity School, 1986), 266.

32. Reformed epistemology drawing on Reid has critiqued Locke as the source of the separation between the knower and the known.

33. Norman Daniels, *Thomas Reid's Inquiry: The Geometry of Visibles and the Case for Realism* (New York: Burt Franklin and Co., 1974), 61, 64.

34. Hilary Putnam, foreword to Daniels, *Thomas Reid's Inquiry*, i-viii.

35. Frederick Dreyer, "Faith and Experience in the Thought of John Wesley," *The American Historical Review* 88 (1983): 12-30, citing "On the Discoveries of Faith," *Works* (Jackson) 7:231; "Remarks on The Count De Buffon's `Natural History,'" 13:454-55, *Works* (Jackson); and *A Letter to Elizabeth Ritchie*, 6:229, *Letters* (Telford). See also *Remarks upon Mr. Locke's "Essay on Human Understanding*," *Works* (Jackson) 13:456.

36. Daniels, *Thomas Reid's Inquiry*, 67.

37. *Thoughts upon Necessity*, §IV.3, *John Wesley*, 487-90.

38. *Remarks upon Mr. Locke's "Essay on Human Understanding,"* *Works* (Jackson), 13:462.

While Wesley recommended Locke's writings and agreed with much of what Locke had to say about epistemology, Peter Browne influenced him more directly.[39] Wesley differed from both Locke and Browne, however, in his understanding of faith. Locke and Browne understood faith as assent to the truth, but Wesley developed an understanding of faith as a sensitive power and, in fact, a faculty of the mind.[40] This had two implications for Wesley's understanding of human knowing that distinguished his emphasis upon starting with experience from Locke's. First, Wesley thought that knowledge of the world through the natural senses was more reliable than many empiricists, including Locke, thought.[41] Wesley's greater confidence in the senses resulted from the influence of Browne, who held that the mind interacted more closely with external reality and was more reliable in its knowledge of that reality.

The second, and most important, way that Wesley differed from Locke and other empiricists was his acceptance of the idea that humans could be given spiritual senses.[42] Because there could be no idea or knowledge of reality without experience of that reality, spiritual senses were necessary for knowledge of the invisible or spiritual world.[43] The spiritual senses provided apprehensions of God that gave rise to ideas of God, which in turn made knowledge of God possible. Even though Wesley generally refers to "spiritual senses" (in the plural), he did not develop any distinction between different types of spiritual senses. Most likely he referred to these senses in the plural as parallel to multiple physical senses. The closest Wesley came to giving a description of the spiritual senses was to describe them as a feeling by the soul.[44] The soul appeared to be the focal point of the spiritual senses because Wesley, using analogies, described the spiritual senses as the "eye," "ear," "palate," and "feeling" of the soul.[45] He often referred to the spiritual senses

---

39. Dreyer, "Faith and Experience," 25.
40. Ibid., 26.
41. Randy L. Maddox, *Responsible Grace: John Wesley's Practical Theology* (Nashville: Kingswood Books, 1994), 27.
42. Wesley was not an innovator with this concept, which can be found in others prior to and during his time. See Maddox, *Responsible Grace*, 27-28, and Matthews, "Religion and Reason Joined," 234.
43. *An Earnest Appeal to Men of Reason and Religion*, §§32-33, *Works* 11:56-57.
44. Ibid., §7, *Works* 11:47.
45. Ibid.

as faith. In this context, he understood faith as discovering what could not be known in any other physical way.[46] "Faith" in this context did not mean rational assent or trust; it meant spiritual experience.[47]

The spiritual senses, however, were not for Wesley always a functioning part of every person's perceptual structure. He said that only believers—those who had accepted what God had done and who had been born again—utilized the spiritual senses.[48] But Wesley also thought that spiritual senses made it possible for the sinner to hear God's voice.[49] In every case, spiritual senses were gifts from God.[50] Wesley insisted that salvation does not come through human effort as a result of a natural or innate ability or as a result of individual efforts. This is true for both the individual's initial conversion and ongoing Christian life. At the same time, however, the spiritual senses are not automatic; they are not effective apart from their use.[51] An individual must use the God-given spiritual senses in order to gain the knowledge available through the use of those spiritual senses. Basically, spiritual senses were available to all through God's grace but developed only as an individual responded to the initial awareness of God's call to sinners. The failure or refusal to respond to that call precluded any knowledge of God.

Wesley believed that a variety of different things were known through the spiritual senses. His inclusive description of what was known was the "invisible world,"[52] which he also referred to as "divine"[53] and as "spiritual."[54] Spiritual senses make it possible for

46. Sermon 117, "On the Discoveries of Faith," §4, Works 4:30.
47. Matthews, "Religion and Reason Joined," 17. This is the most complete discussion of Wesley's use of "faith" in this sense.
48. An Earnest Appeal, §7, Works 11:47; Sermon 119, "Walking by Sight and Walking by Faith," §2, Works 4:49; Sermon 117, "On the Discoveries of Faith," §12, Works 4:34-35; and Sermon 40, "Christian Perfection," §I.1, Works 2:100-101.
49. An Earnest Appeal, §7, Works 11:46-47.
50. Ibid., §9, Works 11:47-48; A Farther Appeal, §I.4, Works 11:106-107; and Sermon 119, "Walking by Sight and Walking by Faith," §2, Works 4:49.
51. An Earnest Appeal, §32, Works 11:56-57; and Sermon 119, "Walking by Sight and Walking by Faith," §2, Works 4:49.
52. An Earnest Appeal, §§6, 7, 32, Works 11:46-47, 56-57; Sermon 117, "On the Discoveries of Faith," §§3, 13, Works 4:30, 35; and Sermon 119, "Walking by Sight and Walking by Faith," §5, Works 4:50.
53. An Earnest Appeal, §33, Works 11:57.
54. A Farther Appeal, §I.4, Works 11:106-107.

a person to know God's existence, God's presence, God's love,[55] the wisdom of God's providence, what God requires from humans,[56] and God's call to sinners.[57] In addition to giving knowledge about God, spiritual senses provide knowledge about the eternal world or existence after death,[58] spiritual good and evil,[59] and the workings of the Spirit.[60]

Wesley described the relation of the spiritual senses to the natural, physical senses by means of analogy. Just as physical senses provide data about the physical world for the mind to judge and organize, spiritual senses provided data necessary for knowledge of the spiritual world.[61] Although similar in function, the two senses differ: Physical senses deal with physical objects while spiritual senses deal with invisible realities. While physical senses are ordinarily present in all persons, spiritual senses are available to all through God's grace, but develop only as an individual responds to the initial awareness of God's call to sinners. The failure or refusal to respond to that call precludes any knowledge of God.

While Wesley made a clear distinction between the knowledge obtained from physical senses and the knowledge obtained from spiritual senses, he did not completely rule out a connection.[62] Wesley thought it was possible that some ideas about God were not based upon the spiritual senses.[63] An individual could come to

55. *An Earnest Appeal*, §7, *Works* §11:46-47; and Sermon 40, "Christian Perfection," §I.1, *Works* 2:100-101.

56. Sermon 40, "Christian Perfection," §I.1, *Works* 2:100-101.

57. *An Earnest Appeal*, §7, *Works* 11:46-47.

58. Sermon 117, "On the Discoveries of Faith," §8, *Works* 4:32-33.

59. *An Earnest Appeal*, §32, *Works* 11:56-57.

60. Sermon 40, "Christian Perfection," §I.1, *Works* 2:100-101.

61. *An Earnest Appeal*, §§32-33, *Works* 11:56-57.

62. Wesley thought that it was a possibility that the higher physical senses (sight and hearing) might continue after death. At that point, though, they would be connected to the soul rather than to the body. Cf. Sermon 51, "The Good Steward," §I.6, *Works* 2:288-89.

63. Wesley also allowed a religious role for a natural philosophy and for knowledge constructed through the physical senses. He compiled a compendium of natural philosophy from what others had written (see his *Survey*), and he frequently utilized arguments from natural philosophy in his sermons (See Sermon 69, "The Imperfection of Human Knowledge," §I.4 and §II.1, *Works* 2:570-71, 577-78; Sermon 118, "On the Omnipresence of God," §II.1, *Works* 4:42-43; and Sermon 119, "Walking by Sight and Walking by Faith," §8, *Works* 4:51-52). Randy L. Maddox summarizes the relationship between knowledge based on the natural senses and knowledge based on the spiritual senses by distinguishing between indirect and direct knowledge of spiritual realities. Maddox says that Wesley allowed for the indirect knowledge of God through inference from experience of the world and the external testimony of Scripture. Direct knowledge of God, however, comes only through the spiritual senses (Maddox, *Responsible Grace*, 27).

believe in the *idea* of God and the invisible world by hearing the accounts of others and reasoning that there must be a reality giving rise to those accounts. This belief is not knowledge *of* God because it lacks any basis in the individual's experience (due to the absence of the spiritual senses).[64]

THE LIMITATIONS OF KNOWLEDGE IN WESLEY'S EPISTEMOLOGY

Wesley recognized that human knowledge was limited. He described this limitation in terms of the absence of certainty, of human sinfulness, and of the human ability to exercise some control over the reception and use of sensations. Basing knowledge upon experience does not provide certainty in knowing, according to Wesley; he was satisfied with probability in most knowledge. Where there was no conclusive evidence (as, for example, on the question of life on other planets), Wesley was satisfied with probability and rejected claims to certainty.[65] Ultimately, Wesley accepted probability rather than certainty for his knowledge claims because he believed that God created a world too complex for human understanding (thereby protecting humans from pride).[66] Later in life, Wesley advised others to be very cautious about what they claimed to know with certainty.[67] The reason for this caution was the complexity of reality. He recognized that great advances in knowledge had been made during his time. At the same time, he realized that there might well be things that would never be known.[68]

Wesley did claim to know with certainty the spiritual knowledge that God had given him.[69] Even in this realm, however, he acknowledged the uncertainty and limited nature of his knowledge. He claimed certainty only for the knowledge that was necessary for salvation.[70] Basically, Wesley believed that God made it possible for

---

64. Sermon 117, "On the Discoveries of Faith," §13, *Works* 4:35.

65. *A Letter to the Editor of the "London Magazine"* (1 January 1765), *Letters* (Telford) 4:283-85.

66. Sermon 69, "The Imperfection of Human Knowledge," §3, *Works* 2:569, and Sermon 140, "The Promise of Understanding," §III.1, *Works* 4:287.

67. Sermon 51 "The Good Steward," §I.7, *Works* 2:289, and *A Letter to the Editor of the "London Magazine"* (1 January 1765), *Letters* (Telford) 4:286.

68. *A Survey of the Wisdom of God in the Creation*, "Preface," §5, *Works* (Jackson) 14:301.

69. *A Letter to the Editor of the "London Magazine"* (1 January 1765), *Letters* (Telford) 4:286.

70. See Sermon 40, "Christian Perfection," §I.4, *Works* 2:100-101; Sermon 69, "The Imper-

humans to know what was necessary for life both physically and spiritually. Beyond that, there was no certainty.

According to Wesley, another limitation on human knowledge was sin. He believed that human sinfulness was pervasive and thus affected knowledge gained through both the physical senses and the spiritual senses.[71] The impact of sin upon knowledge, obtained through the natural senses, was indirect and did not challenge the basic reliability of sensation to convey information about the object of sensation. Sin affected the individual's judgment more than awareness. While Wesley did not explicitly develop this analysis, he demonstrated an awareness of it in his explanation of various events. For example, he recognized the effectiveness of Bacon's emphasis upon observation rather than the retention of scholastic doctrines of nature.[72] So also, the commitment to prior doctrinal positions, rather than the willingness to observe creation, expressed human choice, which could be distorted by sin.[73]

The primary significance of sin for epistemology in Wesley's thought is found in his description of the role of sin as hindering knowledge gained through spiritual perception. The absence of spiritual perception made it impossible for a person to know spiritual truths and realities. Spiritual perception was, of course, lacking in individuals who had not accepted God's gracious provision of spiritual senses. Despite the fact that God sought to provide life both naturally and spiritually to all, humans could choose to reject God's purposes. In doing this, they rejected God's gift of faith, a gift that would enable spiritual perception and insight.[74] The presence of sin in human judgment for an empiricist such as Wesley can also be found in the human influence on the reception as well as the use of sensations. Wesley did not hold that a person

---

fection of Human Knowledge," §II.1, *Works* 2:577-78; *Remarks on the Limits of Human Knowledge, Works* (Jackson), 13:498, and Matthews, "Religion and Reason Joined," 311.

71. Matthews, "Religion and Reason Joined," 304-305.

72. "Of the Gradual Improvement of Natural Philosophy," §6, *Works* (Jackson), 13:483.

73. Wesley understood the failure of medical research to continue the process of observation to be the result of sin. Physicians became distracted by theories and ignored the effectiveness of traditional practices in order to maintain their positions, according to Wesley. Cf. *Primitive Physic: Or, An Easy and Natural Method of curing most Diseases*, "Preface," §§9-10, *Works* (Jackson) 14:310-11.

74. See Sermon 117, "On the Discoveries of Faith," §4, *Works* 4:30, and Matthews, "Religion and Reason Joined," 298. See also Sermon 19, "The Great Privilege of those that are Born of God," §II.8 *Works* 1:439-40 for Wesley's description of the process which led to David's inability to see God.

was passive in the reception of sensations. Instead, he held to the possibility of individual control over sensations. An individual could choose to accept, reject, or (more frequently) modify[75] an impression. Wesley did not accept physical existence as necessarily determined and cited the experience of controlling sense impressions as experiential evidence for his view.

EPISTEMOLOGY AND WESLEY'S ORIENTING CONCERNS

A complete discussion of Wesley's epistemology requires examination not only of his explicit statements about human knowledge, but also of his wider vision expressed in the context of his practical theology and his concern for the spiritual well-being of those to whom he ministered. The worldview, or basic assumptions, that guided Wesley's theological work may be understood as his "orienting concerns."[76] Because these orienting concerns also play an important role in philosophical activity, addressing them is crucial for any effort to bring the Wesleyan theological tradition to bear upon the question of knowledge.

The first orienting concern guiding Wesley's theology is his stress on the presence of God's activity and initiative in caring for humans and, indeed, for all creation. This concern for God's presence in all of creation expressed itself in Wesley's claim that the doctrine of God's omnipresence must be accepted before God's omnipotence can be believed. For Wesley, God's presence to all of reality was more important than God's power over all of reality.[77]

Furthermore, God's caring for humans influences human knowledge. As we have seen, Wesley held that God takes the initiative in our coming to knowledge, and that this initiative is expressed in knowledge through both the natural senses and the spiritual senses. Wesley was not as pessimistic as Locke about the corre-

---

75. *Thoughts upon Necessity*, §IV.3, *John Wesley*, 489.

76. Randy L. Maddox's proposal that Wesley's theology be identified in terms of orienting concerns provides a helpful suggestion for the examination of the implications of Wesley's practical theology for epistemology (Maddox, 17-19). The titles of two recent studies of Wesley's thought and its implications for contemporary Christianity express Wesley's orienting concerns. Maddox's work is entitled *Responsible Grace*; John B. Cobb Jr.'s work on this subject is entitled *Grace & Responsibility* (Nashville: Abingdon Press, 1995).

77. Sermon 118, "On the Omnipresence of God," §II.6, *Works* 4:44.

spondence between an individual's ideas and reality or about the possibility of reliable knowledge through the natural senses. At the same time, God provides all with spiritual senses apart from which it would be impossible to have more than a general awareness of God based upon what others did and said, what God had done in creation, and what God had revealed in Scripture.

A second characteristic concern of Wesley's was his emphasis on human response to God's grace. Wesley never failed to assert the importance of God's activity and initiative in every aspect of human activity. At the same time, he insisted that without a human response, divine activity was insignificant. Wesley was opposed to any understanding of divine predestination that negated the possibility of human response. The significance of human response especially finds expression in his affirmation that humans have at least some control over the receptiveness of their sensory organs.[78] Wesley's emphasis on human response was also supported by his denial of innate ideas. For Wesley, all knowledge comes from experience, whether that experience involves the natural senses or the spiritual senses.

Wesley's theological perspective cannot be accurately represented by simply identifying divine initiative and human response as his organizing concerns. His particular construal of the interaction between God and humans must be acknowledged as a third orienting concern. For Wesley, God's activity and human activity are inseparably dynamic rather than only a function of an initial relationship. This was exactly the point of contention between Wesley and the Deists: God is not merely the creator but continues to be active in the world and in the lives of all people. Also, God's relationship with humans is not unilateral. God responds to human responses rather than acting without regard to human responses. This concern can be seen in Wesley's response to Jonathan Edwards. Wesley found inadequate Edwards's belief that those who turned away from God's salvation had never been saved. Wesley rejected that explanation because it denied the experience of the individual.[79] For Wesley, God's action did not take place regardless of the action of the individual; instead, it took place in response to the individual.

---

78. *Thoughts upon Necessity*, §IV.3, *John Wesley*, 489.

79. See Wesley's edited republication of *A Treatise on Religious Affections: In Three Parts. By the Rev. Jonathan Edwards*, "To the Reader," §1, *Works* (Jackson) 14:269-70.

This human action should not, however, be separated from God's initiative. Only a clearly dynamic understanding of God's initiative and human response can do justice to Wesley's theological concerns. This is shown most clearly in Wesley's rejection of any human initiative in salvation. For Wesley, faith is a gift from God prior to any human response, and knowledge of God is possible only because of God's actions. Spiritual senses develop because God removes the obstacles hindering awareness of spiritual realities.[80] This development occurs because of human response to grace. God responds to our response by giving spiritual sensation that enables us to experience God directly. That experience of God transforms an individual so that he or she lives differently.

Wesley's concept of natural philosophy also demonstrates his commitment to the interaction between God's initiative and human response. Natural philosophy could provide some knowledge about God through the human activity of reasoning about experiences but was incomplete without the experience of God through the spiritual senses. Wesley illustrated this when he said that heathens know that God is present in the world as a whole but do not realize that God is present both to atoms and to worlds. The awareness of God's omnipresence comes only through spiritual senses.[81]

Wesley's specific ideas about knowing and the orienting concerns of his theology offer several insights to contemporary efforts to understand how people know anything in general and God in particular. In the first place, Wesley's affirmation of God's initiative supplies the insight that God can be experienced and known. Knowledge of God comes through experience of God rather than through inference from other experiences or through processing ideas that are present in a person's mind. The experience of God is of a different kind than the experience of physical objects, but it is the basis for knowledge of God as much as the experience of physical objects is the basis for knowledge of those objects. Wesley was certain that the experience of God was not merely believing what an individual wanted to believe but an actual experience of God.[82] Belief in God is not the result of an individual's

---

80. Sermon 132, "On Faith," §18, *Works* 4:200.
81. Sermon 118, "On the Omnipresence of God," §II.1, *Works* 4:42-43.
82. *A Letter to the Editor of the "London Magazine"* (1 January 1765), *Letters* (Telford) 4:285.

belief-forming capacity; it is the result of experiences of God in response to God's actions.

The foregoing implies that natural theology or philosophy, while limited, does have significance for Wesleyans. Natural theology presupposes God's prior activity. It may lead to the belief that God exists and has acted, but it does not bring about the kind of life change that occurs as a person responds to the experience of God's love. Knowledge gained through natural theology, because it depends on inferences from God's prior activity in the world, lacks a basis in one's own experience of God that is needed for true knowledge. This means that one's experience of God provides the basis for knowledge of God rather than belief serving as the basis for knowing. Experience of God as the basis for knowledge does not rule out the importance of reason for knowing in general or for knowing God specifically. The process of coming to knowledge involves the ability of the individual to reason and make judgments based upon experience.

In addition to the Wesleyan affirmation that knowledge of God comes through experiencing God, a second characteristic of a Wesleyan epistemology is the recognition and acceptance that knowledge primarily involves probability rather than certainty. Probability is what is available to human knowing because of the complexity of God's creation, human sin, and human involvement in knowledge. God's complexity does not result in the impossibility of knowing God or God's creation, but divine complexity does limit knowledge to what is useful or necessary for living physically and spiritually. While increases in knowledge will occur and often lead to explanations for events, it is neither necessary nor possible for one to expect to attain complete knowledge of all reality or explanations for every event. Complete certainty would require knowing God comprehensively.

Human sin certainly has an impact upon knowledge through the role that human choice has in receiving, modifying, and utilizing impressions received through the senses. Yet, this does not make knowledge impossible because, ultimately, knowledge does not depend entirely upon human action. As important as the individual is in knowing, our experience is not entirely subjective because of God's existence and God's creation of, and presence within, the physical world. The destructiveness of sin is not complete; it is limited by divine grace.

Human knowing is limited to probability, of course, because of human involvement. Because humans do not merely accept or reject sense impressions but modify them, make judgments, and thereby create knowledge in these judgments, the element of human choice in that process precludes any certainty about the outcome (as long as choice is meaningful choice).

Finally, not only is certainty not possible, it also is not necessary. It is not necessary because God is reliable. God's love for creation and humanity as known through experience of God demonstrates that God will care for humans and creation. In fact, the demand for certainty can displace the experience of God in the effort to establish one's well-being by means of one's own efforts.

In spite of the importance of Wesley's insights, they cannot be directly applied to the contemporary philosophical discussion. Even in situations in which the existence of God is not an issue, knowledge of God often is. Wesley assumed that God was known as external to the knower through one's experience of God. The basis for this knowledge was the spiritual senses that God made available to individuals. But appeals to a special sense of God carry little weight in contemporary epistemological discussions. Wesley had little to say beyond personal experience to defend the existence of these senses. If personal experience is the basis for the claim that there are spiritual senses, then the universality of knowledge becomes problematic. Even if universality is not crucial to a claim to knowledge, and even if knowledge is limited to certain communities, the objectivity of the experience of spiritual senses appears limited to those that respond to God. In the contemporary context, that limitation appears even more restrictive than the limitation of knowledge to a community's consensus or construction because not everyone is a member of this community. Apparently, only those who respond to God's grace constitute such a community.

The complexity of the nature of the spiritual senses raises the issue of the reliability of natural and spiritual sensation. Wesley clearly based this reliability upon the experience of God. That basis will not be granted in the contemporary context because it is limited to those who have already experienced God as reliable. At best, a certain community may find this to be an adequate basis for constructing knowledge. This undercuts the claim that God is experienced rather than merely constructed on the basis of the experiences of the community. Ultimately, this problem raises the central issue of contemporary discussions about knowledge, namely, the reliability of the connection between the knower and the known and between the idea and the reality. Wesley acknowledged the distinction between the idea and the object and rejected any attempt to identify the object as existing in the substance of the reality. The closest he came to demonstrating the reliability of the senses was to point to the demonstration of the experience of God in the changed life of the believer. Insofar as this establishes the actuality of the experience of God as external to the individual, it may provide some basis for the claim that the senses are generally reliable. It will provide neither any certainty nor any identifiable degree of probability beyond that based upon careful evaluation of evidence and adherence to principles for judgments for any specific claim to knowledge.

PROCESS PHILOSOPHY AND THE DEVELOPMENT OF A WESLEYAN EPISTEMOLOGY

A variety of philosophical perspectives offer assistance to Wesleyans seeking to bring Wesley's insights into contemporary epistemological discussions.[83] Several thinkers have suggested process

83. See, for example, William P. Alston, "Christian Experience and Christian Belief," in *Faith and Rationality*, 103-34. Alston offers a defense of the validity of Christian experience as a source of knowledge, arguing that religious experience and perceptual experience function in the same way. The reliability of both perceptual and Christian beliefs can be assumed if there is no evidence that the specific practices leading to each type of belief are unreliable. Wesley holds that Christian experiences are reliable when they fulfill their purpose of facilitating a relationship with God.

W. Stephen Gunter proposes developing Michael Polanyi's identification of personal involvement as part of knowledge rather than a response to knowledge. Polanyi did not seek certainty but instead sought a coherence that was both personal and communal. Finally, knowledge as personal for Polanyi included a transformative aspect of knowledge that changes the individual rather than being external to the individual. Gunter suggests that Wesleyans utilize Polanyi's concept that knowledge involves a tacit aspect that provides contact with reality. Cf. W. Stephen Gunter, "Personal and Spiritual Knowledge: Kindred Spirits in Polanyian and Wesleyan Epistemology," *Wesleyan Theological Journal* 35.1 (2000): 130-48.

Additionally, Mark H. Grear Mann suggests that Charles Sanders Peirce's understanding of knowledge as empirical, probable, and existential relates well to Wesleyan

philosophy as a resource.[84] While some have challenged the compatibility of process philosophy with Christian theology (and thus with Wesleyan theology as a form of Christian theology), it is clear that several similarities do exist between Wesley's epistemology and orienting concerns, on the one hand, and a process epistemology, on the other.

Thomas Jay Oord, in his discussion of David Ray Griffin's constructivist postmodern process philosophy, noted that both Griffin and Wesley hold empiricist understandings of knowledge.[85] More specifically, both Wesley and Griffin insist that direct perception of God is possible, but this perception does not come through the natural senses.[86] Wesley and process thinkers also identify feeling as crucial to knowledge of God. This use of "feeling" refers neither to the physical sense of touch nor to an "emotional" response. Instead, both Wesley and Whitehead used "feeling" to describe a more elementary relationship between the knower and other realities. For Whitehead, the relationship between actualities involves the feeling of one actuality by another. Griffin describes this feeling as nonsensory perception, which involves the causal influence of events upon other events. This is an internalization of an external reality.[87] Similarly, Wesley utilized the term "feeling" to describe the spiritual senses that make knowledge of God possible:

---

theology. Peirce's position that spiritual reality is known through a different means than physical reality particularly supports Wesley's epistemology. Cf. Mark H. Grear Mann, "Postmodernity and Pragmatic Wesleyanism: Peirce, Wesley, and the Demise of Epistemic Foundationalism," Annual Meeting of the Wesleyan Theological Society, 6 March 1999.

Certain similarities exist among these resources. All recognize the importance of the individual in knowing. The individual is both affected by and affects what is known. Another commonality is that all of these perspectives hold that there are ways of knowing in addition to sensuous perception. This non-sensuous way of knowing involves an intuitive feeling that is not dependent upon physical structures. Finally, there is a repudiation of certainty as a characteristic of knowledge. Instead, these authors hold that knowledge is recognized as being more or less probable rather than certain.

84. Thomas Jay Oord addresses this most directly in "Toward a Postmodern Wesleyan Philosophy: Elements Drawn from David Ray Griffin's Constructive Postmodern Vision," *Wesleyan Theological Journal* 35.1 (2000): 216-44. John B. Cobb Jr. addresses this issue generally in *Grace and Responsibility*. The series of essays about process theology in *Wesleyan Theology Today: A Bicentennial Theological Consultation*, ed. Theodore Runyon (Nashville: Kingswood Books, 1985) provides discussions of the general relation between process theology and Wesleyan theology.

85. Oord, "Postmodern Wesleyan Philosophy," 219, citing David Ray Griffin, *Founders of Constructive Postmodern Philosophy* (Albany, N.Y.: State University of New York Press, 1993), 14.

86. Ibid., 236-37.

87. Frederick Ferré gives a similar process account of the relationship between the knower and the known by talking about feelings of the influence of other events and the response

---

It is the feeling of the soul, whereby a believer perceives, through the "power of the Highest overshadowing him," both the existence and the presence of him in whom he "lives, moves, and has his being," and indeed the whole invisible world, the entire system of things eternal. And hereby, in particular, he feels "the love of God shed abroad in his heart."[88]

Wesley identified this process of feeling as being inwardly conscious or, in other words, being influenced by the reality known through feeling.[89]

John B. Cobb Jr. points out that process philosophy and Wesleyan theology share the conviction that God is present and active in the world.[90] Likewise, the concept of a mutual relation between God and the world provides a shared basis for epistemological similarities. For Wesley, God's grace makes possible the human response to God. Spiritual senses are given by God's grace and enable the person who is separated from God to recognize that separation and respond to God. However, grace can be resisted. In that case, God does not unilaterally cause the person to be in relation to God. God does not determine a person to be saved or damned. The reality of a past acceptance does not maintain the relationship with God in the present. But, as the individual responds to God's grace, that grace becomes increasingly effective and transformative. While God makes possible the mutuality between God and humans, that mutuality depends upon human response for its continuation and development.

Process thought can assist in the development of a Wesleyan contribution to epistemology in several ways. Process thought offers an explanation of the claim that perception includes more than sense perception. This can be described as nonsensory perception (Griffin) or as perception in the mode of causal efficacy (Whitehead). Process thought also provides a metaphysical explanation for why probability is sufficient for knowledge and for why certainty is neither necessary nor possible. The ongoing interaction

of the person who has these feelings. Cf. Frederick Ferré, *Knowing and Value: Toward a Constructive Postmodern Epistemology* (Albany, N.Y.: State University of New York Press, 1998), 294.
88. *An Earnest Appeal*, §7, *Works* 11:47.
89. *A Farther Appeal*, §V.2, *Works* 11:139-40.
90. Cobb, *Grace and Responsibility*, 75.

between actualities and the knower means that knowledge itself continually develops. The variety that results from various feelings of past events is not the destruction of knowledge but the opening of new possibilities. Certainty destroys the interest in other possibilities. Finally, process theology provides a metaphysical explanation of the relationship between God and the world that overcomes a separation that makes knowledge of God impossible in any meaningful sense. Wesley is convinced that knowledge of God is possible. He also recognizes that not everyone knows God or is even capable at the present moment of knowing God. Given that reality, if there is no explanation of the relationship of God to the world that allows for interaction between God and the world, then there can be no knowledge of God. Any claim to know God, even a claim based on God's initiative, is impossible if God is not present to the world in order to be known.

CONTEMPORARY WESLEYAN EPISTEMOLOGY

A contemporary Wesleyan epistemology, which draws from Wesley's theologically concerned epistemology and contemporary philosophical resources—especially process thought—will be characterized by three themes. The first theme is that knowledge of God is possible and is not limited to being based upon belief. Knowledge of God is possible because all humans are capable of experiencing God. Furthermore, the experience of God is more than experience through sensory perception. While limited knowledge of God and belief about God may be arrived at through inferences based upon physical sensation, this limited knowledge will always fail to bring about the transformation of an individual's life that experience of God provides. Humans experience God and come to transforming knowledge of God through grace, which also enables us to recognize the possibility of experiencing God. Recognition of God and response to this grace enables us to experience an ongoing transformation of life in a community of those who are also being transformed.

The second theme is that knowledge requires human involvement. Knowledge is not merely a response to an actuality or a passive reception of input from an external object. Instead, as created by God, each individual is capable of directing his or her experiences and of modifying the perceptions involved in those experiences. Experience of external realities conveys information about external realities, but this information is never complete or simply a representation. Instead, knowledge is partially constituted by the response of the perceiver to what is perceived. This creativity, based upon divine creativity, enables humans to engage the past and the present in order to live for the future. The future is created, to a significant degree, by the knowledge that the individual creates in a community. Thus, knowledge is neither the simple reproduction of the past nor completely the result of human creativity in a social context.

The third theme is that knowledge is characterized by probability rather than certainty. Physical sensation provides a high enough degree of probability to enable us to exist (even though we must always engage in the ongoing correction of errors in perception). Likewise, perception of God is adequate to bring about transformation in the individual who accepts God's graciousness. For these reasons, certainty is not necessary for human knowledge. In fact, the desire for certainty, apart from the experience of God's reliability, can become a substitute for the experience of God. This is the case even when the basis for certainty is belief in God if that belief is not characterized by the experience of knowing God. Furthermore, the knowledge of God, through experiencing God, provides neither comprehensive knowledge nor certainty about all that God may do. The basis for assurance of the reliability of perception of both physical and spiritual realities is the experience of God's reliability in loving the individual. It is the experience of this reliability and love to which certainty is limited.

Based upon these three themes, a self-consciously Wesleyan approach to epistemology will demonstrate a number of specific characteristics. The first of these is a modesty about claims to know. Wesley's hesitancy to claim complete explanations of either physical or spiritual realities is an appropriate model. The obviousness of the need for past and future revisions precludes claims to certain knowledge. Ultimately, the priority of divine grace and the limitations upon human knowing make all claims to knowledge open to revision.

A second characteristic of a Wesleyan approach to epistemology is the recognition of the value of human efforts to know. This does not mean that knowledge is simply the creation of a fertile imagination or of a community defining itself. Rather, knowledge involves experience of a reality that is more than the knower. This reality may be divine or nondivine, but it is there to be known by persons seeking to experience it. This characteristic affirms the role of human creativity in knowing.

A third characteristic of a Wesleyan epistemology is the affirmation of the universal availability of the knowledge of God. Based on Wesley's understanding of the presence of divine grace to every individual, Wesleyans claim that the experience and knowledge of God is available to all. While some may choose not to utilize that grace, there are no limits upon its availability. God does not choose to transform some and destroy others. God offers everyone the possibility of the transforming experience of the knowledge of God.

A fourth and final characteristic is the acceptance of community in knowing. The complexity of God and of the created world, along with the creative role of humans in knowing, make knowledge a communal activity rather than a merely individual activity. This is true because of the need for both assistance and correction in the process of coming to know.

A Wesleyan epistemology, then, offers a mediating position in the contemporary context. Such an epistemology recognizes that human thought and activity are crucial in coming to knowledge, as claimed by the classical foundationalists. A Wesleyan epistemology affirms the postmodern understanding of knowledge as socially constituted. At the same time, with Reformed epistemology, a Wesleyan epistemology explains how it is possible to know God. A Wesleyan epistemology recognizes both the constructed nature of knowledge and the possibility of knowledge of an external reality. It offers a comprehensive perspective that provides support for options that receive limited attention in the contemporary discussion of knowing. Concepts such as knowledge of God, knowledge of external realities, and the socially constituted nature of knowledge are rarely held in conjunction with each other. A creative development of this mediating perspective can assist both philosophers and nonphilosophers in understanding this Wesleyan alternative to the dominant epistemological perspectives.[91]

---

91. Theodore Runyon, "The role of experience in religion," *International Journal for the Philosophy of Religion* 31 (1992): 87-194 is one of the few articles that has been published articulating an explicitly Wesleyan approach to epistemology.

CHAPTER ELEVEN

PUTTING REASON IN ITS PLACE:
WESLEYAN THEOLOGY OR ONTOTHEOLOGY?[1]

ALAN G. PADGETT

There has been a happy marriage between Wesleyan theology and process philosophy for the last several decades. Other chapters in this book attest to the continuing vitality of this union of a particular Christian theological tradition and a specific metaphysical school. My purpose in this chapter is to raise a voice of caution. In the past, process theology has tended to privilege reason, or metaphysics, over Scripture and tradition. In this essay, I give some reasons why this has been a problem and may indeed continue to be unless care is taken by process thinkers. The question here is not *whether* faith and reason, or theology and philosophy, belong together. The question is *how*. My entry into this question will be through Martin Heidegger's well-known rejection of ontotheology, although in the end I will turn Heidegger on his head.

Recent work in process theology has moved in the direction of humility in metaphysics and rationality, combined with a greater respect for tradition. Examples of this include John B. Cobb Jr.'s recent book on Wesleyan theology, Charles Hartshorne's collection of essays on moderation in philosophy, and Marjorie Hewitt Suchocki's book on sin, along with her recent essay on John Wesley's theology of prayer.[2] This is a salutary movement in process theology and one I would like to commend. The present volume of essays continues this important change in at least some

---

1. I would like to dedicate this essay to John B. Cobb Jr., a man of many virtues, intellectual and personal, and a model of Christian grace in scholarship.
2. John B. Cobb Jr., *Grace and Responsibility: A Wesleyan Theology for Today* (Nashville: Abingdon Press, 1995); Charles Hartshorne, *Wisdom as Moderation: A Philosophy of the Middle Way* (Albany, N. Y.: State University of New York Press, 1987); Marjorie Hewitt Suchocki, *The Fall to Violence: Original Sin in Relational Theology* (New York: Continuum, 1994); and Suchocki, "The Perfection of Prayer," in *Rethinking Wesley's Theology for Contemporary Methodism*, ed. Randy L. Maddox (Nashville: Kingswood Books, 1998).

process thinkers who are also Wesleyans. In the past, however, process thought was neither so humble nor so interested in valuing the sources of Christian thought in Scripture and tradition. My basic concern is that when working with Scripture and tradition, process theologians may continue to give explanatory priority to metaphysics and/or philosophical rationality. Process theologians have rightly complained that classical theism is too tied to Greek metaphysics. My caution is that Wesleyan theology should not be too tied to process metaphysics.

This essay is primarily about method: method in metaphysics and method in theology. A careful and thorough reply to process theology would include a detailed critique of process metaphysics, especially the work of Alfred North Whitehead. Although we have neither time nor space for such a venture here, I do want to note that I have found a number of important doctrines in process philosophy. There is, after all, much value in process thought. I have chosen to focus on the key problem with process theology—a problem in metaphysical and theological method—rather than any particular doctrine. This problem is well captured by Heidegger, one of the greatest philosophers of the twentieth century.

The problem can be stated very briefly. In the past, process theology allowed philosophy to set the terms for the Christian theological quest to know God. However, because Christian theology is based upon revelation, it can and must resist this move. The path to truth about God is based upon faith and comes through revelation, especially that revelation in Jesus Christ that is made available to us in the witness of Scripture, as the Spirit gives us new eyes to see the truth.[3] Tradition, spiritual practices, reason, and experience are secondary to the primary witness of scripture. Philosophy may indeed teach us something about God. But for a theology dedicated to the truth about God in Jesus Christ, special revelation is the primary source of truth about God. Philosophical theology must accommodate itself to revelation—not the other way around—if indeed revelation is what it claims to be: knowledge of God beyond reason (but not contrary to reason).

---

3. "The necessary and fundamental form of all scriptural exegesis that is responsibly undertaken and practiced in this sense must consist in all circumstances in the freely performed act of subordinating all human concepts, ideas and convictions to the witness of revelation supplied to us in Scripture." Karl Barth, *Church Dogmatics* (Edinburgh: T. & T. Clark, 1956), I:2, §21.2.2, 715.

This is an old debate and process thinkers have, for example, already replied to Barth and his school. But the postmodern twist has put new bite into the criticism of the pretensions of philosophical systems, or metanarratives, to encompass all of reality—including God—into one vast regime of Truth with a capital T. Of course, we could have learned this lesson if we had listened carefully to John Dewey's Gifford Lectures of 1929 on the quest for certainty.[4] But Dewey was ahead of his time and did not write in French! The philosophy of Whitehead represents the last great philosophical system in Anglo-American thought (at least so far) and is a primary example of that at which postmodern critics have aimed, that is, a totalizing metanarrative. To grasp the power of the postmodern critique, however, we should begin with Martin Heidegger.

Heidegger's own very early metaphysical speculations developed into his classic phenomenological study of human Being *(Dasein)* in *Being and Time* (1927).[5] In this text, he begins his path toward the suspicion of metaphysics. Take, for example, his section "Destroying the history of ontology" (Introduction, II.6). Heidegger famously takes Western, traditional metaphysics to task for forgetting Being in its focus on things. His main task in this book remains a positive one, attempting to explicate the "positive aspects" of Being.[6] After this work, Heidegger becomes more suspicious of metaphysics and eventually argues we should "overcome" it. One text along this journey is his 1957 volume, *Identity and Difference.*[7] In this work, Heidegger sets forth the ontotheological constitution of metaphysics but is critical of it. We cannot do justice to the whole of Heidegger's text here but seek only to outline his implicit argument against process metaphysics and, indeed, against all metaphysical systems that claim a systematic, unitary knowledge of God and existence. While Heidegger's critique is couched in terms of Aristotelian philosophy, Whitehead's system is just as problematic and falls under the same ontotheological critique.[8]

---

4. John Dewey, *The Quest for Certainty* (London: Allen and Unwin, 1930).

5. I will cite the pages of *Sein und Zeit* (Tübingen: Max Niemeyer, 1953). The two English translations refer (in their margins) to this edition. See *Being and Time*, trans. John Macquarrie and Edward Robinson (London: SCM, 1962) and *Being and Time*, trans. Joan Stambaugh (Albany, N.Y.: State University of New York Press, 1996).

6. Ibid., 44.

7. German with English translation, ed. Joan Stambaugh (New York: Harper & Row, 1969).

8. Process theologians, wishing to reply to my critique, should distinguish between

The problem, Heidegger states, is how God comes into philosophy. Theology cannot be allowed to dictate answers to philosophy, according to Heidegger. "God [der Gott] can come into philosophy only insofar as philosophy, of its own accord and by its own nature, requires and determines that and how God enters into it," he claims.[9] And again, "We can properly think through the question, How does God enter into philosophy? only when that *to which* God is to come has become sufficiently clear: that is, philosophy itself."[10] In my own language, Heidegger is concerned for the integrity of philosophy as a rational disciple of the University and for the methodological focus and limits of philosophy. If any other science or discipline can dictate answers in advance for philosophy, he holds, then philosophy loses its purpose. He states, "It would be rash to assert that metaphysics is theology because it is ontology,"[11] fully aware that Aristotle called part of his metaphysics "theology." He makes this clear in an earlier lecture, *Introduction to Metaphysics*:

> Anyone for whom the Bible is divine revelation and truth has the answer to the question "Why is there beings rather than nothing" even before it is asked: everything, that is, except God himself, has been created by him. God himself, the Incarnate Creator, "is." One who holds to such faith can in a way participate in the asking of our questions but he cannot really question without ceasing to be a believer and taking all the consequences of such a step.[12]

Because Christian theology is based upon Christian revelation and Christian faith, it cannot be philosophy and should never pretend to be. For Heidegger, the ontotheological problem of metaphysics is this: In assuming that it knows all about God, it short-circuits the due attention that Being deserves and distorts both God and Being in the process.

I believe Heidegger makes some valid points here, ideas we may find in other writers but which are nonetheless important. But I want

finality and *totality*. I accuse Whitehead of the latter, but not the former. He was aware of the need to abandon claims of "dogmatic certainty" (i.e., finality) in metaphysics.

9. *Identity and Difference*, 56 (translation altered).

10. Ibid., 55 (translation altered).

11. Ibid.

12. Ralph Manheim, trans., *Introduction to Metaphysics* (New Haven, Conn.: Yale University Press, 1959), 6-7 (translation altered).

to defend the distinction between philosophy and theology from the other side, that is, from the side of theology. Just as the philosopher rightly defends the autonomy of his or her discipline against theological preemption, so the theologian can and must defend revelation, and the theology based upon it, from philosophical preemption.

In the past, the writings of process theologians accepted Scripture and Tradition to the extent and degree that they fit into a Whiteheadian metaphysical system, or into an *a priori* conception of what counts as rational.[13] But what is wrong with this? If a system of metaphysics is true, do we not want to fit our theology to the truth it contains? Should theology be irrational? The problem has to do with, in Heidegger's words, how God enters into metaphysics.

The God of metaphysics, as Pascal knew long ago, is not the God of religion, and philosophy is not concerned with the goals and modes of knowing found in religion, namely, salvation and revelation. Christianity is devoted, first and foremost, to Jesus Christ. The Bible, as the book of Christ, is the primary witness to the revelation of God in Christ, at least for Christians. Ecumenical, long-standing Tradition provides us with a deeply Christian understanding of that Book.

By putting metaphysics, or rationality, on top, some process thinkers tended to distort theology from the very start. The goal of Christian theology is to gain a knowledge of God based upon special revelation. The task of theology is not to develop an abstract notion of God or still less to construct systems of logical propositions. The true task of theology, grounded in religious practice and revelatory claims, is to know God and enjoy Her forever. As Suchocki recently wrote, "Theologians work out the reasonableness of faith within a particular construal of reality that is already shaped by Christian faith. . . . Faith does not have to live from pretensions of universal truth, as if it were a God's-eye perspective."[14]

Why is theology necessarily grounded in revelation? To ask this question another way, why does Wesleyan theology rightly insist

13. See, among many examples, Schubert M. Ogden, *The Point of Christology* (San Francisco: Harper & Row, 1982). Ogden tends to privilege rationality more than Cobb and the Claremont school, which focuses on metaphysics or "philosophical theism."
14. Suchocki, *The Fall to Violence*, 49, 54.

on the primacy of Scripture as source and norm of thinking about God? Contemporary American Wesleyan theologians are well aware of the so-called "Wesleyan Quadrilateral."[15] This phrase, developed by Albert C. Outler, is inadequate in its expression, but the substance captures an important aspect of Wesley's thought: the primacy of Scripture and the importance of Tradition. I call this ordering of theological sources the Wesleyan Norms. In my understanding, both the Spirit and the human community are at work in all of the norms. Good and helpful theological traditions are gestured to in Wesley's own texts under a number of signs: "Christian antiquity," the "analogy of faith," or the "Church of England."[16] Such Tradition was a major factor in Wesley's own theological thinking and should remain a norm for us today under the primacy of Scripture. The substance of the Wesleyan Norms captures in a simple way the priority of norms in Wesley's own theology. Wesley, along with the vast majority of Christian thinkers throughout the world and throughout the history of theology, would put Scripture ahead of reason and metaphysics as source and norm for deeply meaningful religious truth. But are they correct on this score?

Before continuing on with this theme of Scripture and revelation, I should like to briefly consider what role philosophy rightly plays in theology. I do not want my process theology friends to think I am some kind of bibliomaniac, without a place for philosophical reflection in theology. In his contribution to the famous *Christian Century* series entitled "How My Mind Has Changed," John B. Cobb Jr. was critical of christocentric theology, stating: "The attempt to rest belief in God *solely* on Jesus Christ is, from the historical perspective, questionable and, from the perspective of systematic theology, illusory."[17] I agree with Cobb. But the question,

---

15. See Donald Thorsen, *The Wesleyan Quadrilateral* (Grand Rapids: Zondervan, 1990); and W. Stephen Gunter, ed., *Wesley and the Quadrilateral* (Nashville: Abingdon Press, 1997).

16. Listing the analogy of faith (basically, some essential doctrines that guide our reading of the Bible) under Tradition is contrary to Wesley's own practice. He would have put it under Scripture because he thought he could read these doctrines directly out of the Bible. Such an old-fashioned view is hermeneutically naïve and unacceptable in the light of current theory. Wesley in fact derived his version of the analogy of faith from the Bible, Christian antiquity, and the Church of England. So I list it under Tradition. For more on this, see the books on the Quadrilateral in the previous note.

17. John B. Cobb Jr., "Christian Natural Theology and Christian Existence," reprinted in *Frontline Theology*, ed. Dean Peerman (Richmond, Va.: John Knox Press, 1967), 40.

again, is about the role and priority of metaphysical theism. What role does philosophy play in theological reflection?

For one thing, philosophical training can bring clarity and logic to the reflective, systematic, and constructive tasks of Christian theology. Philosophy may also provide key ideas necessary to explicate revelation. More than this, philosophers may pose problems of internal coherence within the patterns of life and thought that is Christian tradition, religion, and theology. This is a valuable service that theologians have not ignored over the long history of engagement with philosophical partners. Philosophy can also pose other questions to the Christian religion, giving shape in sharp and poignant ways to the problems of our place and time. But the content of the concept of God, the Blessed Trinity, for and within the Christian religion, cannot be determined by philosophy, even for its own place and time. The gospel is the center of Christianity and the focus of theological reflection. There is a unique reasonableness to the pattern of gospel truth—a deep grammar theology must attend to—which is logically prior to any and all claims from science, philosophy, and the world to set the universal standards of reason.[18] There may be some very vague notion of common sense among most people, but there is no developed and neutral system of standard truths and logics to which theology must conform upon peril of being irrational. Rather, theology can and must shape that inchoate, incipient common sense to fit the patterns of gospel truth before turning to other proposed logics.

We should not say that gospel truth, and it alone, determines the content of the Christian doctrine of God. But Wesleyan theologians must say that revelation is the primary source of the knowledge of God. To help people outside the faith, we should not jettison our special revelation and our special way of life. On the contrary, to help people grapple with questions and to minister to the suffering, we need the strengths of faith in and revelation from Jesus Christ. In Christian theology and in Christian mission, evangelism, worship, and the struggle for peace and justice, Jesus Christ is Lord. Philosophy must return to its own domain and discipline if it seeks to rule.

18. See William Placher, *Unapologetic Theology: A Christian Voice in Pluralistic Conversation* (Louisville: Westminster John Knox Press, 1989); Basil Mitchell, *Faith and Criticism* (New York: Oxford University Press, 1995); and Trevor Hart, *Faith Thinking: The Dynamics of Christian Theology* (Downers Grove, Ill.: InterVarsity Press, 1995). Among many

But why is this so? Why does Christian theology strive for a knowledge of God that is first and foremost grounded in the revelation and person of Jesus? The first, simple reason is that philosophy has sometimes come to dominate the partnership, setting forth a supposed "rational" and universal picture of God that is then developed in theological terms. In such cases, theology has given up its true role in the Church: the role of seeking a saving knowledge of God in Jesus Christ and special revelation. The second reason is more profound. There is no universal, transcultural, and extraperspectival ground upon which a human being can seek to know God. There are various systems of logic and various traditions of rationality. The various world religions have within them claims to special revelation, but these claims are conflicting and dissonant. Significant and saving knowledge of God—the sort that gives life meaning and purpose—is to be found neither in comparative philosophy of religion nor in metaphysics. We can and must seek deep religious truth in particular religious traditions and communities, which are shaped by their particular vision of Ultimate Reality, the meaning of life, ethical practices and religious worship. The theologian has no special place or pure, rational insight but shares this common human condition relative to a deeply meaningful knowledge of God. As Heidegger rightly wrote about the God of the philosophers, "Humanity can neither pray nor sacrifice to this god. Before the *causa sui* humanity can neither fall to its knees in awe nor can it play music and dance before this god."[19] Generic theology have we none, or at least none that is of any deeply religious significance.

Natural theology may have a place in Christian thought and mission, but it is a severely limited place, as handmaiden to evangelical faith. We cannot agree with Cobb's earlier statement that, to reflect on "the whole range of intellectual questions with which modern [humanity] is fated to struggle, natural theology . . . must eschew appeal to any authority not recognized outside the church, such as Scripture, revelation, tradition, or personal religious experience."[20] As a definition this is fine, but it has not been a happy

predecessors is Augustine, *On Christian Doctrine*, trans. Carroll Mason Sparrow (Charlottesville, Va.: University of Virginia Press, 1947).

19. *Identity*, 72 (translation altered).

20. Cobb, "Christian Natural Theology," 41.

project. In its own terms, natural theology *alone* has not found answers to our deepest questions and longings. This is not to say that natural theology has no place in the church. But my point is that we can and must return to the roots of Christian religion and call people into that deeper truth, which is founded exactly and centrally upon Scripture, revelation, tradition, and personal religious experience.

In his volume *A Christian Natural Theology*, Cobb argued against the popular "God is dead" movement because he believed that we have good reasons to believe there is a God. The reasons Cobb gave are basically those of a Whiteheadean philosophy of religion. He recognized that all philosophy begins from some perspective, but a natural theology must not appeal to specifically Christian sources of truth. This seems correct. Even so, those doing specifically Christian theology must accept some philosophical teachings. We always presuppose some philosophical doctrines in developing systematic theology: "The problem, then, is how the theologian should reach his conclusions on those broader questions of general reflection presupposed in his work. . . . What the theologian thus chooses functions for him as a natural theology."[21] Cobb argued that we must choose carefully the philosophical system that we, as Christian theologians, will "adopt and adapt" into our systematic theology.

There is much value in Cobb's arguments concerning theology and philosophy. My point in this essay is to call into question the need for Christian theology to adopt and adapt a complete philosophical system, or metaphysics. I likewise reject Cobb's argument for the priority of natural theology in doctrinal development. It is true that in developing a systematic theology, we must always include some philosophical ideas. But it seems to me a very large jump from this truism to the claim that Christian theology must adopt and adapt a whole *system* of philosophy. I believe the theologian does better by accepting philosophical notions on a piecemeal basis, seeking the inner coherence of gospel truth and adapting those philosophical doctrines which may help him or her, in particular times and places, to advance that truth.

---

21. John B. Cobb Jr., *A Christian Natural Theology: Based on the Thought of Alfred North Whitehead* (Philadelphia: Westminster Press, 1965), 262-63; see also 11-12.

Theologies find themselves in particular religious traditions, accepting the vision, worship, prayer, and practice that is most meaningful—that is, the way of action and faith within a religion that best makes sense of life. A Christian theology that knows what it is, that is conscious of these facts of particularity, will place Jesus Christ at the center of its quest to know God in a deeply personal way. The traditions and practices of the vast consensus of Christians that came before us—the saints, martyrs, and apostles—will all point to Jesus Christ. And in so pointing, they will also point to his Book, the book of Christ, that is the Scriptures.

Wesley was one with this great witness in declaring himself to be a man of one book. Of course Wesley did not read only the Bible: He was very learned. But the Bible was central to his knowledge of Christ and his practice of Christianity. The Bible is not alone in bearing witness to the truth of God. Ecumenical, classical tradition also helps in understanding Scripture, and it guides us into a deeper understanding of Christ (hence Wesley's "analogy of faith"). An encounter with Christ, in the power of the Spirit, is a massively important source for knowledge of him. But these latter sources are subject to the normativity of the Bible, not the other way around.

The meaning of the Bible as text is never fixed, of course, and this witness comes to us in human language and history. But these facts do not alter the primary claim of the principle that, of all the sources of our knowledge of God in the Christian religion, Scripture is primary. The primacy of metaphysics, or generic rationality, can lead to a distortion of genuine Christian theology and cannot be accepted by a reflective Christian doctrinal method. Such a method must reject all claims to supposed universal reason and experience that arise from philosophical systems. We cannot agree, therefore, with Cobb and Griffin when they state that the solution to the problem of philosophical distortion of theology lies in finding the right philosophy.[22] Instead, a Christian theology that understands its place and role in the world will always and everywhere give epistemic honor to our Savior, Jesus Christ. Philosophical systems *per se* do not enter into it.

Should philosophy, then, have nothing to do with God? Such a

---

22. John B. Cobb Jr. and David Ray Griffin, *Process Theology: An Introductory Exposition* (Philadelphia: Westminster Press, 1976), 159.

view is too extreme and too contrary to history to be accurate. Philosophers can and should discuss God. But metaphysics needs to be much more humble than it is in Whitehead's system and in some of the systems of his descendants. My own view is that, after the postmodern critique of enlightenment pretensions to complete Truth with a capital T, metaphysics must remain close to a variety of experiences, close to life and the arts and sciences, and close to human beings. Rather than seeking grand unified systems, metaphysics should humble itself before ordinary life and before the multiplicities of our various experiences, contexts, and stories as human beings. Metaphysics can proceed, if at all, only in a piecemeal fashion. The age of grand metaphysical systems is over, or at least it ought to be. And even a humble, piecemeal metaphysics remains suspect when it seeks to set the terms for Christian theology.

Whitehead did indeed place too much confidence in his metaphysical system, as a few remarks in his lectures on science and the modern world make clear. In *Science and the Modern World*, he claimed, for example, that "these metaphysical chapters are purely descriptive."[23] Now despite whatever else metaphysics may be, it will always be very theoretical and speculative. I have become convinced through both philosophical hermeneutics and the philosophy of science, that all descriptions are already theory-laden. Since metaphysics is an abstract, philosophical theory of what lies behind our everyday experience, attempting to make sense of results from all the arts and sciences, it is the most theory-laden of all. Whitehead fooled himself when he thought (at the time of these lectures) that his metaphysics was purely descriptive.

Whitehead fell into the same trap—the Enlightenment ideal of pure access to truth—when he argued that the metaphysical standpoint is "[antecedent] to any special investigation,"[24] and claimed that within metaphysics, we "put ourselves at the standpoint of a dispassionate consideration of the nature of things."[25] I believe that Whitehead's project of a critique of abstractions (and this chapter of *Science and the Modern World* is called "Abstraction") is a valuable

---

23. Alfred North Whitehead, *Science and the Modern World* (New York: Free Press, 1925), 158.
24. Ibid., 157.
25. Ibid.

one. But his ambition of perfectly clear, "purely descriptive," "dispassionate" metaphysics, which is "antecedent to any special investigation," is simply unbelievable today for good reasons. Perspective and presupposition enter into all epistemic investigation, and *a fortiori* into metaphysics.

Whitehead developed his early speculations in metaphysics into a grand system of ideas in his Gifford Lectures, *Process and Reality*.[26] In this text, it is clear that Whitehead aimed to construct a totalizing metanarrative—that is, a grand system of ideas into which everything and everyone would fit. He set the task of speculative philosophy as nothing less than the "coherent, logical, necessary system of general ideas in terms of which every element of our experience can be interpreted."[27] The goal of metaphysics, he claimed, is to know the essence of the universe: "This doctrine of necessity in universality means that there is an essence to the universe, which forbids relationships beyond itself, as a violation of its rationality. Speculative philosophy seeks that essence."[28] To be fair, Whitehead goes on to note that this is an ideal, a goal that philosophers would never achieve. He recognized that his understanding of metaphysics seemed "overambitious"[29] but pressed forward because rationality demanded the attempt at a system of ideas that described absolutely everything.[30]

I have come to believe that these goals for metaphysics are problematic. I do agree that philosophy should be *coherent*, but when ideas clash, who gets to mediate the debate? There are no neutral, value-free, universal, and objective criteria by which to mediate between all of the already-partial and already-theory-laden experiences of all human beings. Even the attempt seeks to obliterate Otherness, diversity, and variety—the spice of life. Is it even possible to create a system of *necessary* ideas that will describe the world? Will a philosopher take a God's-eye view, even knowing all necessary truths and the interlocking systems of the entire universe? The overambitious character of these goals, which

---

26. Alfred North Whitehead, *Process and Reality: An Essay in Cosmology* (New York: Macmillan, 1929). Page numbers in the text are to this edition, also found in the corrected edition, ed. David Ray Griffin and Donald W. Sherburne (New York: Free Press, 1978).
27. Ibid., 4.
28. Ibid., 6.
29. Ibid., 20-25.
30. Ibid., 6, 23-24.

Whitehead shares with Leibniz and a host of others, is clear at the end of the twentieth century. Philosophy in general, and metaphysics in particular, must adopt more modest goals and must be more realistic about its limitations. I do accept the idea that philosophy is based, in part, upon rational truth, or *a priori* judgments, which I call noetic insights.[31] But noetic insight must be subject to critical, ongoing, and communal testing. Noetic insights may claim to be based upon reason and intuition but in fact are always and everywhere open to revision. Here, Kant's method in metaphysics must be openly repudiated.

But why? What is wrong with a set of *a priori* categories, analytic and synthetic, given as a provisional, but total, description of reality? One answer is inductive and historical: *A priori* categories have, so far, proved inadequate. Another is the more general point that our access to reality is, at best, distorted. Experience does not give us pure sense data. Rather, experience is already and always "my" experience, rooted and grounded in "my" body and "my" worldview, which is limited to "my" place and time. It is thought, and not experience, that reaches beyond these limitations, if anything does. Finally, such totalizing claims have obliterated Otherness and distorted, and at times even harmed, the ideas and bodies of our neighbors. Here, one thinks of the *a priori* attachment to "doing one's duty," a notion traced back to Kant and found in Adolf Eichmann's memoirs.

Metaphysics should be provisional and grounded in local knowledge, in one's limited understanding of the world in which one lives, and the things one can learn from the arts and sciences. Metaphysics is a descriptive philosophy, as Whitehead saw, but it is a humble, piecemeal task. Grand systems of logically necessary ideas do not, and cannot, describe the rich variety and diversity we discover in the world around us. The analysis of a single concept in metaphysics, if correct, is an amazing achievement and one with which we should rest happy. If proper, then the analysis of that single concept will need to be open to the experience of all humanity and the teachings of all the disciplines of the university. Even when this task is done—and it never will be fully—there will be no reason at all to believe either that a grand *system* of such concepts can

---

31. See Bernard Lonergan, *Insight* (London: Longman, Green, 1957).

ever be constructed or that there will be logical, necessary connections between these contingent, humble, and provisional analyses.

Most of my friends who are attracted to process theism are attracted not because it provides a grand metaphysical scheme but because of its theology and its understanding of God and the world. If one presses them, they will refer to the metaphysics. If one criticizes the metaphysics, they will appeal to the theology. It is time, I think, to end this philosophical shell game.

The justification of theological concepts, even after proposed revisions from philosophy, comes neither from appeal to metaphysical systems nor from alien notions of rationality. Rather, such Christian theological justification comes by the lengthy process of communal discussion and by comparing the concept to careful work in biblical, historical, practical, and moral theology. The pattern of Christian truth is found in Christianity, not in general revelation. Of course, we turn to culture, reason, science, and art to criticize, revise, and apply theology. We also turn to these areas for some of the questions and problems that prompt our quest for understanding God. But in this hermeneutical circle, Wesleyan theology gives priority to Scripture and the consensual Tradition of the Church and returns to these points again for guidance and insight.

In this essay, I have tried to turn Heidegger on his head. He claimed that faith corrupts philosophy. But I have argued in the other direction: that a too strong or too early commitment to philosophy distorts the development of truth and reason from Christian sources of insight, especially the whole Bible read in the light of Christ, and from the unified, pre-European Christian tradition. I now would like to anticipate the criticisms that process theology might make of this position and respond to them.

In the 1960s, John B. Cobb Jr. and James M. Robinson edited a volume on the later Heidegger and theology.[32] Given Cobb's contribution to that volume, I believe I can anticipate some criticisms of my position. First, reference could be made to the fact that the text of Scripture is not unified but diverse and even conflicting. As he wrote then, "Once we acknowledge diversity in the Christian

---

32. James M. Robinson and John B. Cobb Jr., eds., *The Later Heidegger and Theology* (New York: Harper & Row, 1963). Page numbers that follow refer to Cobb's chapter in this book.

witness, we are placed as theologians in a situation closely parallel to that of the philosopher."[33] Second, it should be noted that tradition is at least as harmful and distorting as it is helpful. Again, to quote Cobb: "The history of Christian witness poses—it does not answer—the theological question for our own day. . . . Only by this same act of liberation [from tradition] can we attain a renewed openness to God such as that of primitive Christian witness."[34] Finally, the question could be posed about what happens when those outside the Christian faith demand some proof for our beliefs? Shall we not appeal to philosophy at that point? Here we might cite Whitehead, who once wrote that "religion collapses unless its main positions command immediacy of assent."[35] Even if these criticisms are not those of Cobb today, some response to them seems in order.

First of all, I do not believe the diversity of Scripture puts us in a place similar to that of the philosopher. We have a text that, despite its diversity, has an overall consonance and resonance, especially when read as a whole and with Christ at the center. We have a tradition of reading the text that can give shape to the task of biblical theology today without determining the outcome in advance. I reject the notion that the authority of Scripture is based upon the speculative results of historical critical scholarship. Biblical criticism helps us understand the final form of the text, but criticism does not replace the text. Scriptural authority rests upon the texts themselves. And I do not think these texts are a wax nose that may be shaped into any idea we like: There is a responsible hermeneutics that can guide a faithful reading of the Bible for the purpose of doctrine and life.[36]

Second, I do not accept Heidegger's radical rejection of tradition. Rather, I believe, as Hans-Georg Gadamer does, that traditions are both necessary and sometimes quite helpful. There is a common

---

33. Ibid., 187.
34. Ibid., 188.
35. Whitehead, *Science and the Modern World*, 191.
36. See, for example, Roger Lundin, et al., *The Responsibility of Hermeneutics* (Grand Rapids: William B. Eerdmans, 1985); Anthony C. Thiselton, *New Horizons in Hermeneutics: The Theory and Practice of Transforming Biblical Reading* (Grand Rapids: HarperCollins, 1997); John Goldingay, *Models for Interpretation of Scripture* (Grand Rapids: Eerdmans, 1995); Nicholas Wolterstorff, *Divine Discourse: Philosophical Reflections on the Claim that God Speaks* (Cambridge: Cambridge University Press, 1995); and Kevin Vanhoozer, *Is There a Meaning in This Text?* (Grand Rapids: Zondervan, 1998).

core to Christian tradition, especially in its pre-European, intercultural witness to the catholic faith. Of course, slavish attachment to the past is not something I have in mind, but rather a willingness to go with tradition when in doubt and to be guided and shaped by the living faith of classical Christianity.

Finally, the question of proof, or grounds for belief is certain to come up in discussion with one of America's foremost natural theologians. Here I can only repeat my previous point that natural theology should have a very limited role. It has no place in the development of doctrine because it rejects from the start the very sources of insight upon which Christian truth is founded. At best, it can defend a few limited ideas drawn from Christian theological reflection.

I believe we should give reasons for our faith when called upon. Perhaps we can show that other systems of belief and life have problems or defend an idea or two in an *ad hoc* manner in discussion with a particular person or worldview. But natural theology, by definition, cannot determine the content of Christian doctrine. We may have to be satisfied with simply explaining genuine Christian faith as best we can and inviting others to participate in its life, thought, and worship.

The knowledge of God, I have argued in this essay, depends neither upon philosophical systems nor upon supposedly universal concepts and logics. Rather, human reason must be cleansed and redeemed by faith for a meaningful knowledge of God to progress. We should and can discover the deeper patterns of truth and insight in scripture and tradition in order to guide our minds' progress to God. In this manner, to truly know God and enjoy Her forever is the true goal of theology.[37]

37. My thanks to Sally Bruyneel, Randy L. Maddox, Samuel M. Powell, Thomas Lindell, and Thomas Jay Oord for very helpful comments on an earlier version of this essay.

CHAPTER TWELVE

THE BEAUTY OF THE WHOLE:
AESTHETICS IN PROCESS AND WESLEYAN THEOLOGIES

KENTON M. STILES

The theologian is an artist who paints divine images with carefully colored and formed words. Many contrasting theological portraits hang in the gallery of belief, but each unique composition has value. The diversity of these images may well be theology's greatest strength.

Pairing together the portraits contributed by process and Wesleyan theologies for their aesthetic contents may seem, at first, odd. Wesleyan theology has rarely addressed aesthetic issues. Charles Wesley was a gifted poet and hymnodist, and John Wesley occasionally considered aesthetic issues, but their successors have concerned themselves with other theological and ecclesiastical matters.[1] It is not an exaggeration to state that, philosophically speaking, Wesleyanism lacks an aesthetic tradition. Whiteheadian process theology, on the other hand, is thoroughly aesthetic. The process metaphysic itself may be described as an aesthetic, while many of its major themes, including those of creativity, oneness and manyness, beauty, harmony/disharmony, intensity, feeling, and form, are steeped in aesthetic tradition. The pattern set by Alfred North Whitehead in passages of *Process and Reality* (1929) and *Adventures of Ideas* (1933) has been followed frequently by later process thinkers, most notably by Charles Hartshorne, Donald W. Sherburne, John Gilmour, William Dean, and (in philosophical aesthetics proper) Susanne K. Langer.

In this essay, I propose to explore certain aesthetic ideas relevant

---

1. John Wesley's aesthetic comments appear in three general groupings: *Journal* entries relating observations on nature, culture, and the arts; sermons containing thoughts on nature or the human faculties; and three short aesthetic essays: *Thoughts on the Power of Music* (1779), *Works* (Jackson) 13:465-70, *Thoughts upon Taste* (1780), *Works* (Jackson) 13:470-73, and *Thoughts on Genius* (1787), *Works* (Jackson) 13:477-79.

to both process and Wesleyan theologies and thereby to encourage greater harmony between the two. Specifically, I will consider the following areas: (1) the beauty of the whole, (2) grace as the means of God's beautification and enjoyment of the world, (3) the world's experience of charm and satisfaction, (4) Christ as aesthetic form, and (5) the experience of evil as ugliness. The lines of this study are drawn tentatively; the subject matter is suggestive, not exhaustive. What one sees here is merely an impressionistic sketch in process and Wesleyan aesthetics, but all new creations *must* have a genesis!

Two preliminary matters must be addressed. The first concerns the definition of the word "aesthetic." The aesthetic, broadly conceived, includes certain types of objects, ideas, experiences, and interpretive schema. Here, we are primarily concerned with the influences of aesthetic ideas and schemas on specific doctrines and theological method, respectively. Unfortunately, actual aesthetic objects and experiences will be considered only in support of these other two categories. The second matter concerns John Wesley's usefulness. While a contemporary "neo-Wesleyanism" would undoubtedly be more sympathetic to exploring relationships between theology and aesthetics, it is important to reckon with Wesley's personality and theology directly. This essay therefore follows the example of other recent works that attempt to rediscover Wesley's relevance to the present theological environment.

THE BEAUTY OF THE WHOLE

John Wesley's great theological legacy is his doctrine of holiness and its expression through perfect love. In his writings, Wesley consistently correlates this doctrine with two teachings: (1) Jesus' great Commandments, namely, the loving of God absolutely and of one's neighbor as oneself, and (2) the Westminster Catechism, which defines human happiness as being experienced supremely in the worship and enjoyment of God. Although neither source is explicitly aesthetic, the aesthetic need not be excluded from Wesleyan conceptions of holiness and perfect love. Indeed, theological descriptions of holiness cannot be complete until they include the aesthetic. Similarly, a theological aesthetic can be enriched by creative understandings of holiness and perfect love.

The word "holiness" has significant aesthetic connotations. The Greek words αγιασμοζ and αγιωσνη suggest balance, soundness, and unity. In contemporary theology, the balance and unity of the whole is presupposed by two significant concepts: holism, which identifies human existence as a multidimensional unity (including the mental, emotional, social, physical, and aesthetic); and relationality, which identifies our social reality as a God-self-other nexus. Another important aspect of holiness is *teleological* satisfaction. When something fulfills its creative purpose, its value is said to be complete or whole. The beauty of wholeness is not literal aesthetic perfection, however. The God of Genesis 1, for example, does not state that the world is perfect; rather, the value judgment is that the world is *tov* ["very good"], which includes aesthetic goodness and fullness.[2]

The judgment that the world, as a whole, is good has important implications for cosmology. We find this to be true for both the breadth of all worldly entities and the depth of all types of experiences. First, whether one follows process thought's description of an emergent world in which every actuality experiences some degree of satisfaction unique to itself, or whether one instead holds to the classic view of an *ex nihilo* Creator who feels and pronounces satisfaction *for* the world, the consequence is that each actuality possesses an aesthetic value *of kind*. In other words, whether we regard something as being good either inherently or through its graced relation to God, its real value goes beyond mere function to include aesthetic form and feeling. It is good in itself. This is an incarnational aesthetic. Furthermore, when the whole world possesses some degree of aesthetic goodness, all *experiences*—good, evil, or indifferent and beautiful, ugly, or banal—will have a positive aesthetic value as well. These diverse types of experiences introduce difference, variety, and imperfection into the world—qualities that should not be considered a liability. Rather, they help to orient the world toward the goal of greater aesthetic wholeness and toward beauty and unity within diversity.

---

2. Gerhard von Rad, *Genesis*, rev. ed. (Philadelphia: Westminster Press, 1972), 61; Claus Westermann, *Genesis 1–11: A Commentary*, trans. John J. Scullion (Minneapolis: Augsburg Press, 1984), 165-67.

While creatures may struggle to appreciate beauty and wholeness on a grand scale, process theology stresses that only God can ultimately feel the whole of aesthetic beauty. Appreciation through feelings is true of all relationships, whether cosmically between God and the world, socially between the one creature and others, or subatomically between the smallest occasions of experience in complex bodies.

Another correspondence between aesthetics and holiness theology concerns the moral impulse of perfect love as a pattern for behavior. To love one's neighbor truly is to suspend a utilitarian scale for value judgments and to appreciate the worth of others as they are and on their own terms. Here, the classic aesthetic phrases "psychical distance" and "disinterestedness" parallel perfect love.[3] By distance and disinterest, we refer to the tenuous balance existing between art and viewer, subject and object. Ideally, an encounter between the two is marked by free play: The individual will love the other perfectly by (1) lowering predispositions and biases, (2) allowing it to express itself on its own terms, and (3) responding to it in extended play. Play's autonomy or freedom can be distorted however. When one player is dominant, the result is psychological subjectivity: The individual reads too much of oneself into the encounter. Then again, if the other dominates the play relation, then that individual misses significant opportunities for sustained emotional and intellectual encounter. Susanne K. Langer suggests that freedom within aesthetic play depends upon balancing the poles of "aesthetic quality" and "emotional stimulation," which can only occur when individuals suspend their personal needs and utilitarian motives and learn the "language" of art by developing an aesthetic consciousness.[4]

---

3. On "psychical distance," see Edward Bullough, " 'Psychical Distance' as a Factor in Art and as an Aesthetic Principle," *British Journal of Psychology* (1912): 87-98; reprinted in Stephen David Ross, ed., *Art and Its Significance: An Anthology of Aesthetic Theory*, 3rd ed. (Albany, N.Y.: State University of New York Press, 1994), 458-67. On "disinterestedness," see Immanuel Kant, *Critique of Judgment*, trans. J. H. Bernard (New York: Hafner Publishing, 1951), esp. §§2-4, 29, 41.

4. Susanne K. Langer, *Feeling and Form: A Theory of Art* (New York: Charles Scribner's Sons, 1953), 18; Bullough, 461. See also Donald W. Sherburne, *A Whiteheadian Aesthetic: Some Implications of Whitehead's Metaphysical Speculation* (New Haven, Conn.: Yale University Press, 1961), 108-12; and Eva Schaper, "Aesthetic Perception," in *The Relevance of Whitehead*, ed. Ivor Leclerc (New York: Macmillan, 1961), 281-83, for differing and somewhat problematic interpretations of Kant and, in particular, Bullough.

Relational freedom, put in terms of a theology of love, is freedom *from* the self and *for* the other. To act in this manner, whether the other is an individual or an artistic creation, is to love perfectly. A discussion of loving encounter and play demonstrates that theology, aesthetics, and anthropology can speak a common language. Each discipline suggests that relationships, whether devotional, aesthetic, or interpersonal, ought to be characterized by love, freedom, balance, and wholeness. Philosophical aesthetics helps us express and emphasize this in a new manner.

GRACE AS GOD'S LURE AND ENJOYMENT

Theologians normally describe grace *(charis)* as God's sustaining and saving works given freely for our benefit. But *charis* also has aesthetic connotations that provide a basis for identifying grace as the means of God's involvement with the aesthetic: first, as attractiveness or charm; and second, as a completed state of being that includes elements of joy and gratitude.[5] In the following discussion, these two dimensions of grace will be explored under the designations *lure* and *enjoyment*. In process thought, these significant terms correspond to the two natures and types of divine activity, namely, God's primordial and consequent natures.

The God who lures the world draws it lovingly toward beauty. God always has an eye on the Beautiful; as such, God is the conceptual artist *par excellence*. At every moment and with all given circumstances, God imagines for each entity in the world the best possible form of self-actualization—that is, a manner of existence that is most creative, is marked by the greatest depth of experience and feeling, and offers the maximal potential for harmony and enjoyment. God does not keep this perfect primordial imagination private, however. Rather, God's beautiful vision is *felt* by each actuality as a personal lure or aim toward greater feeling, enjoyment, and satisfaction.

---

5. "χαριζ," in William F. Arndt and F. Wilbur Gingrich, *A Greek-English Lexicon of the New Testament and Other Early Christian Literature*, 2nd ed. (Chicago: University of Chicago Press, 1979), 877-78. See, also, the entry for χαρα ("joy") for similarities between these terms, pp. 875-75. Cf. Hans Urs von Balthasar, *The Glory of the Lord: A Theological Aesthetics*, vol. 1., *Seeing the Form*, trans. Erasmo Leiva-Merikakis (San Francisco: Ignatius Press, 1982), 34-35.

It is important to note the centrality of feeling in existing. This is a crucial emphasis of the process metaphysic—and one that is intentional. Although Whitehead was a mathematician and physicist, he did not consider the biological/chemical evolutionary schema sufficient to explain why the world had become what it was and where it appeared to be heading. Life is instead a matter of spirit; reality thus becomes a question of feeling and value. God's involvement in this process, again, is as the One who envisions and extends ultimate values.

Just because God is God, however, does not mean that Beauty is inevitable. God's aesthetic aims are also, in a sense, works of art. As works of the spirit, they are fragile and at risk, contingent and propositional. The power of God's aims is emotive and subtle, not coercive. These visions of beauty may be inadequately incarnated, intentionally marred, or outright rejected. In this sense, God is dependent upon the world according to process thought: The potential of these gracious lures only becomes actual when entities freely act upon them, incarnating them within themselves. This dyad of creative divine grace and free creaturely response should appeal to Wesleyans for its correspondence with their understanding of prevenient grace.

Just as God lures the world by grace, God also enjoys the world through grace, the divine presence in, and involvement with, the world. God does not know the world as secondhand information or abstract data; rather, God *feels* the world, actively receiving and enjoying all its values and emotions. Furthermore, these feelings make a difference to God. God's consequent nature experiences change as divine fullness increases, and the feelings are cherished everlastingly. We may imagine God's aesthetic pleasuring in the world as that of an artist—a Creator in the truest sense—and filled with tender, caring love. And it is out of this love that God envisions even higher aims for the world.

An important aspect of God's experience of aesthetic satisfaction is judgment. We find evidence of this, first and foremost, in Genesis 1. Process thought holds that both of these operations—the feeling of satisfaction and aesthetic judgment—occur as God receives the world (in the consequent nature). The actual breadth and duration of God's judgment lies beyond the human imagination.

Nonetheless, process theology offers the terms of harmony, unity, and satisfaction as symbols that designate God's continual bringing together of all experiences belonging to the world into judgments of overall Beauty.

THE WORLD'S AESTHETIC EXPERIENCE

If God receives aesthetic pleasure, then the world does also—and from a myriad of sources within itself. The world feels God's aesthetic aims and responds creatively to them. Let us now consider two aspects of this response. The first concerns the response itself and asks the question: Why do we respond to the aesthetic? The second, not surprisingly, inquires into the nature of aesthetic satisfaction. The obvious parallel between this section, the world's experience of the aesthetic *as* charm and satisfaction, and the preceding discussion, God's aesthetic experience through luring grace and enjoyment, is a natural progression for this study.

The classic question of beauty asks what gives an object its aesthetic charm. Beauty was once thought to be a medium of transcendence; art represented its world of ideal forms. These notions are exploded myths for contemporary art historians who view them as social constructs—ideas mirroring a given culture's social, political, and economic ideals. Nonetheless, the questions of aesthetic charm and of the attractive power of art remain.

Surprisingly, Wesley expresses some strong opinions on such matters. In thirty different sermons, nearly one-fifth of the total he published, he classifies everything that charms the human mind and senses according to three categories found in 1 John 2:16: "The desire of the flesh" refers to that which appeals to the five senses; "the desire of the eye" appeals to the imagination and its tastes for the novel, sublime, and beautiful; and "the pride of life" is the desire for power and grandeur (in the aesthetic realm, art collecting, and connoisseurship). In general, while Wesley approaches all worldly pleasures—including the aesthetic—with extreme caution, it is an overstatement to suggest that he regards them to be inherently evil or as direct causes of sin.

Wesley's tripartite theory of perception is relevant to the question of charm. He suggests that perception, which leads to knowledge of both the world and God, occurs through the physical senses, rational inference, and the spiritual senses. Presumably, then, there are three varieties of charm. Unfortunately, Wesley does not elaborate his ideas further in relation to the aesthetic. The aesthetic is not one of his chief concerns. Nonetheless, his ideas on perception are extremely congenial to process theology, which maintains that in each moment, the divine relates to every dipolar entity in the world through God's presence and aims.

The process notion of dipolarity has several useful applications. For example, dipolarity is one corrective response to aesthetic dualisms that bifurcate form and content. And with regard to the question of aesthetic charm, the mental image of dipolarity is like the alluring imbalance found in art. Indeed, art's imbalance, or indefiniteness, implied by traditional aesthetic phrases such as "*je ne sais quoi*" and "purposiveness without purpose," is often identified as the source of its power.

Susanne K. Langer is the greatest promoter of the dipolar nature of aesthetic charm. Her prominent phrases, "significant form," "feeling-forms," and "objectified feeling," plus her definition of art as "the creation of forms symbolic of human feeling," all point toward the notion of dipolarity.[6] Langer's ideas presuppose that the elements of significance or feeling incarnate within an aesthetic creation serve to communicate a nonverbal meaning that must be *felt* for full aesthetic expression to occur. Also presupposed is the idea of aesthetic encounter as event. In Langer's writings, we find an implicit Whiteheadian idea that Donald W. Sherburne forcefully advances, namely, that aesthetic creations are propositions.

In Whiteheadian process philosophy, a proposition is something interesting meant for encounter. An aesthetic creation is a unique proposition for two reasons: First, it is specifically meant to be encountered aesthetically; second, it is self-reflexive. By the latter, we mean that the creation proposes itself as the object of aesthetic encounter, but in so doing it also acts as a subject—a subject that possesses being, freedom, and enjoyment of its own.

---

6. Langer, *Philosophy in a New Key: A Study in the Symbolism of Reason, Rite, and Art*, 3rd ed. (Cambridge, Mass.: Harvard University Press, 1969), 232-35, 240ff.; and *Feeling and Form*, 19-23, 40.

The concept of aesthetic play, which complements the process view of art as dipolar and propositional, is highly influential in contemporary aesthetics and concludes our discussion of aesthetic charm and lure. Aesthetic play, first of all, must be free. To love the aesthetic perfectly is to maintain psychical distance and establish freedom; play thus exists somewhere "in between" the human and aesthetic subjects. Play, in a sense, is suspended animation: suspended when everyday expectations are set aside and animated as play takes on a life of its own, involving, but distinct from, its subjects. Play's power resides in the relational potential presented by an aesthetic creation. Play offers to us an encounter that transcends the ordinary and an experience that is greater than the sum of its parts. Furthermore, the to-and-fro movement of play is inviting because it corresponds to a basic human need for enjoyment.[7] It is important to note, in conclusion, that the concept of aesthetic play reminds us that art lures us into *active* encounter. Art is only itself when reincarnated in play. It propositions the viewer: "Take your own shot. Recreate me. Understand me." And when an aesthetic encounter is over, the art is, once again, incomplete. Art is art only *during* the play-event—this is its relational lure.

The consummation of aesthetic play is feelings of satisfaction. As we consider this second aspect of the world's aesthetic experience, we must recognize that satisfaction is ephemeral. Pleasure fades over time; the novel becomes all too familiar; encounters may lack vitality or become lopsided; interest and attentiveness may lessen due to personal deficiencies. The bottom line is this: The aesthetic offers no guarantees. Not everyone who encounters the aesthetic will be fully taken up in play and will experience satisfaction. Nonetheless, the power of aesthetic play can be overwhelming. Aestheticians frequently use intensely expressive language to communicate play's effects: "It moved me." "I felt like I was in another world." "It was sheer bliss, ecstasy!" "It was truly intoxicating." Such statements obviously represent an extreme and ideal form of encounter, but it is a real one nonetheless.

The satisfaction felt by an artist, as creator of a work of art, deserves

7. See Hans-Georg Gadamer, *Truth and Method*, 2nd rev. ed., trans. Joel Weinsheimer and Donald G. Marshall (New York: Crossroad Publishing, 1989), 101-34. Gadamer, the twentieth century's leading proponent of aesthetic play, is deeply indebted to the work of Kant and Friedrich Schiller, who each significantly developed and popularized this notion.

special attention. All mystique aside, artists do experience unique forms of enjoyment both during the creative process and when a work is completed. But here it is more helpful to turn to theory than to artists' statements because the latter vary greatly and tend to be overly subjective, philosophical, or dramatic. In fact, process theory helps curtail at least one myth of the genius-artist. As we have seen, process theologians maintain that God's initial aims precede all worldly actions. An artist therefore cannot create out of pure imagination; rather, he or she discovers a proposition and cocreates with God. Yet he or she does possess a measure of genius because it is he or she who finds this inspired idea, incorporates his or her own personality and feelings into the work, chooses the medium and expressive techniques, and actually makes the work of art.[8] An artist's satisfaction will then include elements of the transcendence of inspiration, the wonder of discovery, and the joys and pains of the creative act.

Aesthetic satisfaction may also be felt more practically through the transformation of the everyday. In a relational worldview, enjoyment can remain neither private nor restricted to the past. Rather, these feelings act upon the present through transformed personalities, altered tastes, and changed manners of living. An encounter with the beautiful eventually beautifies all other dimensions of life. Once experienced, beauty cannot be escaped or forgotten.

The aesthetic impulse, which here means the personal desire for repeated encounters with the beautiful, parallels the Whiteheadian notion of the art process. Whitehead suggests that life is guided by a "three-fold urge" that is distinctly aesthetic: "The art of life is *first* to be alive, *secondly* to be alive in a satisfactory way, and *thirdly* to acquire an increase in satisfaction."[9] While it is true that aesthetic experience blossoms when creations are treated as ends in themselves (i.e., loved perfectly) rather than as means to an end, this does not mean that the aesthetic offers no practical benefits. Life *is* better with art. This is the conviction behind Sherburne's promotion of an "Art for Life's Sake" ethic.[10] Indeed, because the aesthetic

---

8. Sherburne, *A Whiteheadian Aesthetic*, 180.

9. Whitehead, *The Function of Reason* (Boston: Beacon Press, 1929), 8; quoted in Sherburne, *Whiteheadian Aesthetic*, 196.

10. Sherburne, *A Whiteheadian Aesthetic*, 193-202.

is a necessary component of humanity's multidimensional existence, refusing to experience the aesthetic is denying life in all its
wholeness.

A final type of aesthetic satisfaction we humans feel relates to
divine glory. The glory that produces this satisfaction should not be
confused with the visible splendor of the Shekinah or a mystical
beatific vision. Nor is it specifically the enjoyment felt when one
adequately fulfills humanity's "chief end" in worshiping God. No,
here we must settle instead for something of a more naturalistic
form. The glory in question is subtly felt by encountering "traces"
of God in an art proposition—that is, when God's ultimate creativity is discovered within and behind the lure and play of art. God's
glory is, after all, truly present in the world because God is continually and actively present in the world through initial aims.
Whitehead goes so far as to suggest that the world exists by its
incarnation of God.

Hans Urs von Balthasar, the twentieth-century theologian most
captivated by theological aesthetics, also feels that glory and divine
traces are found in aesthetic creations. He argues that

> the beautiful is above all a *form*, and the light does not fall on
> this form from above and from outside, rather it breaks forth from
> within the form's interior. . . . Visible form not only "points" to an
> invisible, unfathomable mystery; form is the apparition of this mys-
> tery, and reveals it while, naturally, at the same time protecting and
> veiling it. . . . The content *(Gehalt)* does not lie behind the form
> *(Gestalt)*, but within it.[11]

Von Balthasar's location of form within content—yet another
response to aesthetic duality—highlights art's symbolic and almost
mystical nature. While von Balthasar has not stated that God is the
secret form or content of the aesthetic, he does construct his aesthetic within *theological* boundaries and certainly writes for those
who see with the eyes of faith. So while most people can apprehend and appreciate the mysterious qualities that make art art,
only believers can comprehend this. The transfer from beauty to
glory is made by means of analogy.

---

11. Von Balthasar, *The Glory of the Lord* 1:151.

The aesthetics of glory has some difficulties. Process theology's naturalism differs from von Balthasar's analogical method. Furthermore, to find God "behind" art or even "within" the aesthetic seems intellectually dishonest to a secular philosopher. There is also the question of how divine traces, or aims, are felt, much less enjoyed as satisfaction. At the least, however, we can emphasize a simple connection between aesthetics and glory: The God who is the ultimate genesis of beauty and goodness, whether as omnipotent Creator or all-creative Lure, is worthy of worship and may be enjoyed. Regardless of how aesthetic creations come to be, their glory and satisfaction ultimately refer the faithful to God.

CHRIST, BEAUTY'S LIVING FORM

A Christian theological aesthetics, by definition, must come to terms with the aesthetic value of Jesus Christ. Over centuries, this has most commonly occurred in connection with Jesus' role as divine Image and Form, as God's glory, or as Beauty itself. Not all Christologies are aesthetic; indeed, many will not be since the intellectual biases and existential needs appropriate to certain groups and individuals commonly influence how they interpret Christ's significance. Within each hermeneutical circle, a unique portrait of Christ is drawn. But this fluidity in Christ's value should not be viewed as a liability; on the contrary, this flux in interpretive form and content adds vitality to Christian theology by encouraging free aesthetic-theological play. The depth of meaning(s) found in Christ's forms aptly demonstrates Charles Hartshorne's conviction that "deity is the one theme worthy of infinite variations."[12]

Diversity can nonetheless prove to be a challenge, especially for any attempt to harmonize the process and Wesleyan images of Christ. Much of the difficulty lies with a Wesleyan soteriological approach to Christology—a tendency that can be traced back to its founder. While Wesley is somewhat systematic in his work, exploring Christ's mission through the traditional categories of Prophet,

---

12. Charles Hartshorne, "The Aesthetic Dimensions of Religious Experience," in James Franklin Harris, ed., *Logic, God and Metaphysics* (Boston: Kluwer Academic Publishers, 1992), 14.

Priest, and King, his Christology is circumscribed by the larger issue of salvation from, and atonement for, personal sin. Granted, history may judge salvation from sin as the center of the gospel, but such narrow views of Christ and salvation are insufficient in a world that is concerned with more than an individual's soul. Our contemporary setting demands that a Christology is true to multi-dimensional experience and that salvation involves one's whole being—not to mention the world's whole being. Here we return to our theme of "the beauty of the whole."

Process theology offers a grander, more expansive image of Christ—an image that is also inherently aesthetic. While expressions of process Christology vary within the movement, the general point of convergence is the incarnation of the creative Logos within Jesus Christ, the incarnate power of God's creative transformation and transcendence.[13] This Logos is no stranger: It has already been encountered above as God's creative presence that every worldly entity feels in the initial phase of each moment of becoming. Since everything within the world exists by acting upon God's aims (i.e., in response to the Logos), the incarnation of the Logos—Christ—occurs on a cosmic scale. Wherever there is zest for life, novelty, creativity, and beauty, there also is Christ in its midst.

This conception of Christ as a living form in life's art process may seem to diminish the significance of the historical Jesus or the dramatic grace-sin-salvation movement. When viewed from another angle, however, Christ's value and role have been clarified. First, it sets in his proper place a Jesus who, in his role as *Salvator Mundi*, frequently eclipses God. Christ is "divine" as the perfectly incarnated Logos but is still the form *of* God. Second, it reminds us that Christ, while risen to God, is still active in the world. The creative word of Genesis 1 and John 1 has not stopped speaking to creation. Third, and with special regard for this study's understanding of the "whole," it requires that both spirituality and Christology be

---

13. See, for example, John B. Cobb Jr., and David Ray Griffin, *Process Theology: An Introductory Exposition* (Philadelphia: Westminster Press, 1976), chap. 6; Marjorie Hewitt Suchocki, *God-Christ-Church: A Practical Guide to Process Theology* (New York: Crossroad Publishing, 1995), chap. 10; Marjorie Hewitt Suchocki, *The Fall to Violence: Original Sin in Relational Theology* (New York: Continuum, 1995), chap. 2; and, in particular, John B. Cobb Jr., *Christ in a Pluralistic Age* (Philadelphia: Westminster Press, 1975), chaps. 1-4.

kept in perspective. With regard to the former, we are reminded that faith is but one aspect of the larger whole of multidimensional life. The spiritual should not dominate the physical or emotional, for example. As to the latter point, we find that Christ's value need not be determined by soteriology; rather, Christology may now be much more broadly conceived as an organic element of cosmology and Creation.

The words describing Christ as "beauty's living form" are carefully chosen. The beauty in question is, of course, God's creative intentions for the world. In Jesus Christ alone, the competing center of *self* is transparent to God's creative purposes, allowing the Logos to be incarnated in his being. Here, divine content is purely united with human form, revealing Jesus as the Christ—or, in von Balthasar's words, revealing the Logos who "breaks forth from within [Jesus'] interior."[14] And as we have seen above, the influence of this beautifying form is constantly felt in the world.

To follow God's higher aims and incarnate Christ in the world is to live beautifully in the world. Ethics thus offers an appropriate conclusion to this section. With regard to ethics, both process thought and (surprisingly) Wesley find a connection between Beauty and the Good, an idea that frequently surfaces in the history of aesthetics. In his short essay *Thoughts upon Taste*, Wesley suggests that an ethic of love satisfies the human taste for beauty at an even higher level. He writes:

> May we not likewise observe, that there is a beauty in virtue, in gratitude, and disinterested benevolence? And have not many, at least, a taste for this? Do they not discern and relish it, wherever they find it? Yea, does it not give them one of the most delicate pleasures whereof the human mind is capable? Is not this taste of infinitely more value, than a taste for any or all the pleasures of the imagination? And is not this pleasure infinitely more delicate, than any that ever resulted, yea, or can result, from the utmost refinements of music, poetry, or painting?[15]

Both the Wesleyan and process traditions emphasize the need for moral action through perfectly loving others, the world, and self.

---

14. Von Balthasar, *The Glory of the Lord*, 1:151.
15. "Thoughts upon Taste," §10, *Works* (Jackson) 13:467.

To live the life of Christ is to be God's agent of creative transformation in the world, but it is never enough simply to emulate Jesus Christ. One must "be" Christ instead, acting freely and—if need be—radically as a living form through which the Logos affects the world, working toward the new and beautiful. The necessary correlate to moral action is, ironically, a special type of *inaction*. Process thought emphasizes that relational power is found in both influencing others and being influenced by them. Appropriately, a model of moral action is found in the ministry of Jesus, a man who listened to people, received their touches, and deeply felt their pains. After putting others before self, one is then able to act creatively with more compassion, justice, and beauty.

Evil and the Ugly

Since the publication of David Ray Griffin's *God, Power, and Evil: A Process Theodicy*, the possibility of using an aesthetic perspective to address the problem of evil has provoked significant interest. The idea of an aesthetic theodicy is not new. Saint Augustine, best known for his free-will defense of God and evil's existence, also provides one of the earliest and best examples of a theodicy that is aesthetic. What has generally gone unrecognized among Wesleyan theologians, however, is the fact that it is precisely when Wesley considers the subjects of natural beauty and the problem of evil that he comes closest to developing a full theological aesthetic. We find this specifically in two sermons: "God's Approbation of His Works" and "The General Deliverance."

We must be cautious about identifying definite points of correspondence between process and Wesleyan views on the problem of evil. Wesley's own views are underdeveloped and dated, and some process positions would likely cause Wesley—and some of his followers—to squirm. The primary problem is the question of the nature and extent of God's power. Wesley's God, while loving and respective of worldly freedom, possesses a sovereign power that is essentially unilateral in its orientation. Process theology conceives of God's power as dynamic (i.e., creative-responsive) and social. Because God can be resisted and is incapable of sufficient causation, God's power is "omnipotent" in the sense that it extends to everything within the world at every moment and is unsurpassable in its capacity to affect and be affected. This having been said, we now turn to evil and the ugly.

Evil and ugliness are necessary to a theological aesthetic. Aesthetics involves valuation, and valuation requires difference. Harmony, for example, is only felt in relation to disharmony. But where an emanational aesthetic—such as in Augustine or Wesley— interprets evil *derivatively* (that is, as a diminishing or corruption of the good), in the process metaphysic, evil is a *synthetic* and naturally constitutive element that, despite its immediate and lasting destructive effects, possesses a definite and ontologically distinct value. While discussions of many such particulars of Whitehead's theodicy appear elsewhere, a few implications must be considered. The first of these is that evil, in the forms of discord, triviality, disruption, and ugliness, occurs at all levels of life. Whitehead flatly states, "The nature of evil is that the characters of things are mutually obstructive."[16] Opposition is a given. The natural world is contingent, and every actuality, every "one" within it, forms out of the "many."

Evil is therefore required not only for valuation but also for Creativity itself. Evil introduces a jarring element of syncopation into our world of rhythmic processes. Whitehead explains:

> Progress is founded upon the experience of discordant feelings. . . . Thus the contribution to Beauty which can be supplied by Discord— it itself destructive and evil—is the positive feeling of a quick shift or aim from the tameness of outworn perfection to some other ideal with its freshness still upon it. Thus the value of Discord is a tribute to the merits of Imperfection.[17]

The creation and experience of new forms of beauty and goodness entail greater risk—the possibility that loss can occur through great evil and discord. Or, as common wisdom reminds us, "The higher you fly, the further you fall."

Process thought's understanding of evil is more rich, complex,

---

16. Whitehead, *Process and Reality*, corrected ed., ed. David Ray Griffin and Donald W. Sherburne (New York: Free Press, 1978), 340.

17. Whitehead, *Adventures of Ideas* (New York: Free Press, 1933), 257.

and value intensive than Wesley's. The most creative idea Wesley expresses in his aesthetic discussions of evil is the conviction that the world actually existed in an ideal form prior to humanity's fall. Indeed, he waxes poetic as he imagines creation's primordial perfection:

> [Humanity] saw with unspeakable pleasure the order, the beauty, the harmony of all the creatures: of all animated, all inanimate nature—the serenity of the skies, the sun walking in brightness, the sweetly variegated clothing of the earth; the trees, the fruits, the flowers, "And liquid lapse of murmuring streams." Nor was this pleasure interrupted by evil of any kind. It had no alloy of sorrow or pain, whether of body or mind. . . . And to crown all, [humanity] was immortal.[18]

Wesley is so enthralled by the whole of this beauty that he longingly considers the original perfections of almost every level of creation—even down to insects, plants, and rocks!

Wesley feels that the travails of nature and the existence of evil can be traced back to the Fall. As freedom of the will led to sin, and sin led to death, so human death led to the groaning and suffering of all creation. This is not to say, however, that Wesley feels natural beauty and order have been destroyed entirely. Rather, his thoughts on nature and evil parallel his views of humanity and sin: Corruption sickens all relationships and realities.[19] While creation *per se* is still inherently good and humanity still possesses some moral capability, nothing remains untouched by evil's ugliness. Thus, for Wesley, the restoration of goodness, beauty, and wholeness in the world ultimately depends upon God's eschatological intervention in the New Creation.

Evil primarily has a human face for Wesley. The ugliness he sees is personal sin, social injustice, and general rebellion against God. Accordingly, his personal mission is to offer individuals the hope of personal transformation, rather than to engage in metaphysical speculation. It is therefore hardly surprising that when he

---

18. Sermon 60, "The General Deliverance," §1.2, *Works* 2:439-40.

19. See especially Randy L. Maddox, *Responsible Grace: John Wesley's Practical Theology* (Nashville: Kingswood Books, 1994), 73-83, for a discussion of (1) how early Greek Christian writers influenced the development of a *therapeutic* motif in Wesley's theological anthropology, and (2) to what extent one can call humanity "totally" depraved.

does encounter something aesthetically pleasing and describes the experience in his *Journal*, he eventually reminds himself that his own calling and the ultimate enjoyment is higher than the things of this earth.

Both process and Wesleyan theologies agree that evil spawns relational ugliness, but balancing their respective views of evil is difficult. Process thought insists that evil is real, stubbornly persistent, and systematically pervasive. Because of this, evil cannot be instantaneously overcome. God directs us toward the beautiful, but the power of transformation requires actions from nondivine individuals. Furthermore, the process God is affected by pain and ugliness. God feels all mental and physical valuations of evil, God suffers, and God does so continually because nothing is lost in God.

Some Wesleyans will struggle with some of the foregoing ideas, but this does not prevent Wesleyan theology from complementing the process understanding of evil at several points. First, it agrees that evil's ugliness is a systemic and pervasive distortion of actualities and relationships. Second, it maintains that only God can provide the hope for, and vision of, a new and beautiful future. Third, it stresses that God's gracious interactions with the world are preveniently fitted to actual conditions. Fourth, its evangelistic practices imply that the experience of evil provides individuals with an ultimate reference point for qualitatively judging the value of one's life. This is Wesleyan theology's greatest insight in respect to evil. Salvation and the beauty of holiness may be most fully appreciated when compared to the ugliness, pain, and brokenness of life that have been felt in the past. Confronting evil's ugliness thus has evangelistic and didactic significance.

CONCLUSIONS

The power of the aesthetic, while significant, is not sufficient to overcome certain differences between process theology and traditional theistic Wesleyanism. However, the aesthetic does provide a creative and relatively unexplored medium in which theologians can play between the two perspectives. On the one hand, Wesleyan theology can grow and be enriched by experimenting with aesthetic theological methods, such as one finds in process theology, and by thoroughly exploring aesthetic ideas and doctrinal dimensions. The practice of Wesleyan churches will also have deeper value for parishioners when the use of aesthetic methods for personal growth, devotional life, and corporate worship are encouraged and expanded. It matters not where the aesthetic is encountered, whether in a gallery, concert hall, retreat center, or sanctuary, but *that* it is encountered. It is imperative that the aesthetic, in all of its depth and breadth, be explored. On the other hand, as an intellectual movement process theology lacks ecclesiastical and liturgical ties. It may benefit from continuing to interact with Wesleyanism's diverse groups and respective liturgical, theological, and ethical histories.

With final words, we turn to worship, the first words of Christian theology. John Wesley's discussions of happiness and the aesthetic repeatedly remind us that worship is the ultimate human end. True worship, according to the Westminster Catechism, has aesthetic benefits: the enjoyment of God as glory and the beauty that satisfies most fully. We also recognize that aesthetically significant worship adds profound depth and richness to one's encounter with God. Psalm 29:2 exhorts God's faithful to "worship the LORD in the beauty of holiness" (KJV). This verse is an apt reminder that worship and holiness and the beautiful and the whole, are deeply and intricately related.

CHAPTER THIRTEEN

BLACK THEOLOGY AND A MORE PROTESTANT APPROACH TO WESLEYAN-PROCESS DIALOGUE

THEODORE WALKER JR.

In his book *The Church and Morality: An Ecumenical and Catholic Approach*, Father Charles E. Curran describes and prescribes churchly discourse with other denominations, faiths, religions, and secular philosophies with emphasis upon what is common.[1] Curran calls this an "ecumenical and catholic approach." In August 1983, a Bicentennial Theological Consultation entitled "Wesleyan Theology and the Next Century" was held at Emory University for the purpose of exploring "affinities" between the Methodist heritage and contemporary theology and ethics. A working group on process theology and Wesleyan thought explored affinities between Wesleyan thought and process theology. This 1983 exploration of affinities fits with Curran's account of an "ecumenical and catholic approach." Now, at the turn of the millennium, Wesleyan-process dialogue continues to be predominantly ecumenical and catholic in approach.

A MORE PROTESTANT APPROACH

The deliberation in this essay employs a more protestant approach. A more protestant approach is authorized by black churchly relations to white Wesleyan-Methodism. In North America, independent black Protestantism, in general, and independent black Methodism, in particular, originated from black protests against oppressive white Protestant churches. Both The African Methodist Episcopal (AME) Church and The African Methodist

---

1. Charles E. Curran, *The Church and Morality: An Ecumenical and Catholic Approach* (Minneapolis: Fortress Press, 1993).

Episcopal Zion (AMEZ) Church were born of black protests against, and exodus-separation from, white North American Methodism. Given these black protestant relations to white North American Methodism, identifying affinities between the Wesleyan-Methodist heritage and process theology is not an adequate witness to the truth and value of process theology. On the contrary, from the perspective of black theology, affinity with oppressive aspects of white North American Methodism is more discredit than credit. Where black theological social ethics seeks a critical measure of, and constructive contribution to, Wesleyan-process dialogue, there is need for a more protestant than ecumenical approach.

In his August 1983 contribution to the Bicentennial Theological Consultation Working Group on Process Theology and Wesleyan Thought, entitled "Process Theology and the Wesleyan Witness," Schubert M. Ogden identified six "affinities" between process theology and the Wesleyan witness: (1) rational credibility, (2) rootage in experiences including and beyond sense perception, (3) qualified pluralism, (4) authenticity as trust in and loyalty to divine love, (5) bias toward praxis and (6) concern to overcome homocentrism. I offer the following critical deliberation on the last two of the six affinities identified by Ogden: "bias toward praxis" and "concern to overcome homocentrism."[2]

BIAS TOWARD ORTHOPRAXIS AND THE BLACK SEPARATIST WITNESS AGAINST/FOR METHODIST PRAXIS

According to Ogden, Wesley's "bias toward praxis" is bias toward good works essential to salvation and toward "orthopraxis" over mere orthodoxy.[3] Moreover, given modern historical consciousness, Ogden contends that sharing this Wesleyan bias today requires conceiving of Christian theology in terms that are specifically political and liberation oriented.[4] Ogden sees a similar bias in

---

2. Schubert M. Ogden, "Process Theology and the Wesleyan Witness," *Perkins School of Theology Journal* 37:3 (1984): 18-33; reprinted as chap. 1.
3. Ibid., 30.
4. Ibid. See also Schubert M. Ogden, "The Concept of a Theology of Liberation: Must a Christian Theology Today Be So Conceived?" in *The Challenge of Liberation Theology: A First World Response*, ed. Brian Mahan and Dale Richesin (Maryknoll, N.Y.: Orbis Books, 1981), 127-40.

process theology, especially as it has developed more recently. Accordingly, bias toward orthopraxis is a point of affinity between process theology and the Wesleyan witness.

Obviously, bias toward orthopraxis is also a point of affinity to liberation theologies. This affinity has been acknowledged and developed by Ogden and other Wesleyan-process theologians making their own distinctive contributions to liberation theology.[5]

In the case of North American black liberation theologies, especially those black liberation theologies informed by AME and AMEZ origins, this affinity (bias toward orthopraxis) with process theology and the Wesleyan witness yields witness against the historical praxis of North American white Wesleyan-Methodist churches.

For instance, white members of St. George Methodist Episcopal Church in Philadelphia were so oppressive of their black members that in 1787, under the leadership of Richard Allen (a former slave) and Absalom Jones, black members separated themselves from that white congregation and formed their own independent black congregation—the "Free African Society."[6] This growing Allenite congregation built and dedicated Bethel Church in Philadelphia in 1794.[7] Then in April 1816, the "Mother Bethel" congregation united with black separatist Methodists from Baltimore and other places to create The African Methodist Episcopal Church.

Similarly, white members of the John Street Methodist Episcopal Church of New York City were so oppressive of their black members that in 1796, black members, under the leadership of James Varick and Peter Williams (a former slave), separated themselves

---

5. For examples of Wesleyan process theologians emphasizing orthopraxis and contributing to liberation theology, see *Process Studies: Special Issue on Liberation Theology* 14.2 (Summer 1985), ed. Joseph A. Bracken; especially John B. Cobb Jr., "Points of Contact between Process Theology and Liberation Theology in Matters of Faith and Justice"; Schubert M. Ogden, "The Metaphysics of Faith and Justice"; and Marjorie Suchocki, "Weaving the World." See also Schubert M. Ogden, *Faith and Freedom: Toward a Theology of Liberation* (Nashville: Abingdon Press, 1979). Other notable Wesleyan process theologians emphasizing orthopraxis and other points of contact with liberation theology include Jay McDaniel, Mary Elizabeth Mullino Moore, and Henry James Young.

6. Gayraud S. Wilmore, "Richard Allen and the Free African Society," in *Black Religion and Black Radicalism: An Interpretation of the Religious History of Afro-American People* (Maryknoll, N.Y.: Orbis Books, 1984), 80-84.

7. Bishop William J. Walls, *The African Methodist Episcopal Zion Church: Reality of the Black Church* (Charlotte, N.C.: African Methodist Episcopal Zion Publishing, 1974), 28. See especially chap. 3, "The Period of Organizational Consciousness in America."

from that white congregation and formed a separate black Methodist society. By 1800, that society had become "Zion Church." In 1801, Zion Church was incorporated as "The African Methodist Episcopal Church in New York City." In 1820, this now larger congregation of Zionites calling itself the African Methodist Episcopal Zion Church of New York City united with Asbury African Methodist Episcopal Church of New York City and officially "voted themselves out of the Methodist Episcopal Church and published their first Discipline,"[8] thereby creating The African Methodist Episcopal Church in America.[9] The 1820 Founders' Address signed by Abraham Thompson, James Varick, and William Miller called for "little alteration" in the Discipline.[10] According to the Founders' Address, the differences leading to separation were ethical and practical—matters of "ecclesiastical government" and "limited access" to ordination and other churchly privileges "in consequence of the difference of color." [11] At an 1848 General Conference, The African Methodist Episcopal Church in America distinguished itself from the Philadelphia Allenites (also called African Methodist Episcopal Church) and reaffirmed its Zionite origin by changing its name to The African Methodist Episcopal Zion Church.[12]

North American Methodism enjoyed early experiments with black-white racial integration. Unfortunately, even in the best of instances, churchly integration was under racially oppressive terms resembling white-black relations in the surrounding secular world. For example, as early as 1790, the first Methodist church in the Fayetteville, North Carolina, area had a congregation of blacks and whites. And living in "a shed at the pulpit end of the church" was the famous black preacher who founded that church, Henry Evans, called the "father of the Methodist Church, white and black, in Fayetteville" by Bishop William Capers.[13] Unfortunately, even with the black Henry Evans as preacher, seating arrangements favored whites over blacks: Whites were seated first starting from the front and blacks to the rear. As the fame of Henry Evans

---

8. Ibid., 48.

9. Wilmore, "Richard Allen," 85; Walls, *AMEZ Church*, 49.

10. Walls, *AMEZ Church*, 49.

11. Ibid.

12. Ibid., 50; C. Eric Lincoln and Lawrence H. Mamiya, *The Black Church in African American Experience* (Durham, N.C.: Duke University Press, 1990), 57-58.

13. Walls, *AMEZ Church*, 24.

increased and the Sunday morning congregation grew larger, blacks were altogether crowded out of the sanctuary and came to be seated in subsequently constructed wings ("sheds") to the right and left of the pulpit. At this point, the church took on a strangely colored cruciform shape: Evans's residence to the north, black worshipers in the east and west wings, and a white congregation extending south of a pulpit occupied by a black preacher. Obviously, this would not long endure. Evans died in 1810, and this cruciform began to separate by color. Eventually, the black members of Evans Metropolitan Church united with a black separatist strand of the Wesleyan-Methodist heritage, being received into the AMEZ Church in 1866.[14] Other early North American churchly experiments with black-white integration also progressed from black membership under oppressive conditions to black protests (largely ignored by whites) followed by separation and reformation.[15]

The North American black exodus witnessing against oppressive churchly praxis also implied a witness favoring churchly praxis over prevailing secular praxis. For all churchly oppressions of black members, the mere fact that there were black members (typically consigned to seating in the rear or gallery) and black preachers (typically licensed to preach but not ordained as elders) witnessed to a vast improvement over secular master-slave, human-commodity, and white-black relations. For reason of never having included blacks as members, few if any other predominantly white pre-Civil War organizations (social, cultural, political, or economic) could have experienced a significant black exodus. And even today, for this same reason and to their discredit relative to churches, many secular corporations and institutions have never experienced the possibility of a black exodus. Concerning early North American churchly experiments with racial integration, the possibility of nonviolent black protest and exodus indicated significant moral improvement over the prevailing secular white-black relations (slavery), and the actual black exodus indicated a seriously inadequate churchly quest for orthopraxis.

---

14. Ibid., 24-26.
15. A similar historical process of oppressive churchly praxis yielding congregational protests, separations, and reformations as independent black churches is revealed in Francis Kimani Githieya, *The Freedom of the Spirit: African Indigenous Churches in Kenya* (Atlanta: Scholars Press, 1997).

According to the black separatist witness of AME and AMEZ churches, the white Wesleyan-Methodist heritage produced doctrines worthy of black embrace and at the same time produced oppressive social practices calling for black protest and separation. Here, protests, separations, and reformations were over issues of orthopraxis, not orthodoxy. The historical witness of black separatist Methodism is that white mainstream Methodism is much better at theology and doxology than at orthopraxis, notwithstanding John Wesley's own bias toward orthopraxis.

More recently, from within North American black separatist Christianity, black womanist theologians indebted to Alice Walker's womanist thought find that, like mainstream Protestant and Catholic traditions, black separatist Christianity exhibits an unrighteous patriarchal bias oppressive of women and children and oppressive of all erotic experiences outside monogamous heterosexual marriage.[16] The practical and theological witnesses of Richard Allen, James Varick, and other black separatist patriarchs seldom stand against this womanist finding.[17]

BIAS TOWARD ORTHOPRAXIS AND THE METAPHYSICS OF CREATURELY PRAXIS

Careful readers will have noticed at the start of the preceding section "Bias Toward Orthopraxis . . . " that I place "orthopraxis"

---

16. Alice Walker's anti-patriarchal theology and her call for being less restrictive of erotic feelings are given in the witness of "Shug"—a character in her novel, *The Color Purple* (New York: Simon & Schuster, 1985, originally 1982), see especially 199-204. Although all black female theologians following Alice Walker in identifying themselves as "womanist" agree that patriarchal bias oppressive of women and children is unrighteous, not all embrace Alice Walker's call for being less restrictive of erotic possibilities. While Alice Walker's definition of womanist is the originating reference for womanist thought, womanist theologians add and subtract content according to their own critical deliberations. For instance, Cheryl J. Sanders, a womanist theologian, is critical of some parts of Alice Walker's definition of "womanist." See Cheryl J. Sanders, "Christian Ethics and Theology in Womanist Perspective," *Journal of Feminist Studies in Religion* 5 (Fall 1989): 83-91; and reprinted in *Black Theology: A Documentary History, Volume Two: 1980–1992*, ed. James H. Cone and Gayraud S. Wilmore (Maryknoll, N.Y.: Orbis Books, 1993) 336-44.

17. To its credit, relative to other black and white Methodist denominations, the AMEZ Church (also called "The Freedom Church" on account of its underground railroad and abolitionist activities) "was the first among all of the Methodist denominations, including the Methodist Episcopal Church, to extend the vote and clerical ordination to women," Lincoln and Mamiya, *Black Church*, 58.

where Ogden says "praxis." Because Ogden holds that Wesley's bias toward praxis is bias toward "good works" essential to salvation,[18] and because "orthopraxis" is explicitly about works that are good or righteous, but "praxis" fails to explicate good works as distinct from bad or unrighteous works, there is good reason (favoring explicit over implicit) to replace "praxis" with "orthopraxis." Here, "bias toward praxis" means "bias toward orthopraxis."

Praxis is required of all actual creatures in that actuality excludes zero praxis. As Charles Hartshorne says, *"To be is to create"* and "what [individual creatures] create cannot be zero, so long as the individuals exist."[19] Doing absolutely nothing is being absolutely nothing actual.

Every creaturely deed makes at least some differences to at least some local others. In the case of a human creature, these others include other humans—even if only one's own future selves (according to Hartshorne, strictly speaking, future selves are other selves)—and creatures of other species—even if only internal and external microscopic creatures. The world is wholly indifferent to nothing actual, and the differences actual creatures make are of variable values to various subsequent local creaturely experiences.

Very strictly speaking, the metaphysics of creaturely praxis does not admit doing and being as wholly evil in the sense of contributing only harm to all affected others. Even contributing absolutely no good to absolutely no other is a metaphysical impossibility. No creaturely praxis can be wholly exclusive of contributions to the good of at least some others and God.[20] No doubt even Adolf Hitler made his own more or less regular organic contributions to the well-being of a least some maggots, flies, and worms. Strictly speaking, for actual creatures, praxis contributing to the increased well-being of at least some others is not reducible to absolute zero.

And again speaking very strictly, the metaphysics of creaturely praxis does not admit doing and being as wholly good in the sense

---

18. Ogden, "Process Theology and the Wesleyan Witness," 30.

19. Charles Hartshorne, *Creative Synthesis and Philosophic Method* (LaSalle, Ill.: Open Court Publishing, 1970), 1.

20. That no possible creaturely praxis can be wholly exclusive of contributions to the good of some others and God is a metaphysical claim consistent with Ogden's existential claim that no witness—not even witness to unbelief—can be wholly exclusive of witness to faith in God. See Schubert M. Ogden, "The Strange Witness of Unbelief," in *The Reality of God and Other Essays*, 2nd ed. (San Francisco: Harper & Row, 1966), 120-43.

of contributing only good to all affected others. Even contributing absolutely no harm to absolutely no other is impossible for creaturely praxis. No doubt even Jesus of Nazareth made occasional contributions to the unwell-being of at least some fishes and grapes, and he almost certainly stepped on more than one ant or worm and maybe even slapped a mosquito or two. Strictly speaking, for actual creatures, praxis contributing to the decreased well-being of at least some others is not reducible to absolute zero.[21]

"Ordinary factual statements are *partially restrictive* of existential possibilities,"[22] says Hartshorne. Like factual statements about creaturely deeds, every actual creaturely deed is "partially restrictive." The extent to which given partial restrictions are valued as good or bad varies from creaturely experience to creaturely experience. What is very good for some is less good or bad for some others. For example, when I am sick, antibiotics can be good for me by virtue of being bad for selected microscopic others. Similarly, the chicken soup so good to and for me is bad for the chicken therein.[23] Given a metaphysics of creaturely praxis, which holds that every creaturely deed is a sharing of partially restrictive creativity making variously valued differences to some others and God, the distinction between creaturely orthopraxis and unrighteous praxis is not absolute but relative and graduated—a matter of more or less good and more or less significant creaturely creations shared with some subsequent others and God.

Creaturely praxis is always a variation on sharing more or less good and always more than absolute zero and less than all-inclusive. The all-inclusive divine good is the "comprehensive variable"

---

21. William R. Jones deploys this truth about creaturely praxis as part of a "critical apparatus" revealing absurd aspects of classical theism's response to the problem of evil in *Is God a White Racist? A Preamble to Black Theology* (Boston: Beacon Press, 1998, originally 1973). According to Jones's withering critique, classical theism cannot answer his questions (questions such as "Does God eat?" and, if not, "Why does God not liberate creatures from the eater-eatee circumstance?") without contradicting classical conceptions of omnibenevolence and omnipotence. See especially note 9 of the new afterword in the 1998 edition, 248-49.

22. Hartshorne, *Creative Synthesis*, 159 (italics added).

23. Clearly, it is easy to find examples of human deeds producing both good and bad for others where we include both human and nonhuman others. But even where we restrict our concern to human others, the distinction between good and bad is not absolute. In *Love and Conflict: A Covenantal Model of Christian Ethics* (Nashville, Abingdon Press, 1984), Joseph L. Allen insists upon recognizing the abiding reality of varying degrees of harmony and conflict (neither being reducible to absolute zero nor being simply exclusively good or bad) in human affairs. This is also true of the general creaturely circumstance.

and ultimate measure of every less inclusive good, according to Franklin I. Gamwell's *The Divine Good: Modern Moral Theory and the Necessity of God*.[24] Gamwell says that the "all-inclusive activity is the measure of the good."[25] Ethical deliberation requires recourse to a comprehensive variable (the all-inclusively shared divine good) and recourse to possible creaturely actions, which are judged (relative to other creaturely actions) more or less righteous in accordance with their contributions to more or less inclusively shared good.[26] Orthopraxis designates the intentional and habitual practice of sharing more good where it is possible to share less good.

OVERCOMING HOMOCENTRISM AND THE METAPHYSICS OF MORALS

Although Ogden sees an affinity to process theology in one of Wesley's exceptional sayings differing with the spirit/matter and history/nature dualism presupposed by classical homocentrism, he nonetheless finds that "Wesley everywhere takes for granted an understanding of self and the world that is homocentric when viewed from the standpoint of process theology."[27] John Wesley took for granted, and Wesleyan-Methodist traditions embraced, a form of homocentrism Ogden identifies as "exaggerated humanism."[28]

Exaggerated humanism denies or fails to appreciate the intrinsic value of nonhuman creatures and creations. While such humanism is characteristically Methodist, it is not distinctively Methodist because it is also, as Ogden says, "characteristic of modern Western culture generally" and "typical of the whole movement of liberal theology."[29] Humanistic homocentrism is also characteristic of other Christian (Protestant and Catholic) and Jewish traditions.

For Ogden, overcoming humanistic homocentrism is essential to religious orthopraxis. In "Process Theology and the Wesleyan Witness," he insists:

---

24. San Francisco: HarperSanFrancisco, 1990.
25. Ibid., 187.
26. All-inclusiveness plays a similar role in Allen, *Love and Conflict*. Here, the "basic moral standard," governing any rule or subsidiary judgment, is God's all-inclusive covenant love, 52.
27. Ogden, "Process Theology and the Wesleyan Witness," 31.
28. Ogden, *Faith and Freedom*, 103.
29. Ibid.

Because anything concrete and singular is insofar intrinsically good, and is fully accepted as such by God, the neighbors we are to love as ourselves include not only all our fellow selves but also all the others at every level of becoming who can in any way be affected by our own acceptance and action.[30]

The meaning of ultimate reality for us demands that we accept both our own becoming and the becomings of all others as parts of this ultimate whole and then, by serving as best we can the transient goods of all the parts, to make the greatest possible contribution to the enduring good of the whole.[31]

Furthermore, in "Beyond Homocentrism," a section of *Faith and Freedom: Toward a Theology of Liberation*, Ogden says all creatures are to be loved "finally, solely for the sake of God" who is immanent in all human and nonhuman creatures.[32] Ogden holds that the neighbors we are called to love as ourselves include nonhuman creatures and that we are called to love human and nonhuman creatures for the same reason—for the sake of God and for the contribution to the divine good through contributions to human and nonhuman creaturely goods.

With regard to valuing nonhuman creatures and nonhuman creations, to my knowledge, the black separatist strands of the Wesleyan-Methodist heritage have failed to distinguish themselves from mainline Methodism. Like mainline Methodism, black separatist Methodism (AME and AMEZ) embraces without protest a religiosity characteristically unconcerned with nonhuman creatures and creations. In this regard, black separatist Christianity, black theologies, and other liberation theologies share an unfortunate affinity to white liberal theologies.

Homocentric liberation and liberal theologies are faulted by Ogden in *Faith and Freedom* where he says, "Whatever the form of bondage to which they may be oriented—political, economic, cultural, racial, or sexual—it is solely with *human* liberation that they are typically concerned, and if they regard nonhuman nature as having any value at all, it is the strictly instrumental value it has for

---

30. "Process Theology and the Wesleyan Witness," 31.
31. Ibid., 21.
32. Ogden, *Faith and Freedom*, 110.

realizing *human* potentialities."[33] Accordingly, Ogden identifies homocentrism as a subtle form of bondage from which modern Christian theologies, especially liberal and liberation theologies, need emancipation. Overcoming homocentrism is essential to adequate theology.[34]

Overcoming homocentrism is also essential to an adequate metaphysics of morals. Any "categorical imperative" valuing humans over all other creatures is not, strictly speaking, a categorical or unconditional imperative. Human existence is conditional-contingent, not unconditional-necessary. Imperatives specific to human existence are therefore conditional rather than unconditional.

A putative categorical imperative formulated so as to value humans over all other creatures is, at most, a first order hypothetical imperative for humans. As a first order hypothetical imperative, it means when/where/if there are humans, then in every circumstance, humans should be and do thus and so.[35] Such an imperative could be said to apply to humans unconditionally; however, precisely insofar as it is specific to humans, it is specific to humans on the contingent condition of human existence. Hence, such an imperative is not strictly unconditional.

Appeals to human uniqueness, distinctiveness, or superiority relative to other creatures fail to make favoring humans a strictly unconditional imperative. For example, in *The Divine Good*, Gamwell justifies a "preeminent place" for human creativity "in the divine telos" by appealing to humanity's dramatically greater creativity.[36]

---

33. Ibid., 104.

34. Ibid., 108.

35. The metaethical distinction between a first order hypothetical imperative and a strictly categorical imperative is similar to Ogden's metaphysical distinction between "metaphysica specialis" and "metaphysica generalis." A first order hypothetical imperative has a special, or specie specific ("specialis"), application while a categorical imperative has a general ("generalis") application. See Schubert M. Ogden, "The Criterion of Metaphysical Truth and the Senses of 'Metaphysics,'" *Process Studies* 5.1 (Spring 1975). I am also reminded of Eugene H. Peters's account of Hartshorne's distinction between a "hypothetical necessity" and strict metaphysical necessity. Peters finds that, for Hartshorne, a hypothetical necessity denies that such and such could fail to obtain given the actuality of some said contingent entity. Similarly, a first order hypothetical imperative denies that humans could fail to be so obligated, if only humans are actual. See Eugene H. Peters, "Methodology in the Metaphysics of Charles Hartshorne," in *Existence and Actuality: Conversations with Charles Hartshorne*, ed. John B. Cobb Jr. and Franklin I. Gamwell (Chicago: University of Chicago Press, 1984).

36. Gamwell, *The Divine Good*, 186. While Gamwell's appeal to superior creativity fails to make favoring humans a strictly unconditional imperative, he nonetheless succeeds in proving theism is the strictly necessary "ground of any moral claim," 18.

Here, the preeminent place of human creativity is based upon a factual claim about human creative capacity that, even if factually true, is not necessarily true. Even if present human creativity is greater than any except divine creativity, this has not always been true, and it is not likely to remain true for all future times. Even if human creativity is greater, it is only contingently greater. Contingency also applies to claims about the "most distinctive characteristics" of human existence—"capacity for true speech and self-consciousness"[37]—to claims about human souls, and to all other claims for human uniqueness, distinctiveness or superiority. Even if true, these are contingent, conditional, and factual truths. Hence, human favor, preeminence or priority, is not a strictly unconditional imperative.

A strictly unconditional imperative would have to be formulated in terms of how creatures generally should act in every circumstance.[38] Of course, we cannot bypass specific creatures and specific types of creatures, including most especially human creatures. Even though our concern is with the strictly unconditional, we must examine human creaturely experiences with less emphasis upon distinguishing human experiences from all other creaturely experiences, and with more emphasis upon discerning what is common to all creaturely experiences. No species specific imperative can be strictly unconditional (except in the one extreme instance where the specified specie is the whole class of actual and possible nondivine individuals). Overcoming exclusive humanism and other homocentric specifications is essential to formulating a strictly unconditional imperative.

OVERCOMING HOMOCENTRISM AND THE ETHICAL INADEQUACY OF METAPHYSICS AND METHODISM

Overcoming homocentrism is also essential to an adequate social ethic. Strictly speaking, homocentrism is never wholly overcome in

---

37. Ogden, *Faith and Freedom*, 108.

38. A strictly unconditional imperative would apply to every creature, except to God, at least not in any way allowing the imperative (the unconditional ought) to be distinguished from truth (the unconditional is). Normally, ethical imperatives apply where there is a possible difference between what individuals actually do and what they ought to do. God is

creaturely ethics. Only God is wholly free of every form of homocentrism. Because we are less than all-inclusive, the creaturely others we can know, value, and love are merely some relatively few locals, and this only imperfectly. Even if we overcame humanistic homocentrism, we would still remain homocentric with regard to creatures and creations that are not within our same (homo) relatively local space and time. Although absolute zero homocentrism is metaphysically impossible for creaturely fragments, we are called to overcome as much homocentrism as possible.

Regardless of historical facts concerning anthropocentric Methodist and Judeo-Christian traditions, Ogden argues in *Faith and Freedom* that homocentrism is not true to biblical faith. One reason for holding this view is that the Genesis creation narratives witness "as much to the essential unity of man and woman with all their fellow creatures as to their unique difference over against them."[39] However, Ogden says neither this nor any other exegesis of a particular text is crucial to his argument. For Ogden, the "crucial" reason homocentrism cannot be true to biblical faith is because the nature/history dualism presupposed by homocentrism is precluded by "the most fundamental axioms of biblical faith" (including especially the scriptural axiom of creation) and by "the necessary conditions of the possibility of the entire scriptural witness."[40] Furthermore, in "Process Theology and the Wesleyan Witness," Ogden explains that as a consequence of process philosophy's antidualism, "all expressions of process theology are able as hardly any other kind of theology seems to be, to overcome homocentrism both metaphysically and ethically."[41]

Ogden's resources for overcoming homocentrism include attention to the following: biblical axioms, conditions necessary to scriptural witness, conditions and presuppositions necessary to every witness (including even "the strange witness of unbelief"[42]), the

---

unique in that what God does is necessarily identical to what God ought to do. There being no possible distance between the divine is and the divine ought, speaking of what God ought to do (applying an imperative to God) is metaphysically mistaken or redundant. Where such speech is not metaphysically mistaken, it is redundant because its entire possible content is available under the headings of truth and fact.

39. Ogden, *Faith and Freedom*, 109.
40. Ibid., 109-10.
41. Ogden, "Process Theology and the Wesleyan Witness," 31.
42. Ogden, "The Strange Witness of Unbelief," 120-43.

"unique ontological distinction" between creaturely parts or fragments of reality and the "all-inclusive whole of reality,"[43] and other data available through transcendental process-neoclassical metaphysics and theology. These resources are adequate for overcoming homocentrism in the metaphysics of nature and in the metaphysics of morals, but not in ethics.

Ethical deliberations require more than metaphysics and categorical and first order imperatives. For ethics, conditional/contingent facts, probabilities, evaluations, and hypothetical imperatives are also essential. Overcoming humanistic homocentrism in physics and ethics (rather than merely in metaphysics and metaethics) requires concern with various particular species and creatures in specific space-time-social locations, and hypothetical imperatives guided by actual and probable consequences for various particular species and creatures.[44]

Requiring concern for specifics in overcoming humanistic homocentrism is consistent with Ogden's requiring specifically political expressions of Christian theology today. Without recourse to specifically liberating political expressions, Christian theology today cannot be adequate. Without recourse to specific contingent local nonhuman species and creatures, there is no possibility of overcoming humanistic homocentrism in ethics.

Unfortunately, modern Christian traditions (Catholic and Protestant, mainstream and separatist) usually witness to little concern for righteous relations to the nonhuman world in general and near zero concern for righteous relations to particular nonhuman species, creatures, and creations. For a striking example of disregard for particular nonhuman animal populations, consider the history of Methodism on the North American frontier during the eighteenth and nineteenth centuries. Despite sustained missionary and other churchly contacts with the Lakota (Sioux) nations,

---

43. Ogden, "Process Theology and the Wesleyan Witness," 21.

44. According to my formal analysis, social ethical deliberation includes these basic elements: interpretive themes, populations/circles of concern, descriptions (of past and present), predictions (of probable futures shaped by past and present influences), visions (of more righteous alternatives), and prescriptions (for changing probable futures to envisioned more righteous alternatives). All were permeated by values and value judgments. See Theodore Walker Jr., "Neoclassical Thought and Social Ethical Analysis," presented at The Center for Process Studies at the Claremont School of Theology on 13 November 1996, revised 12 March 1997 and published in a special edition of *Creative Transformation* 6.2 (Winter 1997) honoring Charles Hartshorne's 100th birthday (5 June 1997).

relentless Lakota protests and calls for repentance, and political treaties pledging actual repentance, North American Methodism exhibited no churchly concern for surrounding buffalo herds, herds being slaughtered by Methodist and other Christian populations.

In contrast to this, Native American religions often include explicit concern for both relations to creation generally and relations to particular nonhuman species, creatures, and creations.[45] Some Native American religions explicate concern for relations to whales or fish, and not only whales or fish generally, but also specific kinds of whales and specific kinds of fish in specific locations. And some Native American religions explicate concern for relations to other particular species, creatures, and creations, including bison, elk, deer, bears, horses, trees, maze, rivers, lakes, mountains, and the like.[46] Regarding explicit concern for specific nonhuman populations and creations, even with recourse to biblical axioms; Wesleyan-Methodist witnesses (mainstream and separatist), and process-neoclassical metaphysics, modern Christianity is much less adequate than many traditional Native American religions.[47]

---

45. Vine Deloria Jr. of the Lakota Sioux nation frequently emphasizes Sioux and other Native American religious concerns for relations to location-specific land spaces and waterways. See the following books by Vine Deloria Jr.: *Custer Died for Your Sins: An Indian Manifesto* (Norman, Okla.: University of Oklahoma Press, 1989, originally 1969); *God Is Red: A Native View of Religion*, 2nd ed. (Golden, Colo.: North American Press, 1992, originally 1973); and *The Metaphysics of Modern Existence* (New York: Harper & Row, 1979).

46. Comparing our modern calendar with a traditional Lakota calendar reveals much greater consciousness of relations to a local nonhuman world. In *Black Elk Speaks: Being the Life Story of a Holy Man of the Oglala Sioux* (Lincoln: University of Nebraska Press, 1991, originally 1932), Black Elk of the Lakota nations says that portion of the year we call January is called "Moon of Frost in the Teepee," February is "Moon of the Dark Red Calves," March is the "Moon of the Snow-blind," April is the "Moon of the Red Grass Appearing," May is the "Moon When the Ponies Shed," June is the "Moon of Making Fat" (because "that is the time when the sun is highest and the growing power of the world is strongest"), July is the "Moon of Red Cherries," August is the "Moon When the Cherries Turn Black," September is the "Moon When the Calves Grow Hair" and "Moon When the Plums Are Scarlet," October is the "Moon of the Changing Season," November is the "Moon of Falling Leaves," and December is the "Moon of the Popping Trees." Greater consciousness of relations to a local nonhuman world is also revealed by attention to religious calendars. Unlike Lakota and many other Native American religions, our churchly calendars seldom observe or celebrate relations to general nonhuman "creation" and virtually never observe or celebrate relations to specific-local nonhuman species and creatures. Similarly, unlike Lakota and many other traditional Native American religions, the worded content of our worship services (the words in our songs, liturgies, and prayers) is virtually never about relations to specific-local nonhuman species and creatures.

47. I do not know if early Christianity was much more adequate than modern Christianity with regard to specific nonhuman species, creatures and creations. I suspect not. According

There is a considerable literature on Christian-Lakota dialogue. Typically these dialogues take an ecumenical and catholic approach emphasizing affinities. Similar to an electromagnetic interferometer, the areas of overlap, or affinities, amplify each other at the expense of differences diminished by mutual interference. There is also need for a more protestant approach. A more protestant approach seeks to be instructed by both affinities and differences, with more attention to differences, and without a prior conviction that affinities are preferable to differences.

With regard to Lakota and Christian ways of overcoming humanistic homocentrism, an ecumenical and catholic approach emphasizing affinities draws attention to creation in general—as examples: "Mother Nature" and "Mother Earth." Alternatively, a more protestant approach emphasizing differences adds attention to specific nonhuman creatures and creations—as specific examples: buffalo herds and the Black Hills. Here, we are better instructed by a more protestant approach.

---

to some historical accounts, early Christianity had a decisively urban orientation. For example, in *The Origins of Christian Morality: The First Two Centuries* (New Haven, Conn.: Yale University Press, 1993) Wayne A. Meeks says, "It was nevertheless the earthly cities of Rome and its provinces where the Christian movement found the fertile soil for its earliest and most rapid expansion. It was in the neighborhoods and streets and households of those cities where the colonists of heaven had to rub elbows and do business with citizens and fellow residents of Ephesus and Alexandria and Corinth" (13). Christian ministry was urban ministry from the start. And perhaps urban existence tends to alienate humans from the undomesticated nonhuman world. Overcoming humanistic homocentrism in ethics will require a new kind of urban ministry, a ministry seeking more righteous relations to the undomesticated nonhuman world.

CHAPTER FOURTEEN

COMPASSION AND HOPE:
THEOLOGY BORN OF ACTION

MARY ELIZABETH MULLINO MOORE

From time to time, people in Wesleyan and process-relational traditions of theology have engaged in lively conversation. Because many people identify with both traditions, the conversation is often internal. Both traditions are broad and multifaceted; thus, people relating to one or both of them defy neat stereotypes. Despite this diversity and complexity within each tradition, the two broad systems have many intersecting themes; fruitful patterns often emerge in the course of dialogue, raising questions and posing fresh perspectives. The fruitfulness of dialogue is revealed even in the framing of this book project, *Thy Nature and Thy Name Is Love*. This is a book of conversation focused on one of the major thematic intersections between Wesleyan and process-relational theology—the love of God.

One dimension of conversation has heretofore been neglected, or addressed only in ancillary fashion. This is my central theme: *the compassion and hope that have motivated both systems and the praxis methods by which their theoretical assertions have been constructed.* These are obvious to many observers, but the spirit of compassion and hope and the methods of action-reflection are often under-analyzed and underrated. This problem exists even though John Wesley identifies his work as practical divinity, and even though process theologians address existential questions in much of their work, whether wrestling with human oppression, economic injustice, ecological destruction, or spiritual yearning. When neglected or marginalized, the power of compassion, hope, and action-reflection is diminished in the theological enterprise; when taken seriously, we are challenged to develop practices of compassion, hope, and action-reflection as central to scholarly theological work.

To make claims for compassion, hope, and praxis is to engage in a contextualized, future-oriented, and action-based paradigm for studying religion. Judith Plaskow, in her 1998 Presidential Address to the American Academy of Religion (AAR), argued that the study of religion has been shaped by radical shifts in paradigms, motivated largely by real life in the academy.[1] In her presentation, she named a reality, and she advocated even greater participation in that reality. In particular, she named the way by which the participants, structures, subjects, perspectives, and categories of the AAR have been reshaped by the increasing participation of women and people of color. This is not only a descriptive fact but also a reality to be embraced ever more fully as people engage in scholarship that is grounded in the social, political, and religious realities of their world. Plaskow concluded by "commending the notion of the AAR as a space in which we allow current social and political questions to enrich our thinking, even as we seek to respond to and intervene in them."[2] This vision of the study of religion sounds fresh and challenging. The explicitness of the vision is indeed fresh, and the challenges are almost overwhelming given the complexity of the multiple worlds in which we live. Despite this, the vision is not at all new, and we can find clues for charting these waters in both Wesleyan and process-relational traditions.

The purpose of this essay is to explore possibilities of theological reflection that are grounded in compassion, hope, and praxis, drawing from a comparative study of Wesleyan and process-relational traditions, particularly upon the life work of John Wesley and Alfred North Whitehead. The essay is prolegomena for a larger work, so the spirit is exploratory and the issues are generalized. In order for the method to be compatible with the subject matter, the general analysis is introduced with a case study. The center of the chapter follows—a comparative analysis of compassion and hope in Wesleyan and process-relational traditions. The chapter concludes with a critical reconstruction and a return to the case study. The theological analysis is thus framed with critical issues for which people seek fresh insight; ideally, the study will kindle sparks of compassion and hope.

---

1. Judith Plaskow, "The Academy as Real Life: New Participants and Paradigms in the Study of Religion," *Journal of the American Academy of Religion* 67 (1999): 521-38.
2. Ibid., 534.

CASE STUDY

The case study takes place in the year 2000, and although the publication of this volume is more than a year later, the situation has not changed markedly. For this reason, the case is told in past tense, but with an awareness that the case continues into the present time. In the United States of 2000, many Protestant denominations were torn apart by conflict regarding what was the most adequate Christian response to persons who are gay, lesbian, bisexual, and transgendered, and what was the most adequate Christian thinking about homosexuality. Both gay and straight members have been active in this discourse; at the same time, many gay and straight people have also been alienated and absent from the church because of the church's traditions and values to date. Discussions had been lively and often heated, erupting in denominational meetings, legislative assemblies and conferences, court cases, local church gatherings, church publications, small group discussions, and elsewhere. Several questions had been asked with particular frequency: Is a homosexual orientation sinful, or is it natural and good? Is the chuch's mission to judge and seek to transform people who are homosexually oriented, or is it to welcome them, to celebrate and support gay relationships, and to offer ethical guidance? Are gay, lesbian, and bisexual people to be included fully in the ministry of the church, including the ordained ministry? Is the church's agreement necessary for the unity of the church, or can the church be unified and welcoming of all peoples while still being divided in perspectives, even on issues of great concern for many people?

While these questions continue to be raised in many contexts, the particular focus here is the United Methodist context as one particular example that stands within the Wesleyan tradition. In this denomination, the language of the 1996 *Book of Discipline* was: "Although we do not condone the practice of homosexuality and consider this practice incompatible with Christian teaching, we affirm that God's grace is available to all."[3] Proposals had been sent to the General Conference of 2000 urging that this language be

---

3. *The Book of Discipline of The United Methodist Church* (Nashville: The United Methodist Publishing House, 1996), §65.G, p. 89.

maintained, that it be removed, that it be strengthened, or that it be replaced with a passage that recognized diverse views within the larger context of God's grace. In the latter case, the most frequently made proposal was to substitute the following: "Although Christians disagree on the compatibility of homosexuality with Christian teaching, we affirm that God's grace is available to all."[4] The 2000 General Conference did, in the end, decide to maintain the present language and reject alternatives; however, one addition was made following the much-discussed, pivotal sentence. The addition was: "We implore families and churches not to reject or condemn their lesbian and gay members and friends."[5]

With that introduction, the focus of this case is the 2000 General Conference itself; as it unfolded, differences loomed large. One particular debate was spoken with a loud voice: Should the denomination emphasize agreement on ethical judgments regarding homosexuality (and on biblical and doctrinal interpretation), or should it emphasize inclusiveness. Those who argued for the former often argued for unity in the church; those who argued for the latter often argued for justice. Thus, the issue was usually framed as an either/or matter. Consequently, the decision-making processes were framed as either/or as well. Does the church need decision-making pocesses that encourage openness, mutual understanding, doctrinal agreement, and movement toward unified decision, or does the church need processes that encourage decisive action to include or exclude gay, lesbian, bisexual, and transgendered persons? The church, then, was faced with the dilemma of how to address the complex of ethical questions that were raised in this medley of debates and the medley of perspectives on each question. The web was tangled indeed; yet, the tangling could itself be used as a reason to hold the status quo or to act decisively and give up any possibility of mutual understanding in the process. Either choice would itself be an ethical and political decision.

---

4. Several bodies to the 2000 General Conference submitted this wording. The same language was considered and rejected by a slim margin in the 1996 General Conference; in both quadrennia, it was offered by various groups who sought an alternate to the present language. [Editorial note: the 2000 General Conference retained the language of the 1996 *Book of Discipline*].

5. *The Book of Discipline of The United Methodist Church* (Nashville : The United Methodist Publishing House, 2000), §161.G, p. 101.

COMPASSION

With this case in mind, we turn now to the Wesleyan and process-relational traditions of theology. Of great concern for this case and for the two traditions under consideration are the spirit of compassion with which theology is actually practiced and the view of compassion that is developed and articulated. Four hallmarks can be identified as central to both of these theological perspectives as they attend to compassion. Although the two traditions vary in content and emphasis, the comparison promises to illumine the distinctive traditions and bear fruit for theology more generally.

Wesleyan Compassion

The four hallmarks, when viewed in context of Wesleyan theology, underscore the urgency of compassion in theological reflection. First, John Wesley grounded his anthropology and ethics in God's love. Second, Wesley usually wrote sermons, theological tracts, and letters with compassion for a particular person or community. Third, Wesley's own focus of concern was the grittiness of existence and the urgency of attending to the quality of life. Finally, he assumed a connection among all beings and thus a need for people to be responsive and responsible toward others and toward the whole.

The first hallmark of Wesley's compassion is that his anthropology and ethics are grounded in God's love. This emphasis is found throughout his writing, but particularly in his description of Christian perfection, or perfect love.[6] This topic will be taken up again in relation to hope, but the important note here is that Wesley described perfection as a process of "loving God with all our heart, mind, soul, and strength." For him, this meant "that no wrong temper, none contrary to love, remains in the soul; and that all the thoughts, words, and actions, are governed by pure love."[7]

While Wesley's writing is sprinkled liberally with references to love (and virtually every commentator of his corpus makes reference

---

6. See especially, *A Plain Account of Christian Perfection, Works* (Jackson) 11:366-446; *Brief Thoughts on Christian Perfection, Works* (Jackson) 11:446; and *A Letter to Mrs. Maitland* (12 May 1763), *Letters* (Telford) 4:212-13.

7. *A Plain Account of Christian Perfection*, §19, *Works* (Jackson) 11:394.

to this center), the references that are particularly strong are those in which Wesley reflects on God's grace and the impetus for human responsibility. Consider two recent explications. First, Theodore Runyon identifies Wesley's view of God's grace as love that is available to all, but not forced on anyone:

> Because the nature of grace is love, it cannot be forced upon us, nor is it "irresistible," as some predestinarian theories of grace held. "The God of love is willing to save all the souls that he has made. . . . But he will not force them to accept of it." Depriving human beings of freedom is neither the nature of God's grace nor the nature of God's love. Yet grace does "assist" the human response as the stimulus which calls it forth.[8]

Just as love is the foundation of God's gracious action toward us, so love is also the fruit of new birth in God. As Kenneth J. Collins develops Wesley's "scripture way of salvation," he notes three marks of new birth—faith, hope, and love. The greatest of these is love of God, which issues forth (inseparably) in love of neighbor, obedience to God, and regeneration of one's life and dispositions.[9] Finally, we discover that new birth is not the end of loving. Wesley understood sanctification as a process by which people continue to grow in love. Perfection, then, is not a static state, but "the ever-increasing love of God and neighbor."[10] We see from this brief summary that love is the beginning and the end of God's action and human response. This emphasis on love is a persistent mark of the Wesleyan tradition as it has developed and spread.

The second hallmark—acting with compassion for a particular person or community—is revealed in the concerns that Wesley addressed in his speaking and writing. Consider, for example, his many letters to family members, class leaders, politicians, and members of the growing "Methodist" fellowship. Wesley often wrote to the particular issues and concerns with which these people were wrestling. Looking back, one may cringe at some of his advice, especially to

---

8. Theodore Runyon, *The New Creation: John Wesley's Theology Today* (Nashville: Abingdon Press, 1998), 27. Runyon is quoting Sermon 127, "On the Wedding Garment," §19, *Works* 4:148.

9. Kenneth J. Collins, *The Scripture Way of Salvation: The Heart of John Wesley's Theology* (Nashville: Abingdon Press, 1997), 123-26.

10. Runyon, *New Creation*, 88-91.

his sisters.[11] In fact, one biographer of the Wesley sisters, Frederick Maser, identified the seven Wesley women as sisters in search of love. He argued further that the whole family was peculiarly lacking in the warmth of human love: "There was a unity about the Wesley family that was commendable, but it was not a unity cemented by love."[12] In this comment, and in the letters themselves, one can see that John Wesley's compassion was sometimes misguided, and perhaps even overridden by a passion for order or misogynist correctness.

At the same time, Wesley was clearly engaged with the existential issues of the people he knew personally and those whom he knew through representatives and in more generalized ways. Consider the titles of some of his tracts and sermons: "Thoughts upon Slavery," "Thoughts upon Liberty," "The Use of Money," "The Character of a Methodist," "Thoughts on the Present Scarcity of Provisions," "The Doctrine of Original Sin," "On Conscience," "Justification by Faith," and "The General Deliverance." These titles reveal a man who cared about the quality of life and, indeed, the quality of every person's life. They reveal a man who had particular issues and particular communities in mind when he wrote. Wesley focused in at least three ways: on particular social and political practices, on the general state of humanity, and on the quality of life for each and every person.

The third Wesleyan hallmark—concern for the grittiness of existence and the quality of life—is seen in his abundant attention to the realities of human existence and the meaning of God for people in the midst of these realities.[13] One can see these concerns in Wesley's ethical

---

11. For a full development of these relationships, see Frederick E. Maser, *The Story of John Wesley's Sisters, or Seven Sisters in Search of Love* (Rutland, Vt.: Academy Books, 1988).

12. Maser, *The Story of John Wesley's Sisters*, 8; cf. 9-10.

13. See particularly *The Doctrine of Original Sin, Works* (Jackson) 9:196-464; Sermon 5, "Justification by Faith," *Works* 1:182-99; and Sermon 60, "The General Deliverance," §I.1-2, *Works* 2:438-40. Other scholars have noted Wesley's interest in existence: Schubert M. Ogden, "Process Theology and the Wesleyan Witness," in Theodore Runyon, ed., *Wesleyan Theology Today: A Bicentennial Theological Consultation* (Nashville: Kingswood Books, 1985), 65-75 (reprinted in chap. 1 of this volume); Sheila Greeve Davaney, "Feminism, Process Thought, and the Wesleyan Tradition," in ibid., 105-16, esp. 108; and J. Philip Wogaman, "The Wesleyan Tradition and the Social Challenges of the Next Century," in ibid., 389-99. Ogden gives particular emphasis to this existential quality, noting that Wesley was especially concerned with the meaning of God for us. Wesley also placed "overall existential concentration on the power of God's love in Christ to overcome the power of sin over the future as well as the guilt of sin from the past" (70; cf. 66). Davaney notes Wesley's focus on life in this

---

commitments: to guarantee human rights and liberty; to free slaves and eradicate the dehumanization that is inherent in systems of slavery; to care for the poor and eradicate practices that contribute to poverty (like using grain for brewing liquor rather than feeding hungry people); to critique war; to restore farmlands, especially the land of small farmers; and to encourage holiness and happiness in human life.[14] As in the first hallmark regarding compassion for persons, Wesley's actions on these ethical commitments were not altogether consistent; however, he did attend consistently to these passions. On human rights, his Tory politics and critique of the American Revolution led to some complex expressions regarding rights and liberties. Even with that complexity, he never ceased to express concern for providing guarantees, including governmental controls, so that all people might live in liberty. According to Leon Hynson: "[Wesley's] underlying agenda throughout these tracts— whether he speaks of liberty, slavery, authority, revolution, monarchy or democracy, hunger, population, or other socio-political issues—is the foundation, attainment, and preservation of life, liberty, property, and happiness."[15]

In light of this discussion, the consistency and value of Wesley's particular contributions can be discussed, nuanced and debated,

---

physical world, even in his discussions of perfection (108). Wogaman emphasizes that, for Wesley, social questions were always important; further, the bearers of Wesleyan tradition have generally thought that "it is more important to affect reality than it is to hold correct abstract opinions" (390-91).

14. See *Thoughts upon Liberty* (24 February 1772), *Works* (Jackson) 11:34-46; *Observations on Liberty, Works* (Jackson) 11:92-93; *Thoughts upon Slavery, Works* (Jackson) 11:70-75; *Thoughts on the Present Scarcity of Provisions, Works* (Jackson) 11:53-58; Sermon 50, "The Use of Money," *Works* 2:263-80; *The Doctrine of Original Sin, Works* (Jackson) 9:196-464, esp. 221-25; *The Character of a Methodist, Works* (Jackson) 8:342; and Sermon 7, "The Way to the Kingdom," *Works* 1:218-32, esp. 218-21. Discussions of these themes are found in several places, including Theodore Runyon, ed., *Sanctification and Liberation: Liberation Theologies in Light of the Wesleyan Tradition* (Nashville: Abingdon Press, 1981); José Miguez Bonino, "Conversion, New Creature and Commitment," *International Review of Missions* 72 (1983): 330; Leon O. Hynson, "Implications of Wesley's Ethical Method and Political Thought," in Runyon, ed., *Wesleyan Theology Today*, 373-88; Theodore W. Jennings Jr., *Good News to the Poor: John Wesley's Evangelical Economics* (Nashville: Abingdon Press, 1990); Manfred Marquardt, *John Wesley's Social Ethics: Praxis and Principles* (Nashville: Abingdon Press, 1992); Theodore Runyon, *New Creation*; M. Douglas Meeks, "Sanctification and Economy: A Wesleyan Perspective on Stewardship," in Randy L. Maddox, ed., *Rethinking Wesley's Theology for Contemporary Methodism* (Nashville: Kingswood Books, 1998), 83-98; and Peter Grassow, "John Wesley and Revolution: A South African Perspective," in ibid., 183-95.

15. Hynson, "Implications of Wesley's Ethical Method," 374-75; see also Grassow, "John Wesley and Revolution."

but his compassion for the grittiness of existence and the quality of human life is unquestionable.

The fourth hallmark of Wesley's compassion is his assumption that all beings are connected; thus, people are challenged to be responsive and responsible toward others and toward the whole of creation. The center of Wesleyan theology is God's grace, which is consistently associated with human response and responsibility. In that spirit, Randy L. Maddox identifies Wesley's theological center as "responsible grace," and John B. Cobb Jr. identifies grace and responsibility as the key to a Wesleyan theology for today.[16]

Some comparisons between John Wesley and process-relational theologies have focused on the Wesleyan view of an interconnected creation in which God is active and people are called to be responsive. Paul A. Mickey is particularly lucid on these points, arguing that the Wesleyan view of human life is pluralistic: "We are one among many: many faiths, many peoples, many expressions of God's life."[17] This sense of being one part of a larger world leads to a sense of finitude and "cosmic humility."[18] Mickey makes this case, not only in relation to what Wesley preached, but also in relation to what he did:

> Wesley's appeal to the commoner, his preaching in the fields, his revivals among the miners and those caught in the poverty of the industrial revolution, especially in the urban centers like Bristol and London, drew the economically dispossessed and hopeless toward Christ but also produced a political theology that was a practical corrective for the *hubris* that inspired the French Revolution.[19]

This spirit was accompanied by a sense of shared responsibility and awareness of the fragility and resilience of life. Mickey believes "that evangelicals and process theologians share with Wesley that cosmic humility." He further believes that the spirit of humility and catholicity are expressed in several ways: (1) the pluralism of the

---

16. Randy L. Maddox, *Responsible Grace: John Wesley's Practical Theology* (Nashville: Kingswood Books, 1994); and John B. Cobb Jr., *Grace and Responsibility: A Wesleyan Theology for Today* (Nashville: Abingdon Press, 1995).

17. Paul A. Mickey, "Process Theology and Wesleyan Thought: An Evangelical Perspective," in Runyon, ed., *Wesleyan Theology Today*, 76.

18. Ibid., 77.

19. Ibid.

Wesleyan witness (including pluralism among Wesleyan evangelicals); (2) the lack of energy for triumphalism and Moral Majority politics among Wesleyan evangelicals; and (3) the emphasis on having one's heart right with God and one another.[20]

While Wesley's perspectives on the nonhuman environment were limited, his sense of connectedness was actually quite strong. He was able to connect the poverty of large groups of people with the use of grain for making alcohol rather than food; he connected this further with tax structures and problems of alcohol abuse.[21] Similarly, he recognized the urgency of responsible living for both the well-being of the people who exercise responsibility and the well-being of others who need their help.

These marks of Wesleyan compassion are evidenced in John Wesley's actions as well as his words. They are also suggestive of comparisons with process-relational theology, to which we now turn.

Process-Relational Compassion

Process-relational theology is distinct from Wesleyan theology in many respects; however, on matters of compassion, an astounding correspondence can be found. Whether focused on Whitehead's vision of God as the "poet of the world," or on Daniel Day Williams's grounding of theology in "the spirit and forms of love," one discovers compassion at the center of process-relational understandings of God and God's relation with the world.[22]

The first hallmark for comparison, then, is that anthropology and ethics are grounded in God's love. When Alfred North Whitehead turns to the subject of love, the Christian influences on his philosophical theism become most explicit; he describes "the Galilean origin of Christianity," which "dwells upon the tender elements in the world, which slowly and in quietness operate by love."[23] Building upon this central idea, he describes God as *with* the world in creation and as *saving* the world as it passes into God's own life.[24] God

---

20. Ibid., 77, 83-84.

21. In *Thoughts on the Present Scarcity of Provisions, Works* (Jackson) 11:53-59.

22. Alfred North Whitehead, *Process and Reality: An Essay in Cosmology*, corrected ed. (New York: The Free Press, 1978, originally 1929), 346; Daniel Day Williams, *The Spirit and the Forms of Love* (Washington, D.C.: University Press of America, 1981).

23. Whitehead, *Process and Reality*, 343.

24. Ibid., 343-46.

embraces the fullness of the world, including the pain, responding in the way of compassion. God judges with "a tenderness that loses nothing that can be saved"; in fact, God uses "what in the temporal world is mere wreckage." We are left, then, with a vision of God as "the poet of the world, with tender patience leading it by [God's] vision of truth, beauty, and goodness."[25]

At the same time that Whitehead evoked such poetic visions of God and love, he himself was known as a gentle man whose family and teaching relationships were marked by compassion.[26] Although he did not elaborate on concrete connections between daily living and a metaphysics of love, Whitehead's own way of living seemed to be centered in loving relations with God and the world; his daily life was implicitly attuned to his metaphysics.

Process-relational theologians have further elaborated on the loving relationship between God and the world. No one has done this more fully than Daniel Day Williams, who begins with the assumption that "love is at the core of human existence."[27] Identifying love as spirit, Williams distinguishes between God's love as "the ultimate form-giving and life-giving reality" and human love, which is subject to the conditions of finitude. Thus, "God's spirit always remains *one* in the integrity of Holy Love," while the human spirit is "subject to the distortions, estrangement and perversity" of finite freedom.[28]

Process-relational theologians have been particularly concerned to reshape the traditional metaphysics of love. Williams, for example, critiques the Augustinian interpretation of love by noting "a discrepancy between the reality of the loving and acting God and the metaphysical vision of perfect completion and impassibility."[29] Affirming much in Augustine's view, he concludes that this view "leaves us in difficulty through its tendency to put love ultimately beyond all tension and suffering."[30] Williams and other process

25. Ibid., 346.
26. Victor Lowe introduces Whitehead's biography by asking how the life of such a good man can be interesting (Victor Lowe, *Alfred North Whitehead: The Man and His Work, Vol. I—1861–1910* [Baltimore: Johns Hopkins University Press, 1985], 3).
27. Williams, *Spirit and the Forms of Love*, vii.
28. Ibid., 3. This theme is also developed in Ogden, "Process Theology and the Wesleyan Witness," 72-73; and Ignacio Castuera, "Wesley, Process and Liberation Theologies: A Test Case," in Runyon, ed., *Wesleyan Theology Today*, 99-100.
29. Ibid., 101.
30. Ibid., 102.

theologians offer an alternative in which God's creative work continues, even as God feels and responds to pain in the world. Human freedom also continues, even as human beings yearn to be restored to full humanity and to participate with God in loving the world.

The second hallmark for comparison—acting with compassion for a particular person or community—is less explicit in most process-relational theology than in Wesley. At the same time, several process theologians have attended to the particularities of people faced with existential issues: struggles against poverty and racism; efforts to reconstruct schools or psychotherapeutic practices; and ethical decisions regarding war, euthanasia, and other urgent human concerns. Whitehead himself cannot be called a social activist, but he was active in issues of justice within the particulars of his university, as in Cambridge when he defended the tenure of his colleague and friend Andrew Forsyth.[31] He was also an active speaker and writer in education, addressing polytechnic and university faculty in London.[32] Although far less vocal on issues of poverty and oppression than more recent process theologians, Whitehead did critique the English social system, developing awareness of social oppression through honest conversations with servants in his middle-class family home and through reading Charles Dickens.[33] Whitehead also urged metaphysical attention to particularities, as in his description of interrelatedness, in which each organism is described as internally related to all others and thus to the whole.[34]

In a sense, Whitehead also offered an epistemology for acting with compassion toward particular persons and communities. He insisted that the true method of knowing, or discovering, is like the flight of an airplane: "It starts from the ground of particular observation; it makes a flight in the thin air of imaginative generalization; and it again lands for renewed observation rendered acute by rational interpretation."[35] This is a praxis vision of knowing. Even

31. Lowe, *Alfred North Whitehead*, 315-18.

32. Alfred North Whitehead, *The Aims of Education and Other Essays* (New York: Free Press, 1968, originally 1929).

33. Lowe, *Alfred North Whitehead*, 32-40.

34. I have described Whitehead's focus on particularities elsewhere. See Moore, "Ethnic Diversity and Biodiversity: Richness at the Center of Education," *Interchange* 31:2 and 3 (2000): 259-78.

35. Whitehead, *Process and Reality*, 5.

with such a vision, people who have done theology under Whitehead's influence have not always been ground-huggers. They have not always begun on the ground of particular observation nor returned for renewed observation. Likewise, they have not always combined imagination with rationality. Even the grounding and combining that process-relational theologians have embraced has not always been placed in the foreground for self-conscious analysis.

In truth, the accent on particular persons and communities is much less developed in process-relational theology than in the theology of John Wesley. Just as process metaphysics is a world-view that looks at the large picture of reality, so process-relational theologies are often focused on large pictures. Some people who identify themselves as process-relational theologians do indeed attend to particulars in their daily lives, addressing particular issues in their cities and towns, religious communities and academic institutions. These matters are less explicitly woven into their published theologies, however, than was the case for Wesley. They are, therefore, less vulnerable to contextual narrowness but more vulnerable to abstraction and to losing the urgency, anger, and complexity that emerges from particular contexts.

The third hallmark—concern for the grittiness of existence and the quality of life—is seen in process-relational attention to the realities of human existence and the meaning of God for people in the midst of these realities. Process theologians have been engaged in many dimensions of gritty life: ecology, economics, liberation, spiritual practice, interreligious and interracial relationships, educational practice, bioethics, sexuality, and psychotherapy. Just as Whitehead took stands and developed constructive proposals for education in London, Cambridge, and Boston, process-relational theologians have taken stands and offered practical proposals on many issues of concern both to their communities and to the world. While John B. Cobb Jr. and Charles Birch addressed the global ecological crisis, Cobb and Herman Daly addressed the global economic crisis; in both cases, clear alternatives were developed and proposed. Theodore Walker Jr., Henry James Young, Schubert M. Ogden, Sheila Greeve Davaney, and Ignacio Castuera have addressed issues of liberation. Marjorie Hewitt Suchocki has been concerned with violence, on the one hand, and prayer, on the other hand. David Ray Griffin has attended to the possibilities of global government for matters of planetary survival and economic adjudication, while Jay McDaniel has focused primarily on ecological well-being, with particular attention in recent years to animals, economic systems, and spiritual well-being.

The spirit of these works is clearly to express hope for quality of life—for all life, including humans, animals, plants, mountains, seas, and soil. Though some of this work is general or abstract, all of it emerges from a deep compassion for struggles within the grittiness of life.

The fourth hallmark for comparison is the assumption that all beings are connected; thus, people are challenged to be responsive and responsible toward others and toward the whole of creation. Whitehead's own concern was to weave a coherent theory of the universe, and his passion for relatedness led to an emphasis on the pluralistic nature of the universe in which "nothing exists without essential dependence on other things"; furthermore, he viewed God "as eternally *with* the temporal world."[36] As noted earlier, both Whitehead's daily practices and his metaphysical system pointed to God as lovingly related to all elements of the universe.

The depth and complexity of connectedness is far more developed in process-relational thought than in Wesleyan theology. In expounding a process view, Schubert M. Ogden argued that "to be human is to live as a fragment, albeit a self-conscious and, therefore, responsible fragment, of the integral whole of reality as such."[37] The reality and consciousness of connectedness, in Ogden's view, lead to the necessity of responsibility. In his words, "the meaning of ultimate reality for us demands that we accept both our own becoming and the becomings of all others as parts of this ultimate whole and then, by serving as best we can the transient goods of all the parts, to make the greatest possible contribution to the enduring good of the whole."[38]

This leads to an antidualistic ethic in which care of oneself is tied intimately to care of others and vice versa. The ethics of obligation

---

36. Lowe, *Alfred North Whitehead*, 5.
37. Ogden, "Process Theology and the Wesleyan Witness," 67.
38. Ibid.

that emerges is one in which every situation obliges people to seek the fullest realization of "the intrinsic good that lies in each and every instance of becoming."[39]

In addition, process thinkers have also stressed an epistemological connection between feelings and intellect. Whitehead, for example, recognized that people's knowing transcends conscious reflection processes: "Mothers can ponder many things in their hearts which their lips cannot express."[40] This suggests a sense of connectedness with that which defies a fully conscious and rational analysis.

The natural consequence of process-relational metaphysics and epistemology is a sense of urgency for people to share responsibility for the whole of God's creation. Being anti-dualistic, a process-relational ethic can stir people to respond to the needs of every person and community and of every part of the universe; the well-being of each part is intimately connected to the well-being of the whole.

Again, we may find in a process-relational worldview a metaphysical and epistemological structure that supports the theological perspective of John Wesley in many ways. Ignacio Castuera has seen this as true for ethics, for both process and Wesleyan views emphasize involvement with the dispossessed.[41] For many liberationists, the process-relational view points to a critical partnership between God and human beings but cannot guarantee that humans will actually respond as partners or that the world will grow better. In fact, Sheila Greeve Davaney suggests that the process view of divine action is less confident than either a Wesleyan or a liberationist view: "For while God's presence is indeed the source of hope, it is not, for many process thinkers, the guarantee of any ultimate victory, at least for the human race. God's presence permits, nourishes, and provides the ground for ever greater freedom. But with that increased freedom come new and greater risks of evil and tragedy."[42]

We are left with a strong sense of interconnectedness and responsibility but with no naïve assurances that the world will become

---

39. Ibid., 68.
40. Alfred North Whitehead, *Religion in the Making* (New York: Macmillan, 1926), 67.
41. Castuera, "Wesley, Process and Liberation Theologies," 96-97.
42. Davaney, "Feminism, Process Thought, and the Wesleyan Tradition," in Runyon, ed., *Wesleyan Theology Today*, 114.

"bigger and better." In fact, Davaney believes that process theologians could learn from the confidence of the Wesleyan vision that human beings "are, through God's gracious presence, freed to love and enabled to enter into liberating and transforming connectedness."[43]

Compassion and the Case

The four hallmarks of compassion in Wesleyan and process-relational theologies are embodied in people just as they are constructed in ideas. These hallmarks are also pointers for action, even suggestive for the case with which we began. The case poses a nest of problems, which are substantially informed by a reconstructed theology soaked in compassion. A compassion-soaked theology encourages people to: (1) begin and end all deliberations with a sense of God's gracious love and an ethical vision of love for one another; (2) take seriously the concerns and issues of particular persons and communities; (3) accept the grittiness of existence as part of reality and seek quality of life for all persons (recognizing that multiple aches and issues of God's creation require attention at the same time); and (4) recognize connections among all persons (defying "us and them" deliberations or ethical decisions) and encourage responsiveness and responsibility toward one another. These qualities suggest that gay, lesbian, bisexual, and transgendered persons should be fully accepted and included within human community, even while people continue to deliberate their particular perspectives on sexuality issues. Neither a Wesleyan nor a process-relational framework supports a denial of full and responsible living to any group of persons, even when perspectives on particular questions persist.

HOPE

We turn now to questions of hope. These questions become all the more urgent when flames of compassion arouse concern for God's creation, anger at injustice and destruction, and awareness

---

43. Ibid., 115.

of our human inability to know and do truth fully. Wesleyan and process-relational views of hope can be expressed in three key emphases: trajectories of possibility, expectations of the impossible, and calls for participation.

Wesleyan Hope

Wesleyan hope is grounded from beginning to end in God's initiative and action. Because John Wesley trusted in God's undying devotion to the creation and every person within it, he also trusted that God always acts for the good of creation and for the good of each part.

The trajectory of possibility in Wesley's work is most frequently expressed in relation to God's grace at work in individual lives, from the beginning of life to beyond death. Prevenient grace is God's working in persons to awaken conscience. Through prevenient grace, God nudges and begins works of consciousness-raising and healing. The law plays a role by arousing awareness of sin, turning persons to Christ, and guiding people toward growth in grace.[44] Prevenient grace keeps people open to the further work of grace; God continues to offer grace to justify and then to sanctify human life. Justification is what God *does for* us through Jesus Christ, and sanctification is what God *works in* us by the Spirit.[45] For Wesley, justification and sanctification are interlocking movements in God's grace. He refused to ignore one or subsume one under the other (as he thought Luther and the Roman Catholics did).[46] Even the frescoes in Wesley's City Road Chapel in London testify to this unity, for the dove with the olive branch (signifying deliverance, or justification) is inside a circle (signifying healing, or sanctification). This work of grace is never complete. Although the sanctifying work of God can lead to perfection (known as complete sanctification, or perfect love), perfection itself is understood as an ongoing process in which love is strengthened and purified.

For Wesley, the movement of God's grace is a dazzling and persistent trajectory of possibility; people may, however, deny the gift

44. Sermon 36, "The Law Established through Faith: Discourse II," *Works* 2:33-43.
45. Sermon 5, "Justification by Faith," §2.1, *Works* 1:187.
46. Sermon 107, "On God's Vineyard," §§I.4-9, *Works* 3:505-508; and Sermon 5, "Justification by Faith,"§2.1, *Works* 1:187.

or turn away from it or walk with unsure steps. Wesley spoke frankly of the dangers of lapsing, or falling into "the wilderness state."[47] He also warned against pride in the experience of God's salvation.[48] Even with this awareness of danger, however, Wesley put forth the possibility of perfection in human life, and he encouraged practices by which sanctification might be enhanced.

Thus we see that, *in addition to trajectories of possibility, Wesley also expected the impossible from God, both for human life and for the creation.* God's grace points to God's future, as represented by Theodore Runyon's description of Wesley's emphasis on "new creation."[49] For Wesley, future hope included the renewal of all creation and the new birth of human lives.[50] Due to Wesley's strong emphasis on human life, his recognition of the renewal of creation is often overlooked. It is expressed with clarity, albeit less frequently than the *ordo salutis* which focused on the drama of human salvation.

Concerning human lives, Wesley expressed the seemingly impossible in his doctrine of perfection. In this doctrine, he expressed hope that the ideal might become real; by God's grace, he believed this possible. He explained perfection as "loving God with all our heart, mind, soul, and strength." For him, this meant "that no wrong temper, none contrary to love, remains in the soul; and that all the thoughts, words, and actions, are governed by pure love."[51] Lively discussion has raged as to whether Wesley understood perfection as a sinless state. He himself was ambiguous on this point, allowing for the possibility that mistakes could still be made. Despite the ambiguity, Wesley clearly asserted that, through God's grace, perfection is possible. Even as an ideal, however, perfection is not static; it is a continuing growth in perfect love.

Wesley understood the entire path of salvation as one that could be described in terms of an unlimited movement in God's grace. Be-

---

47. Sermon 46, "The Wilderness State," *Works* 2:202-21.

48. *A Letter to Mrs. Ryan* (28 June 1766), *Letters* (Telford) 5:17-18.

49. Runyon, *New Creation*.

50. See, for example, Sermon 60, "The General Deliverance," *Works* 2:437-50; Sermon 62, "The End of Christ's Coming," *Works* 2:471-84 (esp. §III.5, 482-83); Sermon 18, "The Marks of the New Birth," *Works* 1:417-30; Sermon 45, "The New Birth," *Works* 2:186-201; Sermon 4, "Scriptural Christianity," *Works* 1:159-80; Sermon 26, "Sermon on the Mount, VI," *Works* 1:572-91; and Sermon 63, "The General Spread of the Gospel," *Works* 2:485-99.

51. *A Plain Account of Christian Perfection*, §19, *Works* (Jackson) 11:394; cf. "Brief Thoughts on Christian Perfection," *Works* (Jackson) 11:446; *A Letter to Mrs. Maitland* (12 May 1763), *Letters* (Telford) 4:212-13.

cause salvation was seen as a pilgrimage, guidance was critical along the way. Especially important were preaching the gospel andperfect love, self-examination, and meeting in small communities for accountability and discipline.[52]

This leads naturally to the call for people to participate in God's work of hope. Wesley consistently attributed grace to God and simultaneously expressed the importance of people's participating in the means of grace and acting responsibly in the world. As to the means of grace, Wesley listed these differently at different moments of his ministry. One list includes praying, searching the Scriptures, and receiving the Lord's supper.[53] Another list includes attending church, communicating, fasting, praying privately, reading Scripture, and doing temporal and spiritual good in every way one can.[54] What is most important, in Wesley's view, is that these means of grace are ordained by God and contribute to renewing people's souls.[55]

In particular, Wesley emphasized the sacraments. The sacraments are ways by which we participate in God's grace as a Christian community. Participating in the sacraments also heightens awareness of God's grace at work in our lives. Wesley understood baptism as initiation into God's covenant, cleansing of sins, admission into the body of Christ, and regeneration (new birth) as children of God and heirs of God's kingdom.[56] Baptism will ideally lead to a life of repentance, faith, and obedience—the fruits of God's ongoing work in human lives. This understanding of baptism leads naturally to Eucharist, a sacramental act that continually renews the people. Wesley urged people to "constant communion," saying "it is the duty of every Christian to receive the Lord's Supper as often as he can."[57] Wesley understood Eucharist as a remembrance of Christ's self-giving in life and death, as a means

---

52. Sermon 46, "The Wilderness State," *Works* 2:214-21; Sermon 107, "On God's Vineyard," §§II-III, *Works* 3:508-12; "The Nature, Design, and General Rules of the United Societies," *Works* 9:69-73.

53. Sermon 16, "The Means of Grace," *Works* 1:376-97. Wesley also acknowledged the multiple ways that these multiple means of grace might be practiced. A fuller discussion of means of grace—including sacraments and societies, classes and bands—can be found in Runyon, *The New Creation*, 102-45; and Maddox, *Responsible Grace*, 192-229.

54. *Journal* (31 December 1739), *Works* 19:133.

55. Sermon 16, "The Means of Grace," *Works* 1:376-97.

56. See "On Baptism," *John Wesley*, 317-32.

57. Sermon 101, "The Duty of Constant Communion," §I, *Works* 3:428.

of forgiveness and pardon from past sins, as a renewal of our souls and bodies to follow God, as a promise of glory, and potentially as a converting sacrament (conferring grace even though undeserved).[58] Eucharist, like baptism, conveys God's grace and strengthens people to live by that grace.

In addition to participating with God's salvific work in their own lives and sacramental communities, Christians are also called to participate with God in the larger world. The theme of responsibility, as developed earlier, is very present in Wesley, as in others who have carried on the Wesleyan tradition. For example, women who have lived their lives in that tradition—often without access to preaching, teaching and writing theology—generally embody theologies in which spirituality and social responsibility are held together.[59] This emphasis is found in the many Christian communions that grew out of the Wesley legacy; grace is understood as a gift to be treasured and as a call to respond. The response includes personal response to God's grace and a commissioning to public action within the church and world.

Process-Relational Hope

We turn now to a process-relational view of hope—one that bears an uncanny resemblance to a Wesleyan view, at least when one gazes at the broad strokes of each. Similarities notwithstanding, the accents and primary concerns are often different.

The trajectory of possibility in process-relational theologies is most frequently expressed in relation to the ongoing movement of life, especially as influenced by the lure of God. The language for expressing this view is more philosophical than traditionally theological, but the spirit is similar to Wesley's view of grace. One could merge the languages without distortion, aligning a process-relational view with a Wesleyan one: God works in people's lives before they know it (prevenient grace) and works throughout their lives in ways befitting the person's existential state (justifying, sanctifying, and perfecting).

The very process of concrescence, which in Whitehead's cosmology is the basic building block of the universe, is a process of the

58. Ibid., 3:427-39.

59. Rosemary Skinner Keller, ed., *Spirituality and Social Responsibility: Vocational Vision of Women in The United Methodist Tradition* (Nashville: Abingdon Press, 1993).

many becoming one. The concrescence of an emerging entity includes everything that is positively prehended, or felt, by that entity; thus, the world's diversity is embraced in the creation of every actual occasion.[60] At the same time, God contributes an initial aim to every becoming occasion; thus, God offers guidance to every microscopic event and every being in the cosmos. Even though Whitehead does not identify this as grace, the active principle is God's initiative, functioning not by coercion but by persuasion of each emergent occasion to follow the path of divine vision. This reveals a trajectory of possibility that is significant for the cosmos in general and for every being within it, for God's spirit pervades all of reality.

Whitehead views every becoming occasion as emerging in a relational process; he also views God as responding to the world in a relational process. The consequent nature of God "is composed of a multiplicity of elements with individual self-realization"; it is a whole, but it includes discrete and vivid parts. God's consequent nature is thus both multiplicity and unity, and this multiplicity is still "in process of creation."[61] Creation, in this view, is never complete, even in God, and this is the meaning of the kingdom of heaven.

As with Wesley, we see that *these trajectories of possibility imply that people can expect the impossible from God for both human life and the creation.* Whitehead's cosmology is grounded in the idea that the world passes into God's everlasting unity, accomplishing the majesty of God's vision. God accomplishes this majestic vision by absorbing "the World's multiplicity of effort."[62] This bears a striking resemblance to Runyon's description of Wesley's emphasis on "new creation."

One can see in the process-relational view a metaphysical claim that helps undergird Wesley's view that God has given human beings genuine freedom and that human beings have often exercised that freedom to great detriment. At the same time, God's love never ceases to work with persistence and urgency. The result is a world where genuine evil and tragedy exist, but the grace of God

---

60. Whitehead, *Process and Reality*, 40-42, 220, 236-39.
61. Ibid., 350.
62. Ibid., 349.

is so pervasive and powerful that the condition of sin is never the last word.[63] God continues to offer an initial aim to every becoming occasion; the trajectory of possibilities continues, and people can expect wonders never to cease.

This leads naturally to the call for people to participate in God's work of hope. Just as Wesley consistently attributed grace to God and simultaneously urged human response, a process-relational world-view places emphasis in both places. In fact, the good works espoused in Wesleyan tradition might be described as a parallel to the call for action in process-relational tradition. Paul A. Mickey actually combines the Wesleyan and process languages in making this comparison: "The ongoingness of one's life in Christ is an objectifying witness of the transforming power of Christ's redeeming power as initial aim, but one is also called to join in the 'downward pull of the gospel' (Phil. 2:5-11)."[64] In short, he compares Christ's redeeming power to God's initial aim, and he recognizes each as calling forth a response to the gospel.

Naturally, a philosopher (such as Whitehead) did not develop the ecclesial dimensions of this worldview, as in means of grace and sacramental practice; similarly, an eighteenth-century theologian (such as Wesley) did not develop the comprehensive role of human responsibility in the entire ecosystem. Each man, though, critiques and enlarges the other. Furthermore, Whitehead, while placing hope in religious systems, is freer than Wesley to recognize the importance of dismantling those systems as part of human responsibility. Whitehead says, for example:

> There is a greatness in the lives of those who build up religious systems, a greatness in action, in idea and in self-subordination, embodied in instance after instance through centuries of growth. There is a greatness in the rebels who destroy such systems: they are the Titans who storm heaven, armed with passionate sincerity. . . . Philosophy may not neglect the multifariousness of the world—the fairies dance, and Christ is nailed to the cross.[65]

While Whitehead recognizes the value of destroying religious

---

63. A similar point is made by Castuera, "Wesley, Process and Liberation Theologies," 99-101.

64. Mickey, "Process Theology and Wesleyan Thought," 84-85.

65. Whitehead, *Process and Reality*, 337-38.

systems, he does not approach this glibly. He simply recognizes the reality of beauty and evil in the world: "the fairies dance, and Christ is nailed to the cross." This suggests that human responsibility requires response to God's initial aims and the pull toward beauty, truth, and love; it also requires response to the destructive movements of evil. Hope requires both kinds of response.

Hope and the Case

Considering Wesleyan and process-relational theologies woven into a rope of hope, the case with which we began comes back into view. Perhaps this rope simply offers a tightrope to support people as they walk precariously between diverse views and practices regarding sexual orientation. Perhaps the rope is more of a lifesaving device to throw into the swirling currents where people thrash about. In either case, the rope is not all-sufficient for resolving a difficult situation; however, it may promise support to people who have lost hope. It may offer hope that they can find a way to live with differences, can be accepted into religion by grace, and can be offered as God's initial aim.

Drawing from the trajectories of possibility sketched in this section, one might hope that people who live in the middle of this particular case will not cease to trust in possibilities, even as they honestly face conflicts regarding theological perspectives and just action. In fact, possibilities are already in bud and might be nourished into full bloom. At the same time, people might expect the impossible. In both Wesleyan and process-relational perspectives, the resolution to human dilemmas lies less in finding agreement on mental constructs, than in trusting the power of God. Finally, the people might also recognize that this God-talk does not send the issues into the heavens for God to resolve. The God-talk comes back into people's daily lives, calling them to participate in making hope a reality.

CASE STUDY RECONSIDERED

Where does this analysis lead? Certainly it does not answer the questions of the case in a simplistic fashion. It does suggest some broad-stroke similarities between Wesleyan and process-relational theologies—similarities that arise from the heart of both theological systems. It also suggests a basic approach of compassion and hope to life's dilemmas. To be motivated by compassion is to place the well-being of oneself and others above the particular views that one and others hold. To be motivated by hope is to return to the table again and again and to seek and to expect the possibility of resolving the most difficult dilemmas. Even when those resolutions do not emerge, however, compassionate living with one another can sustain the community through its struggles. This suggests that postponing the full inclusion of one group of people until everyone agrees on one theological or ethical view falls short of grace; both compassion and hope are diminished in such a process.

Another implication of this extensive comparison between Wesleyan and process-relational theologies is that God is larger than human disagreements, yet God is also participating in the middle of these disagreements by persuading people toward the most loving responses. At the same time, human constructs of the good and true and beautiful are always flawed; thus, every human construct requires humility, even when people are deeply committed to it.

Both John Wesley and process-relational theologians refuse to place their theological constructs on a pedestal and beyond the possibility of critique and reformulation. Whitehead is particularly explicit on this point, arguing for critical analysis and constructive theory-building and also for acknowledging the inadequacy of any explanatory scheme that is developed. He further recognizes "how shallow, puny, and imperfect are efforts to sound the depths in the nature of things"; he adds, "In philosophical discussion, the merest hint of dogmatic certainty as to finality of statement is an exhibition of folly."[66] We see here a spirit of humility and a spirit of continuing critique and inquiry.

John Wesley certainly engaged in the same sort of hearty debate in his lifetime, and on many matters, he changed his mind. At the same time, he urged that preference be given to having one's heart right with another, rather than having all of one's theological beliefs in agreement. This is not the place for fine-tuning what

---

66. Ibid., xiv.

Wesley meant by these affirmations, but Mickey, speaking on behalf of Wesleyan evangelicals, does interpret Wesley's point in a way that keeps the conversation open. He explains Wesley in relation to process-relational thought, urging that people relate with others through their deepest physical feelings, or prehensions, of the heart; he also recognizes that such deep religious experiences of faith are "objectified and confirmed as beliefs."[67] In short, the line of demarcation between having one's heart right with another and delineating one's beliefs is not as solid and clear as people might wish in the heat of debate. Neither dimension of human relationship can be totally abandoned. Even though people might disagree about what John Wesley intended and what contemporary Wesleyan theologians intend, Mickey's central point does leave the door open for critical interpretations. Furthermore, Mickey turns the question back to love, quoting Wesley on the subject of how we might meet one another: (1) love me, (2) pray for me, (3) stir me up to love, and (4) love me in the depths of truth.[68]

In light of these reflections on the case study, one might hope that both Wesleyan and process-relational theologies were more thoroughly engaged in the particular issues of the contemporary world. One might hope that controversies regarding homosexuality would be addressed in such a way that hurting and marginalized people would not be forgotten in the midst of debates engulfed by abstraction and dichotomized positions. One might hope that the complex connections between issues of sexual orientation and issues of gender, social class, and race would not be ignored. One might hope, also, that aches of the world caused by racial and economic oppression would not be forgotten in the midst of present debates on sexual orientation. Has the human community finally reached a point when simplistic, either/or formulations of controversy might be critiqued and reshaped? To answer this question, we need to engage the critical imagination of hurting people. We need also to engage the depths of Wesleyan and process-relational theologies, beyond the most superficial rhetoric. If we can do these things, compassion and hope will indeed live!

---

67. Mickey, "Process Theology and Wesleyan Thought," 84.
68. Sermon 39, "Catholic Spirit," §II.3-8, *Works* 2:90-92.

CHAPTER FIFTEEN

SPIRITUALITY AND SOCIAL TRANSFORMATION:
PERSPECTIVES ON WESLEYAN AND PROCESS THEOLOGIES

HENRY JAMES YOUNG

Martin Luther King Jr., in his seminal work *Where Do We Go from Here: Chaos or Community?* helps us see what we must do in order to overcome (1) the increasing polarization between the oppressed and the oppressor, the rich and the poor, and (2) the problem of institutional racism, which increasingly brings about the holocaust of victims to an economic reality where a concentration of wealth is lodged in the hands of a small portion of the world's population, while countless African Americans, Hispanics, Latin Americans, Indians, Africans, and others are consigned to varying degrees of poverty and even death.[1] King points out that for centuries, humankind has lived by the premise that "self preservation is the first law of life." He argues instead that the preservation of the other is really the first law of life. The oppressor and all persons in control of economic resources in the world cannot continue to sustain a high quality of existence on the top at the expense of millions of victims at the bottom. As King says, "The structure of the universe is such that the oppression of any social group creates ecological imbalances that are harmful to all."[2] He repeatedly reminds us that injustice anywhere is a threat to justice everywhere. Consequently, he feels that whenever any group experiences oppression, we are all confronted with an imperative to stand and work in concrete solidarity with that particular oppressed social group.

1. See Theodore W. Jennings Jr., *Good News to the Poor: John Wesley's Evangelical Economics* (Nashville: Abingdon Press, 1990), 13-69.
2. Martin Luther King Jr., *Where Do We Go from Here: Chaos or Community?* (Boston: Beacon Press, 1967), 180.

CONTEXT AND METHODOLOGY

My task in this essay is to show that concrete social solidarity growing out of Wesleyan and process theological paradigms can provide a viable hermeneutical key to unlocking the doors of the Christian church and Christian theological discourse and toward making spirituality and social transformation of equal and central importance to soteriology. In other words, in order for soteriology, eschatological hope, and other themes of Christian theology to take socially transforming dimensions, the salvific moment must, by definition, include the process of standing and working in concrete solidarity with the poor, dispossessed, oppressed, physically challenged, and marginalized of society. Here, spirituality and sociality are interpreted as two distinct dimensions of one and the same process. Or, to put it another way, they are two sides of the same coin, making them interwoven, interconnected, and interdependent. If spiritual journeying is at the core of the gospel of Jesus Christ, then social transformation must stand beside it with equal importance. The transformation of the whole person must include spiritual, psychological, and physical dimensions. As I will attempt to point out, this approach to salvation captures the theological orientation of Wesleyan and process liberation theologies. What militates greatly against this type of theological orientation, however, are the many metaphysical problems we have inherited from classical and modern theological paradigms.

For example, the classical theological paradigm—beginning with the Platonic worldview and continuing up to the thought of John Calvin—embraced a metaphysic of dualism with a corresponding split between spirituality and sociality, mind and body, and interiority and exteriority.[3] Classical theological discourse also tended to make the spiritual realm the locus of the real as distinct from the physical realm, which was perceived as metaphysically inferior to the real. The Greeks associated the spiritual with the changeless and static realm, which was believed to consist of the real. The physical realm was thought to consist of the world of change, becoming, and finitude and was seen as inferior to the static and

---

3. Peter C. Hodgson, *Revisioning the Church: Ecclesial Freedom in the New Paradigm* (Philadelphia: Fortress Press, 1988), 11-19.

changeless realm. This resulted in the Christian church and theological discourse accepting the doctrine of otherworldly eschatological hope as the core of the Christian faith—an acceptance that ultimately undermined socioeconomic and political involvements on the part of the faith community. It created false notions of compensatory grace manifested through acts of divine vindication. What followed from this was a spiritualization of oppression and its sanctioning by God.

The modern theological paradigm, beginning with John Calvin and continuing up to the twentieth century,[4] intensified the dualistic worldview of the classical theological paradigm by replacing the speculative metaphysics of Plato and Aristotle with scientific observation, experimentation, empiricism, and objectivity as the normative criteria for truth validation. Truth validation was grounded in scientific materialism, which perceived each aspect of reality to be autonomous, separate, self-contained, isolated, detached, independent, substantial, valueless, complete, and unchanging. With such an orientation in the modern period, we took a private and individualistic approach to salvation, placing a high premium on the self over the community of faith. We can say that the Christian church and theological discourse in the modern period based its theological orientation on the premise of scientific materialism and fostered a movement of its social institutions—including the Christian church—toward social insulationism, cultural isolationism, and individualism. Included in this list should be the exploitation of human and natural resources.[5]

During the Enlightenment, we experienced the collapse of "salvation history" as the fundamental mythos of our culture. This theological vision, deeply rooted in the Jewish and Christian cultural traditions and contending that divine sovereignty will ensure the final victory of good over evil, was secularized and reformulated into a "theory of progress."[6] This theory took an evolutionary orientation and interpreted God's presence in history as associated with the wealthy conquerors of human and natural resources. For this reason, modern slaveholders considered themselves to be good

---

4. Ibid.

5. See Henry James Young, *Hope in Process: A Theology of Social Pluralism* (Minneapolis: Fortress Press, 1990), 1-45.

6. Hodgson, *Revisioning the Church*, 14.

Christians doing God's will. In fact, modern slavery was "created by Christians, it was continued by Christians, it was in some respects more barbarous than anything the world had yet seen, and its worst features were to be witnessed in countries that were most ostentatious in their parade of Christianity."[7]

Process thought, based on a postmodern theological paradigm grounded in relationality, sets the stage for spirituality and social transformation to become the appropriate methodological framework for interpreting soteriology, eschatology, and other themes in Christian theology. It begins by describing the world in its totality, from the smallest level of existence to the most complex and configured. It provides an integration of the within (interiority) and the without (exteriority) of reality. Just as each unit of experience contains a spiritual and physical dimension in process thought, so does the nature of God. The primordial nature of God is mental (spiritual), and God's consequent nature is physical (derivative of the world). Whitehead is cautious not to make God "an exception to all metaphysical principles, invoked to save their collapse"[8] as in the case of Aristotle, whom he considers to be the chief metaphysician in the Western tradition. Whitehead offers a vision of God as the chief exemplification of all metaphysical principles. Thus there is no generic distinction between God and other acts of experience in the world. God contains the basic stuff that makes up all other forms of reality, namely, quanta of energy. A fundamental difference, however, is that God is nonperishable and infinite in nature, while all other creatures are finite and perishable.

Such an orientation brings soteriology and social transformation into an integrated nexus of inseparability. Each unit of experience contains inherent spiritual and social dimensions. In the classical and modern worldviews, a substance-oriented outlook leaves the spiritual and the social realms autonomous without any inherent interconnectedness. Process thought makes the two socialized, that is, related both internally and externally.[9]

In the dualistic worldview of classical thought and the materialistic worldview of modern thought, reality is interpreted on the

---

7. W. E. Burghardt Dubois, *The World and Africa* (New York: Viking Press, 1946), 53.

8. Alfred North Whitehead, *Process and Reality: An Essay in Cosmology*, corrected, ed., ed. David Ray Griffin and Donald W. Sherburne (New York: Free Press, 1978), 343.

9. Ibid., 18-30.

basis of a philosophy of substance. By definition, a substance depends on nothing else for its existence. It endures change, remaining the same regardless of how it relates to others. As John B. Cobb Jr. points out, the Greeks defined an atom as a unit of substance. Modern mechanism builds its metaphysics on this notion. Things that are not atoms are thought of as nothing but a structure of atoms. Atoms, therefore, are not affected by the structure in which they are arranged. They behave like machines and are not inherently affected by their relations with other things. Other forces can affect a structure of atoms by taking parts of the structure and separating some atoms from others. But the character of the separated parts is not affected.[10]

Process thought contains a metaphysics that seeks to discover the general ideas that are indispensably relevant to the analysis of everything that happens. Whitehead makes it clear that the reality described should not be revised in an attempt to force it into conformity with a metaphysical scheme already constructed. Process thought begins with experience as the basic methodological framework. Appropriating the scientific method and speculative metaphysics, it then extrapolates from particular acts of experience into broad universal generalities. The method then returns to the particular acts of experience to test its hypothesis.[11]

It is important to note that experience itself is both one and many, individual and diverse. Traditional classical and modern theologies projected the experience of Caucasian males as dominant and normative for all other experiences. Consequently, experiences of ethnic minority social groups and women were not considered as viable points of departure in theological discourse. This is the reason that contextualization is so essential for doing theology today. We have learned from scholars in the field of the sociology of knowledge that all knowledge is structured by factors growing out of social, political, and economic realities. Totally objective knowledge removed from ideological elements just does not exist. Whenever North American Caucasian male theologians project universal categories about the nature of God, humanity,

---

10. John B. Cobb Jr., "Ecology, Science, and Religion: Toward a Postmodern Worldview" in David Ray Griffin, ed., *The Reenchantment of Science: Postmodern Proposals* (Albany, N.Y.: State University of New York Press, 1988), 107.

11. Whitehead, *Process and Reality*, 3-17.

Christ, the Holy Spirit, and eschatology and are presumed to be objective, they fail to acknowledge, or even question, the biases undergirding their own presuppositions and assumptions. They assume these biases to be absolute and consistent with truth validation. Process thought helps to overcome this problem.

In process thought, experience is affirmed as both one and many. In fact, in God's consequent nature, God incorporates multiple experiences, change, potentiality, complexity, and so forth. Here, God's creation and the host of experiences in the world enrich the reality of God. In God's primordial nature, God conceptually envisages all possibilities that might be realized as experiences in the world. We can extrapolate that multiple experiences manifested through multiculturalism, ethnic minority social groups, women, and diverse religious expressions are normative.[12] Experiences are pluralistic and diverse, not monolithic.

In Wesleyan thought, experience interacts with scripture and serves as the medium through which truths found in the Bible are validated. Religious experience informs all other experiences a person may have, and vice versa. The experience of "new life in Christ" brings spirituality and social transformation to a pivotal point in the life of the individual and the corporate community of faith. When "new life in Christ" is incorporated into an individual's lifestyle and is shared by the corporate faith community, the Christian church suddenly will be able to celebrate spirituality and social transformation as its reason for being.[13]

Wesleyan thought takes creaturely fallenness seriously. Although prevenient grace is available to all persons, humanity has fallen from righteousness and is not able to realize holiness apart from being born again in Christ. Divine grace and the empowerment of the Holy Spirit enable humanity to do what is pleasing and acceptable to God. We stand justified before God in righteousness, not because of our own works but because of our belief in Jesus Christ. Experience takes upon itself a dynamic quality in that, as persons stand justified before God, they become partakers of the divine nature of God through regeneration. This

---

12. Young, *Hope in Process*, 84-108; Susan Thistlethwaite, *Lift Every Voice: Constructing Theologies from the Underside* (New York: Harper & Row, 1990), 6.

13. See *The Book of Discipline of The United Methodist Church* (Nashville: The United Methodist Publishing House, 2000), ¶ 104, pp. 81-82.

newness of experience is a continuous process; it is not static and complete. It takes place over and over again in the life of Christians. We are constantly repenting and being regenerated before God. This constant renewal of experience in Jesus Christ is inclusive of one's commitment to a preferential option for the poor, to the social transformation of the world, and to the protest against all forms of social injustice. For both process and Wesleyan thought, good works are essential to making spirituality and social transformation happen effectively in the world, but neither happens apart from the intentional efforts of God and humanity.[14]

In Wesleyan thought, one does not earn salvation or take credit for the grace that transforms the world. We cannot force grace into spirituality and social transformation. We can only create the occasion for grace. In process thought, God is affected both negatively and positively by all creaturely decisions. When we respond positively to God's possibilities, God participates in the joy of the salvific moment. When we reject God's possibilities and thereby fail to create the occasion for social transformation to take place, God suffers the shame with us.

THE REALITY OF GOD: SANCTIFICATION AND CHRISTIAN PERFECTION

In Wesleyan thought, good works are the fruits of faith and follow the experience of regeneration. Sanctification is the work of God and cannot be earned meritoriously. Sanctification takes place after standing justified before God in righteousness as a person grows into holiness by the empowerment of the Holy Spirit.[15] Here, the person attempts to avoid committing outward visible sin; but because inward sin continues, a process of sanctification is required in order to conquer inward sin.[16] This process of sanctification continues on an inward and outward basis as the person regenerated in Christ moves toward perfection. One is never completely exempt from committing sin in this life but is always living in a state

---

14. Ibid.
15. Harald Lindström, *Wesley and Sanctification* (Wilmore, Ky.: Francis Asbury), 83-125.
16. Sermon 5, "Justification by Faith," *Works* 1:181-99.

of renewal in Christ. Regardless of the maturity of a person, for Wesley, the "perfected" individual is never free from the possibility of error, temptations, illness, or death. The Christian faith does not shield the Christian from the normal problems associated with finite existence; nor does it immunize humanity from finite limitations. In spite of the many problems related to our finite existence, the Christian faith enables us to participate in the vision of God's kingdom being manifested in the world.

The great challenge of Wesleyan thought—a challenge that I will attempt to show is compatible with process thought—is the mission and ministry of the Christian church to make social holiness characteristic of lifestyle. In other words, repentance, justification, regeneration, and sanctification are not aimed at making persons candidates for heaven but are instead aimed at making persons candidates for standing and working in concrete solidarity with oppressed creatures, which will make the quality of life more consistent with the values embodied in the kingdom of God. Even though a belief in living with God after death is present in both Wesleyan and process theologies, neither system of thought begins and ends with it. Both theologies are about making social justice, love, righteousness, mercy, goodness, and honesty characteristic of life on earth. The values of the kingdom of God—or God's vision for the world—demand a radical stance from Christians. Whenever the values of the kingdom of God are inconsistent with the goals, objectives, purposes, and functions of social structures in the world, the task of the Christian community is to stand and work in concrete solidarity with members of the oppressed by holding these social structures accountable to God. Such is the prophetic dimension of preaching, teaching, and Christian leadership. Sanctification provides persons with the passion needed to face the increasing demonic forces of social injustice.

In Wesleyan and process thought, "perfection" is interpreted in a dynamic manner. For Wesley, the individual Christian moves gradually toward perfection;[17] and in process thought, the moment of perfection comes when acts of experience are self-actualized. God provides, through persuasion, the highest possibilities for creaturely existence, and these possibilities flow from God's primordial

17. See Sermon 76, "On Perfection," *Works* 3:70-87.

nature into the world for self-actualization. In this manner, God functions as the principle of concretion, for God limits the possibilities so as to maintain order in the world rather than chaos. This is the transcendent conceptual pole of God. It consists of the reservoir of all possibilities for the world. These possibilities are inexhaustible and infinite. In this manner, God functions as our "help in ages past and our hope for years to come."

Some of these possibilities are lost in the process of flowing from God's primordial nature, but others reach concretion in God's consequent nature. So, perfection takes an existential and historical dimension. In traditional existential philosophies and theologies (e.g., Martin Heidegger, Rudolf Bultmann, and Søren Kierkegaard), the existential moment of self-actualization is grounded in subjectivity as opposed to objectivity. Kierkegaard makes the point that truth is subjectivity and refers to the experience of authenticity as "the existential leap of faith." For Heidegger, authenticity grows out of a phenomenological and epistemological response from the self as a finite being confronted by Being-itself while in the quest for authentic existence. Bultmann refers to it as the eschatological act of faith. Each moment of authentic existence is separate and detached from the other. In each case, subjectivity is the locus of meaning. In Wesleyan and process theologies, however, the duality of subjectivity and objectivity accepted by existentialist philosophies is rejected. For process thought, subjectivity and objectivity are interdependent and inseparable. Both process and Wesleyan theologians take the existential moment out of a fixation with the present and integrate it into tradition, culture, past, present, and future.[18] But what happens to experiences after they reach different levels of perfection? What happens to them when they become complete and perish? It is in response to these questions that process thought and Wesleyan thought can offer challenges and eschatological hope in overcoming oppression.

RESOURCES IN PROCESS AND WESLEY FOR OVERCOMING OPPRESSION

After creaturely experiences reach levels of perfection, they perish but are not lost. God enjoys the perfection of these experiences

---

18. Whitehead, *Process and Reality*, 342-51.

in God's consequent nature. They are then forever preserved in God's faultless memory with neither loss nor obstruction. Because of this faultless memory, God preserves our sufferings, sorrows, failures, joys, and triumphs and transforms them into a harmony of universal expression. They become immediate, always multiple and diverse, always one, and always containing degrees of novel advance in moving forward but never perishing. Evil, suffering, and oppression in the world are combated in God's consequent nature. As Whitehead says, "The revolts of destructive evil, purely self-regarding, are dismissed into their triviality of merely individual facts; and yet the good they did achieve in individual joy, in individual sorrow, in the introduction of needed contrast, is yet saved by its relation to the completed whole."[19] Whitehead's image of God is that of patience and tender love so that nothing in the world is lost. The tenderness of God is so profound that God loses nothing that can be saved in the world. God's love and patience are infinite.

We can see that divine vulnerability and concrete social solidarity are not afterthoughts with God. They are at the very heart of what it means to be divine. In process thought, God cannot be invulnerable, unloving, impatient, and uncaring. The nature of God is to share and preserve all creaturely experiences. However, in response to victims of social injustices, political domination, sexism, or institutional racism, we have to go much further than merely saying that the beauty of our past experience, with all of its joys and sufferings, is preserved once and for all in the storehouse of beauties, or in the infinite memory of God. We must also go further than merely saying that all we are and will become—whether good or bad—is destined in spite of our many weaknesses "to be imperishably loved by the cosmically social being."[20] The Wesleyan sense of appropriating radical ethics, implementing social strategies, making our prophetic voices heard, and forever challenging all social structures, helps to integrate the theoretical overview of Whitehead's metaphysical construct into praxis.

God seeks to overcome evil, suffering, and turmoil by the completion of God's own nature. God's role is not to use force in the

---

19. Ibid., 346.
20. Charles Hartshorne, *Reality as Social Process: Studies in Metaphysics and Religion*, (Boston: Beacon Press, 1953), 42-43.

world to change oppressed conditions toward the good. It is through persuasion, not coercion, that God uses the overpowering rationality of conceptual harmonization to transform the world. In Whitehead's comprehensive metaphysical scheme, evil, suffering, failures, and faults are resolved ultimately in the nature of God. Through God's infinite wisdom, love, and patience, problems of evil and suffering are transformed.

We need to integrate Whitehead's vision with the Wesleyan notion that repentance, regeneration, and sanctification directly challenge oppressors to a modification of lifestyle, a redistribution of economic resources, and preferential treatment for the poor. In order to accomplish this integration, a number of questions must be answered. Although the overpowering rationality of God's conceptual harmonization ultimately resolves the problem of evil and suffering metaphysically, how can humanity use this cosmic vision in order to transform immediate systemic structures of oppression? What needs to happen in the church and society to make this happen? What should be done about the monopolies on decision-making processes in social institutions geared toward perpetuating a selected group of elite Caucasian male managers, while women and members of ethnic minority social groups have no chance of moving up the social ladder? What about social structures that sustain economic colonialism in Africa, Latin America, the United States, and other parts of the global village? What about the increasing presence of war and violence throughout the global village? Is America commissioned by God to police the world into peace, harmony, and economic solvency? We need only look at the increasing presence of poverty, racism, sexism, and disenfranchisement of members of ethnic minority social groups in America in order to realize that there is something fundamentally inconsistent about our efforts to bring freedom and liberation to the global village when oppression in our own backyard is growing in epidemic proportions.

CHRISTOLOGY, VULNERABILITY, AND SOCIAL TRANSFORMATION

The critical point of departure that is essential for the liberation of both the oppressors and the oppressed is the experience of vulnerability. Here, the question is not one of power and control but one of being able to enter into an entirely modified lifestyle in which the quest for power and control is not essential. The oppressed are on the bottom of the socioeconomic ladder and without a place to retreat from the forces of social injustice. But interpreting the life and ministry of Jesus Christ from within the Wesleyan tradition as embracing a preferential treatment for the poor, a new point of departure comes to define the mission and ministry of the Christian church. The oppressors must experience the pain and vulnerability associated with going out from themselves and taking on the pain and suffering of the oppressed. It is not until the pain, misery, and suffering of the oppressed are identified with by, and become the problems of, the oppressors that social transformation is likely to reach a substantive level of significance. As long as the suffering of the oppressed is identified solely as the problem of the oppressed, we are not likely to witness social transformation of systemic forces. Jesus Christ went to the poor and made their problems his own. This is what it means to stand and work in concrete solidarity with others.

In process thought, the nature of God is understood within a metaphysics of inclusiveness where vulnerability and concrete solidarity are characteristic of social reality. This is the reason that, through mutual immediacy, the highest possibilities available for creaturely existence are preserved everlastingly in God's nature at each dimension of temporality. Jesus Christ represents the special paradigmatic point in which these possibilities culminate and become the *kairos*, or the point of salvation for the world. Incarnation in process thought is pluralistic, not singular as in both classical and modern theological paradigms. In other words, from a process perspective, we can say that the history of the world represents the history of God's incarnation, reaching the special point of salvific manifestation in Jesus Christ. In this sense, Jesus Christ is our Savior and paradigmatically remains the hope of humanity.[21] For the world, Jesus Christ represents the symbol of the New Age. He represents the new sociopolitical order of social justice, freedom, liberation, and righteousness. The heavenly age of redemption and freedom from sin and death is available in him.

---

21. See John B. Cobb Jr., *Christ in a Pluralistic Age* (Philadelphia: Westminster Press, 1975), 177-258.

Here, we find a resolution to the christological controversies that plagued theological discourse in the early centuries of Christianity with an attempt to relate the *ousia* (being) of the Logos to the *ousia* (being) of God. The christological questions of Jesus' person and of the relationship of the nature of God to the nature of humanity are both dealt with in process thought by recognizing that each event, including the incarnation of God in Jesus Christ, consists of an integration of divine and creaturely activity. The nature of divine and creaturely being is not substantial; rather, it consists of two inseparable dimensions of the same process. Wesleyan theology is more traditional in its christological formulation. It accepts Jesus Christ as truly God and truly human. It affirms a "two-natures" theory, in which the natures are perfectly and inseparably unified in Jesus Christ. In this manner, Christ is perceived in Wesleyan thought as the eternal Word of God incarnated and made flesh. Jesus Christ is the only begotten Son of God.[22]

The extent to which we move into the world preaching the gospel of Jesus Christ, teaching about the Good News, and transforming oppressed conditions is the extent to which we become heirs of Jesus Christ. We become followers of Jesus Christ as we acknowledge him as our Christian paradigm and then transform the world accordingly.

CONCLUSION

The hope of humanity resides in the extent to which we are able and willing to make the atoning work of Jesus Christ characteristic of the mission of the Christian church—just as Jesus Christ made himself vulnerable and gave his life for the sins of the world. We must go forth into the world and give our lives through concrete solidarity in overcoming systemic forms of oppression. Only then can the gulf between the oppressors and the oppressed be overcome. We must repudiate all forms of paternalism, handouts, and expressions of charity. Oppressors must both internalize and experience the pain and evils of oppression before the atoning work of Jesus Christ can become redemptive in the world. Before we can

22. *The United Methodist Book of Discipline*, ¶103 pp. 59-60 and 64-65.

consider ourselves fully members of the Body of Christ, the structures of oppression must be abolished. What will make this happen more effectively is the Christian church and theological discourse articulating the gospel of Jesus Christ in a manner that holds spirituality and social transformation in creative tension.

With the Wesleyan notion of sanctification understood dynamically and with the idea that each unit of experience contains both spiritual and social dimensions as found in process thought, the church can foster a new sense of ethical accountability. At each level of soteriology, whether we are speaking of conversion, sanctification, justification, or redemption, the element of social accountability is to be found. We cannot abstract spirituality from its social dimensions as the church has done in the past. For example, during the modern period, slaveholders were perceived as good Christian people. The church elevated spirituality above social accountability. When we perceive them as inseparable, however, salvation is taken out of a privatistic and individualistic focus, and the church is enabled to regain the corporate meaning of faith. In other words, we are not saved until the systemic structures of evil and sin, which perpetuate the increasing gulf between the oppressed and oppressors, are overcome.

The Whiteheadian notion that the kingdom of heaven is with us today, and the Wesleyan notions of sanctification and social holiness help the church to see that we have all the resources necessary to eradicate all forms of systemic oppression.

CHAPTER SIXTEEN

JOHN WESLEY, PROCESS THEOLOGY, AND CONSUMERISM

JAY MCDANIEL AND JOHN L. FARTHING

We write as college professors who have been teaching at a church-related, liberal arts college for twenty years. Over the decades, it has been obvious to us that an overriding reality in our students' lives—and in ours as well—is consumerism. We also write as Christians. We are struck by the many ways in which consumerism contradicts the ideals of Christ as depicted in the New Testament. If Christianity is to have influence in our time, we believe that it must offer an alternative to the consumer-driven habits that shape so much modern life. Our subject, then, is Christianity in the age of consumerism.

Our thesis is simple. It is that John Wesley in his way, and process theologians in theirs, invite us into postconsumerist ways of living and thinking. We develop our thesis in three sections. In the first, we explain what we mean by consumerism. In the second, we explain how, in his historical context, John Wesley proposed a countercultural way of living that directly contradicted, and still contradicts, the lifestyle and attitudes of consumerism. And in the third, we suggest ways in which process theology can affirm, complement, and contribute to Wesley's counterconsumer insights.

WHAT IS CONSUMERISM?

By consumerism we mean two things: (1) an overconsuming lifestyle practiced by about one-fifth of the world's population, and aspired to by many among the other four-fifths, and (2) a set of attitudes and values that support and reinforce this lifestyle and that can be caricatured as an unofficial, corporate-sponsored world religion. Our analysis of the overconsuming lifestyle comes from Alan Durning's *How Much Is Enough? The Consumer Society and the Future of the Earth.*[1]

The Lifestyle of Consumerism

According to Durning, the overconsumers of the world live in North America, Western Europe, Japan, Australia, Hong Kong, and Singapore and among the affluent classes of Eastern Europe, Latin America, South Africa, and South Korea. Typically, they—we— drive privately owned automobiles, eat prepackaged foods, depend on throwaway goods, drink from aluminum cans, enjoy temperature controlled climates, thrive on a meat-based diet, fly in airplanes, and release inordinate amounts of waste into the atmosphere. Collectively, we consume approximately 40 percent of the earth's fresh water, 60 percent of its fertilizers, 75 percent of its energy, 75 percent of its timber, 80 percent of its paper, and 85 percent of its aluminum. Our aerosol cans, air conditioners, and factories release almost 90 percent of the chlorofluorocarbons that cause ozone depletion. Our use of fossil fuels causes two-thirds of the emissions of carbon dioxide. If the whole world consumed as we consume and polluted as we pollute, the life-support systems of our planet would quickly collapse.

Of course, many of us say that we are "struggling to make ends meet." And indeed we are, though not because we lack food to eat or the basic necessities of life. We are struggling because we spend much of our time trying to maintain a way of living that we are taught to call the good life, but which often leaves us breathless and frantic. Caught between the demands of work and family, of personal desire and civic responsibility, we fall into a compulsive busyness, always on our way toward a happiness that never quite arrives. We yearn for a simpler life, one that is more spiritual and caring.

Amid our yearning, however, we ought not to romanticize our situation. Instead, we should remember the other four-fifths of the world's population, many of whom might deem our need for "spirituality" somewhat self-indulgent. According to Durning, the other four-fifths of our human family is divided into two groups: the sustainers and the destitute.

---

1. Alan Durning, *How Much Is Enough? The Consumer Society and the Future of the Earth* (New York: Norton, 1992).

The "sustainers" form about three-fifths of the world's population and live mostly in Latin America, the Middle East, China, and among the nonaffluent in East Asia. Typically, they earn between $700 and $7500 a year per family member, eat more grains than meats, drink clean water, ride bicycles and buses, and depend more on durable goods than throwaways. They are "sustainers" because they live at levels that could be "sustained" into the indefinite future if global population were stabilized and clean technologies employed.

The "destitute" are the abjectly poor of the world. They are about one-fifth of the world's population and live mostly in rural Africa and rural India. They earn less than $700 a year per family member, eat insufficient grain, drink unclean water, and travel by walking. Their lives are in no way "sustainable." Their deepest need is to rise to the level of the sustainer class.

What, then, is the best hope for our planet? It is that (1) the population of the world cease growing, (2) nations begin to rely upon clean technologies to feed and furnish their citizens, (3) the truly poor of the world rise from their poverty with some combination of external assistance and local self-development, and (4) the overconsumers learn to live more simply. In short, it is that the overconsumers and underconsumers meet in the middle, where the sustainers live. Durning hopes—and we do, too—that the religions of the world can find inner resources to help realize this hope.

The Religion of Consumerism

If Christians are to contribute to this hope, they—we—will have to recognize that consumerism is also more than a lifestyle. It is a set of attitudes and values that support and reinforce the overconsuming lifestyle and that are now preached twenty-four hours a day throughout the world in advertisements on radio and television, in magazines, and on billboards. In order to explain these attitudes and values, it helps to imagine them as part of an unofficial, corporate-sponsored world religion.

Perhaps the central organizing principle of this religion—and thus its god—is Economic Growth. We borrow this idea from John B. Cobb Jr., who suggests that the past one thousand years of western history can be divided into three periods: the ages of

Christianism, Nationalism, and Economism.[2] The age of Christianism was the Middle Ages, in which the central organizing principle of much public life, for good and ill, was the Christian Church. In the seventeenth century, partly in response to the religious wars of the sixteenth century, a new organizing principle emerged that has considerable power today: the nation-state. Slowly but surely, people's needs for security and adventure, for meaning and creativity, came to be satisfied through "service to the nation" as opposed to "service to the church." The age of Nationalism emerged.

In our time, the age of Nationalism is being replaced by an age of Economism, which has itself emerged, not only through the rise of capitalism and science, but also in response to the two world wars and many regional wars fought in the name of nationalism. The central organizing principle of an Economistic Age is not "the church" or "the nation" but "the economy," or more precisely, material prosperity as produced through a growing economy. In the age of Economism, many people's needs for security and adventure are satisfied, not by "service to the nation," much less "service to the church," but by "service to the corporation." The interests of business take priority over the interests of government and church. Corporate headquarters, not the nation's capital or the church, are the symbolic centers of society.

If Cobb is right and we are entering an age of Economism, then economic growth has become a god of sorts, albeit a false one; and "consumerism" names that cultural ethos—that religion, if you will—that serves this god. The priests of this religion are the public policy makers—corporate executives, economists, and politicians—who understand growth and promise us access to it. The evangelists are the advertisers who display the products of growth and convince us that we cannot be happy without them. The laity are the consumers themselves, formerly called "citizens" in the age of Nationalism. The church is the mall. And salvation comes—not by grace through faith, as Christians claim—but by appearance, affluence, and marketable achievement.[3]

---

2. John B. Cobb Jr., *The Earthist Challenge to Economism: A Theological Critique of the World Bank* (New York: St. Martin's Press, 1999), 10-25.

3. Marcus J. Borg, *Meeting Jesus Again for the First Time* (San Francisco: HarperSanFrancisco, 1994), 87. Our caricature of the means of salvation in consumerism borrows directly from Borg's assertion that Jesus challenged the conventional wisdom of his day, in which "achievement, affluence, and appearance" were the dominant values.

We might also imagine consumerism as having its doctrines and creeds. Its doctrine of creation would be that the earth is real estate to be bought and sold in the marketplace and that other living beings—animals, for example—are mere commodities for human use. Its doctrine of human existence would be that we are skin-encapsulated egos cut off from the world by the boundaries of our skin, whose primary purpose is to "have our needs met." And its basic creeds would be "bigger is better," "faster is better," "more is better," and "you can have it all." Admittedly, our caricature is negative and cynical. Still, we think there is truth in it. If we are entering an age of Economism, then there does seem to be an ideology—a set of attitudes and values—that functions like a religion: that is, a way of organizing the whole of life, inner and outer. Thus, a serious question emerges: Can middle-class Christians in high-income countries, who have been so deeply co-opted into the ideology of consumerism, nevertheless find resources within their heritage, past and present, for critical and creative response to this lifestyle and its accompanying religion?

WESLEY AND THE NEW MONASTICISM

In light of this question, we turn to John Wesley. What Wesley offers most deeply is an image—a hope—that life can be lived in a simpler and more frugal way. In what follows, we highlight six overlapping Wesleyan ideals that, taken together, form a radical alternative to consumer-driven living: (1) sharing with others, (2) freedom from inordinate attachments, (3) freedom from affluence, (4) freedom for the poor, (5) freedom for simplicity, and (6) freedom for the present moment. These ideals were challenging in his time, and they are challenging in ours.

The Primacy of Sharing

One key to understanding the spirit of the Methodist movement is to view it as a Protestant analogue to Roman Catholic monasticism. As envisioned by Wesley, the movement looks rather like a lay order within the Church of England.

At points, of course, the analogy breaks down. Wesley never

entertained any thoughts of imposing a vow of celibacy as a precondition for membership in the Methodist societies. Nevertheless, there are many instructive parallels between the spirit of early Methodism and certain distinctive features of Roman Catholic monasticism. Consider the three monastic vows: chastity, obedience, and poverty.

Chastity is an ideal that Wesley found, if not compelling, at least alluring. The radical simplicity of lifestyle that he regarded as the outward expression of inward holiness is clearly more accessible to those who remain unentangled in domestic responsibilities. During the first several generations of Methodism, the rigors of the itinerant ministry involved a lifestyle that was hardly compatible with the more settled routines of home and hearth. While never imposing celibacy as a criterion of discipleship or as a precondition for membership in the Methodist societies, Wesley was himself drawn to the celibate form of discipleship.[4]

Additionally, the authoritarian strand in Wesley's relationship to the Methodist societies recalls the monastic virtue of obedience. The structure of primitive Methodism, like that of monasticism, was not democratic but hierarchical. Wesley managed the affairs of the United Societies with an iron fist; in relation to the Methodist movement he was, in effect, a father superior. The early conferences were not decision-making bodies but rather opportunities to transmit decisions made by Wesley in an utterly top-down fashion. "We are no republicans," he declared, "and never intend to be."[5]

But it is at the point of the monastic ideal of poverty—the rejection of private property in commitment to the lifelong practice of self-denial—that the analogy between monasticism and Methodism is most striking.[6] Wesley noted that in the earliest centuries of the history of the Church, the more affluent of the churches were the first to fall into corruption, while the pristine integrity of primitive Christianity was retained longest by poorer congregations. Wesley attributed the loss of the church's original simplicity to the pernicious influence of prosperity, with its attendant temp-

4. See *Thoughts on a Single Life*, *Works* (Jackson) 11:456-63; and Stanley Ayling, *John Wesley* (Nashville, Abingdon Press, 1979), 215-31.
5. *A Letter to John Mason* (13 January 1790), *Letters* (Telford) 8:196.
6. See Sermon 48, "Self-denial," *Works* 2:238-50.

tations and distractions. Wesley argued from the apostasy of Ananias and Sapphira that the earliest symptom of the loss of innocence in the New Testament church is seen in the abandonment of the community of goods enjoyed by believers shortly after Pentecost.[7] Accordingly, Wesley envisioned Methodism as moving toward a restoration of both the spiritual vitality of the primitive Church and its economic concomitant, the community of goods.[8]

It was only with reluctance that Wesley accepted the existence of private property among Methodists, and only as an interim arrangement on the way toward a more perfect *koinonia* in imitation of the Church at Jerusalem (Acts 2:44-45, 4:34-35). The community of goods was not a curious relic from an irretrievable Golden Age for Wesley. It was an ideal for the present and future: an image of the beloved community to which Christians were called.[9]

Here the word "community" needs to be stressed. Wesley was far from embracing the radical individualism of consumerism, with its image of the human self as a skin-encapsulated ego. On the contrary, he articulated a vision in which *love* occupied such a central position in Christian living that the whole of the Christian life was seen as essentially relational. Thus, a Wesleyan spirituality is intensely communitarian, for there can be "no holiness but social holiness."[10]

To be sure, the primary function of the qualifier "social" in that phrase was to warn against the religious narcissism to which mystics were sometimes prone; it was a pointed reminder that no one can go to heaven alone.[11] But Wesley's fascination with the community of goods—both as an expression of solidarity among Christians and as a liberation from egocentricity—suggested that "social holiness" involves transformation of economic relationships

---

7. Sermon 61, "The Mystery of Iniquity," §12, *Works* 2:456.

8. Among the Rules of the Select Societies is found the following: "Every member, till we can have all things common, will bring once a week, *bona fide*, all he can spare towards a common stock." Minutes of the First Annual Conference (28 June 1744), *John Wesley*, 144.

9. See John Walsh, "John Wesley and the Community of Goods," in *Protestant Evangelicalism: Britain, Ireland, Germany and America. Essays in Honor of W. R. Ward*, ed. Keith Robbins (Oxford and New York: Basil Blackwell, 1990), 25-50.

10. *Hymns and Sacred Poems* (1739), "Preface," §5, *Works* (Jackson) 14:321.

11. See *A Letter to Frances Godfrey* (2 August 1789), *Letters* (Telford) 8:158, "It is a blessed thing to have fellow travelers to the New Jerusalem. If you cannot find any, you must make them; for none can travel that road alone."

among the sanctified here and now. In its pristine state, Wesley argued, Christianity was marked by a mutuality of commitment that expressed itself economically in a socialism of love. He dared to hope that a renewal of primitive Christianity would involve the restoration of an economics of sharing.

This community of goods would not be a matter of discipline or legislation. Instead, it would be a spontaneous reflection of the intimate fellowship and pervasive charity that characterized believers' life together—a foretaste of the perfection of Kingdom living. It was only with reluctance then that Wesley accepted private property, and only as a practical necessity until the Methodists had reached the perfected communion toward which the Spirit was leading them.

It is in this context of sharing that Wesley recommended an economic ethics designed to minimize the spiritual ravages of a capitalistic economy. His famous formula was: "Gain all you can," "Save all you can," and "Give all you can."[12] On the one hand, *gaining* and *saving* presuppose the diligence and rigor associated with religious idealism. *Giving*, on the other hand, is a bulwark against the spiritual temptations that are inevitable in the midst of material prosperity. For Wesleyan piety, *giving* becomes virtually a sacrament—a channel of grace, a means of salvation. Wesley's appeal could hardly be more emphatic: "Do you gain all you can, and save all you can? Then you must in the nature of things grow rich. Then if you have any desire to escape the damnation of hell, *give* all you can. Otherwise I can have no more hope of your salvation than for that of Judas Iscariot."[13]

Freedom from Inordinate Attachments

Saving and giving (rather than consuming) determine the contours of Wesley's view of the linkage between economics and spirituality. Here emerges another crucial connection between the genius of primitive Methodism and that of Roman Catholic monasticism: At the heart of Wesleyan religion, as of the monastic tradition,

---

12. See Sermon 50, "The Use of Money," §§I-III, *Works* 2:268-77.

13. Sermon 122, "Causes of the Inefficacy of Christianity," §18, *Works* 4:96. On Methodist philanthropy, see Walsh, "John Wesley and the Community of Goods," 45, with references to the work of Manfred Marquardt, M. J. Warner, R. F. Wearmouth, and Leon O. Hynson.

lies *an ascetic spirituality*. It is true that the most rigorous of Wesley's ascetic demands are not intended for all members of the Methodist societies. Wesley reverts to the Catholic view (rooted in *The Shepherd of Hermas*, Clement of Alexandria, and Eusebius) that the Body of Christ consists of "two orders of Christians," corresponding to the Roman Catholic distinction between the religious (monks and nuns who sought perfection through radical renunciation) and Christians living in the world (who "did not aim at any particular strictness, being in most things like their neighbors"[14]). But even for Wesleyans of the less rigorous sort, Wesley recommended an austerity that contemporary Methodists might find shocking.

Especially striking is his indictment of conspicuous consumption.[15] Wesley summoned the people called Methodists to a kind of asceticism that is, in Albert C. Outler's well-crafted phrase, "less a loathing of God's good creation than a declaration of independence from bondages of worldliness and self-indulgence."[16] The ascetic element in Wesleyan spirituality is "rooted in traditions of monasticism, finding its expression in a *contemptus mundi* that raises the human spirit above all inordinate attachments to "this world.""[17] Wesleyan asceticism sought to counteract the spiritual effect of affluence that Wesley labeled *"dissipation,"* defined as "the uncentring the soul from God."[18] Here Wesley's language plays on an analogy of sun and wind:

> The original word properly signifies to "disperse" or "scatter." So the sun dissipates, that is, scatters, the clouds; the wind dissipates or scatters the dust. And by an easy metaphor our thoughts are said to be dissipated when they are . . . unhinged from God, their proper centre, and scattered to and fro among the poor, perishing, unsatisfying things of the world.[19]

---

14. Sermon 89, "The More Excellent Way," §5, *Works* 3:265.

15. See especially Sermon 88, "On Dress," §26, *Works* 3:259-60, in which he denounces extravagance in attire: "Let me see, before I die, a Methodist congregation full as plain dressed as a Quaker congregation. Let your dress be *cheap* as well as plain. Otherwise you do but trifle with God and me, and your own souls."

16. Outler, "Introduction," §IV, *Works* 1:61.

17. Ibid. Outler notes that after 1727 Wesley immersed himself in the asceticism of Thomas à Kempis, William Law, Gaston de Renty, and Gregory Lopez, among others. His mature theology and ethics bear the indelible imprint of that encounter.

18. Sermon 79, "On Dissipation," §11, *Works* 3:120.

19. Ibid., §10, *Works* 3:120.

What Wesley had in mind was not just philanthropy but self-denial for the sake of the health of one's own soul. Wesleyans are challenged to give to the needy—not only because the poor need to receive but also because *the affluent need to give.* Wesley sensed that *what I need to do for the poor is precisely what I need to do for myself:* I who have too much to eat must give to the hungry—and not just so that they may survive: for the health of my own soul, I need to eat less in order to make the point that my appetites are not sovereign over me. Even if there were no hunger in the world—even if none of my sisters and brothers were starving—I would still need to declare my independence from the compulsion to consume. By a marvelous symmetry, it turns out that what I need to do *for them* is precisely what I need to do *for myself.*

This was Wesley's context for understanding the importance of fasting as an antidote to the tendency toward self-gratification: "While we were at Oxford the rule of every Methodist was (unless in case of sickness) to *fast* every Wednesday and Friday in the year, in imitation of the primitive church, for which they had the highest reverence."[20] Wesley reported that in Methodism's most expansive phase membership in a Methodist society involved a commitment to self-denial through regular abstinence from food. Systematic fasting was observed by the Methodists, Wesley reports—not just by a heroic elite, but

> by them all, without any exception. But afterwards some in London carried this to excess, and fasted so as to impair their health. It was not long before others made this a pretence for not fasting at all. And I fear there are now thousands of Methodists, so called . . . who are so far from fasting twice in the week . . . that they do not fast twice in the month. . . . But what excuse can there be for this? I do not say for those that call themselves members of the Church of England, but for any who profess to believe the Scripture to be the Word of God? Since, according to this, the man that never fasts is no more in the way to heaven than the man that never prays.[21]

Fasting belonged to the regimen of systematic self-denial that Wesley considered key to the effectiveness of early Methodism; but

---

20. Sermon 122, "Causes of the Inefficacy of Christianity," §14, *Works* 4:94.
21. Ibid.

the loss of this ascetic impulse he regarded as a principal reason for the decline of the movement's original vitality. He laments the loss of serious practices of self-denial among the Methodists and found in that development a key to understanding why Christianity—especially among the Methodists—had turned out to be woefully ineffective in its impact on the life of the world.

Freedom from Affluence

If the loss of the practice of self-denial explains the growing impotence of Methodism, what is to explain the decline of asceticism among the Methodists? Wesley's answer was: *affluence.*

> Why is self-denial in general so little practised at present among the Methodists? Why is so exceeding little of it to be found even in the oldest and largest societies? The more I observe and consider things, the more clearly it appears what is the cause of this. . . . The Methodists grow more and more self-indulgent, because they *grow rich.* Although many of them are still deplorably poor yet many others, in the space of twenty, thirty, or forty years are twenty, thirty, yea, a hundred times richer than . . . when they first entered the society. And it is an observation, which admits of few exceptions, that nine in ten of these decreased in grace in the same proportion as they increased in wealth. Indeed, according to the natural tendency of riches, we cannot expect it to be otherwise.[22]

The ascetic note in Wesleyan spirituality includes a call for simplicity of lifestyle and thus turns definitions of *rich* and *poor* upside down. Wesley pointed to a radical disconnect between prosperity and happiness: "Are the richest men the happiest? Have those the largest share of content that have the largest possessions? Is not the very reverse true?"[23] If we may believe Wesley, the fulfillment and contentment that material wealth promises will always prove to be illusory because the satisfaction of material desires has the ironic effect of stimulating rather than satisfying human appetites: "Who would expend anything in gratifying these desires if he considered that to gratify them is to increase them? Nothing can be more certain than this: daily experience shows, the more they are indulged, they increase the more."[24]

---

22. Ibid., §16, *Works* 4:95.
23. Sermon 87, "The Danger of Riches," §II.10, *Works* 3:240.
24. Sermon 50, "The Use of Money," §II.5, *Works* 2:275.

To explain why the conventional view of the relation between possessions and happiness was hopelessly misleading, Wesley resorted to the metaphor of emptiness. Since the gratifications provided by money were lacking in eternal substance, the pursuit of happiness through a strategy of "being-by-possessiveness" was doomed to frustration. To seek contentment on the basis of acquisition and consumption was like trying to fill a bottomless pit: "You know that in seeking happiness from riches you are only striving to drink out of empty cups. And let them be painted and gilded ever so finely, they are empty still."[25] At the same time, Wesley says, "A man may be rich that has not a hundred a year, nor even one thousand pounds in cash. Whosoever has food to eat and raiment to put on, with something over, is rich. Whoever has the necessaries and conveniences of life for himself and his family, and a little to spare for them that have not, is properly a rich man."[26]

Wesley does not advocate self-denial to the point of abject destitution or injury to one's health, but his moderation should not be mistaken as a compromise with worldly values or as an indulgence of worldly ambitions. Each Methodist, he argued, should retain "a little to spare"—not to accumulate for oneself but to be able to give to others who are in greater need.

Freedom for the Poor

Wesley had a special empathy with the poor, especially the urban proletariat, in whom he found a greater hunger for salvation and a deeper seriousness about the life of the spirit. The social constituency of early Methodism, after all, was concentrated in the less affluent classes that were less susceptible to the illusion of self-sufficiency: "But 'who hath believed our report?' I fear, *not many rich*."[27] A recurrent motif in Wesley's sermons was his withering critique of the plutocracy that dominated British political and economic life. By temperament, he was always more comfortable with rednecks than with bluebloods. Unlike his brother Charles, he had a barely disguised contempt for members of the social aristocracy—"gay triflers," he called them—who were more concerned about

---

25. Sermon 87, "The Danger of Riches," §II.10, *Works* 3:240-41.
26. Sermon 131, "The Danger of Increasing Riches," §I.1, *Works* 4:179.
27. Sermon 87, "The Danger of Riches," §II.9, *Works* 3:240 (emphasis added).

etiquette than about eternity. He was appalled by the "shocking contrast between the Georgian splendours of the newly rich and the grinding misery of the perennial poor (not least, those lately uprooted from ancestral villages and now huddled in and around the cities and pitheads)."[28] Perhaps it would be too much to claim that Wesley anticipated the "epistemological privilege of the poor" that has been thematized in recent liberation theologies, or the notion of God's "preferential option for the poor." But his own option is clear: He instinctively identified with people from the lower socioeconomic strata—"*Christ's poor*"—and always insisted that he was not trying to elaborate a sophisticated theology for the learned but rather to provide "plain truth for plain people." His option for the poor and his misgivings about the spiritual tendencies of affluence combined to inspire his apprehensions about the *embourgeoisement* of Methodism. Wesley's longing for a community of goods among Methodists, his warnings about the dangers of riches, and his insistence on the imperative to "*give all you can*" must all be understood in that context.

Perhaps the publication of Adam Smith's *Wealth of Nations* in 1776 reinforced the resistance of the Methodist *nouveaux riches* to Wesley's third maxim *("Give all you can")*. There is abundant evidence suggesting that by the last decade of Wesley's life, many Methodists—perhaps most of them—had fallen into the habit of appropriating his economic ethics with a striking selectivity: *gaining* was far more widely observed than either *saving* or *giving*.[29]

Warnings about the danger of surplus accumulation became a leitmotif in Wesley's thought throughout the 1780s. From December 1780 until September 1790 (less than six months before his death), Wesley's sermons reflected a growing anxiety—virtually an obsession—about the corrosive impact of affluence on the spiritual integrity of the people called Methodists. His journals include numerous references to the ephemeral nature of the wealth that a capitalist culture encourages us to accumulate, coupled with

---

28. Outler, "An Introductory Comment," Sermon 50, "The Use of Money," *Works* 2:263.

29. "Of the three rules . . . you may find many that observe the first rule, namely, 'Gain all you can.' You may find a few that observe the second, 'Save all you can.' But how many have you found that observe the third rule, 'Give all you can'? Have you reason to believe that five hundred of these are to be found among fifty thousand Methodists?" Sermon 122, "Causes of the Inefficacy of Christianity," §8, *Works* 4:91.

stern warnings against putting trust in the kinds of security that wealth can provide. On Tuesday, 4 July 1786, for instance, Wesley reflected on his visit to Wentworth House, "the splendid seat of the late Marquis of Rockingham. He lately had forty thousand a year in England and fifteen or twenty thousand in Ireland. And what has he now? Six foot of earth."[30] On Friday, 15 September of that same year, Wesley identified "the chief besetting sins of Bristol: love of money and love of ease."[31]

Wesley grew ever more insistent in his warnings about the moral and spiritual consequences of surplus accumulation. Wealth brings in its wake, he argued, an inclination toward the sin of idolatry: Affluence sets up the temptation to trust in one's own resources rather than in God.[32] But since riches are essentially empty of power and life, to rely on them is not just *sinful* but *foolish* in the extreme: At the point of loss or despair or sickness or death, the material goods to which we look for security are inevitably shown to be false gods that cannot save.[33]

Freedom for Simplicity

The lifestyle of a Methodist, then, will be marked by a conscious rejection of the tendency to accumulate; to continue amassing creature comforts is, after all, an overt act of disobedience to the word of Christ:

> "Lay not up for thyself treasures upon earth" [Matt. 6.19]. That is a flat, positive command, full as clear as "Thou shalt not commit adultery" [Exod. 20.14]. How then is it possible for a rich man to grow richer without denying the Lord that bought him? Yea, how can any man who has already the necessaries of life gain or aim at more, and be guiltless? "Lay not up", saith our Lord, "treasures on earth." If in spite of this you do and will lay up money or good . . . why do you call yourself a Christian?[34]

---

30. *Journal* (4 July 1786), *Works* 23:405.
31. *Journal* (15 September 1786), *Works* 23:419.
32. "One thing thou lackest—The love of God, without which all religion is a dead carcase. In order to this, throw away what is to thee the grand hindrance of it. Give up thy great idol, riches." *NT Notes* on Mark 10:21.
33. Sermon 28, "Upon Our Lord's Sermon on the Mount, VIII," §§18-21, *Works* 1:623-26.
34. Ibid., §22, *Works* 1:626-27.

Thus, Wesley explicitly rejected the axiological premise of consumerism: He challenged Methodists to repudiate the assumption that the meaning and value of human life are defined in terms of an ever increasing bottom line.

And Wesley practiced what he preached. His own lifestyle exemplified *voluntary renunciation, divestiture,* and *kenosis.* In a letter dated 6 October 1768 (to his sister, Patty Hall), Wesley indicated his attitude toward the riches that came his way: "Money never stays with *me.* . . . I throw it out of my hands as soon as possible, lest it should find a way into my heart."[35] When the pious Margaret Lewen died and left him a personal bequest of 1000 pounds, he immediately set about devising a system for distributing it to the poor. When he made 200 pounds from sales of his *Concise History of England,* he had given it all away within a week.[36]

Living in the Now

Reinforcing Wesley's critique of "being-by-possessiveness" is a realized eschatology that views the Kingdom of God not as a distant reality but as a contemporaneous experience. Commenting on Ephesians 2:8 ("For by grace are ye saved through faith"), Wesley argued that the proper orientation of Christian existence is toward immediate experience in the present rather than a deferred fulfillment in the future:

> The salvation, which is here spoken of, is not what is frequently understood by that word, the going to heaven, eternal happiness. It is not the soul's going to Paradise. . . . It is not a blessing which lies on the other side of death, or (as we usually speak) in the other world. . . . It is not something at a distance; it is a present thing.[37]

In keeping with this existential orientation toward the present moment, Wesley encouraged believers not to live in the past or in the future but radically in the now.[38] If the spiritual life is focused

---

35. *A Letter to Mrs. Hall* (6 October 1768), *Letters* (Telford) 5:108-9.

36. Ayling, *John Wesley,* 259.

37. Sermon 43, "The Scripture Way of Salvation," §I.1, *Works* 2:156.

38. See for example Sermon 29, "Upon Our Lord's Sermon on the Mount, IX," §§24-29, *Works* 1:645-49. Wesley advises Methodists to avoid the kind of preoccupation with the future that is implied in the impulse to accumulate worldly possessions: "Enjoy the very, very now" (§28, p. 648).

on authenticity in the present rather than on security in the future, then a major source of the impulse toward acquisition and accumulation melts away. For instance, a major incentive to surplus accumulation is the desire of parents to provide a substantial inheritance for their children. Wesley admitted that he was amazed at "the infatuation of those parents who think they can never leave their children enough."[39] Those who live in the present will not feel impelled to accumulate possessions in order to make the future secure for themselves—*or for their children*. Wesley's censure of personal self-indulgence extended to a critique of the impulse to accumulate possessions for passing on to one's heirs: Parents who themselves live modestly, abstaining from self-indulgent accumulation and consumption, have made little progress if what they decline to spend on themselves they lay up in store for their children. To provide inordinately for one's progeny is but a refined form of self-indulgence—with the added liability that inherited wealth threatens to implicate one's children in all the moral problematics associated with increasing affluence: "What! cannot you leave them enough of arrows, firebrands, and death? Not enough of foolish and hurtful desires? Not enough of pride, lust, ambition, vanity? Not enough of everlasting burnings!"[40]

Living in the present is incompatible, finally, with a lifestyle based on indebtedness. It is safe to say that Wesley would be appalled at the excesses of a credit-card culture such as our own. Primary among his objections to a debt-based lifestyle was his assertion that indebtedness restricts the ability to be generous to others. The culture of credit inhibits the philanthropy that Wesley saw as the only refuge from the pernicious effects of affluence:

> A person may have more than necessaries and conveniences for his family, and yet not be rich. For he may be in debt; and his debts may amount to more than he is worth. But if this be the case he is not a rich man, how much money soever he has in his hands. Yea, a man of business may be afraid that this is the real condition of his affairs, whether it be or no; and then he cannot be so charitable as he would.[41]

---

39. Sermon 50, "The Use of Money," §II.7, *Works* 2:276.
40. Ibid.
41. Sermon 131, "The Danger of Increasing Riches," §I.2, *Works* 4:179.

PROCESS THEOLOGY

From what has been said we hope it is clear that, for contemporary Christians in high-income countries who dwell in relative affluence, Wesley offers a countercultural challenge. He recommends a way of living—a new monasticism, if you will—that is at odds with "the American dream" of bigger is better, more is better, faster is better, and you can have it all. As we listen to him with middle-class ears, we almost feel that he took Jesus too seriously. He was, to put it bluntly, "too Christian."

Nevertheless, there may well be a voice within many of us— however still and small—that resonates with the six ideals just named: (1) the primacy of sharing, (2) freedom from clinging, (3) freedom from having too much, (4) freedom for the poor, (5) freedom for simplicity, and (6) freedom for the present moment. This is where, in a contemporary setting, process theology can be helpful. It can help us in three ways.

First, it can help us interpret the "still small voice" as originating in the very God who dwells with each creature on our planet, who calls the universe into existence, epoch by epoch and moment by moment, and who is at work in each human life relative to the situation at hand. Thus, process theology helps show that as middle-class Christians respond to an inwardly felt call toward simple and compassionate living, we are being faithful, not only to the anti-consumerist teachings of the New Testament and the example of Jesus or Wesley, but also to a deeply creative Calling within the universe. It then adds that this Calling—the creative and healing Lure—is omni-adaptive and thus relative to the needs and situations of each creature. In the life of an overconsumer, for example, the Lure is indeed toward simplification of lifestyle and service to the poor; but in the life of a person who is destitute, the Calling may well be toward an accumulation of more goods and a battle against poverty. In this way, process theology helps contextualize, while affirming, Wesley's insights concerning the workings of the Holy Spirit within human life.

Second, process theology offers a wholesale critique of the "theology of Consumerism" identified earlier, showing that two of its doctrines—its idea that human beings are skin-encapsulated egos and its doctrine of creation as real estate—are properly replaced by a more relational and life-appreciative way of thinking. Thus it offers a worldview that (1) supports and builds upon Wesley's own insights concerning the social nature of Christian existence and (2) enriches Wesley's seminal but undeveloped insights concerning the value of animal life. In the first instance, process theology shows that what Wesley believed true of Christian existence, namely, that it is profoundly social, is true of all human life. Thus, process theology offers a philosophical anthropology to support the Wesleyan viewpoint, thereby suggesting that there are important ontological insights in Wesley's analysis of Christian existence. In the second instance, process theology widens Wesley's perspective into an ecologically rich point of view, the seeds of which are already found in Wesley.

Third, process theology supports and adds to Wesley's own emphasis on "living in the present" by offering an event-oriented cosmology that displays the universe itself as unfolding, not simply epoch by epoch or even day by day but rather—in a more Buddhist vein—moment by moment. In so doing, process theology opens the door for a creative dialogue with another religious tradition, which can, in its own way, further help Christians transcend the acquisitive and goal-driven ethos of consumer culture. In what follows we want to say a word more about each of these three contributions.

The Lure of God

Let us assume that in many middle-class Christians there is a hidden yearning—a still small voice—that transcends the acquisitive nature of consumerism and that calls toward a simpler and more frugal way of living. From a process perspective, this inwardly felt Lure—this Holy Spirit—is already within all over-consuming persons on our planet, even prior to their asking for it and quite apart from whether they are self-identified Christians. This is an example of what Wesley would mean by prevenient grace.

As process theologians understand this grace, it is (1) the presence of fresh possibilities for healing and wholeness relative to the situation at hand and (2) the presence of a divine desire—a divine eros—within those individuals and communities that these possibilities be actualized. What Wesley shows so clearly is that, for the overconsumer of our world, there are fresh possibilities for sharing and simplicity, for solidarity with the poor and freedom from affluence, for relinquishment from inordinate attachment and living in the present moment. Process theologians would then add that our desire to actualize these possibilities—to make them real in our lives—is itself God's prayer within our lives. It is not simply that God calls us into simpler living; it is that God needs us to live more simply so that others (the poor and the other creatures) might simply live. Our task as humans is not simply to pray to God; it is also to hear and respond to God's prayer within our own lives.

This hearing and responding is what Christians call "discernment." It consists of listening to the various voices within us and deciding which are neutral, which are from the enemy of our better self (sometimes called "the devil"), and which are from God. Wesley felt deeply that the voices of consumerism were from the enemy, and that those toward simplicity and frugality were from God. Process theologians agree and then invite us to listen deeply to these positive voices, with the help of scripture, tradition, reason, experience, and also with the help of spiritual disciplines such as Wesley emphasized, including fasting. What process theologians will add is that such fasting rightly includes not only fasting from food but also fasting from television, radio, computers, and other "modern conveniences," to which many of us are so deeply addicted. In a contemporary context, one of the deepest fasts may be a fasting from electricity.

Process theologians will further add that this life of discernment, as enriched by fasting and other disciplines, is not so much a decisive and dramatic act but rather an ongoing process that, in time and with the help of God, becomes a habit of the heart, partly conscious but largely unconscious. The hope then is that, with divine guidance, Christians and others can come to respond to the divine Lure toward simplicity in a more spontaneous and instinctive way.

Additionally, process theologians will emphasize that this divine prayer—this divine Lure within human life—is also found throughout the cosmos and within other creatures. Birds respond to the Lure by flying, fish by swimming, dogs by barking, and cats by purring. We humans respond by becoming wise, compassionate, and free in our daily lives. In so doing, we do not leave the world behind; rather, as Wesley emphasized, we leave our inordinate attachments behind, so that we can live more lovingly with others.

It follows then that the "sharing" to which we are called, by Wesley and of course by Jesus, consists of not only sharing money, time, and resources with other humans but also sharing space with other creatures such that they, no less than humans, can obey the divine command to be fruitful and multiply.[42] And it follows that the relinquishment of inordinate attachments includes a "letting go" of the idea that humans, and humans alone, have a right to inherit the earth. This takes us to the second way in which process theology can build upon Wesley: namely, its doctrine of creation and its doctrine of human existence.

Earth as Alive

The tendency within consumerism is to reduce the earth and its creatures to commodities for exchange in the marketplace. The phrase used in process theology to explain this reductionism is "instrumental value." The idea is that the theology of consumerism wrongly reduces the whole of nonhuman life to its instrumental value to human beings, forgetful of (1) the "intrinsic value" that each living being has in and for itself, (2) the value that each living being has for God, and (3) the unique value that all of the creatures, humans included, have as a diverse whole in God's ongoing life. It is tempting to speak of the second value just named as a creature's "instrumental value" for God, but this way of speaking would go against one of the deeper intuitions of process theology, which is that God values each creature "in and for itself." Thus we can speak of a creature's "intrinsic value" in and for itself and also its "intrinsic value" for God.

In process theology, this appreciation of intrinsic value is central to love, both human and divine love. We humans "love our neighbors as ourselves" when we approach them as ends in themselves, not simply means to our ends and when we empathize with their own inner states, as best we can. Such empathy lies in "feeling the feelings" of other humans and other creatures in vague, intuitive,

---

42. See Sermon 64, "The New Creation," §17, *Works* 2:508-9; Sermon 67, "On Divine Providence," §§9-12, *Works* 2:538-39.

and meaningful ways. Process theologians believe that what we feel indistinctly, God feels more fully. Thus, God is not only the Lure within each creature toward healing and wholeness relative to the situation at hand but also the Great Empathy—the divine Companion—who shares in the sufferings and joys of all creatures, each on its own terms and for its own sake.

A process theology of creation thus emphasizes that we humans can share in the divine Empathy in limited but meaningful ways, feeling the very presence of the earth as a communion of subjects, not a collection of objects, and understanding ourselves as parts of this very communion.[43]

Accordingly, a process theology of human existence emphasizes that we humans become fully human when we awaken to the communal nature of our own existence, understanding that we ourselves are not individuated substances with self-contained walls but are open spaces—fields of feeling and awareness—whose very natures include, rather than exclude, the feelings of others. We awaken to the truth about ourselves in acts of love, which have epistemological value in their own right. When we let go of our defenses and allow the feelings of others to move us, sharing in their joys and sufferings, we discover who we truly are: empathizers made in the image of that deeper Empathy that is God.

Moment-by-Moment

Finally, a process theology emphasizes that this life of sharing in the joys and sufferings of others requires a willingness to slow down, be patient, and attend mindfully to what is happening in each present moment. This attention does not involve forgetting the past or neglecting the future. From a process perspective, we are inevitably and deeply shaped by all that has happened in the past and by the presence of the future as pure potentiality. We are individualized fields of awareness, constituted not only by what we see, hear, touch, and taste, but also by what we remember and anticipate, consciously and unconsciously. Nevertheless, it remains the case that, from a process point of view, we are never in the past

---

43. The phrase "communion of subjects, not a collection of objects" is often used by the ecological author Thomas Berry. We borrow the phrase from several of his oral presentations.

gazing at the future, and we are never in the future gazing at the past. Rather, at any and every moment of our lives, we are living in the present, shaped by what has been and by what can be. If we are to meet God anywhere at all, it will have to be in the present moment, right where we are standing or sitting, laughing or crying, living or dying.

While Wesley points us in the direction of such "living in the present moment," Buddhists take us still more deeply into it.[44] They suggest that if we truly awaken to the reality of the present moment, we will realize that it is a coming together of the entire universe—all its joys and sufferings, all its beauties and horrors—and that we ourselves are made of all these things. This means that we cannot separate ourselves from others: the suffering ones, to be sure, but also those who cause their suffering. Each present moment is a communion of subjects, not just a collection of objects. Buddhists further suggest that we cannot objectify the present moment as an object among objects because we ourselves are the present moment. As the moment comes into existence and then perishes to be succeeded by another moment, which does the same, we ourselves are this coming into existence and perishing, and then rising up again.

As process theologians appropriate this insight, they—we—learn to see that the traditional Christian idea that we should "live and die daily with Christ" has a deep meaning. It means that the whole of an individual's life, understood most deeply, is an ongoing process of death and resurrection, of living by dying, at ever deepening levels, with no two moments the same. As we awaken to this truth, we then realize that we cannot and need not "hold on" to life or to ourselves, as if objects for permanent possession. We cannot live by acquisition, by owning things, by possessing things. We can only live-by-letting-go into a deeper grace that can never be owned, as if it were a commodity among commodities, but can always be trusted. Wesley's name for this deeper grace was "God."

---

44. Sermon 67, "On Divine Providence," §17, *Works* 2:542-43; see also Sermon 91, "On Charity," §II.3, *Works* 3:296, where Wesley explicitly renounces Christian exclusivism by saying, "But this we know, that he is not the God of the Christians only, but the God of the heathens also; that he is 'rich in mercy to all that call upon him', 'according to the light they have'; and that 'in every nation he that feareth God and worketh righteousness is accepted of him.'"

He saw this grace revealed uniquely, but not exclusively in Jesus Christ. We do, too.

What consumerism most obstructs is a capacity to live from this grace. It encourages Christians and others to live willfully, not willingly: to utilize their creative energies to "get things" and "achieve recognition" rather than to love and let go of things when they pass away. We hope that this essay has shown that both Wesley in his way and process theology in its way offer a challenge to lifestyle, attitudes, and values of consumerism.

CONCLUSION

The question remains as to whether contemporary Christians, including us, can learn from this challenge and enter into that "still most excellent way" that Paul called life in Christ. This is the urgent challenge of our time, upon which the well-being of life on earth sorely depends. For process theologians, it is not fully known—even to God—whether we will respond to this challenge. Our decisions partly determine the outcome of what, at present, are two possibilities: a continuation of the ways of overconsumption, in which case so many others will suffer, or a learning to live more simply so that others might simply live. But one thing is clear, at least for process theologians and for Wesley. There lies within each of us a divine prayer that we will choose the second option: that we choose life over money, community over commodity, love over greed. Given the presence of this prayer within each of us, everything does not depend on us. We need not willfully engineer a destiny of our design. Our only need is to listen and respond to a healing and creative Spirit at work in the world, who steadfastly seeks the well-being of life.

WESLEYAN THEOLOGY, BOSTON PERSONALISM, AND PROCESS THOUGHT

THOMAS JAY OORD[1]

In a number of significant ways, the present dialogue between Wesleyan theology and process philosophy parallels an earlier dialogue between Wesleyan theology and personalist philosophy. Given the basic affinities between Wesleyanism and personalism, on the one hand, and between personalism and process thought, on the other, it may be that the present correlation of Wesleyan theology with process thought is a natural development. In this appendix, I trace some Wesleyan proclivities toward the Boston Personalist movement of the twentieth century and identify some affinities and differences between Boston Personalism and process thought.

BOSTON PERSONALISM AND WESLEYAN THEOLOGY

John H. Lavely defines personalism as "a philosophical perspective or system for which person is the ontological ultimate and for which personality is thus the fundamental explanatory principle."[2] As Edgar Sheffield Brightman explains, "any theory that makes personality the supreme philosophical principle (that is, supreme in the sense that the ultimate causes and reasons of all reality are found in some process of personal experience) is given the name *personalism*."[3] While in a broad sense many philosophers and

---

1. Special thanks is due to Bryan P. Stone, who not only read and made various suggestions regarding this essay, but also contributed a few sentences here and there. I believe the essay is much stronger because of his help.

2. John H. Lavely, "Personalism," in *The Encyclopedia of Philosophy*, ed. Paul Edwards (New York: Macmillan, 1967) 6:107.

3. Edgar Sheffield Brightman, *An Introduction to Philosophy*, 3rd rev. ed., ed. Robert N. Beck (New York: Holt, Rinehart, and Winston, 1963), 330.

schools of philosophy could be called personalist, the school of thought at Boston University known as "Boston Personalism" is the most representative of the more narrowly designated personalist tradition and the most closely associated with the Wesleyan tradition.

Given personalism's emphasis upon the person as ultimate explanatory principle, philosophers in this tradition have understandably concentrated upon explicating just what personhood entails. Brightman, for example, defines person as "a complex unity of consciousness, which identifies itself with its past in memory, determines itself by its freedom, is purposive and value-seeking, private yet communicating, and potentially rational."[4] Personalism, at least in its Boston form, is also identified with the philosophical tradition of idealism—specifically, a theistic form of idealism. As Brightman explains, "idealistic personalism, or personal idealism, makes the . . . assertion that persons and selves are the only reality, that is, that the whole universe is a system or society of interacting selves and persons—one infinite person who is the creator, and many dependent created persons."[5] At its core, this project of theistic idealism is a metaphysical enterprise by which one seeks to develop the most coherent and plausible theory possible to account for what is given in conscious experience.[6]

The initiator of Boston Personalism was Borden Parker Bowne (1847–1910). During the late nineteenth and the early twentieth centuries, Bowne's personalist influence upon American Christianity was immense. In 1936, Henry Nelson Wieman and Bernard Eugene Meland claimed: "[Bowne's] thinking has probably reached the minds of more professing Christian people than any other philosophy of religion in the United States."[7] This far-reaching influence is demonstrated by Bowne's influence upon scholars such as Brightman, Lavely, Peter A. Bertocci, L. Harold DeWolf, Ralph T. Flewelling, Georgia Harkness, Albert C. Knudson, and Walter Muelder.[8] His influence even extends to well-known religious leaders such as Harry Emerson Fosdick and Martin Luther King Jr.

4. Edgar Sheffield Brightman, "Personalism," in *A History of Philosophical Systems*, ed. Vergilius Ferm (New York: The Philosophical Library, 1950), 341.

5. Brightman, *Introduction to Philosophy*, 330.

6. Ibid., 331.

7. Henry Nelson Wieman and Bernard Eugene Meland, *American Philosophies of Religion* (Chicago: Willett, Clark and Co., 1936), 134.

8. Others strongly influenced either directly or indirectly by Bowne's brand of personal-

That personalism should have such a broad impact suggests that many religious leaders found its worldview intellectually and religiously satisfying. Indeed, Boston Personalists attempted quite consciously to provide what they considered to be the most adequate philosophical structure for Christian theology.[9] Apparently, many theologians considered this effort successful. Wieman and Meland stated flatly, "a survey of prevalent philosophies yields the conviction that of them all the philosophy of personalism is most true to the Christian tradition."[10]

Of those influenced by Boston Personalism, clearly Wesleyans were in the majority. Bowne's thought was more important for the work of Wesleyan-oriented scholars in America than that of any other philosopher in the early decades of the twentieth century. He provided Wesleyans, says Thomas A. Langford, with "a philosophical foundation for theological construction."[11] This made Bowne "the originative source of the most generally influential school of theology produced by American Methodism."[12] Bowne and those in Boston's personalist tradition guarded "the intellectual life in religion," says F. Thomas Trotter, and "clung to the Wesleyan insistence on the practice of vital piety."[13] This insistence on vital piety in the Wesleyan spirit coincided with the Boston Personalists' private theological inclinations; all were Methodist.[14]

One reason that Bowne-inspired personalism was so influential in America comes down to sheer numbers. Ministerial students from Wesleyan traditions flocked to Boston University and later left the school to serve as college presidents, professors, and church

ism include John W. E. Bowen, Olin A. Curtis, Paul Deats Jr., Nels F. S. Ferre, Carroll D. Hildebrand, Francis John McConnell, Richard M. Millard, Wilbur Mullen, Harris Franklin Rall, Edward T. Ramsdell, Carol Sue Robb, J. Deotis Roberts, S. Paul Schilling, William H. Werkmeister, H. Orton Wiley, and J. Philip Wogaman.

9. In the words of Albert C. Knudson, Boston Personalism "seeks to provide religion with a philosophical underpinning, to give it a cosmic framework in which it will fit, to create for it an intellectual atmosphere in which it will thrive" (*The Philosophy of Personalism: A Study in the Metaphysics of Religion* [New York: Abingdon Press, 1927], 328).

10. Wieman and Meland, *American Philosophies of Religion*, 133.

11. Thomas A. Langford, *Practical Divinity; Volume 2: Readings in Wesleyan Theology*, rev. ed. (Nashville: Abingdon Press, 1999), 113.

12. Thomas A. Langford, *Practical Divinity: Theology in the Wesleyan Tradition*, rev. ed. (Nashville: Abingdon Press, 1998), 164.

13. F. Thomas Trotter, "Boston Personalism's Contributions to Faith and Learning," in *The Boston Personalist Tradition in Philosophy, Social Ethics, and Theology*, ed. Paul Deats and Carol Sue Robb (Macon, Ga.: Mercer University Press, 1986), 21.

14. Paul Deats, "Introduction to Boston Personalism," in *Boston Personalist Tradition*, 13.

leaders. Partly because of these graduate masses, personalism was the dominant philosophical position in scores of colleges and churches across the land.[15]

For what reasons did personalism come to hold such an attraction for Wesleyans? First, one of Boston Personalism's core conceptions was congruent with a basic Wesleyan tenet: God is personal, interactive, and relational.[16] "What we especially have in mind, when from the religious view we speak of the personality of God, is the thought of fellowship with him," says Knudson. "He is a Being who knows us and loves us and whom we can trust."[17] "On every count," argues Brightman, "the metaphysics of personality interprets [deity] more adequately than does any competing view." To illustrate, he notes that

> prayer, contemplation, mystical communion, ethical loyalty, are all personal attitudes and experiences, which acquire their highest worth when directed toward a personal object. Any impersonal view of God is either vague or unsuited to serve as the object of prayer and worship. . . . Such experiences as redemption and salvation have to be interpreted most awkwardly and unnaturally on the basis of an impersonal view of God. The eternal ideals of goodness and beauty, truth and holiness, by which we seek to measure our human vales, are given a clear and rational metaphysical status when thought of as the conscious goals of God's purpose.[18]

It comes as little surprise that Wesleyans would be attracted to such a conception of deity. John Wesley understood God as a relational deity who intimately interacts with the created order.[19] Certainly the God who is personal in this way is amply attested to

---

15. Ibid.

16. Brightman and his students presented this in a more coherent way. Bowne argued for a personal, interactive, and/or relational God but rejected divine mutability and temporality. For a discussion of the problems Bowne faced because of this rejection, see Jose Franquiz Ventura, *Borden Parker Bowne's Treatment of the Problem of Change and Identity* (Rio Piedras, Puerto Rico: University of Puerto Rico, 1942).

17. Albert C. Knudson, *The Doctrine of God* (New York: Abingdon-Cokesbury Press, 1930), 298.

18. Edgar Sheffield Brightman, "Personality," in *Personalism in Theology: A Symposium in Honor of Albert Cornelius Knudson*, ed. Edgar Sheffield Brightman (Boston: Boston University Press, 1943), 62-63.

19. See Randy L. Maddox's discussion of Wesley's relational, interactive God in *Responsible Grace: John Wesley's Practical Theology* (Nashville: Kingswood Books, 1994), chap. 2.

throughout the biblical witness. Still, this conception of God was not well represented by other metaphysical schemes that have dominated the theologies of Western Christianity. Personalism's alternative metaphysics came as a breath of fresh air to Wesleyans who sought a philosophical basis for their central convictions about relations with a personal God.

A second reason that Wesleyans found Boston Personalism attractive was that it emphasized the freedom of persons,[20] while opposing mechanistic, behavioristic, or theistic theories that denied persons a measure of self-determination. The personalist claim that God created persons with the capacity to act freely corresponds well with the central Wesleyan doctrine that prevenient grace enables humans to act in free response to God. It can also be said that this notion of human freedom dominates the biblical witness. Wesleyans felt that the philosophies at the heart of theologies espoused by Augustine and Aquinas, and those at the heart of the Reformed theologies of Luther and Calvin, were not conducive to this emphasis upon genuine personal freedom. Boston Personalism offered a philosophical alternative to these traditions—one that was more consistent with the spirit of Wesleyan thought.

Third, Boston Personalism offered Wesleyans a structure to support the Christian demand for personal morality and social responsibility. "Personality implies freedom and moral responsibility," as Knudson states.[21] Personalists claim that the world is social; it is a world of mutually dependent and interacting moral beings. "In such a world," says Knudson, "love is necessarily the basic moral law."[22] For Ralph T. Flewelling, this implies that society "should be so organized as to present every person the best possible opportunity for self-development, physically, mentally, and spiritually."[23] Given statements such as these, those who agreed both with Wesley's rejection of antinomianism and with his conviction that there is no holiness but social holiness, were likely to find personalism inviting. The fact that Georgia Harkness, the first female

---

20. Knudson reports that "personalism . . . holds to the libertarian as against the deterministic view of [humans]" (*Philosophy of Personalism*, 74).

21. Ibid., 83.

22. Albert C. Knudson, *The Principles of Christian Ethics* (New York: Abingdon Press, 1943), 118.

23. Ralph T. Flewelling, "Personalism," in *Twentieth Century Philosophy: Living Schools of Thought*, ed. Dagobert D. Runes (New York: The Philosophical Library, 1943), 325.

theologian at an American seminary, and Martin Luther King Jr., the most well-known American civil rights leader, were personalists suggests that personalism played a vital role in how some American Christians were responding to matters of gender and race.

The final reason Wesleyans were attracted to Boston Personalism was its emphasis upon love. The primacy of love in Wesleyan theology is illustrated by Wesley's own words: "Love is the end of all the commandments of God. Love is the end, the sole end, of every dispensation of God, from the beginning of the world to the consummation of all things."[24] Wesley also reminded us, "It is not written, 'God is justice,' or 'God is truth' (although he is just and true in all his ways). But it is written, 'God is love.' "[25] Boston Personalists likewise argued that God's primary volition is love.[26] Furthermore, the nature of love requires interpersonal relationships, both for deity and creatures. Brightman contended that, "if God is love, his love needs free companions who return his love."[27] God seeks to increase love in others: "The personal God is one who works—whether with us or in spite of us—to attain the highest values and the most perfect love."[28] What made personalism so attractive to those who placed love at the center of their theological construction, then, was its personal and interpersonal categories. These categories made possible a lucid analysis of divine and creaturely love relations.

The fact that many Wesleyans were drawn to Boston Personalism in the twentieth century does not mean, however, that it was accepted by everyone as the most adequate philosophy for the Christian faith. Some Wesleyans were suspicious of the idealism at the root of personalism; they preferred instead the realism of a commonsense philosopher such as Thomas Reid.[29] Others opposed various novel theological formulations proposed by specific Boston Personalists. For example, many considered Brightman's notion of a finite God, for whom evil is something of

24. Sermon 36, "The Law Established through Faith, II," §II.1, *Works* 2:38.
25. *Predestination Calmly Considered*, §43, *John Wesley*, 445.
26. Borden Parker Bowne, *Studies in Christianity* (Boston: Houghton Mifflin, 1909), 94.
27. Edgar Sheffield Brightman, *Is God Personal?* (New York: Association Press, 1932), 64.
28. Ibid., 46-47.
29. One who makes this claim is James E. Hamilton, "Epistemology and Theology in American Methodism," *Wesleyan Theological Journal* 10 (1975): 70-79.

a "given" within the divine self, religiously inadequate. So too, some recognized that traditional Christian doctrines were not easily couched in the theistic idealism of personalism. Even Knudson admitted that "the traditional doctrines of the Trinity, Incarnation, and Atonement do not easily fit into the framework of our current personal idealism." He maintained, however, that "this may point to the need of the reformulation of these doctrines rather than to any want of harmony between personalistic philosophy and the essentials of the Christian faith."[30] Wesleyans varied among themselves regarding the extent to which they thought such doctrines needed reformulation.

BOSTON PERSONALISM AND PROCESS THOUGHT

With even this introductory sketch, we can perhaps already recognize some significant commonalities between Boston Personalism and Whiteheadian-Hartshornian process thought. This helps explain why personalist and process philosophers have been generally appreciative of each other's views since the early decades of the twentieth century. In fact, Brightman called both Whitehead and Hartshorne "personalists," and he praised Whitehead, saying that "the greatest Anglo-American philosopher of recent times, A. N. Whitehead, came from a realistic tradition, but his doctrines . . . all point to panpsychistic personalism."[31] Brightman's published work and personal correspondence reveal that, through his reading of Whitehead and his exchanges with Hartshorne, he slowly drifted away from hard-core personal idealism toward doctrines more characteristic of process thought. By contrast, although Hartshorne considered Brightman to be a process theist and was influenced somewhat by him, Whitehead did not appear to be significantly influenced by Bowne, Brightman, or others in the Boston Personalist tradition.[32]

A number of similarities—both thematic and methodological—

---

30. Knudson, *Philosophy of Personalism*, 80.
31. Brightman, "Personalism," 344.
32. The key word in this sentence's claim is "significantly." On this and related subjects, see Randall E. Auxier, "God, Process, and Persons: Charles Hartshorne and Personalism," *Process Studies* 27.3-4 (Fall-Winter 1998): 175-99.

between process and personalist philosophies have proved to be of great interest to Wesleyans. Both philosophies are adventures in speculative metaphysics; both are grounded in an analysis of experience, which leads to the testing and construction of metaphysical suppositions in light of that experience. The resulting philosophy is hypothetical; it is always subject to reassessment and revision.[33] Lavely suggests that "the affinities between and the common motifs of personalism and panpsychism are such that both positions have more at stake in reinforcing each other than in repudiating each other. . . . Jointly panpsychism and personalism may be the . . . best hope of metaphysics."[34]

The epistemological point of departure for both Whiteheadian process thought and Boston Personalism is self-experience. Bowne contends that self-conscious and active intelligence is the presupposition for knowledge of ourselves, others, the world, and God.[35] "What we immediately experience as the starting-point of all our thought and action and the present fact at all times is our own self" says Brightman.[36] Personalists claim that what we find in our personal relationships provides the basis to construe everything in terms of personality. Here, however, process thought differs from personalism as to the types of self-experience that inform epistemology. Boston Personalists limit their notion of self-experience to experience that is conscious, sensory, and value-based. Process philosophers, in the tradition of Whitehead and Hartshorne, also acknowledge the epistemological validity of unconscious and nonsensory experience. This broader approach to experience is seemingly more suitable to Wesleyan concerns for how God relates to creation and, specifically, how God guides and assures us by means of what Wesley called the "spiritual senses."

Especially appealing to Wesleyans is another current running through both personalist and process philosophies—namely, the relational metaphysics of each. For process thought, all actual existence involves, in Whitehead's words, "an essential interconnect-

---

33. Brightman, "Personalism," 345-47.

34. John H. Lavely, "Personalism Supports the Dignity of Nature," *The Personalist Forum* 2.1 (Spring 1986), 37.

35. Borden Parker Bowne, *Personalism* (Norwood, Mass.: Plimpton, 1908, 1936), 217.

36. Edgar Sheffield Brightman, "Personalism as a Philosophy of Religion," *Crozer Quarterly* 5:4 (October 1928): 383.

edness of things."[37] Bowne, sounding like a relational metaphysician, also argued that "the notion of interaction implies that a thing is [influenced] by others, and hence that it cannot be all that it is apart from all others. . . . Its existence is involved in its relations."[38] Late in his life, Brightman spoke of interconnectedness when claiming that personalism posits "an interacting and intercommunicating universe," which means that the basis for this philosophy "is essentially interpersonal, and therefore social."[39] However, as contemporary personalist Rufus Burrow Jr. admits, "it must be conceded that neither Bowne nor Brightman worked out the fuller implications of a relational metaphysics."[40] An illustration of this failure to work out a relational metaphysics is Brightman's denial of literal participation of selves in one another; he concludes that "monads have no windows through which existences or concrete realities may interact. Only purposes may interact."[41] Whitehead and process metaphysicians contend that monads do have "windows," whereby each actuality is internally related to others who have preceded them.[42] The unique process way of conceiving real internal relations shares strong affinities with the Wesleyan emphasis on the prevenience of grace and the transforming presence of God within all creation.

We have already noted that the emphasis on God as personal, which resides at the core of Boston Personalism, is attractive to Wesleyans. Although the similarities between Whitehead and Hartshorne are so great that both are generally regarded as the primary inspirations for process theology, Hartshorne's thought is decidedly more congruent with Boston Personalism at this point; his doctrine of God more easily generates a conception of God as personal. In *The Divine Relativity*, he argued that God should be conceived "as a supreme person."[43] As person, God enjoys

37. Alfred North Whitehead, *Adventures of Ideas* (New York: Free Press, 1933), 227.

38. Borden Parker Bowne, *Theism* (New York: American Book Co., 1902), 57.

39. Brightman, "Personalism," 347, 350.

40. Rufus Burrow Jr., *Personalism: A Critical Introduction* (St. Louis: Chalice Press, 1999), 232.

41. Brightman, Letter of 13 May 1939, quoted in Auxier, "God, Process, and Persons," 181.

42. Later in his life, and subsequently due to deeper reflection upon the thought of Hartshorne and Whitehead, Brightman attempted to correct his deficient hypothesis regarding internal relations. See Auxier's article regarding Hartshorne's influence upon Brightman pertaining to this matter ("God, Process, and Persons," 175-99).

43. Charles Hartshorne, *The Divine Relativity: A Social Conception of God* (New Haven, Conn.: Yale University Press, 1948), 142. See also Hartshorne, "God, as personal" in *Encyclopedia of Religion*, ed. Vergilius Ferm (New York: The Philosophical Library, 1945), 302-303.

successive "states" of existence analogous with the states of existence enjoyed by other personally ordered societies of occasions of experience.[44] Whitehead's God, however, does not lend itself to Personalist categories because deity subsists in a single, ever-becoming state.[45]

Process theism also shares important similarities to personalism with regard to theodicy. A glimpse at how prominent scholars in these traditions address the problem of evil reveals that, in general, both personalism and process thought seek to reconceptualize divine power to account for divine love. Sounding like Whitehead, although writing nearly twenty years earlier, Bowne rejected classical theology's construal of divine power: "A great deal of our theology was written when men believed in the divine right and irresponsibility of kings, and this conception also crept into and corrupted theological thinking, so that God was conceived less as a truly moral being than as a magnified and irresponsible despot."[46] Wesley reconceived divine power similarly, although his construal was hammered out in the context of broader soteriological concerns, especially related to the question of predestination.

Chief among notable answers to the problem of evil given by Boston Personalists was the relatively controversial one offered by Brightman. The fact of evil, he claimed, "indicates that the Supreme Self is achieving value in the temporal order under difficulties."[47] The impetus of these difficulties is found in the improper use of human freedom and in God's own self-imposed conditions of reason and goodness, but these impetuses do not account entirely for the presence of evil. A crucial aspect of what Brightman considered an adequate theodicy developed through his reflection upon the

---

44. Charles Hartshorne, "Whitehead's Idea of God," in *The Philosophy of Alfred North Whitehead*, ed. Paul Arthur Schilpp (New York: Tudor Publishing, 1951), 530.

45. Whitehead's doctrine of God does not easily lend itself to speaking of God as personal, because he conceived God to be a single, ever-concrescing, actual entity. Although interaction with others is part of what it means to be personal, it is difficult to imagine how a single actual entity, which everlastingly becomes, can affect other actualities. That is, if interaction requires an individual to oscillate between being and becoming, or object and subject, as Whitehead contends, then it is unclear how God could interact personally. For a critique of Whitehead on this point, and for an alternative doctrine of God similar to Hartshorne's, see the classic work on the subject: John B. Cobb Jr., *A Christian Natural Theology: Based on the Thought of Alfred North Whitehead* (Philadelphia: Westminster Press, 1965).

46. Bowne, *Studies in Christianity*, 94.

47. Brightman, "Personalism as a Philosophy of Religion," 385.

divine nature. He speculated that, residing within Godself, is a measure of recalcitrance and perversity he calls "the given." This resistant and retarding factor "constitutes a real problem to divine power and explains the 'evil' features of the natural world."[48] Although neither created nor condoned by God, this nonrational given inevitably conditions the divine experience internally making it impossible for God to overcome all evil.

In contrast to Brightman's controversial solution, Boston Personalists have generally simply affirmed divine self-limitation as a way to preserve perfect divine love in the face of genuine evil. In providing power for freedom to creatures, they say, God became self-limited; most prefer the notion of divine self-limitation, then, to Brightman's notion of a finite God. Although many process theists also reject the language of divine finitude, they do not embrace the personalist notion of divine self-limitation. Process theology's criticism of a self-limited God is that this deity, who incessantly enjoys the capacity to become unselflimited, ought to overcome self-imposed limitations periodically in the name of love.[49] Process theologian David Ray Griffin, for example, rejects Brightman's notion of a God internally burdened with a nonrational given and calls this deity an imperfect Being unworthy of worship.[50] Unlike Brightman's God, whose internal conflict prevents unqualified expressions of love, the process deity Griffin proposes expresses perfect love everlastingly, albeit through the metaphysical conditions that God and all other actualities embody.

Both Personalism and process thought emphasize the immanence of God. Speaking like a naturalistic theist in the process tradition, Bowne begins his book, *The Immanence of God*, with these words: "The undivineness of the natural and the unnaturalness of the divine is the great heresy of popular thought."[51] However, Boston Personalists speculate that God's immanent relation with the world, in contrast to the immanent relations of process God, is volitional rather than necessary. Personalism "insists on God's free

48. Ibid.

49. Among pertinent material criticizing divine self-limitation from a process theological perspective, see Tyron L. Inbody, *The Transforming God: An Interpretation of Suffering and Evil* (Louisville: Westminster John Knox Press, 1997), 148-50.

50. David Ray Griffin, *God, Power, and Evil: A Process Theodicy* (Philadelphia: Westminster Press, 1976), 246.

51. Bowne, *The Immanence of God* (Boston: Houghton Mifflin, 1905), preface.

relation to the world," says Knudson.[52] Or, as Bowne says more subtly, God "is the most deeply obligated being in the universe. And, having started a race under human conditions, he is bound to treat it in accordance with those conditions. God is bound to be the great Burden-bearer of our world because of his relations to men."[53] Process thought, in contrast, denies that God voluntarily relates with nondivine creatures, or, as Whitehead says, "the relationships of God to the World should lie beyond the accidents of will." Instead, these relationships should be founded "upon the necessities of the nature of God and the nature of the World."[54] This implies that some realm of finite actualities or another has always existed;[55] God does not omnipotently dispose "a wholly derivative world" *ex nihilo*.[56]

Ultimately, the greatest differences between process and personalist thought can be traced to the philosophical traditions upon which they draw; process thought draws heavily from realist traditions and Boston Personalism draws heavily from idealist traditions. These different starting points lead each to regard the nonpersonal entities of nature quite differently. For Bowne and other theistic idealists of the Boston Personalist tradition, unconscious entities (e.g., rocks, plants, and cells) have no degree of independent reality. One reason that nonpersonal entities possess no independence whatsoever is that, for these personalists, individual "experience" is synonymous with "consciousness." Personalists account for the presence of the nonpersonal world by claiming that it depends entirely upon, and acts as an element of, the divine mind.[57] Brightman states this idealist position succinctly:

> Personalism may be taken to be that philosophical system which holds that the universe is a society of selves, unified by the will and

---

52. Knudson, *Philosophy of Personalism*, 329.

53. Bowne, *Studies in Christianity*, 144.

54. Whitehead, *Adventures of Ideas*, 168.

55. This does not deny, in principle, the theory that our particular universe may have begun with a "big bang," only that such an event, if it occurred, was not the beginning of finite existence.

56. Whitehead, *Adventures of Ideas*, 166. For an examination of the relevance of God's voluntary or necessary relations with the world, see Thomas Jay Oord, "Matching Theology and Piety: An Evangelical Process Theology of Love" (Ph.D. Dissertation, Claremont Graduate University, 1999), chaps. 6-7; and Mark Taylor, *God Is Love: A Study in the Theology of Karl Rahner* (Atlanta: Scholars Press, 1986), chap. 11.

57. Borden Parker Bowne, *Kant and Spencer* (Port Washington, N.Y.: Kennikat, 1967), 133ff.

immanent causality of a Supreme Self, and which, therefore, defines matter and the whole system of physical nature in terms of the active, conscious will of that Supreme Self, while it regards human selves (and whatever other selves there may be) as enjoying an existence of their own, dependent, it is true, upon the will of the Supreme Self, yet no part of it.[58]

Process theism, arising out of realist philosophies, postulates that the unconscious actualities of the natural world *do* have a degree of independence, and even autonomy, *vis-à-vis* God. Without this postulation, say process philosophers, persons have no good reason to claim that unconscious entities even exist, let alone possess intrinsic value. The postulation that nonpersonal and unconscious actualities have a measure of independent reality does not lead process thought to espouse mindless materialism, however. Instead, process thought puts mind in matter; experience occurs at all levels of existence. This avowal of panpsychism or, more happily, panexperientialism[59] offers a way to affirm the reality of mentality generating purpose, freedom, and value; it also offers a way to affirm the commonsense notion that a real world of unconscious natural actualities exists with a measure of autonomy. One way to characterize process panexperientialism, then, would be to claim this doctrine considers "personhood" to extend from the most complex to the least complex of all entities in the world. In this postulation, personhood need entail neither consciousness nor the degree of complexity required to sustain enduring individuals. At the risk of oversimplification, one might say that if, as Boston Personalists contend, idealism is the antithesis of materialism, then panexperientialism is the synthesis.

The implications of panexperientialism for process thought are significant, and the extent to which these implications result in significant differences between process theology and the idealism of Boston Personalism is far-reaching. I mention three briefly. First, although Boston Personalists sometimes argued for a responsible environmental ethic, their idealist presuppositions made it difficult

58. Brightman, "Personalism as a Philosophy of Religion," 382.

59. David Ray Griffin suggests that "panexperientialism" better depicts what is entailed in process philosophy's version of panpsychism ("Some Whiteheadian Comments," in *Mind in Nature: Essays on the Interface of Science and Philosophy*, ed. John B. Cobb Jr. and David Ray Griffin [Washington, D.C.: University Press of America, 1977]).

to formulate ethical schemes that regard nonhuman individuals and the elemental actualities of nature as intrinsically valuable.[60] Only persons are really real, which implies that only persons can be intrinsically valuable. Second, Boston Personalism, because of its adherence to idealist premises, struggles to provide a satisfying solution to the mind-body problem; it provides no adequate theory for how a person (human self or mind) could interact naturally with a person's bodily members (matter). Third, because of its idealism, Boston Personalism aligned itself with a position in the science and religion dialogue that many today find unsatisfactory.[61] Knudson expresses this position when he argues that "if both scientists and theologians had understood that science is by its very nature confined to the phenomenal realm and that religion by its nature is concerned simply with the ultimate power and purpose that lie back of the phenomena, most of the conflicts between them in the past would have been avoided."[62] "It is [best]," he concludes, "to adopt Bowne's distinction between phenomenal and ontological reality, and then to say that science is concerned with the former and religion with the latter."[63] Process thought rejects the distinction between phenomenal and ontological reality and, therefore, also rejects a hard and fast distinction between science and religion partly because of its doctrine of panexperientialism.

Although Wesleyans still shape and are shaped by personalism—and personalism is by no means a dead philosophical school[64]—the last half of the twentieth century has witnessed a stronger Wesleyan attraction to process thought. Reasons for this attraction have been addressed in this essay; a fuller exposure of such reasons is found in the essays of this book. My present task, however, has involved proposing a rationale for why it is that Wesleyans have been attracted to personalism in the past and for why this attraction naturally carries over to a contemporary process thought.

---

60. Rufus Burrow Jr. wrestles with this criticism in *Personalism*, 235-40.

61. For a brief explanation and criticism of the kind of position Boston Personalists take regarding the relationship between religion and science, see Ian G. Barbour, *Religion in an Age of Science* (New York: Harper & Row, 1990), 10-16.

62. Knudson, *Philosophy of Personalism*, 253.

63. Ibid., 330.

64. Contemporary personalists include Douglas R. Anderson, Randall E. Auxier, Thomas Buford, Rufus Burrow Jr., Charles Conti, Mark Y. A. Davies, Frederick Ferré, Erazim Kohak, James McLachlan, and Josef Seifert.

ABBREVIATIONS

Hymns   *A Collection of Hymns for the Use of the People Called Methodists*, ed. Franz Hildebrandt and Oliver Beckerlegge (Nashville: Abingdon, 1983); volume 7 of *Works*.

John Wesley   *John Wesley*, ed. Albert C. Outler (New York: Oxford University Press, 1964).

Letters (Telford) *The Letters of the Rev. John Wesley, A.M.*, ed. John Telford, 8 vols. (London: Epworth, 1931).

NT Notes   *Explanatory Notes Upon the New Testament*, 3rd corrected ed. (Bristol: Graham and Pine, 1760–62; many later reprints).

Survey   *A Survey of the Wisdom of God in the Creation: Or, A Compendium of Natural Philosophy*, 4th rev. ed., 5 vols. (London: J. Paramore, 1784).

Works   *The Works of John Wesley*, begun as "The Oxford Edition of the Works of John Wesley" (Oxford: Clarendon, 1975–83); continued as "The Bicentennial Edition of the Works of John Wesley" (Nashville: Abingdon, 1984—); 15 of 35 volumes published to date.

Works (Jackson)   *The Works of Rev. John Wesley, M.A.*, ed. Thomas Jackson, 3rd ed., 14 vols. (London: Wesleyan Methodist Book Room, 1872; reprinted Grand Rapids: Baker, 1979).

CONTRIBUTORS

John B. Cobb Jr., Emeritus Professor of Theology, Claremont School of Theology, Claremont, California.

John Culp, Professor of Philosophy, Azusa Pacific University, Azusa, California.

John L. Farthing, Professor of Religion and Classical Languages, Hendrix College, Conway, Arkansas.

Tyron L. Inbody, Professor of Theology, United Theological Seminary, Dayton, Ohio.

Michael E. Lodahl, Professor of Theology, Point Loma Nazarene University, San Diego, California.

Randy L. Maddox, Paul T. Walls Professor of Wesleyan Theology, Seattle Pacific University, Seattle, Washington.

Jay McDaniel, Professor of Religion, Hendrix College, Conway, Arkansas.

Mary Elizabeth Mullino Moore, Professor of Religion and Education, Candler School of Theology, Emory University, Atlanta, Georgia.

Schubert M. Ogden, University Distinguished Professor Emeritus, Southern Methodist University, Dallas, Texas.

Thomas Jay Oord, Assistant Professor of Philosophy, Eastern Nazarene College, Quincy, Massachusetts.

Alan G. Padgett, Professor of Systematic Theology, Luther Seminary, Minneapolis, Minnesota.

Samuel M. Powell, Professor of Philosophy and Religion, Point Loma Nazarene University, San Diego, California.

Kenton M. Stiles, Ph.D. Cand., Graduate Theological Union, Berkeley, California.

Bryan P. Stone, E. Stanley Jones Professor of Evangelism, Boston University School of Theology, Boston, Massachusetts.

Marjorie Hewitt Suchocki, Ingraham Professor of Theology, Claremont School of Theology, Claremont, California.

Theodore Walker Jr., Associate Professor of Ethics and Society, Southern Methodist University, Dallas, Texas.

Henry James Young, Professor of Systematic Theology, Garrett-Evangelical Seminary, Evanston, Illinois.